WITHDRAWN

THE
EVOLUTION
OF
MODERN PSYCHOLOGY

BY

RICHARD MÜLLER-FREIENFELS

TRANSLATED BY

W. BÉRAN WOLFE, M.D.

NEW HAVEN
YALE UNIVERSITY PRESS

PUBLISHED ON THE FOUNDATION ESTABLISHED IN
MEMORY OF AMASA STONE MATHER
OF THE CLASS OF 1907 YALE COLLEGE

The present volume is the fifteenth work published by the Yale University Press on the Amasa Stone Mather Memorial Publication Fund. This Foundation was established August 25, 1922, by a gift to Yale University from Samuel Mather, Esq., of Cleveland, Ohio, in pursuance of a pledge made in June, 1922, on the fifteenth anniversary of the graduation of his son, Amasa Stone Mather, who was born in Cleveland on August 20, 1884, and was graduated from Yale College in the Class of 1907. Subsequently, after traveling abroad, he returned to Cleveland, where he soon won a recognized position in the business life of the city and where he actively interested himself also in the work of many organizations devoted to the betterment of the community and to the welfare of the nation. His death from pneumonia on February 9, 1920, was undoubtedly hastened by his characteristic unwillingness ever to spare himself, even when ill, in the discharge of his duties or in his efforts to protect and further the interests committed to his care by his associates.

TRANSLATOR'S PREFACE

IT is a great privilege to introduce Professor R. Müller-Freienfels' splendid history of the evolution of modern psychology to English-speaking students. When first the Yale University Press commissioned my translation I hesitated to essay such a tremendous project, earlier translations of German psychological works having taught me how thankless a task the work of making not only the ideology, but the very sensations and emotions of German psychologists comprehensible to English-speaking audiences can be. The translation of German psychological studies is extremely difficult, for in many instances no equivalents for many of the German scientific terms exist, and the translator is compelled to indulge in wearisome circumlocutions or tread the dangerous path of inventing neologisms. Of the two courses I have usually chosen the latter, with what success the reader himself must judge.

A cursory examination of the manuscript was not calculated to encourage a hesitant translator. The translation of *The Evolution of Modern Psychology* from the Müller-Freienfels' typescript involved not only purely psychological terminology, but also necessitated the translation of the technical terminology of physiology, medicine, philosophy, and epistemology, not to speak of modern psychiatric and psychoanalytic terms and concepts. The further I read in the typescript, however, the more convinced I became of the splendid perspective the author commanded, and the greater became my respect for his encyclopædic knowledge, his broad sympathies, his remarkably keen intuition. When I finished reading Müller-Freienfels' book, I felt *compelled* to translate it.

Free from the bias of the professional academician, with a fairness rare among the psychologists who pride themselves upon their so-called objectivity, Müller-Freienfels has discussed the various schools of thought, evaluated their contributions, pointed out their shortcomings without rancor, and indicated how one great school of psychological thought grew organically into the next.

In my psychiatric practice and in my lectures I am often asked, "Just what is the difference between the teachings of Freud, Jung, and Adler?" I know of no other book which has answered this moot question of modern psychology so succinctly and so understandingly. Müller-Freienfels' discussion of the various branches of social and racial psychology seems peculiarly appropriate at this time when the broader social and national aspects of psychology occupy the minds of every serious student of human nature. Important as these contributions are, it is my belief that Müller-Freienfels' greatest contribution to the American student of psychology is a legacy of divine discontent. He who reads these pages must forever after be dissatisfied with the psychological blind spots of the prevalent academic psychology.

Müller-Freienfels' book should come as a tonic and refreshing breeze. *The Evolution of Modern Psychology* is a worthy monument to the spirit of Müller-Freienfels' American teacher, William James. My work as translator has already been more than repaid by the pleasure I have had in making this exceedingly instructive and stimulating text available to English readers. If, in addition, I have thereby enabled other students to broaden their psychological perspectives, or to regain their faith in psychology, the months of arduous preparation will not have been spent in purely selfish enjoyment.

W. Béran Wolfe, M.D.

New York City,
    June, 1934.

CONTENTS

INTRODUCTION: *Plan and Point of View*

The Emergence of a "New" Science of Psychology

The Genealogy of Modern Psychology

The Grand Strategy of Modern Psychology

Fundamental Levels of Modern Psychology

PART ONE: *How Psychology Became Conscious of Consciousness*

Consciousness as the Nuclear Problem of Psychology

The Problems of the Analysis of Sensation

The Synthesis of Consciousness on the Basis of Sensory Psychology

Synthesis of Consciousness from Two Elements

PART THREE: *The Psychology of Action and Conduct*

The Psychomotor Problem in the Past

William James as the Founder of a Psychomotor Psychology

Contents

FOREWORD

THESE *pages endeavor to present a survey of the entire field of modern psychology and its related sciences. While giving due consideration to the experimental method, I do not view this method as the only possible means of constructing a science of psychology. The following presentation will show that from the very beginning, the reciprocal influence between experimental practice and theoretical research has been the very factor making for progress. All experiment is preceded by theory; and the history of all sciences is primarily a history of their theoretical approach to certain problems. I have therefore written this history of modern psychology as a history of its theoretical problems. Only in this way can we gain an insight into the innermost operations of research. In confining ourselves to the detailed work of the laboratory, we are too apt to lose sight of our ultimate goals.*

It has been my intention to do more than merely enumerate external events and compile a catalogue of titles. I have tried to lay bare the interrelations of various tendencies and thus obtain a systematic survey of modern psychological research in all its rich variety. The history of modern psychology is a history of the emergent evolution of the conceptions of mental life. But it is also the history of a tremendous expansion of the scope of research. The result is that today there is no corner of life which has not gained some new perspective from modern psychology.

I must add a word concerning the vast results of psychological research in the United States. An exhaustive discussion of existing American material has been impossible for me to attempt. Since this book has been written in Europe, only those American scholars who have achieved considerable European influence have been discussed, for even the largest European libraries do not afford a complete picture of American psychology. It is my hope that this book will arouse particular interest in the United States for the very reason that it treats the evolution of psychology from a European point of view, which, while including well-known American trends, emphasizes certain European schools which are not so well known in America.

I want also, at this time, to acknowledge my personal indebtedness to the United States, and especially to William James, for having decisively determined my direction of thought. I was encouraged in my first attempts at independent research by this great man and scholar. May this book, therefore, be a token of my gratitude for everything that I have received from the United States.

RICHARD MÜLLER-FREIENFELS

INTRODUCTION

PLAN AND POINT OF VIEW

EVOLUTION OF MODERN PSYCHOLOGY

THE EMERGENCE OF A "NEW" SCIENCE OF PSYCHOLOGY

IT is a significant fact, and by no means a fortuitous circumstance, that at the very time that science, using every refinement of modern research methods, undertook to investigate what we call the "soul," religious studies of the human soul were beginning to decline. Many of the new investigators did not even believe in the existence of the human soul in the earlier sense of the word. They pursued a "soulless psychology," and while utilizing the concept of the old-fashioned soul they sought to demonstrate that such a thing did not really exist. But the most amazing result of these trends is the fact that in the course of the investigations the formerly ostracized soul won readmission, and with full honors, to the halls of science. Today, indeed, there are again psychologists who not only believe in a real soul but even openly grace their conviction with a metaphysical and religious coloring.

The formal proclamation of psychology as a really exact new science, and the mobilization of an international army of scholars for the conquest of the unknown inner world occurred almost uniformly in all civilized countries during the second half of the nineteenth century. All that had formerly gone by the name of psychology was loudly denounced as no science at all; only now, it was declared, were we in possession of sure-fire methods of getting at the essence of the soul. While formerly psychology was studied only as an adjunct of philosophy, now separate chairs of psychology were being set up everywhere. In fact magnificent institutes, such as hitherto only physicists and chemists possessed, were being built for psychologists. These psychological laboratories were equipped with shiny metal apparatus like so many medieval torture chambers. And no one doubted, in the presence of all this complicated machinery, that the soul eventually would be compelled to deliver its deepest secrets to the psychologists.

As we have said, this sudden efflorescence of psychology was no fortuitous accident, but evolved necessarily from the existing historical situation. Since the beginning of the sixteenth century inorganic nature had been carefully investigated and with the help of mathematics had been converted, as it were, into a solved arithmetic problem. After the middle of the eighteenth century a new biology developed which not only thrust the world of living things into the focus of scientific research, but also extended this research back to the very dawn of time. The nineteenth century, moreover, created a critical science of history which, on the basis of authoritative sources, brilliantly illuminated the obscure corners of the civil and cultural life of mankind. Only the human spirit, to whose genius we owe this upswing of all science, remained a *terra incognita* which had not yet been probed by scientific investigation.

When it came to the soul, men either contented themselves with popular or theological explanations or listened to the widely discordant speculations of the philosophers. The accepted psychology of the day was quite incapable of arousing any interest comparable to the popular preoccupation with physics or Darwin's theory. Its methodology, too, was not nearly so systematically developed as that of the other sciences. This deficiency became apparent largely because the spirit of the new era, permeated as it was with empirical and critical research, could no longer be appeased by traditionally muddled beliefs about the essence of the soul. There is small wonder, therefore, that a universal demand for a strictly scientific psychology arose, and that simultaneously throughout the civilized world learned investigators devoted themselves to the research of this important problem. As the Bible says, "The time had come."

Psychology, hitherto the Cinderella of the sciences, was suddenly called upon to help everybody everywhere. No longer was the human mind to be scrutinized simply for its theoretical interest. Pedagogics and politics, medicine and jurisprudence as well as the historical and social sciences hesitated to approach their problems without preliminary consultations with psychology. And the lay public went even further and began looking to the psychological laboratories with expectations of fantastic results, which happily were rejected rather than nourished by the more serious psychologists.

Half a century has already passed since this era, and it is now possible to make a critical survey of the evolution of the new psychology for the purpose of ascertaining how far the early expectations associated with the new science have been fulfilled. We are going to narrate this history, which, despite its mere fifty years of existence, is a story of rapid development, strong reaction, passionate party battles and even turbulent revolutions. To be sure, this history is not always dramatic and we must also tell the story of a protracted campaign in which the height of heroism was often manifested not in great battles but, as in modern warfare, in obstinate endurance and weary detail work. We shall also be compelled to record disappointments and mistakes. In psychology, as in every science, truths are frequently discovered solely by the elimination of errors. But the history of nations, too, is not a mere record of victories; many a defeat has signified a psychological victory for the future destiny of a nation. I relate the history of the new psychology in this spirit, fully aware that some of the results which were loudly glorified at first were finally exposed as bizarre mistakes. Our presentation will show that in spite of apparent zigzags the basic evolution of psychology has followed a clear and definite path.

THE GENEALOGY OF MODERN PSYCHOLOGY

1. My presentation proper will begin with the history of the "new" psychology, as it was named *circa* 1880. I shall

preface it with a brief review of the earlier history of psychology ranging over thousands of years. We can do this without much danger today whereas in the beginnings of the new movement we would have been accused of being hopelessly entangled in the mazes of mythology. The new psychology's attitude toward the old has changed. Despite the fact that modern psychologists at first contemptuously disclaimed any kinship with the old theories and actually boasted that they knew nothing about them, they admit today that many a grain of truth lies hidden in them. One reason why the modern science was considered so completely "new" was that the old psychology was only superficially known.

Meanwhile certain distinguished champions of the new science did not think it beneath their dignity to examine the old psychology in the light of modern historical and psychological methods. And then a change took place. Instead of boasting about the absolute originality of the new psychology, the new investigators pointed with pride to a noble genealogical family tree whose roots were anchored in thousands of years of antiquity. Proud of their distinguished ancestors, the professors in the new institutes of psychology began to hang nicely framed pictures of Aristotle, Descartes, Leibniz, and many others on the walls.

We shall show that many of the newest phases of the new psychology are merely more profound reconsiderations of studies that were already some hundreds or thousands of years old. We do not detract from the value of Columbus' accomplishments by admitting that long before his day the Vikings had discovered the coast of the new Continent. As far as the world is concerned, it is not mere priority of discovery, but the exploitation of the thing discovered that is really significant. Herein lies the task of the new psychology, when it consciously or unconsciously seeks to knit the raveled threads of tradition into its modern tapestry.

In speaking of the old soul probings as "psychology" we must make one important reservation: these were rarely "pure" psychology. The old psychology's problems and aims were frequently confused by theological, metaphysical, ethical, epistemological, and even biological considerations. A "pure" psychology is only now slowly taking crystalline shape, and it is by no means its aim or ideal to remain isolated for all time.

2. Our first premise, then, is that psychology is not a new but an ancient science, perhaps the most ancient of all the sciences. If we define the essence of this science as the attempt to understand and control reality by mental means, we are compelled to accept many of the proceedings of primitive medicine men and shamans as primitive science, for their magic practices, absurd as they may seem to us, are based, as can be shown, on elaborate theoretical conceptions. I grant you these theories from our present point of view seem absurd yet, in the opinion of the Eskimos or Melanesians who practice them, they are just as scientific and valid as is our own science in our opinion. There is no justification in belittling the soul theories of primitive peoples. It is rather our business to examine and comprehend them as singularly interesting psychological phenomena.

Today we have amassed vast stores of data concerning the mind theories of primitive peoples. The study of these data reveals the amazing fact that primitive men not only had a highly developed psychology, but also that they pursued all other sciences, such as medicine and astronomy, as part of psychology. We cannot escape the fact that all primitive thought is focused in the conviction that not only people, but also animals, plants, mountains, and stars have "souls" —in short, that the whole world and everything in it is "animated" by a soul. This well-nigh universal, primitive, philosophical attitude is, therefore, named "animism."

Whether animism was preceded by a pre-animistic period must remain an insoluble theoretical problem, because of the lack of all direct evidence. The important fact is that not only do we find animism in the early stages of every culture, but also that this animism is crystallized and systematized wherever we find it. Many schools of the newer psychology, such as psychoanalysis, moreover, take the leather-aproned or feather-adorned primitive psychologists very seriously, and seek to rediscover in their savage totems and taboos the basic results of their own research, clothed in mythological forms. These primitive medicine men were undoubtedly past masters of certain up-to-date psychological techniques such as suggestion, hypnosis, and mental training long before modern science had any idea of them.

We may as well forego our civilized arrogance toward these primitive psychologists as, indeed, we have finally been compelled to do with regard to primitive art, primitive religion, and primitive social life. We must admit that certain central problems of modern psychological science were already recognized in the early days of human civilization despite the fact that they were incased in a cocoon of myth.

The essence of animism is the belief that in every material being there lives a second being—a kind of demon—which, if not entirely insubstantial, is at least of a substance different from that of the body. The vital functions were ascribed to this immaterial ego, the "soul," and it was believed that it left the body in death, or even in sleep and dreams. In any case, it was believed that the soul was capable of independent existence beyond the body. The soul soon came to be identified with the breath (almost every word for soul originally meant breath), and then again it was thought of as a shadow. We even find the concept of a "soul worm," a concept preserved by civilized peoples in the symbolic representations of the soul as a snake. In any case, primitive animism recognized the disparity between psychic phenomena and the material body. Subsequent research into the nature of the connection between the soul and the body became the primitive basis of the problem of psychophysical interrelationships.

Attempts to associate the soul with specific bodily organs,

such as the blood, the nerves, the heart, the sex organs, the saliva (but hardly ever the brain!) were formerly very popular. This, in turn, frequently led to the conception of separate organ souls with different functions, thereby introducing the unity-multiplicity concept, and later the atomization of the soul into various component parts. In primitive psychology particular attention was also paid to pathologic phenomena: intoxication and diabolism, which were explained in terms of the wanderings of the soul. Naturally enough these primitive psychologists were not concerned with psychological theory; they were chiefly interested in technique and method, that is, in the practical problem of magically exorcising the demons that dominated the soul. Absurd as much of this practice may seem to us, a deeper meaning often underlies the seemingly perverse and cruel phenomena of primitive mental life.

3. The psychology of the ancient Hindus leads us unquestionably into the domain of science; for they possessed everything that many people consider the essence of genuine science; namely, technical and learned terminology, thick books, experimental practice, and something of an academic and professional status. The Hindu psychologists, to be sure, were largely intrusted with priestly functions and therefore their psychology was saturated with mythology. However, this should not prevent us from recognizing their science as science. In any case, there is a certain poetic magnificence in the basic thesis of the Vedanta doctrine, that the individual soul (Atman) is identical with the world soul (Brahman). *"Aham brahma asmi"* ("I am Brahma") is the alpha and omega of this philosophy, at least in its esoteric form.

The exoteric Hindu psychology is preoccupied with the individual soul, the psychic apparatus. The latter attaches a Karma, a factor that varies from birth to birth, to the Atman, and it accompanies the Atman throughout all its metamorphoses, without causing the Atman to lose its divine nature; Deussen put it nicely in the form of an analogy "as the crystal is not fused with the color painted on it."

While in the Vedanta doctrine, individuality is only an illusion (Maya), in the Sankhya doctrine "soul" means the individuality of the particular man. Instead of Atman they say "purusha" (that is, man—later, spirit) in order thus to stress the individual. Here, too, the soul as such is changeless light, pure spirit. The light of consciousness derived from the soul falls into the variable nature of man. Thus, nature becomes "as if it were spiritual" and conversely, the soul, "as if it were active." The internal organs and the organs of sense and motion constitute the "fine body" (Lingam), the counterpart of the soul in nature, in truth completely different from it but connected with it.

The Hindu subdivision of the soul is particularly complicated. From the Ahankara, the individuality principle, stem the five Buddhi indryas (sense organs: hearing, touch, vision, taste, smell), and the five Karma indryas (organs of action: speech, hands, feet, genital, and excretory organs). There also appears the Manas, which intervenes between the perceptory and motor organs. This indicates, however, only a few of the subtle distinctions of this psychology. But it is already evident that the Hindus had clearly formulated the central problems of subsequent psychological research: the problem of the essence of the soul and the coexistence of its separate functions. These psychologists invented the practice of the Yoga—a refined technique of mental concentration exercised in nearly all Hindu sects. By control of posture and breathing, the Yoga manages to rise from consciousness to a mystic state of superconsciousness, as a result of which, to be sure, psychology loses itself entirely in metaphysics.

4. The Greeks were nearer to modern psychology than the Hindus, and much that was taught about the human soul in the colonnaded halls and parks of Athenian academies has influenced the development of Western psychology. In fact,

the suggestions embodied in the works of the ancient thinkers have by no means been exhausted by the new psychology. Recent research (for example, Rhode's fine work, *Psyche*) has shown how deeply animism permeated the entire religious, social, and scientific life of Hellas.

Greek psychology is partially a development of folk religious animism, partially a struggle against it, the two often so fused with one another as to be hardly distinguishable. Is it not possible, for example, that the attempt of the earlier philosophers to trace the essence of the soul back to material substance is the first conquest of animism? We know that Thales (Aristotle says Hippo) considered the soul equivalent to water; Anaximenes and others decided it was air, while Heraclitus compared the soul to fire; and Empedocles even made it up of the four world elements— water, air, fire, and earth. It sounds like modern chemistry, but of course it was not meant that way, because it was derived largely from metaphysical concepts. These soul stuffs were not elements in the sense of modern chemistry, but were held to be animated. That is why these old philosophers were also called Hylozoists—theoreticians of "animated matter."

While all of these theories are concerned chiefly with the substance of the soul, later thinkers attempted to determine its form largely by substantializing it. The soul concepts of the atomists like Leucippus and Democritus, who thought the soul consisted of atoms, and of course the smallest, smoothest, and the most mobile atoms, were not yet freed of substance. The soul theory of the Pythagoreans, who defined the soul by number relations or as "harmony," was even more formal, despite its strong mysticism. The Sophists energetically raised the question of individual differences of particular souls, and developed the beginnings of a critical theory of perception.

We have but an incomplete knowledge of ancient psychological theories and we must often reconstruct them entirely from a few existing fragments, just as a paleontologist reconstructs an entire dinosaur from a few bones. In Plato's theory of the soul, however, we find the first system of psychology (and of metaphysics, too, of course). For Plato the soul is not only a principle of earthly life but arises from a divine preëxistence and is immortal after death. Plato sought to solve the difficult problem of the unity of the different functions of the soul in many masterly pictures. We know from the *Phædrus* his comparison of the soul to a team of horses, where Reason, as driver, holds together the two horses, Courage and Appetite. This trisection of the soul is carried out in greater detail in the *Politeia*. And in the *Theætetus*, psychology appears in conjunction with epistemology. In this work Plato states a theory of perception that goes beyond the sensationalism of the Sophists in seeking to grasp the soul as a living unity. All in all, though Plato's soul theory remained well within the bourn of animism, it strongly stimulated analytic psychology.

The psychology of Aristotle was a distinct advance beyond animism. Although Aristotle, too, viewed the soul as metaphysical in origin, he considered it primarily as the life principle. His psychology linked itself with biology. He held that the soul was the creative form of all organisms, a self-unfolding, not a rigid form, an entelechy. Aristotle solved the problem of multiplicity in unity by distinguishing several separate souls: the feeding soul (*anima vegetativa*), which even plants possess; the perceptive soul (*anima sensitiva*), which animals have, and the thinking soul (*anima cogitativa*), which only humans possess, and which rules over the lower souls. The thinking soul, Reason, however, was further subdivided into a passive and an active reason, and only the latter was considered divine and immortal.

Together with these theories of the essence of the soul as a whole, which are only now being revived in present-day psychology, we find in Aristotle keen analyses of sensory experience, thought, and emotion, which are valuable forerunners of analytic psychology. The modern psychologist indeed can still learn a great deal from Aristotle's books

De Anima, Ethics, Rhetoric, while among his encyclopedic writings the outlines of a theory of type and of character are to be found.

Psychology in the last century before Christ was concerned primarily with an ethical way of life. This was so in the school of Epicurus, and more so in that of the Stoics. Despite the fact that the Stoics reverted to a rather materialistic concept of the soul, they nevertheless developed a detailed classification of the mental faculties. They distinguished a guiding principle in the soul (the *begemonikón*), and opposed to it the emotions and the instincts. The emotions and passions were conceived as perversions of reason and had, therefore, to be subdued. The final phase of Greek psychology was neo-Platonism. The soul of the neo-Platonists, to be sure, was wholly engulfed by mystico-religious concepts, but these thinkers nevertheless achieved some significant insight into the life of the individual consciousness.

The Greek studies of the soul, as we see, also traveled the road from theological and metaphysical speculation to a biological and empirical faculty psychology. Greek psychology returned to a theological point of view only toward the end, because in this era it merged with new Occidental historical trends and was absorbed in a new chain of evolution.

5. During the Christian Middle Ages, just as in medieval Arabian science, psychology was a matter of zealous concern. Here again the starting point was theological speculation. The aim of all Christian learning was the eternal salvation of the soul. We can understand, therefore, why the early Christians demanded the deepest possible knowledge of this soul. Medieval psychology, like all medieval science, was directed toward reconciling ancient learning with Christian revelation. The Christian theory of the immortal soul is strongly animistic, in so far as it conceives of the soul as sharply divorced from the body and composed of immaterial substance which strives to unite with God.

The chief aim of Scholastic psychology was to prove that the human soul, although it is bound to the body and has to fulfil various earthly functions, is nevertheless a super- natural essence. We must not, however, view medieval psychology as altogether dependent on ancient psychology. It raised new problems of its own. Augustine discovered something entirely new when he focused attention on the will as well as on the intellect. And in the late Middle Ages the controversy over the primacy of the intellect or the will stirred the minds of such great schoolmen as Thomas Aquinas and Duns Scotus. Nominalism likewise raised problems, such as that of the purely symbolic character of consciousness, which are still being debated today.

6. The psychologists of the Renaissance had an altogether different conception of the soul from that of the monkish psychologists of the Middle Ages. Just as science in general during the sixteenth and seventeenth centuries concerned itself less with supernatural than with natural problems, so the psychologists of the Renaissance were more occupied with the earthly reality of the soul than with its heavenly future. Analyses of consciousness anticipating modern the- ories are to be found in the works of the Italian Telesio, the Spaniard Vives, the Englishman Bacon, and many others. It is true that they are mingled with fantasies, as in Tel- esio's assumption of "life spirits" which are supposed to emanate from the cerebrum and spread through the body.

7. The psychology of the sixteenth century had already be- gun to study mental life with scientific methods. In the seventeenth century when mathematical physics, under the inspiration of Galileo, opened up unforeseen perspectives, the scientific method made great strides. At the same time psychology became part and parcel of metaphysical systems. Descartes explained only that part of psychic phenomena which is bound to the body, along mechanistic lines. Des- cartes divided the world into two substances: matter (*ex-*

tensio) and thought (*cogitatio*, sometimes called *conscientia*).
Animals have no souls and are, therefore, machines. In
humans, however, the thinking soul is connected with the
body through the pineal gland. Pure thought as such has its
own laws, and has innate ideas. To the extent that they are
connected with the body, however, all mental phenomena
such as sensations, associations, and reflexes had to be explained mechanistically. The emotions also were held to
arise from the union of body and soul. The soul did not
generate motion—it could only change its direction. Descartes' mechanistic concepts had an especially fruitful influence. The dualism between body and soul brewed difficulties
which the successors of Descartes: Geulinx, Malebranche,
and Spinoza, sought to settle.

Spinoza invented a parallelistic monism in the body-soul
question which exerts its influence to the present day. On
the other hand, the materialistic-mechanistic theory was
further developed by Hobbes, who denied the existence of
innate ideas. All thought in his theory was supposed to
derive from experience, and all consciousness was bound to
the motion of bodies. Sensation, association, desire, and
aversion, including the will which was held to be strictly
determined, Hobbes explained mechanistically.

8. The eighteenth century studied psychology less in connection with metaphysics than as an adjunct of epistemology.
In England and France it followed mainly a naturalistic-
sensualistic path; in Germany and Scotland, an idealistic-
rationalistic trend. In the case of Locke, whose *Essay Concerning Human Understanding* had already appeared at the
end of the seventeenth century, interest lay not, as with
Hobbes, in physiological psychology, but in an analysis of
the acts of cognition. Locke assumed two sources of consciousness: sensation and reflection. His distinction between
primary and secondary qualities was to prove specially
stimulating to the future. Although Locke's major interest
was epistemological, not psychological, the new association

psychology was greatly influenced by him. Certain inconsistencies of his were eliminated by his successors.

Berkeley, for example, dropped the primary qualities and arrived at a spiritualism in which only souls or spirits were valid. He also produced a first-rate empirical analysis of space perception and an ingenious critique of imagination thereby continuing the analysis of consciousness begun by Locke. This was carried to an extreme by the venturesome D. Hume, who recognized only impressions and the association of ideas, but no substantial soul, even as he attempted to dispose of substance in the external world.

Hume, in addition, pursued psychology as did Adam Smith and his school, in connection with problems of morals and politics. Together with Hume we must name D. Hartley among the pioneers of modern analysis of consciousness. However, Hartley placed the greatest stress on the connection of mental events with cerebral and nerve processes. The sensationalism of these English philosophers was pursued further in France, especially by Condillac and Bonnet, and culminated in the materialism of La Mettrie.

In contrast to the empiricism and sensationalism of the English and French thinkers, an *a priori* and rationalistic tendency in psychology was advanced in Germany. The contrast appears most sharply in Leibniz, whose too little-known masterpiece in psychology, *Nouveaux essais sur l'entendement humain*, refutes Locke's essay point for point. It had already been written in 1704, but first appeared in print in 1765. In it Leibniz fought primarily against the *tabula rasa* theory and insisted on the activity of the souls which, as monads, were to him the only real things in the world. It is also significant that he was the first to introduce the concept of the "unconscious" with his *"petites perceptions."*

One of Leibniz' disciples, C. Wolff, is known as the founder of faculty psychology. Like Leibniz, he assumed a monadic soul to which he ascribed two faculties, the knowing faculty and the desiring faculty. His disciple, Tetens, added emotion as a third faculty, while others further increased the number of faculties. Kant, too, set out from Leibniz and Wolff. It was Kant who brought psychology into great disrepute when he declared it could not become an exact science because it was not amenable to mathematical proof. In his *Critique of Pure Reason* he allowed the concept of the existence of a substantial soul, but not as an object of experience. In this respect he approached the position of Hume. Nevertheless, as opposed to Hume, Kant stressed the unity of apperception, the unifying force of consciousness, rather than the multiplicity of sensation. Kant sought to fathom the categories in which experience first arises in consciousness, because it never comes into being through sensation alone. Yet, in the *Critique of Practical Reason* the soul was still introduced as a supernatural essence and its immortality attested.

Scotch philosophy struck out against the tendency of Hume yet in a manner unlike that of the German thinkers. T. Reid appeals to "common observation," direct consciousness. He taught that we have innate mental forces that do not arise from external experience. Contrary to the associationists, he stressed the unity and cohesion of the soul.

Thus, the contradictions that exist in psychology today were already assuming shape in the eighteenth century: passivism vs. activism; sensualism vs. rationalism; empiricism vs. apriorism—all, of course, then closely connected with epistemology and ethics.

9. We shall now give only a cursory view of the developments of psychology in the first half of the nineteenth century. For our survey of the recent trends, we shall frequently find it necessary to refer again to the psychologists of this period, and of earlier periods, too. One of the fundamental theses in our history of modern psychological research is that modern psychology is by no means so independent of its predecessors as one might believe. The first founders of a psychological laboratory had to begin at the beginning, it is true, and then build up a new science on

the basis of their experiments. But they themselves did not always know how many old theories they carried with them, nor how far their very experiments were influenced by the old psychology. That is why we shall give only a historical survey here, and shall indicate later what part of this generation's doctrines have been carried over to the "new psychology."

The German philosophers of the early nineteenth century, Fichte, Schelling, and Hegel, were contemptuous of psychology. What they called spirit or soul was primarily a metaphysical consciousness or rather a superconsciousness, whose individuation in particular people was treated regularly as a secondary matter. Nevertheless, a series of psychologists arose from the school of "natural philosophers" several of whom, such as K. G. Carus, have been revived today. Along with the metaphysicians who sought to exclude psychology from the realm of philosophy, there were other thinkers like Fries and Beneke who wanted to base all philosophy on psychology. Herbart worked out an intellectualistic system of psychology that even applied mathematical calculations to mental life. Herbart exerted a particularly great influence on pedagogics. Among his pupils was Drobisch, who, like Herbart, rejected the "mental faculties" and turned out a penetrating description of the life of consciousness. Lazarus and Steinthal represented the association psychology which they applied primarily as folk psychology to ethnologic problems with great success. Lotze worked out an ingenious system in which the substantial soul (in the sense of Leibniz) reappeared. Johannes Müller, Helmholz, and others enriched psychology through their contributions to physiology.

Psychology was no less cultivated in other civilized nations. In France, about 1800, Cabanis and Destutt de Tracy connected psychology with physiology. Bichat and Pinel were already advancing that medical psychology in which the French of later days were to render such significant services. Maine de Biran cleared the way for a psychology of will. Independently, Jouffroy chose Scotch psychology as his point of departure. About the middle of the nineteenth century H. Taine, the most widely read psychologist of France, appeared. He developed a sensationalistic, positivistic psychology and also drew on pathologic phenomena to explain normal mental life. Of Renouvier and Fouillée, philosophers of this period, we shall write later, because they gave a great impetus to the new psychology, especially that of William James.

In Great Britain, Thomas Brown proceeded on the basis of Scotch psychology but approached association psychology besides. Hamilton, too, extended the Scotch line with his emphasis on the activity of the soul. James and John Stuart Mill, on the other hand, were ardent champions of a positivistic, association psychology, which suffers the active ego to recede entirely to the background. A. Bain emphasized the significance of motion and kinesthetic sensation for mental life, and became thereby one of the forerunners of more recent trends, such as behaviorism. Herbert Spencer treated psychology within the framework of his system of evolution and in that way brought into psychology the concept of development which was destined to play a significant rôle in later days. This concept was also taken up by other English investigators like Sully, Francis Galton, Tylor, Romanes, and others.

We shall come back to all these psychologists later, for the transition to the so-called "new" psychology is not so abrupt as it is sometimes represented. It is true that the attention of these psychological investigators was still strongly riveted in epistemological, ethical, and social problems; nevertheless, the purely psychological problem already stood out clearly, and this is a distinguishing mark of the "new" psychology.

10. A stately train of pioneers blazed the trail for modern psychology! Painted Indians and tattooed Polynesians; pious Brahmans and worthy Greeks; Dominicans in black

robes and Franciscans in brown robes; men of the baroque period in proud wigs; braided men of the age of enlightenment—all had attempted to fathom that mysterious essence which men, ever since men existed, have called their soul. Partly in solitary introspection, partly through observation of their neighbors, partly through a study of physical events, partly in logical and religious speculation, they had attempted to grasp the soul. What they so glibly called the "soul" was an extremely variable entity. Like Proteus of the Greek legend, it always changed its form as soon as one attempted to grasp it. And still all these interpretations of the mystery called soul were not arbitrary whims, for each attempt captured some essential quality of the soul, no matter in what fantastic disguise. This is reflected in the fact that most of these soul concepts reappear in some form or other in modern psychology.

Let us recapitulate, therefore, some of the more significant concepts of bygone psychology, and investigate how they have been revived again in modern research. Primitive animism lives once more in crude form in modern occultism and in parapsychology at the same time that it still plays a part in purely psychological observations. The biological conception of the soul as the living form of the organism is revived in the neovitalistic theories. The sensationalistic association psychology has forerunners in the Sankhya psychologists, in Democritus and the Epicureans, in nominalism, and in the Englishmen from Bacon to Spencer. Rationalism has a distinguished ancestry from Plato through Descartes to Kant. Voluntarism, too, was prepared for by St. Augustine, Duns Scotus, and many others. Even for such a seemingly modern theory as that of the unconscious, we found a forerunner in Leibniz. And the theory of the superindividual superconsciousness is presaged in the psychology of the Upanishads and many later thinkers.

In short, it requires some temerity for the new psychology to flaunt its "newness" before the world. And psychology was the first to be aware of this. As the first modern psychologist, William James expressed it with all frankness in his *Talks to Teachers:* "I say at once that in my humble opinion there is no 'new psychology' worthy of the name."

If we look back over the path of the old psychology we will find that it has gone through a number of clearly distinguishable stages, although not in strictly chronological order. Both in India and in Greece, and then again in the Middle Ages, the soul was conceived as a superindividual, supernatural essence, which is individualized only by connection with the body during life, and which, after death, returns to its metaphysical home. Thus it was with the Vedantas, with Plato, and with the Schoolmen. Then the structure of this soul was also investigated, its faculties and organs, and the forces from which it derives consciousness and motion. These investigations, too, were already carried on by Plato and Aristotle, and by the later rationalistic psychology. However, the soul was not always mere consciousness, but a substantial essence that happened to possess consciousness. The fact that the essence of the soul is consciousness and that the problem of psychology is the analysis of consciousness first dawned in the writings of Descartes. The analysis of consciousness later became the chief aim of the English association psychology. Paralleling this came the research methods which sought to explain mental life through the movements and organs of the body, that is, in terms of physiology. These are found already in Aristotle, then in Hobbes and later in the materialists of the eighteenth and nineteenth centuries.

The interesting part of the latest developments is that the old order of the problems apparently has been reversed. Now we begin with the analysis of the consciousness and its physiological accompaniments. Then we turn to a study of motor activity on the one hand, and on the other hand to the study of the structure of the soul with especial emphasis on the unconscious mental life. Finally we come to the problems of superindividual psychology which, however, we do not attempt to probe by metaphysical speculation.

If you object that we are back again in the realm of speculative psychology, bear in mind that not the problems but the methods of the old psychology were unscientific and speculative. Modern psychology attempts to take up these problems, but with a rigorously scientific technique.

The development is reversed in still another way. We saw that a pure psychology took shape very slowly. It had first to sever its problems and methods from their associations with theological, metaphysical, ethical, and epistemological systems. The new psychology begins with "pure" psychology, but applies its results more and more to epistemological, ethical, social, and even metaphysical and religious problems. This process, too, as we shall show, need not become unscientific, but when correctly executed may result in really rich possibilities of psychological research.

THE GRAND STRATEGY OF
MODERN PSYCHOLOGY

THE new method of psychology when closely examined is not a purely psychological method, but is essentially the application of a scientific method to the data of psychological research. The soul, viewed as something supernatural in the old days, was now to be treated entirely as an object of nature, just as a physical phenomenon or a chemical substance. And psychology, originally a discipline of philosophy, set its heart upon freeing itself as far as possible from philosophy and becoming a natural science. There were professors of the new psychology who boasted that they knew nothing about philosophy. To some the very word psychology was distasteful because it sounded too much like philosophy. They dug up new names in order to emphasize in their trade-mark, so to speak, their kinship with natural science: Psychophysics (Fechner), Mechanics of the Mind (Verworn), Mental Chemistry (J. S. Mill), Physiopsychology (Wundt). Not one of these really took root. In fact today we have a *"geisteswissenschaftliche Psychologie"* and a "philosophical anthropology" all over again without anyone suspecting them of being no more than primitive superstition.

Psychologists no longer become indignant when you speak about their philosophic spirit, although in the beginnings of the new psychology this was an insult. The psychologists then had a veritable inferiority complex toward the exact sciences whose great successes were celebrated in the nineteenth century, and it is for this reason that at first they borrowed the methods of physics and chemistry without questioning whether or not they were really applicable to the soul.

What these new psychologists really borrowed from the natural sciences were precision and the exclusion of all preconceived ideas and speculation. They demanded facts, more facts, and only facts! Basing their conception of facts on the model of the physical sciences, they refused to accept as a fact anything which could not be observed with certainty or documented with tangible evidence. Since it was difficult to control the introspection practiced at this time, the new psychologists sought to replace it by experiments or other expedients. Many psychologists wanted to exclude introspection from their studies altogether. They no longer wished to rely upon the intuitive talents of individuals, but upon extensive controlled determinations which could be checked by many investigators. The organized work of entire schools of well-disciplined psychologists is, therefore, one of the tangible differences between the new psychology and the old. The ancient soul investigators advanced into the uncharted realm of mental life like the pioneers of the California gold rush. They found many veins of gold, to be sure, but they were not interested in planned colonization.

Modern psychology proceeds like an organized expedition working with field measurements, geological and mineralogical investigations, and systematic plans for colonial development. If previously the search for the soul was a solitary hunt, it has now become a systematic round-up in which the frightened game is attacked from all sides. The modern psychologist not only investigates his own consciousness, but in collective work he investigates the mental life of others, and ends by submitting his own mind to objective investigation by others.

In the beginning, to be sure, this method was defective in so far as the laboratory psychologists investigated only the minds of specialists, with the result that the new psychology first became a mere psychology of psychologists. But the domain of psychology was soon extended to include women, children, babies, Eskimos, Polynesians, Bushmen, and other exotic objects in its sphere of interest. The psychologists began to investigate animals such as apes, dogs, bees, and amœbas for their mental characters. Even plants were examined for their sense organs by Haberlandt. In this way psychological research attained a completely unanticipated extension of its horizons.

The new psychology, having discarded all preconceived notions, now developed a set of special methods as a result of these precise collective efforts. These special techniques were either modeled on the methods of the physical sciences or evolved spontaneously through the association of psychological research with physiology, medicine, and other sciences. The new psychology now proceeded to play its trump ace. The psychological experiment was to be the means of getting reliable results which would compare with the data of physics and chemistry. The psychologists set up complicated apparatus by means of which they hoped, if not to eliminate uncontrollable introspection entirely, at least to restrict its influence. We shall see that the field of sensation and simple reactions yielded rich data to this method. The development of experimental techniques which produced insight into the higher mental life was a natural consequence of earlier experimental methods.

The mathematical method, which was so closely related

to the experimental in its early days, was the pride of the young psychology. The compromising statement of the great Kant, that psychology could not become an exact science as long as mathematics could not be applied to it, had to be refuted. Psychology, after all, had been associated with mathematics often in the past; among the Greeks, during the Renaissance, and very elaborately in the nineteenth century by Herbart. But all this remained inadequate. Really serious work along these lines was first done by E. H. Weber and G. T. Fechner (whom we shall learn to know better later on) by the introduction of mathematical methods in the measurement of the mind. Since their appearance on the scene, workers in psychological laboratories frequently compose endless arrays of statistical tables, or draw curves and construct geometric diagrams, in order thus to subject the mental life to the discipline of mathematics.

Great success has attended the psychopathological method, that is, the process of drawing conclusions about the minds of healthy people from the observation of mental patients. It may seem absurd at first sight for the new psychology to attempt to gain insight into the normal mind by studying the inmates of sanitaria and insane asylums. It is to be considered, however, that by this very method—the study of bodily disease—our knowledge of the physiology of the healthy body was advanced. French investigators were among the first to apply the pathological method, but, recently, many others have also made use of it with great success.

One of the early conclusions derived from this method was the realization that the so-called "normal" mental life was by no means always as "normal" as was originally assumed. It was in this very domain that the young psychology made a series of discoveries that at first almost enticed it into public exhibitions. Charcot's clinic, where he publicly presented hysterical women in the 1880's, became a fashionable vaudeville. Luckily, all that theatricality is forgotten now; but the pathological method remains as a pillar of modern psychology. It has, in fact, acquired entirely new forms through psychoanalysis.

The methods we have briefly indicated here are, on the whole, the methods of the psychology of 1880. While they are all still cultivated today, they have undergone great changes. We have withheld all criticism, because the history of the twentieth-century psychology is in itself the history of the criticism of the methods of the expiring nineteenth century. The new psychology of that time had already become an old and, in spots, an obsolete one. New methods have arisen and psychological research strives for new goals. But this is a chapter in the main body of our book.

FUNDAMENTAL LEVELS OF MODERN PSYCHOLOGY

1. Before venturing into the history of contemporary psychology I must speak again briefly about method, namely, the method of historical description. We might proceed purely chronologically, as did the historians of former days; this process, however, is hardly germane. We are not dealing with a coherent succession or a straight line development, but rather with the simultaneous development of various violently conflicting tendencies. A purely chronological presentation would serve only to confuse the whole subject beyond repair.

We could also, as I have done in an earlier book, unravel the history of psychology in terms of the development of these different tendencies. In this way we would obtain not a history of the new psychology but a history of the new psychologies. But, as I have already remarked in an earlier book, this process obscures the undeniable unity of psychology and gives a one-sided picture. Similarly, if I attempted to treat the different methods separately and sought to write the history of experimental, comparative, psychopathological, and other psychologies, no unified survey would result.

Therefore, I choose a different approach. I propose to arrange the material about the dominant problems and points of view, that is, about the different and successive conceptions of the character and essence of the soul that were investigated. As it happens, this concept developed in a quite definite fashion—a fashion which paralleled the chronological development, at least in its broader aspects. This point of view requires a certain simplification of the problem for it is not my purpose to name every single work and every author who has ever accomplished anything in any special field of psychology. But what is lost in breadth, we gain, perhaps, in depth. In this way my book will attempt to attain not only a purely historical presentation, but also some validity as a systematic survey, for the sequence of phases which will be presented will necessarily follow one another because of their intrinsic relationships.

I shall, therefore, organize my material in accordance with the transformations that the general concept of the soul underwent in the new psychology, since each separate inquiry depends upon this central concept. Although the "soul" of the psychological science of 1880 is something entirely different from what was called the "soul" in 1900 and in 1930, many psychologists today continue to study the soul of 1880 or the soul of 1910 and to defend their concepts against any innovations! But the majority of psychologists, and surely the more proficient ones, include the results of the more recent research in their works, even when they adhere fundamentally to an older soul concept. Sometimes they are entirely unaware of their practices, as, for example, the psychologists who, conceiving the soul as consciousness, like the generation of 1880, nevertheless usually speak of "structure" or of the "unconscious" too. For the variations of the soul concept are essentially extensions and deepenings of the soul concept which progressively include more and more new and previously unobserved fields of mental life.

The conquest of the terrain of the soul by the army of

psychologists proceeds like the conquest of an enemy country by an army of soldiers. The army does not press forward in a straight line, but advances first on one sector and then on another, as one battalion finds a breach and takes advantage of it. Some battalions are constantly engaged in reinforcing the positions in previously conquered sectors and safeguarding the ground that has already been conquered. But just as the military reports deal mainly with advances and conquests, so in the history of research, the latest developments of the youngest generation of investigators always seem the most interesting.

2. The first phase in the conquest of the soul I have called becoming conscious of the conscious.* When the investigators of this period spoke of the "soul," they meant only consciousness, or, more exactly, the manifestations of consciousness. We shall have to clarify the paradox that the facts of consciousness must first be made "conscious" in our later discussions. At this point our chief concern is to isolate, measure, and arrange the conscious experiences that occur in the confused stream of consciousness. The early investigators were convinced that they would understand the essence of the soul if they succeeded in untangling the Gordian knot of the stream of consciousness into its individual threads, and if they could discover the laws of their association. In the course of these investigations the psychologists shifted their interest more and more to the problem of the totality of consciousness. This problem, however, could not be solved by the mere aid of consciousness itself, and so gave rise to a new problem, the problem of the totality of the ego.

A second research trend was being developed parallel with the studies in pure consciousness: the study of the connection between consciousness and physiological organs. At first the research was directed toward the dis-

*Translator's note. In America we would say becoming "consciousness-minded."

covery of distinct brain areas which corresponded to and controlled the different states of consciousness. This was the problem of cerebral localization. As in the study of consciousness, a deviation from the technique of isolation gradually occurred with regard to cerebral localization. Here, too, the problem of totality entered inevitably into the picture. New trends such as vitalism, psychovitalism, and studies in human constitution appeared on the scene and focused psychological interest on an entirely different plane, by establishing the primacy of the purely psychological over purely physical phenomena.

A third phase in the development of psychological research made movement, not consciousness, the essence of the soul. In this trend the soul emerged primarily as the motor and steering apparatus of the body. The older representatives of this school pointed to the fact that all consciousness is connected with movement and that movements are not only the consequences but often also the causes of conscious experiences. William James was the pioneer in this field. His more radical disciples eliminated consciousness altogether and declared that the description of overt conduct and behavior is the sole task of psychology. The soul theory of the behaviorists and the Russian psychoreflexologists is that the mind is no more than a physical reflex apparatus.

A fourth trend that has become extremely significant since the beginning of the twentieth century advanced in still another direction. It comprehended the task of psychology not as analysis of consciousness, but as the probing of the inner totalitarian structure of mental life. These psychologists expected a solution of their problems neither from physiology nor from the study of motor activities. It became apparent that the consciousness concept was focused solely on the superficial waves and eddies of the stream of mental life, only to overlook the dynamic forces that generated these waves and whirlpools. The concept of the mind as an empty stage upon which the states of consciousness automatically moved about appeared entirely inadequate. What was really behind the scenes? And how were the strings and pulleys which moved the marionettes of consciousness actuated? That was the new problem!

The soul was conceived by this school as though it were a highly complicated lighting apparatus which was entirely different qualitatively from the conscious "light effects" produced by it. The psychologists penetrated into this inner structure of the soul and uncovered its dynamics, its capacities, and its instincts. If the psychology of consciousness was essentially like the botany of Linnæus—a classification of flowers—the new school now wanted to include the roots, stems, and twigs from which those flowers sprouted. The great battle cry of these investigators became "Totality" or "Structure" and by structure they meant more than the mere totality of the consciousness. And presently, quite in contrast to the soulless psychology of earlier days, there emerged a psychology with a soul!

Meanwhile psychiatry made significant discoveries in abnormal mental states which the psychologists utilized practically for the interpretation of the normal mind. The study of hypnosis, hysteria, and other mental abnormalities demonstrated that neither consciousness alone nor consciousness in combination with physical phenomena exhausted the essence of the soul. It had been found that alongside of the primary consciousness there were subconscious or, more correctly, paraconscious phenomena that influenced the primary consciousness and frequently disturbed it considerably. It became obvious that the primary consciousness was not the sole master of human life. Powerful co-rulers and opposing currents were discovered in the soul, and these paraconscious forces were just as much part of the soul as the conscious forces. Psychoanalysis took upon itself the task of investigating these dark recesses of the soul, with the result that some very remarkable and weird things came to light. I have called this phase of recent psychology the Psychology of the Unconscious.

In the meanwhile another tendency arose further extending the horizons of hitherto unexplained psychological phenomena. For this school of psychologists the soul is not purely an individual phenomenon, operative only within the individual organism. These psychologists maintain that there are superindividual phenomena that dominate the phenomena of the individual soul. In this category they place social institutions, speech, morals, political life, and in short those superindividual totalities—civilization and culture—which give individual humans their characteristic and significant hall marks, their common "style of life." Since this style of life is not only superindividual but also superconscious, I have named this phase of psychological research, the phase of the soul, *superindividual superconsciousness*, a superconsciousness whose effect in all individuals is partially conscious and partly unconscious. For this school the soul becomes a superindividual nexus, so that we have folk souls, culture souls, and the like. And lo! the soul which at first was supposed to be nothing more than an entirely empirical reality has become a metaphysical concept again!

As you see, the concept of the soul which the international army of psychologists set out to delimit and to establish has undergone many changes in its development too. Modern psychology finds itself in the predicament of Hercules in his fight with the Hydra: for each head that is cut off the dragon's body, a dozen new heads appear! The "enemy" which the psychologists bravely challenged, far from growing smaller, has become infinitely larger and more complicated. This is no cause for discouragement; while it is not inconsistent with genuine heroism to rejoice at the conquest of an obstacle, good sportsmanship requires that we also rejoice when new and larger problems challenge us. The spirit of the explorer expands as his problems grow. In any case, modern psychology, despite all its zeal, has found confirmation of an expression uttered many centuries before Christ by the great Heraclitus: "You will not discover the limits of the soul though you should wander through each and every avenue; so deep lie its foundations."

And with that we set out to investigate the terrain into which the advancing columns of the army of modern psychologists have marched.

PART ONE

HOW PSYCHOLOGY BECAME CONSCIOUS
OF CONSCIOUSNESS

CONSCIOUSNESS AS THE NUCLEAR PROBLEM OF PSYCHOLOGY

1. What surprises the layman upon first entering the portals of the science of psychology is that he must leave behind him all previously entertained ideas concerning the "soul." For modern psychology at the very outset defines its task as the investigation of consciousness. Its subject matter is, therefore, no longer the "soul," but the facts of consciousness. The relationship of these facts of consciousness to external objects and to the physiological phenomena connected with consciousness is then studied as a corollary procedure.

At first, however, only "consciousness" is posited as the object of psychology. "The attributes of our consciousness, and *only* these, have psychological significance," writes Ziehen and thereby expresses the opinion of almost all his psychological contemporaries. This solemn proclamation can be understood in two ways: on the one hand, as a negative renunciation of all research that probes behind consciousness for a material "soul" or for a mystical psychic force; and, on the other hand, as the positive assertion that it is just this consciousness which is the firm foundation upon which a strictly scientific psychology must be erected. This is assumed rather dogmatically. It is, as a matter of fact, a heritage of the modern idealistic philosophers from Descartes and Berkeley to Kant and Fichte, although the psychologists who preached this doctrine were unaware of the fact. However, they conceived this doctrine in a strictly empirical sense and took pains to remain empirical.

Extreme radicals among the empirical psychologists were even more cautious. They thought that the eclectic concept of consciousness contained an inference which was no longer empirical; it assumed a unity and totality of the conscious which was not confirmed by inner experience. They maintained that psychological phenomena must, first of all, be conceived of in the plural, and that only after doing this could it be determined whether and to what extent man possesses a unified consciousness.

In the course of the development of psychology, it became evident that the supposedly solid foundation of consciousness was much more insecure than had at first been assumed. The phenomena to be investigated became more and more numerous and complex; more and more new perspectives loomed up leading to unknown horizons. Indeed, a few decades after the construction of an empirical psychology upon the basis of consciousness, psychologists and behaviorists denied that this basis is even accessible to empirical science.

2. In point of fact history shows that human beings have not always been aware of possessing consciousness. At least a word for it does not exist in most colloquial languages. The primitive "soul" was a material entity and in no way identical with consciousness. The word "consciousness" is an artificial word which occurs rather late in history and has only gradually assumed its present connotation. In Greece, the concept "συνειδησις" first appears in Democritus and the Stoics and later goes over into Latin as *conscientia*. But even in this form it is not yet represented as a fundamental antonym to the physical. In Plato and Aristotle a great deal of what we today call consciousness is ascribed more to the body than to the soul in its immortal aspect. Descartes was the first to draw a sharp distinction between "consciousness" (*cogitatio*, but also *conscientia*), and the material world. He termed the mind a "substance"; but he classified the passions and emotions as being more physiological than otherwise. His concept of consciousness does not, however, signify the empirical state of consciousness, but a cosmic "substance."

The pioneers of the modern study of consciousness are the Englishmen: Locke, Berkeley, and Hume. Their point of departure was the individual consciousness, although they shifted the emphasis to those very emotions and concepts which Descartes had deprecated. With Leibniz, the line of demarcation between consciousness and unconsciousness is again obliterated, since his "perceptions" could be both conscious and unconscious.

In Germany the word *"Bewusstsein"* (a translation of *conscientia*) first appears in the eighteenth century in the works of Christian Wolff. Very gradually it comes into usage as a composite idea for all feeling, thinking, sensation, and volition. But with Kant and his followers consciousness (*Bewusstsein*) is still not only the sum of conscious experiences, but also includes the inner structure of the mind, the "potentialities," and the essentially unconscious "categories." Consciousness is no purely empirical fact but a somewhat metaphysical one, an interpretation which is very apparent in Fichte, Schelling, and Hegel. They speak of "consciousness in general," which is something quite different from the empirical consciousness of modern psychology. To this very day the psychological and the dialectical Kantians are still disputing as to whether Kant in his theory of knowledge was speaking of individual or cosmic consciousness (*panlogos*).

At any rate, it remains an historical curiosity that for centuries consciousness has been studied by science only as a metaphysical phenomenon. Yet even in the nineteenth century, when consciousness was understood as essentially the empirical consciousness of individuals and was sharply distinguished from the unconscious, there still remained ambiguities in the concept, and the more deeply consciousness was penetrated, the more intangible became its division from the unconscious.

3. Meanwhile, even when we speak of "conscious phenomena" only in the sense of empirical psychology, a "science of consciousness" seems to involve a paradox. For what is science? Exactly understood, it undoubtedly means "making the universe conscious." If I study the natural

sciences, I desire to make the facts and laws of nature conscious; if I study the science of history, I desire to become conscious of the personalities and events of the past. Consciousness or the facts of consciousness, however, are already conscious, at least by definition. What therefore is the purpose of making consciousness conscious?

The paradox is not as involved as it seems. In other sciences, too, the central purpose is not an irrelevant process of consciousness, but systematic description, classification, and determination of laws. Botany as a science does not consist of the mere awareness of the existence of plants but in their description and classification together with insight into the laws of vegetative life. The purpose of the science of consciousness is quite similar. It, too, desires to describe, classify, and determine the laws of the phenomena of consciousness enacted within us in an apparently accidental sequence and chaotic multiplicity.

In the beginnings of psychology, there was very little brain-racking over the fact that consciousness is necessarily divided into dynamic knowing and static known components. The chief interest was in static consciousness, consciousness objectively considered, and the weighty dilemma that consciousness is also subjective was not taken into consideration. This much was sure: when I think about my consciousness, I discover emotions, ideas, feelings in it. These are to be described exactly as the botanist describes his plants and the historian his medieval wars. There was no deterrent in the difficulty that consciousness, which submits its own states to observation and description, thereby changes and distorts those very states. One thing was clear: that it was not immediate consciousness that was being described but a consciousness already gone by that was recalled from memory. The subjective was treated objectively and description and classification were blithely embarked upon without further ado.

4. In view of the function of scientific psychology just out-

lined, it was evident that it had no completely virgin soil to work upon. On the contrary, in colloquial speech and in preëxisting science it already found words and concepts dealing with the conscious life. And since science must make use of language, it must needs work with the linguistic material already in existence.

The mere language of daily life already describes and classifies states of consciousness. Although it has received the word "consciousness" from science, nevertheless, colloquial language long ago possessed words for thinking, feeling, loving, hating, desiring, and for many other even more differentiated states of consciousness. It is, indeed, richer in its nuances of meaning than are the generalizings of science. Whereas science speaks in a generalizing way of pleasurable feelings, colloquial speech distinguishes joy, pleasure, abandon, glee, comfort, delight, happiness, and a dozen other states. It is the more general concepts that are loosely defined and often coincide with one another. In German *empfinden* and *fühlen*, *denken*, and *wollen* often coincide in meaning. I can use *empfinden* with love as well as *fühlen*. I say, "I intend (*denke*) to do something." And the same is true of all other highly developed languages. The French word *sentir* can signify *fühlen* as well as *empfinden*, and has the same distinction as the German words in the derivatives of *sentir*, *sensation*, and *sentiment*. *Sentir* often bears the special meaning of "to smell." In English, in a like manner, the words "to feel" and "to think" are extraordinarily loose in their connotations. One says, "I see," when there is absolutely nothing visual to see but only something to be mentally understood.

Now science has from its very inception tried to give words an exactly defined meaning. Because of the fact that most scientists had their own terminology, the confusion grew even worse. The word "ἰδέα" in Plato means something quite different from the corresponding word (idea) in Locke and Berkeley, where it means something more resembling our modern word "perception" or "image."

With Kant and Herbart, "idea" signifies not only the reproduction of a perception but the perception itself, and it
also can mean "concept" (*Begriff*) which today is sharply
distinguished from "idea" (*Vorstellung*). Many philosophers and psychologists actually developed a private language, as, for example, R. Avenarius, who did so as late
as 1890 or thereabout.

5. The initial task of modern psychology consisted of shaping colloquial language and older scientific terminology so
that it became unambiguous and clearly defined. This labor
was accomplished to a considerable extent in the last decades of the nineteenth century. Most surprising of all, an
international agreement in the matter has even been instituted. Today the possibility actually exists to so designate
the chief types of psychic states that the specialists of all
civilized nations can understand each other to a fair degree.
Without an international committee having been chosen
for the task, a quiet unification of terminology was gradually effected.

In Germany the authority of Wundt, who was conver-
sant with French and English literature, caused his terminology to prevail. For France, the works of T. Ribot on
English and French psychology established a means of
communication among the neighboring countries and
standardized the use of the language. Since many Englishmen and Americans, foremost among whom were William
James, G. Stanley Hall, and Titchener, studied in Europe,
the standardization touched America, until finally such
progress was achieved that today in all countries there exists for the chief types of psychological states an unambiguous, lucidly defined terminology. This defining of technical
terms is the firm basis for all research. These technical
terms must be mastered in order to understand the many
new discoveries and changes within the science.

The following distinctions are made:

a. Sensation (*Empfindung*). This is the act of becoming

aware of an isolated external stimulus by means of a specific sense organ.

b. Perception (*Wahrnehmung*). This is the act of becoming aware of related stimulus complexes by means of one or more sense organs, during which the stimulus complex is mentally translated into an object. You "sense" blue; you "perceive" the sky.

c. Idea or Image (*Vorstellung*). There is no external stimulus in this case. The response is stimulated from within but confines itself mostly to perceptible objects.

d. Concept (*Begriff*). This is essentially a word, that is, a body-motor act that designates a concrete or abstract object and is accompanied by a visual or nonvisual awareness of that object.

e. Simple Feelings (*Einfache Gefühle*). These are the pleasurable or nonpleasurable reactions of the subject which, as subjective attitudes, are supplementary to sensations, perceptions, ideas, or concepts.

f. Emotions (*Gemütsbewegungen, Affekte*). These are mental occurrences mostly accompanied by internal and external body movements and instinctive reactions toward perceived or imagined objects. This concept includes: hate, sympathy, anger, fear, sexual excitement, and similar states.

g. Will (*Willensvorgänge*). This denotes mental states which have a positive or negative relationship to objects, and which strive toward purposeful action; this is also expressed in body movements.

These are the fundamental types of states of consciousness met with in almost all psychological textbooks.

Research has drawn finer distinctions among these fundamental types and has also attempted to reduce them into terms of each other. For the most part, one or more of these fundamental types has been set up as the one and only type, and an attempt has been made to regard the others as derivative from this one type. This, however, is no longer a simple determination of facts, but interpretative theory.

6. A perusal of our outline of the fundamental types of consciousness immediately brings up the question as to whether they really are fundamental types of consciousness. Our answer is: "Yes and no!" Beyond any doubt, each of these fundamental types corresponds to a special, verifiable type of consciousness. But they are distinguished not only by means of consciousness but also by means of their relationship to extraconscious phenomena:

a. by means of their relationship to objects.

b. by means of their relationship to body organs and physiological processes.

From this point of view, an examination of these fundamental types will disclose that each one is distinguished both by a definite relationship to objects and by a relationship to body organs and processes.

This is no arbitrary qualification but derives from the very nature of consciousness which always includes a relationship to extraconscious phenomena and is inseparably bound up with physical occurrences. Making consciousness an absolute, as many philosophers from Berkeley and Fichte on have attempted to do, can only be valid within the bounds of a special philosophical system.

The direct experience of consciousness simultaneously includes the fact that it is related to extraconscious objects and that it is connected with body organs and processes. This fact is recognized by practically all psychologists and it is the basic premise of all psychological research. For two individuals can communicate their experiences of consciousness only in so far as they refer them to some object relationship and to the accompanying body phenomena. The solipsistic point of view that only *my* states of consciousness are real, and that I can have no knowledge of objects, nor of physical occurrences, nor of consciousness, excludes the very possibility of a science.

Every science, including the science of psychology, must make the realistic assumption that outside of consciousness there is an objective world to which the body belongs. It must also assume the possibility of people being able to understand one another. These assumptions are necessarily accepted by all psychologists of consciousness.

In addition to the introspective analysis of our own states of consciousness, rational communication with others also belongs to the science of psychology. Psychology as a science has meaning only when we assume that other people have states of consciousness similar to our own and that there exists the possibility of mutual understanding. This, however, is only feasible if we can place our consciousness into a definite relationship with external objects and at the same time observe the outward reactions of others in regard to the same objects.

When I have a color sensation which I designate as "violet" and should like to know whether someone else is experiencing the same thing, all I have to do is to procure a violet-colored object and determine from the direction in which that person is gazing first of all whether he sees the object, and then whether he also designates the resultant sensation as "violet." It is noteworthy that most colloquial terms for color are already identified with the object which they designate as, for example, the color just mentioned, "violet," which also designates the flower of the same name. With ideas, concepts, feelings, and emotions, such identification with the object designated is not so simple; but it is always present, just as are the accompanying physical reactions.

In accordance with this, we can definitely state that the study of consciousness is always more than the consistent analysis of consciousness; it always implies the relationship to objects and to physical reactions. Indeed, we shall see that even the school of psychology that emphasizes consciousness never confines itself to a mere analysis of consciousness but also always ventures in the direction of object relationship and concomitant physiological phenomena.

In our treatment of the subject we shall, for methodological reasons, make a distinction that is not always observed in psychological research. In this chapter we shall treat only the analysis of consciousness in relation to its objective facts. The relation of consciousness to physical organs and processes will be considered in the following chapter.

7. As for scientific method in modern psychology, the fact that the study of consciousness is not merely a matter of individual introspection has become particularly important because it made possible the use of the experimental method. Introspection was not completely eliminated, as is often claimed, but, bolstered up by experiment, became extraordinarily subtle and to a large extent controllable.

Experiment makes possible the exact control and variation of objective stimuli in relation to the process through which they become conscious. That is why experiment has become especially important in the study of sensation. By means of the artificial variation and combination of stimuli new states of consciousness have been discovered. Many experiments have also been made with thinking, attention, feeling, and will, by means of the creation of special external conditions. Almost always, however, the relation of consciousness to external objects has also intruded into these experiments.

The study of consciousness especially includes those experiments which undertake to measure the states of consciousness. For, besides description and classification, the psychology of consciousness sees its chief task in the measurement of states of consciousness.

The natural sciences served as an example to psychology in this instance. In physics and chemistry the substitution of the quantitative for the qualitative had already been accomplished. Mass, energy, wave length, and wave frequency are quantitative concepts in physics. Heat, voltage, light, and sound are measured. In analogy to these, the attempt was made to measure the facts of consciousness and as far as possible to reduce quality to terms of quantity. The results thus attained shall be listed later. To anticipate, however, we should like to state now that psychomathematics, strictly speaking, never measures consciousness as such; it measures either the relation of consciousness to physical stimuli or to concomitant physiological phenomena. Both of these present genuine scientific problems but nevertheless do not belong precisely to the study of consciousness. •

8. The paradoxical idea of making consciousness conscious has now assumed a definite meaning. What it means is that static consciousness is merged with dynamic consciousness. The earlier generation of psychologists accepted the fact that the appearance of the pictorial image of an object already included the process of becoming conscious of that object. To most psychologists perceptions, ideas, and feelings are not only statically but also dynamically conscious.

Leaving this question for the moment, the science of consciousness consists of the description and precise designation of static states of consciousness. Anticipating the result of these efforts, we can say that the number of types that were distinguished became increasingly greater, and the types themselves were broken up into more and more special, subordinate groups. We shall see how consciousness, which, at the beginning of modern psychology was believed reducible to one, or at the most, to a few elements, proved to be increasingly complicated.

Indeed, the question has been raised whether it is even permissible to speak of "elements" of consciousness at all. The more complex consciousness becomes, the more problematic the unity of consciousness seems. And the question arises whether the consciousness of unity is the unity of consciousness. In other words, the question is whether consciousness as a uniform whole is equal to the sum of its parts. We shall see how this changes the problem of the psychology of consciousness.

THE PROBLEMS OF THE
ANALYSIS OF SENSATION

1. Modern psychology chose the sensations as its initial and most important sphere of study, that is to say, those very experiences which previous thinkers, like Plato and Descartes, had ascribed not to the soul but to the body. It was believed that sensations were particularly well suited for exact examination. Here was an instance in which consciousness stood in a definite relationship to the external world; here the methods of experiment and measurement could most easily be applied. Here also, as in optics and acoustics and in physiology, previous research was available which in itself almost amounted to a valuable contribution to empirical psychology. Besides, it was an earlier belief that the sensations were the "elements" from which all the higher facts of consciousness were developed. That is why all early textbooks of psychology begin with a discussion of the sensations. In tracing the history of modern psychology, we, too, must begin with a study of the sensations. But we shall not at this particular point present all the innumerable minor details since they are to be found in every current textbook of psychology.

We already know the definition of sensation: the act of becoming conscious or aware of a sense stimulus. From this act everything which because of memory, thought, or any other factor is related to it must be subtracted. In everyday life sensations generally appear as complexes. Approximately simple sensations can be derived only under the special conditions of the laboratory. Even here the so-called "simple" sensation is not entirely simple; it becomes a question of determining those of its characteristics which can be varied and separated from one another. In this manner the distinctions arrived at in all sensations are:

    a. type.
    b. intensity.
    c. spatial characteristics.
    d. temporal characteristics.

Belonging with these, according to many psychologists, is the "feeling tone" (*Gefühlston*) which, however, is conceived today as an experience of consciousness entirely different from sensation. In addition, specific characteristics are evinced by the simple types of sensation. These will also be referred to later.

The problem of the psychology of consciousness is, therefore, not merely the isolation of the sensations, but beyond that, the analysis of the sensations in terms of their characteristics.

2. With regard to the types of sensation, modern psychology, allied to physiology, immediately goes beyond the popular classification. In addition to the proverbial "five senses" a number of other types of sensation, each one of which corresponded to a specific organ or to a specific nerve connection with the central system, was discovered. It became evident that the popular distinction of five classes was not universally valid. Thus the boundaries between smell and taste are not very precise because a great deal of what is ordinarily ascribed to the gustatory sense really comes to us through the olfactory sense.

The basis of all study of sensation is the Law of the Specific Energy of Nerves established between 1830 and 1840 by Johannes Müller. It is formulated today as follows: "A sensory nerve always reacts in its own particular manner to any possible stimulus that can cause it to react, and therefore registers only its own specific type of sensation." This law, as Lotze has already remarked, is essentially a physiological one. But it has also become basic for the psychology of sensation the problem of which was to learn which various experiences of consciousness could be determined by stimulating definite organs and varying the stimuli. Johannes Müller's law must not be understood in the sense that the stimulus itself is completely irrelevant. It simply defines the relation of specific types of sensation to specific neurones.

Through the coöperation of physiology and psychology

sensations in addition to the five known ones were isolated. These were the sensation of heat, pain, motion, equilibrium, and also a "general sensation" (*Gemeinsinn*) which embraces the sensations of internal organs. We shall not take up the single types of sensation until we have first discussed the old types which were related to their characteristics. We shall also summarize a few of the more elementary sensations like pressure, heat, and pain under the term "epidermal sensations"; and the kinesthetic, static, and "general" sensations under the term "endogenous visceral sensations."

3. The second characteristic of sensation, intensity, was already known in daily life but had never been systematically investigated. Many psychologists regard as the birthday of all modern psychology the morning of October 22, 1850, when Gustav Theodor Fechner, lying in bed, realized the possibility of measuring the intensity of sensations and bringing these numerical measurements into causal relationship with the numerical measurements of external stimuli. Whether it is right to celebrate that particular day is doubtful; first of all, because Fechner was not without predecessors in his procedure, and secondly, because his results have been too badly belabored by modern criticism, although this, of course, does not necessarily invalidate their historical significance.

In any event, the dignified figure of Fechner has the right to claim a place of honor in every history of psychology, even if the most profound impetus for his methodology, which strove toward the maximum of exactitude, was of a metaphysical and speculative nature. This discoverer of the microscopically detailed method of psychology was also a bold philosopher, who conceived the entire universe as a conscious whole and endowed the fixed stars and planets with "souls."

Presumably, it was his conviction of the consciousness of the universe which impelled him to trace the parallel between mind and body in the experiences of humankind. He, himself, made no claim of absolute priority for his conception of consciousness, but gratefully made use of the work of several predecessors, particularly that of E. H. Weber. He undertook a prodigious amount of detailed labor in counting and measuring; he gathered endless statistics and made endless computations before publishing his investigations in 1860 in a work entitled *The Elements of Psychophysics*.

Fechner's aim was to find a unit of measurement which would permit one to speak not only in general of greater or lesser intensity, but also to say, "this sensation is two or three times as strong as that one." From Herbart, who had spoken quite generally of the "threshold of consciousness" (*Bewusstseinsschwelle*), Fechner adopted the notion of "threshold." He coined the term "stimulus threshold" (*Reizschwelle*) for the point which a stimulus must reach in order to become a sensation. But, in further intensifying stimuli, not every degree of intensification registers; here, too, there are limits which must be exceeded before the intensified stimulus becomes conscious. In such an instance, Fechner speaks of "differentiating thresholds" (*Unterschiedsschwellen*). Using these as a basis, he developed three methods of measuring the intensity of sensation. These are illustrated by the example of sensations of pressure originating from lifting a container with various weights in it.

The problem of measuring the intensity of sensation occupied the earlier generation of modern psychologists to a feverish degree. The announcement of the Weber-Fechner Law concerning the relation of stimulus intensity to the quality of sensation was rated as a scientific feat comparable to Galileo's discovery of the laws of the lever and of falling bodies. Unfortunately, the continuation of these investigations did not confirm the general applicability of this law, and as shortly afterwards as the early 1890's, William James remarked that precious little had come out of that tremendous success. Today it must be admitted that the intensity of sensation is not only dependent upon the stimulus, but also upon a host of concomitant physical and psychic influences. This proves, consequently, that the problem of intensity is not to be solved by means of the isolated analysis of sensations, but only within the sphere of studying the organic whole.

4. Passing on to the spatial characteristics of sensation, we find that we can never refer to a space perception or to space images, into which mental functions not a part of the sensation itself do not enter. When I look out of my window and see the trees in the garden, the towers of the city, and the river disappearing into the distance, I gather these into an organic spatial picture possessing depth and width. This spatial picture originates not only from the sensations of my retina, but also from multifold motions, images, and concepts which are involved with it.

The single sensations that presuppose each spatial picture do not come to me as a chaos, a "turmoil," as Kant said, but they must in some way be spatially conditioned. Not only do stimuli strike the eye in an order that I cannot voluntarily change, but sensations corresponding to these various stimuli also possess such an order.

This necessarily inferred spatial quality of the sensations was first emphasized by Lotze, who introduced the expression "local sign" (*Lokalzeichen*) to designate it. Lotze worked out a theory of the tactual and visual senses. Every contact with the skin brings about a distinctive "local sign" which in itself is not spatial, but is rather a differentiation of intensity upon the basis of which, however, we can localize sensations. With the visual "local sign" the movements of the eye play an important rôle. These "local signs" of sensation are, according to Lotze, the basis for the complex spatial picture which the mind constructs out of them. Incomplete as the theory of "local signs" is, it has not been supplanted by anything better.

Meanwhile the problem as to whether the localization of

sensation lies within sensation itself, or whether it occurs in the entire consciousness must be faced. This problem would lead us beyond the pure psychology of sensation.

5. Problems of the temporal characteristics of sensation seem much more simple than those of spatial characteristics. Laymen are of the opinion that the occurrence and duration of stimuli are exactly defined. But experimental investigation has shown that such a simple state of affairs does not exist.

Here we shall discuss the temporal characteristics of sensation only. These have not always been sharply distinguished from complex temporal perceptions, where, with the aid of memory, expectation, concepts, and judgments, we create a special consciousness of larger temporal complexes; as, for example, when we think of a melody or a long lecture in terms of elapsed time. In order for such a temporal state to come into being, we must ascribe to every single sensation a definite temporal quality. In analogy to "space index" the term for this phenomenon is called "time index."

Experimental research has industriously occupied itself with the relationship of sensation and time. More than anything else, the "reaction time" has been studied, i.e., the length of time that elapses between the application of a stimulus and the motor reaction to it. This study has yielded no uniform numerical measurements. It is difficult to separate the time required for the sensation to register from the time required for the motor reaction.

Not only the starting time but also the stopping time of a sensation offers difficulties. Here, investigation has determined the existence of positive and negative residual sensory images and related phenomena, which are often scarcely distinguishable from the sensations themselves.

The very fact that the temporal quality of sensations is subject to deception forces us to realize its special problems. Indeed, as with the "local signs," the question arises whether temporal characteristics are to be found within the sensations themselves or within the whole consciousness which arranges sensations in an organic order.

6. In addition to all these characteristics common to every type of sensation, distinctions had to be instituted within each separate type; and from the myriad different aspects within each type, certain basic generalities had to be drawn. These were then presented as basic characteristics whose variation composed all the single aspects.

Thus, in the case of visual impressions, colors, color tone, brightness, and saturation were distinguished, and the "color octagon" was constructed. Every shade can be distinguished in the "color octagon" by considering the basic characteristics mentioned above.

With auditory impressions, "sound" based upon regular vibrations was distinguished from "noise" produced by irregular vibrations. Sounds were arranged into a regular series according to "pitch." Although "timbre" is also a distinguishing characteristic of sound, it is much more difficult to classify. It borders upon the uncertain and intangible sphere of noise.

Olfactory and gustatory sensations have also been classified; six basic characteristics were arrived at in the former, and four in the latter, all schematically arranged.

The tactile sense was differentiated into the sensations of pressure, temperature, and pain, but, within these, new forms were also discovered, as for example, Katz's vibration sensations.

With internal sensations, the distinctions were kinesthetic sensations and organ sensations, although they are not very different from one another.

The neurones corresponding to all these types and subtypes and the accompanying physiological facts have been studied since the middle of the nineteenth century. Since 1900, the addition of new material concerning sensation may be said to have been practically concluded. Finer distinctions may yet be made, but it is hardly possible that any more essentially new material will be discovered.

The problem of the relation of sensations to external stimuli is quite a different one. Here, there is no such simple causality as had at first been hoped for, even as regards characteristics. In the beginning, marked individual differences were made the subject of study. Color-blind and tone-deaf individuals, that is to say, definitely abnormal types, were thoroughly examined and an insight into the physiology of color vision and hearing was gained from them.

But even with so-called normal persons, it was found that a given stimulus did not always correspond to the same sensation. Neighboring stimuli brought forth manifold contrasting reactions. Furthermore, the investigation of mixed stimuli revealed that often very complex stimuli corresponded only to simple sensations. Studying the effects on consciousness of mixed colors, sounds, and odors became an expansive field of investigation that set itself many different tasks with reference to the various types of sensation. The results of these investigations are now part of every psychology textbook.

As with the quantitative measurement of sensations, we must take cognizance of the fact that the qualitative coördination of sensation and stimulus is subject to grave uncertainties inexplicable in terms of sensation itself. The qualitative investigation of sensation also indicates that the problem is one of consciousness as an organic whole. While the generation between 1850 and 1900 succeeded in creating some order in the study of sensation, it soon became evident that each of the various problems led beyond the earlier psychology of isolated sensations.

7. That is why it is necessary, with all due acknowledgment of the sound work of the psychologists of sensation, to raise a few fundamental objections against their procedure as a whole, against the position to which they relegated sensations as "elements" of the whole study of consciousness. In the first place, it is questionable whether sensations as such

may even be considered part of consciousness. Secondly, it is doubtful whether they really are "elements." And in the third place, it is uncertain whether there is any such thing as a general causal law in the relationship between stimulus and sensation. All these objections have been brought to the fore by the advancement of the psychology of sensation.

The first objection implies that we never experience a sensation isolatedly but only within complexes in which the separate sensations are merged somewhat like atoms in a molecule. It can be argued, therefore, that when I read a book my eye is struck by black and white impressions; but my consciousness is occupied with the meaning of what I am reading so that no consciousness of black and white arises in me. But even when I deliberately direct my attention upon the black and white, the consciousness of that act of attention is joined to the pure sensation and then makes the pure sensation conscious. The "pure" sensation of the laboratory is, therefore, a "borderline case," and it is doubtful whether it can, as such, still be called conscious. That is the reason why philosophers from Plato to Bergson and Münsterberg have not considered sensation as part of the mind but have credited it rather to matter or to the body. Of course that seems rather extreme to us, but our attitude does not settle the question whether sensation, in a complete sense, is "conscious."

We shall frequently realize the fact that there are few so badly defined concepts as the concept of consciousness. Leibniz drew a distinction between perception and apperception, wherein perception, particularly the *"petites"* perceptions, could be unconscious, whereas complete consciousness referred only to apperceptions. At any rate, "pure" sensation is not conscious in the same sense as, let us say, perceptions or concepts, and experimental psychology can be reproached because it has never studied simple sensations at all, but only simple perceptions or apperceptions.

What psychology calls "simple sensations" means only the concentration of the entire mind upon simple stimuli.

Even in an apparently simple sensation, it is the entire ego that is actually involved, and the "simplicity" can be obtained only as a result of complicated acts of thinking.

The second objection is that sensations, even when they are artificially isolated, are nevertheless not yet "elements" in the sense of "atoms," i.e., indivisible units. In physics, too, since Rutherford and Bohr, the atom has been obliged to submit to further division and no longer rightfully bears its name of "indivisible." The same can be said of the sensations. Psychology itself has contributed its share toward the division of sensations into a mass of separately variable characteristics that can be isolated. It has also discovered separable stimulus sources in a great many sensations. Certainly several such characteristics occur together in all sensations; indeed, it is impossible to conceive of a sensation without temporal characteristics. Besides, these characteristics as a rule are not "apperceived" but only perceived. However, they are "apperceptible" when isolated. They presuppose for the most part separate physical and psychological conditions.

Herbert Spencer tried to probe beyond sensation and searched for psychic atoms. But this was only an hypothesis. Even when we confine ourselves to consciousness, as a matter of principle we are forced to admit that the so-called simple sensation is still further divisible and that, consequently, even a simple sensation is of an eclectic nature. Such an eclectic entity can no longer be called a sensation, but must be a unique synthesis which, beyond the mechanical reception of stimuli, suggests an attitude of mind tending toward organic unity.

The third objection is that psychophysics has found no exact coördination between stimulus and sensation. On the contrary, by its very study of color blindness, tone deafness, and other abnormalities, it had confirmed the fact that between stimulus and sensation there is always an obtrusive physiological factor which is not always constant. The difficulty is thus passed on to a third factor, but is in no way solved. Mental acts such as the degree of attention, the general "tone" of feeling, and the like, so modify pure sensations that all coördination between stimulus and sensation is only approximate or average, but never exact. From a positive angle, therefore, it must be affirmed that there is no such thing as a sensation *per se*, but only sensations as part and parcel of the whole ego. This shifts our problem more and more away from the search for general and average causal laws toward the study of individual differences.

In conclusion, we must realize that despite the many successes of the analysis of sensation, a host of problems has remained unsolved, problems that cannot be solved by this method alone. Their solution can only be found, as we have tried to show from instance to instance, by adopting a point of view that embraces the whole of consciousness and the physical constitution, confronting their totality (*Ganzheitsbetrachtung*).

THE SYNTHESIS OF CONSCIOUSNESS ON THE BASIS OF SENSORY PSYCHOLOGY

1. In studying sensation, psychologists were on firm ground, at least to a partial extent. They united the most disparate tendencies into a larger common purpose. The separation of these tendencies does not begin until the higher functions of consciousness are subjected to a closer scrutiny. Until about 1890, during the early stages of modern psychology, there was general agreement that the main task of psychological science consisted in constructing a synthesis of the higher mental processes on the basis of the more elementary ones. But the very question of how many component types were to be recognized prepared the parting of the ways.

Three parallel tendencies can be traced. First of all there is sensationalism or sensory psychology which considers only sensation and its changing aspects as components of consciousness. Secondly, there is the Wundt school which declares that the entire mind consists of only two components: sensations and feelings. And in the third place, there is a group of many dissenting voices which accepts three or more components.

We shall first discuss sensory psychology. Its basic principle has the scientifically desirable advantage of "economy," since it tries to get along with only one class of components. These components also appear in reproduced form as ideas, and they are bound together by association. That is all. All higher mental processes are to be explained in terms of sensation together with its reproductions and associations.

The chief pride of the sensory psychologists is not only the economy but also the empiricism of their explanation. We have shown above that sensory psychology developed in the eighteenth century in connection with an empirical theory of knowledge. The premise was that all sensations are facts of experience and all experience is founded upon sensations. And the conclusion consequently was that the only way to remain upon a basis of experience was by strict adherence to sensations.

In tracing the way in which sensory psychology developed its system, it is surprising to find that the most radical sensory psychologists at the end of the nineteenth century were to be found in Germany, a country that in the eighteenth century had most energetically rejected sensory psychology. The chief proponents of this school were: Ernst Mach, Theodor Ziehen, Georg Elias Müller, and, with a few reservations, Hermann Ebbinghaus. In principle they are all sensory psychologists, although it will soon be seen that the history of sensation psychology is at the same time a history of the advance beyond sensationalism in various directions.

Psychologists in other countries were also partial adherents of sensory psychology but they were not as one-sided in their beliefs as the aforementioned Germans. This may partially be due to the fact that sensory psychology had already been advocated for a much longer time in England

and France, and thus its limitations were better known. And besides, in England under the influence of Darwin and Spencer, the mind was regarded essentially from the point of view of evolution, which is no pure factor of consciousness. In France, too, psychology had been so influenced by the great psychiatrists that the prevalent theories of abnormal psychology emphasized the importance of the feelings and emotions. And America, no matter how eagerly she turned to the study of sensation, has never adopted a one-sided sensationalism, chiefly because of the influence of Wundt in the United States.

Since the psychology of sensations was studied mostly in Germany, and had celebrated its first great successes there, it is perfectly obvious why the Germans later attempted to explain all higher mental functions from that particular point of view. That, probably, is also the psychological reason why the Germans, formerly the chief antagonists of sensationalism, now became the most radical sensory psychologists.

2. The premise of every sensationalistic psychology of the higher mental functions is that sensations are revived in the consciousness even without an external stimulus. This reproduction of sensation is called an "idea." A consequent task was to study carefully these ideas or images. A sharp distinction was not always drawn between the reproduction of simple sensations and that of complex perceptions. But since perceptions are regarded as complex sensations or as a union of sensations and ideas, this distinction was not absolutely necessary from the point of view of sensory psychology.

By means of introspection, earlier psychology had separated ideas from sensations. Hume understood the difference between the two as being one of degree. After him, ideas and images were differentiated from perceptions by a lesser degree of intensity and vividness. Lotze emphasized the fact that there also existed types of difference. In this he was followed by modern sensationalism which emphasized the transitoriness of images, their poorer content, and their sketchy nature.

The task now was to determine exactly what these differences were. At first the questionnaire method was used by a number of men—Fechner, later by Galton, and more recently by Titchener, G. E. Müller, and others. Great individual differences of vividness and clarity were thus established. Whereas certain individuals, especially artists, have such clear images that they can sketch objects in all their detail from memory, scholars can form no pictorial images, according to Galton. This led to a distinction between concrete and abstract visual types. Most individuals, of course, stand somewhere between these extremes and can form clear images in some fields but not in all.

The psychology of images was particularly inspired by the discovery of further visual types. French scientists, foremost of all Charcot, found that abnormal persons formed only visual images and, after the loss of visual memory, also lost the power of verbal thought. In a similar way, an auditory type was discovered, to which, in turn, a motor type was subclassified. Whether a similar, yet individually different, reproductive capacity could be assumed for the other senses, was not investigated to the same degree.

In distinguishing a "motor" image type, a concept was introduced which disrupted the idea of strict sensationalism: this was the "motor image" to which "speech image" was also added. Could "motor image" be directly coördinated with visual, auditory, and other reproductions of sensation? It was only certain that reproductions of kinesthetic movements might occur even if they were not separately identifiable in consciousness.

The Viennese physician Stricker, obviously a strong motor type, determined that in "motor images" motion is not imagined at all, but is suggestively enacted. And Ribot explained, upon the basis of his investigations, that the so-called motor image is an actual motion in the process of being born. This was widely confirmed by subsequent investigators. A motor image is, therefore, something basically different from a visual image. It is certainly no reproduction of a sense impression, but the production or reproduction of a motion; in other words, an extraconscious occurrence that becomes conscious only through kinesthetic sensations (not reproductions)!

The same applies to "speech images" or "word images." To the motor type, these too are actual suggestive motions, a sort of *langage intérieur*. A great number of investigations were devoted to speech motions, viz., those of Ballet, Egger, Dodge, Meumann, Bärwald.

Although these studies were at first made from the point of view of sensation psychology, they really go beyond sensationalism, even beyond the psychology of consciousness itself; for motions as such are not consciousness, and the kinesthetic sensations which they generate are not images. Unlike visual images, they have nothing to do with primary experiences. Consistent sensationalism is quite inconsistent in subordinating motions to images.

3. With the investigation of ideas as such, little has been attained. We must find out how they are connected with each other and with sensations if we wish to learn the broader relationships of all mental processes.

For this purpose, the older psychology offered the notion of association, a term we have already met in Aristotle, Hume, Hartley, and others. Consistent sensory psychologists used to think that they could explain all higher mental processes through this idea, and that is why today they are often called "associationists."

The concept of association fits into the system beautifully in so far as it reduces the association of images to the association of sensations. Older psychology recognized two main laws of association: the law of contiguity and the law of similarity. Both point back to the field of sensations; for, if contiguity is to be operative between reproductions, it must already have existed in sensations or perceptions. If two images are similar, the primary experiences as a result of which they were formed must have been similar. The objection has therefore been made that the actual problem of ideational phenomena is not one of association but of dissociation; the problem then, is, how does it happen that not all contiguous and similar associations, but only a very few, are aroused?

As a matter of fact, the problem of dissociation has always had a prominent place in associational research. The idea of association intensity was introduced. When A is associated with B,C,D, the most intensely associated idea prevails; i.e., it dissociates the other associations. A main problem for experimental research was, consequently, the measurement of association intensity.

Experimental psychology within the last decades has turned its attention toward the quantitative study of association. In doing this, it drew an insufficiently narrow distinction between associations of ideas and associations of motions. This, however, is a very fundamental distinction, as I shall show later on.

In these experiments it soon became evident that association intensity can depend upon dissimilar facts: upon the frequency of association, clarity, feeling tone, and "constellation," that is, the state of susceptibility or preparedness of all image tendencies associated with the main idea. Endless experiments were made in order to study the dependence of association frequency upon repetition, stimulus intensity, the feeling tone, and other factors. A major portion of the experimental work of the '80's and '90's extends into this field.

The chief sphere of the application of associational research became experimental mnemonics, which was introduced by Ebbinghaus. His work on the memory * (1885)

*Ebbinghaus, *Über das Gedächtnis* (Eng. tr., *Memory*, 1913).

was epoch making. He worked with nonsense syllables and also with meaningful memory material. In the former case, meaning and the feeling tone were eliminated and their significance was estimated in comparison with the learning of syllables connected in meaning. With indefatigable perseverance extending over a period of many years, Ebbinghaus tested the permanency of associations and drew up exact statistical tables of the number of readings necessary for retention of content, of the progressive forgetting of content, and so forth. His investigations were taken up to an even greater degree by G. E. Müller and his co-workers, F. Schumann, A. Pilzecker, and others. Later Meumann and his assistants worked along in the same direction.

We shall not criticize the practical value of these experiments. We only wish to call attention to the fact that the same objection must be raised here which we raised in the case of the idea theory; namely, that the difference between idea association and motor association is not brought out with sufficient emphasis. Since almost all associational and mnemonic research works with linguistic material, the act of mental reproduction was in many instances only the training of motor mechanisms, something that is entirely different from ideational association.

The theory of association was no mere analysis of consciousness in yet another instance. In many cases, since associations seemed to "jump," the existence of unconscious interconnections had to be assumed. And furthermore, is "association" as such really conscious? This, too, must be denied. The only thing that is conscious is that which has been associated, not the associating connection itself. All unconscious interconnections were not empirically determined but only hypothetically inferred. And even the "constellation" is totally unconscious; it was supposed to have been based upon the "state of susceptibility or preparedness" of association, of which only very few actually became conscious. If, however, in addition to the one idea in a state of nascent consciousness, many others simultaneously arise, it becomes apparent that the mind as an organic unit operates together with every "constellation."

4. The sensory psychologists hoped that they could explain all other mental functions on the basis of ideas and associations. They sought to get at the nature of perceptions, i.e., the coördination of sensations to space-time complexes, and, further, to the concrete grasp of "things."

They considered first of all space perception, and particularly optical space perception. Kant's view that single sensations are only regulated by the "form of seeing" was opposed to this. Sensationalistic empiricism, on the other hand, emphasized that stimuli and sensations were already in themselves regulated and characterized by local signs. Nevertheless, innumerable problems remained for the solution of which eye movements were studied, viz., accommodation, eye convergence, and binocular parallaxes. The determination of depth and three-dimensional vision offered especially difficult problems toward whose solution the physiologists and psychologists worked together at the end of the nineteenth century.

The optical illusions were a favorite subject for research, as was the ability to judge the size of spatial objects. The studies of congenitally blind persons whose vision was restored by surgical operations were particularly fruitful. Similar to the problems of optical space perception are those of tactual space perception. Here, too, there were all sorts of illusions regarding the localization of objects in space to be interpreted; and here, too, the study of blind persons was very productive of results.

The controversy revolved chiefly about the question of the extent to which space perception originated in experience, and the extent to which it was innate. In general a compromise solution was achieved by assuming an innate organization of space perception which, however, must be developed through experience. But, since this innate organization was related to the organs of motion, and since investigation proved that all space perception was related to muscular movements, the limits of the pure psychology of consciousness were thus overstepped. A quality of innateness must also be granted to innate organs of motion, even when they are developed through experience.

Parallel with the study of space perception went the study of temporal and motor perceptions. Countless experiments were made upon the subjective judgment of time, the temporal relations of two impressions, the comparison of time intervals and rhythmic experiences. And again the empiricists and the "nativists" were opposed; and again it became evident that especially in involuntary rhythmic movements motor acts play an important rôle. In general, such psychologists as Ebbinghaus, Mach, and Schumann, who worshiped sensationalism on principle, granted the innate quality of the apprehension of time. Undoubtedly, acts of thinking and judgment hardly explicable from the viewpoint of sensation psychology are involved in the judgment of time.

For motor perception, the sensory psychologists adopted memory images as explanatory devices. But the very theory of motor perception casts doubts on the sensory associational interpretation of motor perception as consisting of single perceptions plus their associations, and views them as *Gestalten* or totality experiences (Wertheimer).

Perception is only partially explained in terms of space and time. To these must be added *Gestalt*, recognition, character of reality, and "objectification." Sensory psychology explains all these by "ideas." Thus we have G. E. Müller's definition: "An idea just being formed is (1) complemented or interpreted by other ideas either already existent in a state of susceptibility or called into existence by that idea, or (2) is brought into some other relationship with some previous experience." The opinion that a special process of "apperception" was to be assumed was absolutely rejected, contrary to Wundt's view. The sensory psychologists would far rather believe that everything was explicable in terms solely of ideas and associations.

Ziehen explained the procedure more thoroughly than anyone else. According to him, when I see a rose, an entire series of memory pictures is formed by the complex of visual sensations: a tactual image, an olfactory image, an acoustic idea of the word together with the motor idea of its articulation. The totality of these elements results in the complete idea, the apperception of "a rose."

The object of the experimental investigation of apperceptive phenomena is the testing of the *"Gestalt* problem." The method utilizes such apparatus as the tachistoscope in the investigation of optical illusions, the mechanics of reading, and the like. Most of these experiments tend to discredit the sensory associational explanations of the phenomena.

At this point, we shall attempt only to decide whether the sensory explanation of perception remains true to its principle. It must be remembered that this explanation did not originate from the direct analysis of consciousness, because introspection tells us nothing about associated ideas. Ziehen, therefore, also speaks of the "sympathetic harmony" (*Anklingen*) of ideas, or of the arousal of such auditory elements as contain the residues of those images. This, of course, deserts the point of view of consciousness and introduces unconscious ideas.

5. A thorough-going investigation of attention was also at this time made from the angle of sensory psychology. Attention was characterized on the one hand as the narrowing of the field of consciousness, and on the other hand as the intensification of the degree of consciousness. Herbart had already attempted to explain attention as the rise and ebb of competing ideas. Modern associationism follows him in that. It attempts to explain attention in terms of the objective qualities of those sensations or ideas that are attended to; in other words, in terms of external conditions,

such as novelty, intensity, and importance. But all these only lead to "passive" attention and neglect its "active" aspect which is just as frequently experienced.

Experimental research in the field of attention produced many offshoots. An attempt was made to measure the span of attention,* its power of distribution, and its intensity. The temporal characteristics, divertibility, and variability of attention were experimentally tested. The pathology of attention was studied by Vaschide and Meunier (1908) and by Specht (1908) after Ribot had already done pioneer work in the field.

In the course of these investigations, physiological motor facts entered the field of observation; e.g., tension of the eye muscles, of the scalp, even changes in the entire tonus of the body. Ribot pointed out these factors and an attempt was made to relate the consciousness of activity in "paying attention" to the kinesthetic sensations thus aroused. While this rescued sensory psychology from all doctrines that sought for some special apperception or influence of the will in attention, it shifted the problem from the sphere of pure consciousness into the motor sphere. Does this shift explain the direct experience of an organic direction of consciousness toward the object that attention designates? Here, too, strictly empirical analysis must lead to an organic theory that associationism cannot satisfactorily give us.

6. What is the relationship of sensory psychology to general ideas and concepts? Berkeley, who denied the possibility of general ideas, had already surmised these difficulties. The more modern sensationalists followed him in this to a certain degree; they spoke of blendings, "the phenomena of fading" (Brod and Weltsch), and the like. Ebbinghaus describes the matter thus: "I am thinking of a tree or of trees. The extent to which my mind is involved is ex-

*Wirth, *Ph. St.*, 1902; Geissler, *Am. J. Psych.*, 1909; Dullanbach, *Am. J. Psych.*, 1913.

tremely little. I think of the name, perhaps of something tall and branched, but scarcely more. All the countless details which characterize certain trees or a certain species of tree, as well as the great multiplicity of these species are far removed from my consciousness; they do not burden my mind. Therefore, I can very easily manipulate my idea of trees; I can relate it to others and think, for example, that trees can attain a very great age and grow only to certain heights, and the like. But as soon as the play of my thoughts produces a relationship which is incompatible with any one of those unthought-of characteristics of trees and their divers species, they immediately become alive and reject what is opposed to them. They have not, therefore, been simply nonexistent in my mind, even though previously they had not been consciously brought forward. On the contrary, thinking of the general idea also smoothed the paths of the details together with which the idea had been visually experienced, and from which it then was detached. In some manner these details are brought into proximity with the conscious, and when a slight impetus is added to one or the other of them, they are associatively awakened. . . . The general idea has become an inclusive surrogate for the details. The general idea becomes a 'concept' when it is associated with a comparable symbol, that is to say, a word, which then becomes a center of association in a similar manner."

We admit that this explanation attempts to retain the associational point of view in a very cogent manner. Nevertheless, here too, just as with the associational theory of perception, we must observe that this is no longer pure analysis of the conscious, but a hypothetical construction that refers back to unconscious associations. The psychology of consciousness and particularly sensation psychology is overstepped, moreover, when words and speech are taken into consideration. Articulate speech as we have repeatedly emphasized is not a pure act of consciousness and has nothing sensory about it; it is a process of motion and as such falls beyond the self-appointed limits of sensation psychology.

7. The field of mental processes that seems farthest removed from that of sensory psychology even though sensationalism invokes it for the explanation of the associations of attention, is the field of the emotions. Stumpf, who is otherwise not to be counted among the sensation psychologists, has even upheld the theory that pleasure and displeasure are only special types of sensations (feeling sensations). In general, the sensation psychologists like James Mill, Bain, Nachlowsky, and recently Ziehen, see in the feelings only "characteristics" of the sensations. G. E. Müller also accepted the view that feelings occur solely in conjunction with sensations. Almost all the sensory psychologists maintained that only pleasure and displeasure are to be regarded as elementary feelings. The experiments of the sensory psychologists were primarily designed to investigate the dependence of feelings upon sensations, their quality, intensity, and duration.

At first these experiments were confined to artificial laboratory conditions. Any undogmatic study would eventually result in the conclusion that feelings are only partially dependent upon stimuli and, in the main, are dependent upon the general disposition of the entire self, as when even the "most appetizing" food can arouse anorexia or disgust when the organism is oversatiated.

The more complex states of feeling, such as emotions and passions, were also subjected to a sensory interpretation. The earlier sensory psychologists like Ziehen wanted to explain the emotions as the combination of ideas and feelings, the feelings being, however, only "tones" of ideas. The "peripheral" theory of emotions, which was announced almost simultaneously by the Danish psychologist C. Lange and by William James in 1884, is apparently even more extreme from a sensory point of view. This theory traces the emotions back to internal sensations which, according to Lange, are bound up with vasomotor activity, and, according to James, with visceral processes.

There is no agreement as to whether emotions are pure sensory combinations, or whether they are, as James conceded and as Störring later sharply emphasized, the feeling tones tied up with those sensations which constitute the consciousness of emotions. In any event, this doctrine, extremely sensory as it seems to be at first glance, actually extends beyond sensationalism when it relegates the nature of emotions to movements which, as such, do not belong to consciousness.

8. Acts of will fall into the same category. Most sensory psychologists agree that there is no such thing as will as an elementary experience of the consciousness. The traditional associationists like Herbart, Spencer, and Ziehen tried to see the nature of will in ideas; yet, at the same time, they could not help realizing that the motions related to those ideas were essential factors of will. Ebbinghaus went back to instincts whose rise to consciousness he explains in a sensory fashion by emphasizing the rôle of kinesthetic sensations. But he admits that sensations of motion presuppose a motion which as such is not mental. Will is instinct which has become anticipatory. But he maintains that nothing but sensations or feelings of pleasure and displeasure are present in will; at most, strong fusion of these elements was believed to exist. But all this is true only of the conscious side of will, which, however, presupposes motor acts—a fact no sensationalist disputes—so that once again the limits of the psychology of consciousness are exceeded.

Experimentally, only simple reactions were studied to any great extent by the older psychology. This psychology concerned itself with the measurement of reaction time, the influence of fatigue, and other problems which referred more to motor activity than to the accompanying consciousness. As soon as this was taken into consideration, chiefly because of the work of Ach, a refutation of sensory psychology was found.

Much greater psychological difficulties, however, are involved in the understanding of those extensive attitudes of will, such as planning and project making, which life demands of every one. The attempt to solve the problem by means of a dominant "super-idea" (*Ober-Vorstellung*) as Liepmann, for example, attempted to do, reveals even more clearly the complete inability of associational psychology to explain acts of conscious volition.

9. In spite of this, sensationalism attempted to completely resolve the total consciousness, the "self," into sensations and ideas. Following Hume, Ernst Mach emphatically and radically stated that "The self is irretrievably lost!" According to him, the ego is nothing but the result of sensations, under which he also included ideas, feelings, and concepts. Later sensationalists, like Ebbinghaus, emphasized the particular importance of organ sensations for the consciousness of self. These, experienced as a unit, form the solid nucleus of the self which is designated as the "most dominant mental idea." All this, however, refers only to the "idea of self," the consciousness of self; but even extreme sensationalists granted that consciousness of the self is inconceivable without the body that goes with it. This makes sensationalism no longer a pure analysis of consciousness. Elsewhere, too, the boundaries of pure consciousness are crossed. When, for example, Georg E. Müller designates "all capabilities or types of reactions," as the potential content of the consciousness of self, he necessarily admits the existence of "capabilities," which are not pure facts of consciousness. The problem of self reveals most clearly that every synthesis of isolated sensations and ideas must perforce remain an incomplete picture.

10. Reviewing the sensory synthesis of the higher mental

capabilities, we must admit that it attained many valuable results, although its principle of research is open to much criticism. It unveiled the process of perception in all its complexity; it demonstrated the importance of previous experiences, the significance of motor acts in perception and related experiences. Moreover, it cast light upon the complex world of ideas and demonstrated interesting individual differences in the formation of ideas. The distinction between visual and motor memory, of especial importance in the field of mnemonics, also produced practical results. Because of its demonstration of the importance of motor processes in memory, the study of attention also proved significant in mnemonics. And in many other ways a multitude of interesting facts were discovered by this psychological movement.

All this is undoubtedly to be entered upon the credit side of sensory experimental psychology. Whether the basic principle of sensory psychology, that all higher mental functions are based on sensation, was consistently upheld is an entirely different matter. If we pursue this question to its logical conclusion, we are compelled to come to the astonishing result that the history of sensory associationism is also its own refutation. For the doctrines of the sensationalists prove in themselves that the sensory principle is inadequate.

In the first place, we need feelings in order to explain memory, imagination, attention, emotion, and will; and it is not enough to reduce feelings to nothing but sensations. They are neither sensations themselves nor are they characteristics of sensations. And even if they were, they would still be something different from "pure" sensation.

In the second place, the history of sensory psychology shows that it was compelled to refer to an ever increasing degree to motor processes. The sensationalists themselves mentioned all manner of motor processes in connection with perceptions, ideas, concepts, attention, and emotions. In accordance with their principle, they justifiably emphasized the kinesthetic and visceral sensations related to motor acts, but they overlooked the fact that these sensations are not the motion itself, and that motor processes are something entirely different from sensations. If this is granted, then the basic principle of sensationalism is shattered. In other words, the history of sensation psychology demonstrates that it is impossible to understand the higher mental processes in terms of sensations and their recollection and associations.

Sensory psychology is really as inconsistent as at first sight it seems to be consistent. It endeavored to give us an analysis of consciousness and constantly went beyond consciousness: in one instance by the introduction of unconscious mental connections in association and constellation, and, in the other instance, by the inclusion of motor acts. Sensory psychology cannot maintain that it remains within its premises in introducing motion, because it has always emphasized that all processes of consciousness are to be coördinated with physiological processes. This does not apply to motion because there is no parallelism in instinctive acts and acts of the will. On the contrary, motions partly precede and partly succeed consciousness.

Even the strongly emphasized empiricism of sensory psychology has a doubtful status. It exists in intention, not in execution. The very assumption that sensations alone are grounded in experience is dogma, not empiricism. Our direct experiences in no way tell us that feelings, acts of will, thoughts, and the like consist only of sensations. Sensationalism had to "prove" this by main force and by means of distortive theories. These theories, however, not only were not derived from direct experience, but also directly contradicted experience. There are unquestionably inner experiences which cannot be reduced to sensations. My experiences, when I feel, think, and will, are not based upon sensations, even when we grant the sensationalists that sensations and ideas play a significant rôle in them.

This brings us to a third shortcoming of sensory psychology: its passivism. It claims that sensations arise through the passive reception of external stimuli. The most direct experience of consciousness, however, is a feeling of activity which appears in attention, thinking, and volition. Sensationalism ascribes the consciousness of activity, when it does not overlook it entirely, to motions and their reflected kinesthetic sensations. There is a degree of truth in this, but it does not explain the entire phenomenon. For this reason, sensory psychology was subjected to sharp criticism even by the Wundt school which otherwise often agreed with it. The criticism has been even more severe from all those schools which claimed the total activity of the self as the elemental experience of our consciousness, as opposed to the atomizing passivism of the sensationalists.

All such criticism converges upon the fact that sensory psychology, which minces consciousness into atoms of sensation and then laboriously ties these atoms up with threads of association, does not achieve totality. The attempted synthesis remains incomplete. It makes consciousness a mosaic of sensations, not a living whole. That is why sensory psychology was compelled by subsequent schools to take the defensive. It made the problem of totality painfully evident just because it stuck to its basic principle so stubbornly. Its historic mission was to lead beyond itself.

SYNTHESIS OF CONSCIOUSNESS FROM TWO ELEMENTS

1. The "consciousness" of the sensory psychologists was but a passive mirror of the objective world, despite all their attempts to explain active subjectivity from their point of view. Since the relegation of activity to body-motor functions contradicted the experience of activity in consciousness, active elements were sought in consciousness itself. In fact, there is a second school of research which energetically denied that the totality of consciousness is composed of only one type of elements. It maintained that there

were two principal classes of elements to be distinguished: sensations and feelings, which are in no way reducible to sensations. These feelings, it was affirmed, were not merely important as such; they also merged partly with each other and partly with sensations and ideas in various relationships, in such a manner that the entire higher consciousness was inexplicable without the feelings.

The chief representative of this school is Wilhelm Wundt. As the founder and director of the Psychological Institute of the University of Leipzig, he exercised a powerful influence not only in Germany but in all other countries. Not that he limited himself to the feelings in his investigations. He was also a leader in the psychology of sensation and industriously studied the phenomena of ideation. His was an encyclopedic mind of magnificent dimensions. He began as a physiologist, wrote giant works on all branches of philosophy, on logic, and ethics, and finally outlined his own system of philosophy. He was acquainted with all the older scholars and followed the work of his contemporaries with interest and occasionally with trenchant criticism. Innumerable students gathered about his lecture pulpit, where, over his great beard, he calmly and undramatically delivered himself of his immense knowledge.

His chief work, *Principles of Physiological Psychology*, contained, in three volumes running to 2000 pages of small print, all that he had to say concerning psychological questions. This book was for decades a standard work in the library of every psychologist and grew in size with every new printing. A shorter outline of psychology followed in 1895. But Wundt's views on the psychology of the individual were conclusively formed about 1890. In his ten-volume work, *The Psychology of Peoples*, which occupied him until his death in 1920, he turned his attention toward the problems of the superindividual relationships of the mind.

2. Since Wundt considered feelings and sensations as equally

important elements of mental life, he had first to prove that feelings are not reducible to sensations, as had been maintained by the sensation psychologists. To do this, Wundt pointed to the psychological fact that clearly conceivable external organs can be aligned with sensation, whereas the physiological phenomena accompanying feelings are of a central (cerebral) nature. He maintained emphatically that the aspect of consciousness in the case of feelings was entirely different. Their particular characteristic is motion in opposites, which is revealed by the designation of their basic forms such as pleasure, displeasure, excitement, tension, and relief.

Another decisive factor is the circumstance that related feelings can be connected with entirely different objective sensations. A sound, a color, a taste—each is entirely different from the other; all of them, however, can summon forth in us in a very similar manner pleasure or displeasure, excitement or calm. Sensation is objectively conditioned; feeling is a variable subjective reaction thereto while the sensation remains the same. The feeling of pleasure in a melody can turn into displeasure through frequent repetition even though the sensations of sound remain the same. From this Wundt concluded that feelings must be elements of consciousness entirely distinct from sensations. For the rest, Wundt agrees with the sensory psychologists that all higher states of consciousness are composed of elements.

In his more detailed analysis of feeling, Wundt diverged from the sensory psychologists in that he did not merely distinguish the opposites of pleasure and displeasure. He affirmed the existence of a three-dimensional diversity, i.e., the three contrasts:

a. pleasure—displeasure.

b. excitement—calm.

c. tension—relief.

Beyond these three-dimensional feelings, Wundt also sponsored a pluralistic theory of feeling. He taught that the single feelings of pleasure or of tension are not quite the same, but at most something similar to one another. The pleasures in an harmonious chord, in appetizing food, in a moral deed are similar, in so far as they are feelings of pleasure, but they are different when compared to each other. The number of possible feelings, therefore, is much greater than the number of possible sensations and ideas.

3. In sensations and feelings we would have, therefore, the elements of consciousness. We must now make the higher experiences of consciousness comprehensible in terms of these elements. Wundt attempted to accomplish this by means of a system which is naturally much more complicated than that of sensory associationism, since the feelings intrude at every juncture.

From sensations and feelings Wundt synthesized the mental "constructs." The classification of mental constructs is relative to their component elements. If sensations are predominant, the constructs are called "images" or "ideas"; if feelings are predominant, they are called "emotions." The chief forms of ideas or images (*Vorstellungen*) are:

a. intensive images or ideas.

b. spatial images or ideas.

c. temporal images or ideas.

The chief forms of emotions (*Gemütsbewegungen*) are:

a. intensive feeling combinations.

b. affects (emotions *per se*).

c. volitional acts.

Mental constructs furthermore are connected with each other in the most diverse ways. Images or ideas are combined in part into greater simultaneous idea complexes, and in part into regular idea sequences. In a similar way, feelings and volitional acts are combined, sometimes with each other, sometimes with ideas as well. The nexus of mental constructs thus becomes a class of synthetic processes of the second degree, erected upon the simpler primary images and ideas. Sometimes of a simultaneous nature and sometimes sequential, these mental constructs are further differentiated according to the kind of attention directed toward them. If the consciousness remains passive, Wundt speaks of "associations"; if it is active, then he refers to "apperceptive combinations."

4. We must consider separately this concept of "apperception" which is of such central importance in Wundt's psychology. Apperception presupposes association, the one factor the sensory psychologists admitted. It is distinguished from association in the subjective consciousness by a concomitant feeling of activity; association occurs passively, apperception actively. It is not objectively conditioned by an associated image, but is subjectively conditioned by the entire previous development of consciousness. By this means, the apperception attains the character of a volitional act. Apperception certainly presupposes disposable associations; but it selects from their number only those which correspond to the given situation. Sometimes it combines ideas or images and sometimes it divides them. In every case, however, it is a relating function, and in that it differs most clearly from association, which takes place without relation to a future goal.

Volition is the basic phenomenon in which all mental processes based on feelings take root. In the process of apperception volition comes into direct relation with the idea content of consciousness. Because of the fact that volitional processes, however, are conceived as related and similar in spite of the differences of their content, a direct feeling of this relationship arises. This is first tied up with the feeling of activity which accompanies all will, but later extends itself throughout all the contents of consciousness. This feeling of the relationship of all individual mental experiences, Wundt designates as the "self." This is no image, no idea, but a feeling which, of course, is bound up with general sensations and the ideas of one's own body.

A third level of relationships which Wundt designates as "mental developments" is constructed above the connections of mental images and ideas. These are divided into developmental processes of various kinds. Developmental processes of the narrowest type are those which relate to the development of the intellect, of the will, of the feelings, or even merely to the development of a separate component of these forms of function, as, for example, the development of esthetic or moral feelings. The sum total of these mental developments dominates the single instances.

Beyond the study of these various levels of combination of mental elements, ideas, relationships, and developments, stands the task of formulating the principles governing the general laws of mental phenomena, the task of revealing the mental causality expressed in all these processes.

The problem of the "soul" is the focus of these researches. For Wundt, the soul was only an auxiliary concept intended chiefly for the purpose of causal interpretation. He rejected the concept of the soul as a substance, and replaced it with a concept of actuality which considered the direct reality of mental processes themselves as the essence of the soul. From this angle the body-mind problem assumed a new aspect. It was no longer a question of two different substances, but of two different points of view in regard to the same experience. To a certain degree Wundt relinquished the notion of psychosomatic parallelism, but he retained the elements and constructs. Their characteristic connective and relating forms, together with concepts of value and purpose, are not subsumable to the principle of psychosomatic parallelism.

Consequently, independent psychological causalities had to be assumed for the three general principles. In the first place there is the principle of "psychological resultants" which states that every mental construct displays its own characteristics which cannot be understood in terms of the qualities of its components, and yet is more than the mere sum of its component elements. In this principle, therefore, a creative synthesis is recognized. Wundt believed an increase in mental energy was possible while physical energy remained constant. Wundt moreover distinguished the principle of mental relationships and of contrasts. Applied to broader mental relationships, these principles yielded the general laws of the evolution of mental growth, of the heterogeneity of purposes and the evolution of opposites.

5. Wundt's system in its entirety is a much more complicated structure than the system of the sensory psychologists. The reason for this is that in almost all mental experiences, two types of elements coöperate. Nevertheless, his description of consciousness is a much closer approach to direct experience than the hypothesis of the sensory psychologists. Wundt does more justice to the experience of subjective activity than do his opponents, who relegated all activity to physical motion, and in this regard Wundt held to the standpoint of consciousness more consistently than they. Indeed, he censured and absolutely rejected the notion that motor acts and the sensations derived from motor activity could explain attention, emotions, and volitional acts, thereby depriving his psychology of the undeniable value of these facts.

If we want to understand Wundt historically, the most important fact to remember is that Wundt was the great champion of the German tradition in psychology. Sensory psychology, even among its German representatives, continued the English and French tradition which began with Locke and led to the Mills and Taine. The psychological tradition of Leibniz and Kant, who discarded the *tabula rasa* theory of the sensory psychologists and emphasized the subjective attitudes in consciousness, is still alive in the Wundtian psychology.

It is not easy to understand the historical ramifications of Wundt's influence. He was, undoubtedly, an inspiration of the first order and most psychologists of the younger generation have either been his direct pupils or have been influenced by him. What is most remarkable, however, is that the very theories which he considered of primary importance in his system have not been accepted by the most active of his disciples. Certainly they accepted his doctrine of the feelings as independent elements, and they agreed with him about their great significance for the higher mental processes, especially volition. But they rejected the other doctrines of three dimensionality, of the pluralism of feelings, and Wundt's theory of apperception. Most of Wundt's pupils recognized the nature of feelings as elements, but beyond that endeavored to explain the higher mental processes according to the tenets of sensory psychology, that is, they created a synthesis of Wundt and sensory psychology. It was the tragedy of Wundt's life that he attracted many pupils but held only a few. Meumann, Külpe, and many others studied at his feet but eventually went their own ways.

6. This is also true of E. B. Titchener, an Englishman working in America, who founded his own school in the United States. He took over from Wundt the recognition of feelings as independent elements, but approached the sensory psychologists more nearly in his interpretation of the higher mental processes. Titchener discarded Wundt's three-dimensional idea and his notion of pluralism as regards the feelings, and like most of the sensory school recognized only pleasure and displeasure as primary feelings, going so far as to dispute the possibility of "mixed feelings."

Titchener also followed an independent path in his theory of attention. Like the sensory psychologists he rejected the idea of a special activity of consciousness in attention, and explained its real nature only in the greater clarity of visual experience, in its increased "vividness" or "intensity." His kinship with the sensory school also showed itself in his violent opposition to the Würzburger school, which tried to introduce nonvisual mental elements. Titchener's influence in America was very great. Although he was a pioneer of a new science in the beginning, he gradually became the representative of conservatism in psychology and eventually found himself opposed not only to the new German tendencies, but also to the new American trends toward "functionalism," the study of individual skills, and behaviorism.

Not only the orthodox Wundtian school but even its independent followers were destined to represent venerable and even antiquated traditions in the twentieth century. While it must be granted that Wundt considered the problems of subjectivity, of activity, and of the totality of mental life much more rigorously than the sensory psychologists, his solutions, nevertheless, have proved themselves untenable. And Wundt himself was never able to rid himself entirely of the tendency to "atomize" consciousness, despite the fact that he limited this trend by many theoretical conditions.

SYNTHESIS OF CONSCIOUSNESS FROM THREE AND MORE ELEMENTS

1. Along with the psychologists who believed in one and two elements of consciousness, there were certain workers in the '70's and '80's who were unwilling to limit the fundamental elements so closely. They felt that a more comprehensive survey of mental components was more important than the reduction of all mental life to a few elements. In this section we shall group a series of thinkers who recognized three and more elementary experiences in mental life. In considering these "elements" we must emphasize that they no longer retain the character of "elements" in the meaning of the sensory psychologists, but are already designated as acts, positions, and fixed characteristics.

The most widely influential school that posited three basic elements of mental phenomena was that of Franz Brentano. This school predominated in Austria at a time when the national boundaries were much more extensive than at present. Most of the chairs of psychology in the universities were gradually filled by pupils of Brentano, although he himself lost his position because, in spite of having been a Catholic priest, he married. He went to live in Florence and in Switzerland as a free-lance scholar. The fact of his priesthood is mentioned here because it is important for the understanding of his psychological system.

From his clerical past, he brought along a knowledge which was at the disposal of none of his Protestant colleagues: a profound acquaintance with Aristotle and the scholastic psychology of the Middle Ages. And all this was no dead mass of information to him, for he breathed new life into it. Now the old Schoolmen had known something about consciousness which was later forgotten or disregarded. They had pointed out with great emphasis that consciousness is never an immanent condition, but in all its forms is focused upon something which does not lie within consciousness itself.

In the Middle Ages, this was called the "intentional or mental inexistence of objects." Brentano shaped out of this his doctrine of the intentional character of consciousness, a doctrine which was to become fruitful in the development of logic and epistemology. Brentano's chief psychological work, *Psychology from the Empirical Standpoint*, appeared in 1874. Its first volume appeared at about the same time as Wundt's *Physiological Psychology*. A part of the second volume appeared in 1911 under the title *The Classification of Mental Phenomena*. A third volume, *The Sensory and Noetic Consciousness*, did not appear until 1928, ten years after the author's death. It is therefore very difficult to define Brentano's historical position. He developed an extensive school but it is difficult to determine how much of his fame was due to the personal inspiration of his lectures, for little remains in his written works to account for his great following.

We are chiefly concerned with Brentano's analysis of consciousness, or, as he says, of "mental phenomena." He agrees with most of his contemporaries that at first the "elements" of mental life must be ascertained. He distinguishes three basic classes of such elements: ideas, feelings, and judgments. It is particularly the recognition of judgments as basic classes which differentiates his psychology from that of other schools.

Brentano did not conceive of the notion of the "idea" in the narrower sense of "a reproduced perception," but in the broader sense used in the terminology of older German philosophy. According to this, all perceptions and concepts are "ideas," just as are experiences of memory and imagination. In many ways Brentano's notions are more complicated than those of most other psychologists who maintained that an idea was a mere "picture" of external objects without attempting to account for the process whereby such a "picture" became conscious.

Brentano emphasized the doctrine that every idea also included an idea of that idea. When we have an idea of a sound, we are conscious that we have it. That, however, does not mean that there are two different ideas; on the contrary, both belong to the same psychical act. It is only conceptually that we can separate the idea of that idea by separating the dual connection between two different objects, a physical and a mental one. "In the same mental phenomenon in which a sound is imagined we grasp at the same time the mental phenomenon itself according to its dual nature (1) in so far as it contains the sound, and (2) in so far as it is simultaneously present as a mental content. The sound is the primary object of the sound; hearing it is the secondary object of the sound."

These hair-splitting distinctions were quite foreign to the sensory psychologists who considered only the idea, not the process of having ideas itself, as consciousness. We have given Brentano's distinctions such prominence because they stimulated an entirely new tendency in research with which we shall become acquainted later. It is the distinction of act from content of consciousness, which is the basis of the so-called "act psychology."

For the present discussion Brentano's doctrine of judgments as mental elements is of paramount interest. The notion of "judgment" is not to be understood in the sense in which it is used in logic, as the combination of a plurality of concepts. The question is one of the affirmation or rejection of an idea; for judgment does not appear independently, but as an adjunct to an idea which is first recognized by judgment. This concomitant inner recognition is included in the concomitant act itself, but it is not, however, a combination of subject and predicate. It can appear in different degrees of intensity, that is, of conviction.

Like Wundt, Brentano recognizes feelings as elementary phenomena. For him, as for the sensory psychologists, feelings were limited to the contrast: pleasure and displeasure. Brentano also conceded differences of intensity in feelings but thought these differences in feeling intensity were only irregularly related to the intensity of accompanying ideas.

The three elements—ideas, judgments, and feelings—are not to be thought of as substantial entities; they are to be conceived rather as three facets of the same mental acts. All our simultaneous mental activities belong to a real unity. Whether, and how, successive mental acts form a unity, Brentano never decided clearly. He left the problem of the unity of consciousness unsolved from several angles.

Brentano's psychology was contained for a long time in his first volume, and even in the subsequent publications he did not round it out to a complete picture. Brentano's interests later turned more toward philosophical questions. Yet his influence in psychology was considerable. In the beginning there was an orthodox Brentano school which adhered religiously to the master's teachings, Brentano himself having always been very resentful of unorthodox interpretations of his words. In spite of this, he could not prevent the defection of the Meinong school, nor hinder the subsequent development of *Gestalt* psychology, act psychology, and phenomenology from his doctrines.

2. The resistance of the sensory psychologists to admitting further fundamental mental phenomena had already been broken by Brentano. Brentano's successors added still an-

other set of elements: desires. The responsibility for this addition rests with Alexius Meinong, of Graz, Austria, who began with Brentano but then founded his own school which indulged itself in the scholastic delights of classification. A. Höfler's popular textbook, following the lead of Meinong, lists four classes of elementary mental experiences:

a. ideas.
b. judgments.
c. feelings.
d. will.

These groups, however, are even further split up by the Meinongites. The ideas were divided into real and imaginative ideas. With judgments come "assumptions" which are related to actual judgments as imaginative ideas are related to real ideas. Similarly, in the field of emotions, real and imaginative emotions are to be distinguished. And desires, too, fall into desires for knowledge and desires for value.

But this does not exhaust the subtle distinction of the Meinong school. From the multifarious interrelations of elementary experiences arise still further complications which we cannot follow here.

Meinong's analysis of the experience of value (*Wert-Erleben*) has proved itself very fruitful. Although he does not consider "value" merely as a psychological problem he concedes that it has a psychological aspect. There is a dispute in the Meinong school as to whether the experience of value is based more upon desire, that is to say, upon will, as Von Ehrenfels maintained, or whether it is to be reduced to feeling, as Kreibig tried to prove. These and other scholars have formed themselves into research groups to study the theories of values and validity.

As you see, the schools of Brentano and Meinong went their separate ways, and the process led them far astray from the other 1880 schools which were working upon the clarification of consciousness. The other schools remained faithful to their problems because neither the relationship of consciousness to physiological processes nor its exact coördination with external stimuli had yet been investigated. As a rule, experiment played a minor rôle in this school, although several of its younger representatives, such as Witasek and Benussi, approached more closely the other schools of psychology by including experimental research.

3. Rehmke's psychology, although not directly connected with the Austrian school, bears a certain resemblance to it. He was a professor at the remote University of Greifswald and his textbook of psychology first appeared in 1894. Like Brentano, Rehmke distinguishes three "basic determinations" of the mind: the objective, circumstantial, and thinking consciousness. This triple division corresponds somewhat to the images, feelings, and thinking of other psychologists.

Rehmke's characteristic conception of the soul as "the essence of consciousness" puts him in the ranks of the psychologists of consciousness, but at the same time he conceives of the soul as a "simple single entity," which promises that those "determinations" of the mind are not "elements" but metamorphoses of the unitary soul. The soul, however, is essentially differentiated from the body with which it enters only into a functional unity.

Taken singly, Rehmke's analyses of consciousness are penetrating, but they bear little relation to the other tendencies of psychology. They are historically interesting because, at a time when everyone was dividing consciousness into "elements," Rehmke insisted strongly upon the unity of the soul. Rehmke's later works are mainly in the field of philosophy, which he wanted to establish anew as "the fundamental science," and his philosophy, like his psychology, was characterized by the use of subtle and often hair-splitting definitions of concepts.

4. The Danish psychologist, Höffding, whose *Psychology* appeared in 1882, is less abstract and in closer contact with experimental psychology. He separates three states of consciousness: apperception, feeling, and volition, which, how-

ever, are not identical with the "elements" to be found in them upon closer examination. The "elements" are different aspects or qualities of those states of consciousness. "In apperception (to which in psychology we reckon sensations and ideas) a picture is formed of the external world and of the individual himself as a part of that world. In will (to which we reckon not only instinct, planning, and decision, but also involuntary forms of activity), the individual reacts upon the external world. The elements of feeling, of the inner rhythms of pleasure and displeasure, are always so bound up with certain ideas and thoughts or actions that they very easily become mixed with these."

Höffding assumed that the triple division was not basic but had gradually differentiated itself in the course of psychological evolution. It must be said in Höffding's behalf that he never participated in the contemporary custom of atomizing consciousness, but, on the contrary, pointed the way to future research by his insistence on the unity of mental life.

5. Like Höffding, the English psychologists of this period distinguished psychic phenomena but never isolated them as elements. In his famous article in the *Encyclopædia Britannica* of the year 1886, James Ward tried to do away altogether with the superconcept of "state of consciousness," and its coördinated subdivisions. In lieu of apperception, emotion, and desire, he recognized analytically only three separate and irreducible facts: attention, feeling, and ideas (or objects), which, together in certain combinations, constitute a concrete "state of mind." According to the participation of attention, these states of mind are either sensory (receptive) or motor (active); in the former case, feeling follows upon attention; in the latter, it precedes attention. In everything mental, Ward assumed a relationship with the subject as "pure ego," which he did not identify with the metaphysical doctrines of the soul or "mind stuff." Ward rejected the attempts to exclude this "ego" or "self."

The ego, according to Ward, was always in the background as a totalitarian point of relationship, and because of it Ward completely separated himself from his contemporaries, who dissolved the mind into a chain of single states.

In the '90's, G. F. Stout followed the pioneer trails of Ward. Stout treated psychological problems in several subsequently critically revised works. He went beyond the psychology of elements and considered judgment (with which he still classified assumptions), feeling, and striving not as "elements" of consciousness but as "attitudes" which are joined to "simple apprehension." In the course of elaborating his system, Stout closely approached the general concepts of the psychologists who understand the higher acts of consciousness as the product of the concatenation of simple sensations.

6. The one thing that was common to all these different psychologists, whose works appeared in the '70's and '80's, was the emphasis placed upon direct analysis of consciousness. Their theories differed from sensory associationism and from Wundt's apperceptionism in that experiment played either a minor rôle or no rôle at all. The "measurement" of the phenomena of consciousness did not primarily interest them, and for this reason they did not proceed to segregate "elements" of consciousness. They did not try to reduce the multiplicity of mental phenomena to the least possible number of elements, but emphasized more sharply the interplay of single phenomena. Consciousness as a point of view was consistently emphasized by them. This theoretical consistency was, however, of no practical advantage because the further evolution of psychology was destined to profit greatly by the study of motor processes, a study from which Brentano's school was particularly far removed.

THE 1890 CRITICS OF THE PSYCHOLOGY OF CONSCIOUSNESS

1. At the very time when psychological institutions where human consciousness was being analyzed into its component elements, where its fundamental states were being measured and estimated, were increasing in every civilized country, a countermovement appeared which cast such microscopic mental dissection into grave doubt. This happened in the year 1890. The opposition was dangerous because it did not originate from the ranks of the older generation but from scholars who knew modern methods of research intimately. Consequently, it was not to be disposed of by simply labeling it as "reactionary"; no, this opposition claimed to have the future all to itself. Furthermore, the leaders of this movement were brilliant, spirited writers who did not demand of their readers the endless patience which the experimental psychologists required of their subjects and of their readers.

A critical attitude against the dissection of consciousness was common to all these scholars, among whom the three most prominent were the Frenchman Bergson; the American William James; and the German Dilthey. They, too, took consciousness as their point of departure and tried to clarify it. But their procedure was not primarily one of division into elements, of "atomizing." Each one of them in his own way taught that consciousness is a totality. Special phenomena can be understood only within the totality of this consciousness which is more than the consciousness of totality.

In so far as they include motor acts and human conduct in psychology, they transgress the limits of pure psychology, and we shall trace the direction of their research in another connection when we study the psychological tendencies which consider the motive principle of life rather than consciousness as the primary quality of the soul. So far as we are concerned now, we are essentially interested in their analysis of consciousness, which is not only a trenchant criticism of the "atomists," but is also an enrichment of our knowledge of consciousness.

It is to be hoped that the fact that these three thinkers were not only "pure" psychologists but also philosophers is no reproach today, as it surely was at the time when they first examined the development of psychology. They were, for that reason, not inimical to empirical research; on the contrary, they all claimed to represent a better and more encompassing system of empiricism than the earlier atomists of the mind.

2. The first mine planted under the new psychology was prepared in France in the form of a small volume bearing the title *Essai sur les données immédiates de la conscience*. It appeared in 1889 and was written by Henri Bergson, a young mathematics instructor from the provinces who was destined to great fame and an academic chair in Paris. This thin volume contains not only a sharp criticism of the newer psychophysics but a complete system of metaphysics. It bears all the traits of an early work of genius in which (as in the youthful works of Leibniz, Schopenhauer, and Nietzsche) the germs of the author's entire philosophy are contained.

We are essentially interested here in the criticism which disputed not only the possibility of mathematical psychophysics but also the possibility of even referring to intensity and quantity in relation to consciousness. Bergson thus attacks the atomizing experimental psychology at the very point where it considered itself impregnable. Apparent differences of intensity are in truth qualitative and, therefore, not measurable. The concept of intensity presents a dual aspect according to whether one considers states of consciousness directed outwardly or directed inwardly. In the former instance, so-called intensity consists of a certain estimation of the quantity of the stimulus-cause by means of a quality of the reaction; in the second instance, we mean by "intensity" the more or less considerable multiplicity of simple mental facts which we are aware of within the fundamental experience. The experience is one which has been summoned from without in the first instance; in the second, it is confused.

Bergson not only accused the older psychologists of confusing intensity and quality in the description of states of consciousness, but also accused them of the additional error of ascribing spatial characteristics to purely temporal experiences of consciousness. Our states of consciousness do not form a clearly arranged sequence; they flow into and through one another in such a manner that it cannot be said whether they are a unity or a plurality. As soon as you examine and describe them you already distort them. They belong to the realm of *"durée,"* a difficult word to translate because the English word "duration" as well as the German word *"Dauer"* generally denote a continuation of the same state, whereas what is meant here is unity in constant change in which the past still lasts on into the future.

The single phases of this constantly changing stream are not a numerical plurality. When one characterizes them singly one tears them apart. As the result of the social community of our life, we project our states of consciousness into space and conceive the idea of a homogeneous space, that is, we spatialize consciousness; we transpose our experiences into objects and things. Our concepts are in truth only schematic outlines to which we subordinate the passing flux of reality in the service of our activities and our practical needs. The dynamic is changed into the static and even what is externally static is carried over into the inner world. All previous psychology was subject to this error; it spatialized the temporal flux of mental happenings, objectified it, and congealed it.

This was a caustic criticism of psychology which struck home all the more because a professional psychologist of the first order, William James, was soon to fire his shot into the same breach. Bergson himself in his further work devoted himself to formal philosophy. Some of his theories, especially the theory of the relation of the mental to the physical, will occupy us later. For our present train of thought, the important thing is the not entirely disputable fact that psychology, which believes it grasps a direct reality in its description of mental phenomena, in truth changes these moving occurrences into spatial and static things. This is a very abrupt way of putting the matter, and perhaps does not do justice to the intention of the psychologists, but it certainly does describe their accomplishments.

Bergson's criticism of psychophysics was aimed more or less directly at the Belgian psychologist Delboeuf. His criticism of psychophysical parallelism as well as his positive psychological accomplishments, especially his totalitarian doctrine of memory and his theory of instinct, will be discussed later.

3. William James was the second of the three great critics of the psychological mosaic theory. He not only influenced the evolution of psychology by his criticism but also by his creative work. As a personality, he was undoubtedly one of the most interesting figures of the new science; for it is no accident that most of the representatives of an impersonal psychology, despite the fact that they may be conscientious investigators, are seldom very human people.

The spirited, vivid personality of William James is expressed in every one of his works; it can be seen even more intimately illuminated in his published correspondence. For the understanding of his system of psychology, it is important to know that he came from a deeply religious but not clerical family, the son of a man who was inwardly akin to Swedenborg and Emerson. A propensity for transcendentalism never left William James, and indeed it became increasingly evident in his later life. At times one has the impression that he struggled with his deepest nature in undertaking the exact study of physiology and psychology, and that he saw in this study only a means of firmly bolstering up his religious transcendental convictions. At any rate, he struggled intensely all his life for a union of exact science and religious faith. He himself had such an experience of conversion as he describes in his book on the psychology of religion.

He completed his studies for the most part in Europe—in France, Switzerland and Germany—and subsequently often returned to Europe to keep in touch with his colleagues there. After studying medicine, he became an instructor in physiology at Harvard University and later received a professorship in psychology. During the last period of his life he devoted himself mainly to philosophical problems in which he likewise opened up new vistas. His chief work in psychology, *Principles of Psychology*, appeared in 1890 and is a milestone in the development of modern psychology. To this very day, no other textbook of psychology has exceeded it in literary style, broadness of view, and profundity of insight.

We are not yet concerned here with the presentation of William James's entire system, but only with his criticism of previous analysis of the conscious.

This criticism strikes at the impersonality of the customary psychological conceptions. In almost all previous textbooks, mental facts had been simultaneously treated as objective facts, as atoms or components by means of whose synthesis the higher states of consciousness could be constructed. What exists, however, are not these components but a personal consciousness which is a continuity of constantly changing states always representing themselves as parts of that personal consciousness. But these parts are not to be understood as stereotyped entities, as they were portrayed by previous psychology; they are absolutely unique and never recur in the same way within the same personal consciousness.

To be sure, the same object can be subjectively experienced twice, but this subjective experience is never the same. "We feel things differently accordingly as we are sleepy or awake, hungry or full, fresh or tired; differently at night and in the morning, differently in summer and in winter; and, above all, differently in childhood, manhood, and old age. And yet we never doubt that our feelings reveal the same world, with the same sensible qualities and the same sensible things occupying it. . . ." "A permanently existing 'Idea' which makes its appearance before the footlights of consciousness at periodical intervals is as mythological an entity as the Jack of Spades." Undoubtedly psychology had formerly paid scant attention to these many variants of supposedly the same sensations, ideas, and concepts, either in its examination of the same personal consciousness or in its comparison of the mental life of different individuals.

The second chief reproach James leveled against earlier psychologies was that of the erroneous isolation of the facts of consciousness. Ironically he speaks of "domino psychology," since it juxtaposed isolated and objectified states in much the same way a child arranges dominoes. In truth, what we have is a constantly intertwining "stream of consciousness," not to be divided into pieces. Analogies such as "chains" do not get at the core of the matter; "nothing is joined; it flows." Such arguments as the one that a sudden explosion abruptly breaks into the consciousness are invalid, "for even into our awareness of the thunder, the awareness of the previous silence creeps and continues; for what we hear when the thunder crashes is not thunder pure, but   thunder-breaking-upon-silence-and-contrasting-with-it." In the stream of consciousness, one must distinguish between "substantive" and "transitive" parts. "Like a bird's life, it seems to be an alternation of flights and perchings." "The resting places are usually occupied by sensorial imaginations of some sort, whose peculiarity is that they can be held before the mind for an indefinite time, and contemplated without changing; the places of flight are filled with thoughts of relations, static or dynamic, that for the most part obtain between the matters contemplated in the periods of comparative rest."

As certainly as the fact that in the external world there exist not merely solid objects but also relationships between them, so certain is it that there also exists a consciousness of such relationships. "There is not a conjunction or a preposition, and hardly an adverbial phrase, syntactic form, or inflection of voice in human speech, that does not express some shading or other of relation which we at some moment actually feel to exist between the larger objects of our thought. We ought to say a feeling of 'and' and a feeling of 'if,' a feeling of 'but' and a feeling of 'by,' quite as readily as we say a feeling of 'blue' or a feeling of 'cold.' "

The number of transitory states of consciousness does not nearly exhaust the wealth of the life of consciousness. There is a consciousness of expectation, a consciousness of direction, a consciousness of gaps. At least a third of our mental life consists of such "rapid premonitory perspective views of schemes of thought not yet articulate." Every state of consciousness is surrounded by a "halo" of relationships which James calls "psychic overtones" or "fringes."

A third charge that James flings at traditional psychology is that of passivism. Consciousness is not a supine mirror which reflects everything before it without discrimination. Consciousness always makes a choice from among the impressions which besiege it; it incessantly welcomes or rejects. Most of the things surrounding us are not even perceived and the stimuli emanating from these things come into active being and are variously characterized. What we call "experience" is not something purely objective, but is almost entirely conditioned by our habits of attention. Not only our perceptions are selective but also all our experiences of consciousness.

But what does the choosing? Not the single states of consciousness which are only "acted" not "acting." Behind thoughts emerges the problem of the active "thinker," behind consciousness the problem of the "self" which governs the personal character of consciousness. Of course, psychology as an analysis of consciousness discovers only

"the self as known," not "the self as knower." And so
James turns first to the "self as known," the empirical self
or "me." In a brilliant analysis three "constituents of the
me" are distinguished:

    a. the material me.
    b. the social me.
    c. the spiritual me.

Not only our body, but also our clothes and everything
we possess belong to the material Me. The social Me "is
the recognition which a man gets from his mates. Properly
speaking, a man has as many social selves as there are individuals who recognize him and carry an image of him in
their mind." The spiritual Me, in so far as it belongs to the
empirical self, is the totality of all states of consciousness,
all mental capabilities and dispositions. "When we think of
ourselves as thinkers, all the other ingredients of our Me
seem relatively external possessions. Even within the spiritual Me, some ingredients seem more external than others.

"Our capacities for sensation, for example, are less intimate possessions, so to speak, than our emotions and desires; our intellectual processes are less intimate than our
volitional decisions. The more active feelings, states of
consciousness, are thus the more central portions of the
spiritual Me. The very core and nucleus of our self, as we
know it, the very sanctuary of our life, is the sense of activity which certain inner states possess. This sense of activity is often held to be a direct revelation of the living
substance of our soul. Whether this be so or not is an
ulterior question."

In addition to the constituents of the self, "the feelings
and emotions of self" are treated: self-appreciation, which
can appear as "self-complacency" or "self-dissatisfaction."

In the third place comes self-seeking and self-preservation in which the further distinctions of bodily self-seeking
and spiritual self-seeking are made.

All these different selves are partially in rivalry with
each other and partially they form an hierarchy. "In each

kind of Me, material, social, and spiritual, men distinguish between the immediate and actual, and the remote and potential, between the narrower and the wider view, to the detriment of the former and the advantage of the latter." The interest in the self in its various forms is no mere intellectual play but has teleological significance. "Its own body, its friends next, and finally its spiritual dispositions must be the supremely interesting objects for each human mind."

These acute analyses of the consciousness of self are no longer purely critical but a positive creative accomplishment of introspective psychology. And yet they are a devastating criticism of traditional psychology, because here for the first time very central problems were disclosed of which previous psychology had not even dreamed. Indeed, this criticism cast doubt on all the values of previous research because it showed that all the mental processes studied in an isolated form were to be understood only in connection with the self.

For all that, James still remained completely within the realm of the study of consciousness. Thus far he had spoken only of the "self as known." But he also did not hesitate to boldly break through the confines of earlier psychology to reach the "self as knower." He termed it "the I" or the "pure ego." "It is that which at any given moment is conscious, whereas the Me is only one of the things which it is conscious of. In other words, it is the Thinker." That which obliges us to accept the notion of such a thinker is above all the unity of the transitory flux of consciousness. If we follow the sensory psychologists and accept only "a pack of ideas each cognizant of some one element of the fact one has assumed, nothing has been assumed which knows the fact at once. And yet in the actual living human mind what knows the cards also knows the table, its legs, etc., for all these things are known in relation to each other and at once." With the hypothesis that all our ideas are "combination of smaller ideas" very little is gained. For all combinations that we know "are effects, wrought by the units said to be combined upon some entity other than themselves. Without this feature of a medium or vehicle, the notion of combination has no sense."

With these words James encroached upon a field that experimental psychology had thus far studiously avoided. The problem of the unity of consciousness is not to be solved from consciousness itself. Pure analysis of consciousness is, therefore, also inadequate. We shall see later that James's psychology, as a matter of fact, endeavored at all points to advance beyond the realm of consciousness.

4. The third of the great critics of modern psychology was a German who was a philosopher and historian even though he was destined, through his criticism and his clearly defined program, to become the founder of an entirely new psychological school. He was Wilhelm Dilthey, Professor of Philosophy in Berlin. His main scientific goal was a "Theory of Knowledge of the Intellectual Sciences." And in the course of his preliminary studies for this work and in his own historical works on Schleiermacher and the evolution of thought since the Renaissance, it became clear to him how little the "scientific" psychology had to offer him for his purpose.

And so, in his own way, he sought a new psychology which was to be erected by his pupils upon the foundations he had laid. He was a brilliant teacher and speaker who was more interested in formulating his thoughts in speech than upon paper. In print he only published preliminary studies. Whenever he started upon larger works his thoughts were mired in the first volume. Not until his posthumous works were published in several thick volumes was an insight afforded into the wealth of his world of ideas, so his actual influence was not felt until after his death in 1911. His earlier publications were essentially criticisms of "scientific" psychology and represented little more than the outline of his system which, despite its incompleteness, is nevertheless historically significant. In our connection, the most important of his writings was a lecture entitled *Ideas on a Descriptive and Analytical Psychology*, published in 1894.

Dilthey's criticism against "scientific" psychology was bitter; for he, too, had struck at the very point on which modern psychology had prided itself most. This point was the older psychology's belief that it was strictly empirical, that it remained clear of all hypotheses, and that it had nothing in common with the speculative psychology of bygone days. And along came Dilthey, and at a formal meeting in the hall of the Prussian Royal Academy, accused the entire new science of being a purely theoretical system! Dilthey claimed that psychology was not directed toward the factual description and analysis of the actual given mind, but toward an "explanation," i.e., toward the derivation of consciousness from a limited number of exact elements, which themselves are only hypothetical. And the theory of the relationship of these elements was just as hypothetical. The analytic psychologists thought they were describing the mind and did not realize how far they had strayed from experience. What William James had exposed with endearing humor, Dilthey expounded with academic severity, documenting his accusations with a mass of historical erudition.

In offering his opponents the program of an actually descriptive and analytical psychology, Dilthey begins with what he calls the "Intellectuality of Inner Perception." By that he means that inner perception does not occur directly as had generally been thought, but is also shaped by logical categories just as is external perception. We use processes like classification, designation, distinguishing, relating, separating, generalizing, by which we focus the external world upon our consciousness. The remarkable thing is that we directly experience (*"erleben"*) relationships and connections which, brought before the court of the understanding, are inconceivable.

For this reason psychology must start from "Erlebnis," in which phenomena of the entire mind operate together.

This concept of "experience" became very productive in later German psychology and is something quite different from the elements of the "scientific" psychologists. In experience a single occurrence is born by the totality of mental life. In experience that direct, logically unclassifiable connection of the single occurrence with the entire mind is disclosed. The connection is understood, not explained. This act of understanding, so diametrically opposed to explaining, became so important in modern German psychology that Diltheyan psychology was frequently opposed to traditional explanatory psychology as the "understanding" psychology. Dilthey's own definition is: "We *explain* by means of purely intellectual processes, but we *understand* by means of the coöperation of all the powers of the mind in comprehension. In understanding we start from the connection of the given, living whole, in order to make the part comprehensible in terms of it. What we experience in our consciousness of our relationship to the whole makes it possible for us to understand a single sentence, a single gesture, or a single act."

Later in the positive section of his essay Dilthey still demanded description and analysis from psychologists, yet he did not ask that they seek out elements; he demanded that they integrate and make distinctions within the total unity, and it was his thesis that psychological knowledge should be attained by a process which was a refinement of the process by which ordinary human knowledge was obtained.

Dilthey confronted modern psychology with three tasks. The first task was to find the structural whole of the developed mind. He introduced the word "structure" into psychology in a new sense, which we shall have occasion to study in greater detail later on. Dilthey clarified this concept by means of an analogy: psychology, according to his viewpoint, is not interested in the stones, the mortar, and the workmen at a building, but in the architecture of the completed structure, that is, in the inner relationships of the parts. The character of this structure is simultaneously teleological and causal.

The second task is the disclosure of development showing the dynamic growth of mind, not its static condition.

The third task is to determine the effect of the acquired connected whole of consciousness upon each individual act. Only by an insight into this connection can the free vitality of the mind be analytically elucidated. For our knowledge and our plans are not dead possessions but living entities, rich in instincts and feelings which impart interest to a new impression, evoke an idea, or motivate a volitional trend. The understanding of our entire mental life depends upon the understanding of these interactions. The conditioned totality of an individual is manifested in all his creations. No man can tell what he really is by meditating about himself—he must learn by studying his history.

We shall interrupt here, because Dilthey's positive psychological discoveries will occupy us in detail at another point. There is historical justification for this interruption since Dilthey did not himself carry out his program in specialized positive research, because he felt hurt by antagonistic criticisms. Toward the end of his life he did return to his researches when a great many of his students embarked upon the task of transforming his inspiration into practical work.

5. Different as the three 1890 critics of psychology were in personality and scientific attitude, they agreed in the main ideas of their criticism. And their missiles, as we have shown, struck those very targets of modern psychology which were considered most solidly intrenched: the distinction and classification of states of consciousness. All three agreed that this impossible and unjustifiable atomization of a fundamentally indivisible consciousness was worthless. Everything in the way of "elements" and "combinations" which had been elaborated in the laborious anatomy of consciousness, was unmasked in the light of

their criticism as an artificial and defacing theoretical construction, not as the empirical treatment of the facts it had claimed to be. And while no one disputed that the primary task of psychology was the study of consciousness, all three agreed that this study should not degenerate into an "anatomizing" dissection of it.

The result of this criticism was the positive demand for a new conception of consciousness as a primary "totality." In this, too, the three critics agreed, although they differed greatly in details. With Bergson the unifying totality of the consciousness lay within the *"durée"*; with James, it was revealed in the "stream of consciousness," behind which the "ego" stood as a unifying point of reference; with Dilthey, unity and totality were to be found in a connected meaning, in the teleological structure of consciousness. According to Bergson who developed the idea later in his *Creative Evolution* (1907), the comprehension of totality occurs by means of instinct; according to Dilthey, by means of "understanding." Bergson and James became close comrades in arms. Dilthey was probably not yet acquainted with Bergson when he conceived his ideas, but he did know James, whom he esteemed very highly.

Naturally the embattled experimental psychologists defended themselves. Marty, a student of Brentano, made a none too fair criticism of James's *Principles*. Hermann Ebbinghaus, a leader of experimental psychology, took a strong stand against Dilthey, whose pupil he had been. In an essay in the *Zeitschrift für Psychologie* (1895), he parried Dilthey's attacks, by attempting to prove that Dilthey did not strike at modern associational psychology in his attacks, but only at its antiquated representatives, such as Herbart. Ebbinghaus insisted, moreover, that modern interpretative psychology was advancing in the same direction that Dilthey had designated, and was striving toward increasingly broader unities, despite the fact that it began with a consideration of elements.

Dilthey's objection to the use of hypotheses was refuted

by Ebbinghaus when he called attention to the fact that even descriptive psychology could not manage without hypothetical aids, and that the very description of the subject matter itself remained extremely theoretical in many instances. And when Dilthey asserted that the use of the conclusions of associational psychology had in certain isolated cases produced damaging results in the social sciences, Ebbinghaus answered that it was unfair to condemn the methods of psychology as a whole because the premature and uncritical application of those conclusions had led to damaging results. Ebbinghaus concluded with the pronouncement that Dilthey's polemics were aimed at nonexistent opponents.

6. It is not very easy to determine the exact historical influence of the three great critics. It was not to be expected that the atomistic psychologists would give up their position without further ado because of the sharp criticism of their opponents. Most of them simplified the matter for themselves: they ignored the criticism and continued their previous work. Shrugging their shoulders, they rejected as outsiders those critics who had no warm sympathy for psychological research. And still the criticisms gradually penetrated into the laboratories. There was more care in anatomizing consciousness; it was admitted, at least theoretically, that the segregation of elements was only "fictive," and that no one even thought of regarding the elements as independent atoms. The notions of "totality," "structure," and "stream of consciousness" became familiar even in the experimental institutions. We shall see later that the new movements arising after 1900, thought psychology, *Gestalt* psychology and eidetic psychology, approach a totalitarian point of view, although the direct influence of the 1890 critics is scarcely discernible. Yet even in the older movements the problem of the fundamental totality of the mind began to take its place alongside the problems of isolating analyses and hypothetically constructed syntheses.

The positive inspiration of the men of 1890 was far more effective than their negative criticisms and resulted in the creation of research trends which gradually led away from the pure analysis of consciousness. In America a separation into structuralists and functionalists occurred, the Wundt-Titchener school commonly being designated as "structuralist" while the "functionalists," following the inspiration of James, found new leaders in Dewey and others. The functionalists were also inspired by Höffding and Ward. Their purpose was not so much a matter of working out the elements of consciousness and their synthetic reconstruction, as it was the determination of the "functions" which the mind must fulfill in adjusting itself to the external world. The center of interest was shifted, as in James, to action and "conduct" because not only states of consciousness, but also reflexes and motor acts were important in the study of this adjustment.

The problems of terminology present great difficulties in giving a broad historical presentation of modern psychology. For in Europe the very schools which are termed "structural" correspond to the American schools of functional psychology. In Germany the expression "functional psychology" is also used synonymously with "act psychology" and functions denote those mental acts which produce "content." But the expression "structure" of the mind is also used for all those mental phenomena which are not conscious so far as their content is concerned. The expression "structure" is used by the Dilthey school, moreover, to express the totalitarian relationships of mental life. It must, therefore, be clearly understood that what is called "structural psychology" in America connotes the very thing which German structural psychologists attack, and that German structural psychology is much more closely related to American functionalism.

THE DISCOVERY OF THE "NON-SENSORY" PHENOMENA OF CONSCIOUSNESS

1. It was not merely the influence of the 1890 critics that brought about a change in psychology as well as in biology, sociology, and philosophy between 1890 and 1900. There was a well-nigh universal endeavor to be rid of scientific anatomizing and mechanization and to think in terms of "totality." Of the schools of experimental psychology which appeared at this time, I shall first discuss the new psychology of thought and will which, confining itself entirely to the study of consciousness, discovered the existence of new "non-sensory" psychological phenomena which are not referable to primary sensations. These phenomena are not to be confused with the so-called "elements" of the older sensory psychology; they can better be characterized as "acts" or something similar. And here again the problem of activity and, further, the totality of the self, hold the center of the psychological stage.

Perhaps this whole discussion strikes the layman as being thoroughly superfluous. Ask the average man whether he can have an abstract thought and he will answer in the affirmative without hesitation. Most of the old psychologists never doubted in the least that the human mind is capable of "non-sensory" general concepts. In Plato the word ἰδέα or εἶδος originally meant shape or form; but Plato used it in a very abstract sense and emphasized the fact that numerals, or concepts such as equality or similarity, are not derived from sensations. And Aristotle even ascribed thought and sensation to different "souls." In the philosophies of Descartes, Spinoza, and Leibniz, thought and its concepts are not derived from sensory experiences but are diametrically opposed to them. Despite this, the problem of abstract thought has some historical foundation, for among the ancients there existed a sensationalism which reduced all abstract thought to sensations, side by side with a rationalistic psychology. Berkeley and Hume, as we have already seen, disputed the possibility of abstract ideas, and the sensory psychologists strove to maintain this position by means of hypothetical constructions in violation of the facts.

2. The first to approach this problem of abstract thought with modern methods was Francis Galton. He instituted a general inquiry in the '70's concerning "mental imagery." His work *Inquiries into Human Faculty and Its Development* (1883) was a more uniform presentation. He approached the problem from the standpoint of sensory psychology and was not a little surprised that the persons whom he first questioned completely denied the experiences of visual imagery. They were mostly learned people. Galton saw in this a "deficiency" which he compared to color blindness. His questions were answered thus: "These questions presuppose assent to some sort of a proposition regarding 'minds' eye,' and the 'images' which it sees. . . . This points to some initial fallacy. . . . It is only by a figure of speech that I can describe my recollection of a scene as a 'mental image' which I can see with my mind's eye." Galton stops at this purely negative characterization and looks for and finds visual images in uneducated people. He does not attempt to investigate the positive side of the problem and learn what occurs in abstract minds when they think.

French scholars like Ribot and Binet also investigated this problem. Ribot in the study of memory types discovered that there are people who scarcely work with visual memory images but instead utilize the image of the printed word. Binet, in his *Psychologie du Raisonnement* (1886), was still strongly under the influence of sensualism, yet he came to the conclusion that there are experiences of consciousness which are not traceable to sensory impressions in his *Étude experimentale de l'intelligence* (1903), which he wrote in connection with his studies of children. The problem, therefore, in 1900, was in a thoroughly chaotic state.

3. In Germany non-sensory consciousness was made the object of experimental research in the first decade of the twentieth century by a group of younger psychologists who were often collectively referred to as the "Würzburg school." The instigator of this tendency in the study of consciousness was a pupil of Wundt, Oswald Külpe. The execution of his plans was taken over by a large circle of his students at Würzburg, where he first taught, and later in Bonn and Munich. Külpe himself had already issued an *Outline of Psychology* (1893) in which he still held essentially the fundamental doctrines of Wundt. His *Lectures on Psychology*, edited by Bühler in 1920, treats in detail only the lower spheres of consciousness. A reference to the psychology of thought and will is relegated to an appendix in which he summarizes the investigations of his school.

The novelty of the Würzburg school is its method, because here for the first time experiment was consistently applied to the higher mental processes. These psychologists utilized the reaction experiments which had been made to measure the time elapsed between the application of the stimulus and the reaction. At first, they measured the time in experiments on thought, but later the mechanical apparatus was put aside. A mental problem was posed and the subject of the experiment had to seek the solution, as well as to observe the conscious processes involved. Exact records were taken of his statements. The problems posed were sometimes arithmetic examples, sometimes the establishment of logical connections between concepts, and then again the interpretation of difficult passages from the poets and philosophers. Whether we call the process "introspection" or "experiment" is a minor matter; it is a kind of introspection that is systematized and checked against certain sources of error. In ordinary self-examination there is danger that the examiner will find what he wants to find; here, however (at least in theory), the subject of the experiment did not know what it was all about. Whether this method was always observed in practice is a matter which will occupy us later.

4. The *Archiv für die gesamte Psychologie* became the organ of all the work of the Würzburg school. In it appeared "Experimental: Contributions to a Theory of Thought" by H. J. Watt, in which non-sensory and nonverbal thought were determined but an exact definition of these states was not held possible. C. O. Taylor's dissertation in which the understanding of words and sentences was treated appeared soon afterwards. With N. Ach, in his book *On the Activity of Will and Thought* (1905), the newly discovered states at least acquired a name. They were now called "awarenesses" (*Bewusstheiten*) and were considered the consciousness reflex of memory contents which were in a state of preparedness but not completely reproduced.

These investigations were continued by A. Messer who, in his work on *Sensation and Thought*, brought the non-sensory contents of consciousness into relationship with the "intentional acts" emphasized by Brentano and his pupil, Husserl. Messer sharply distinguished these intentional acts from all sensations, ideas, and words. A closer definition of the new experiences, however, was still lacking in Messer's work.

Non-sensory contents of consciousness were somewhat more clearly characterized by Carl Bühler, who called them "thoughts," as O. Schultze had already done before him. Bühler, too, lays emphasis upon the variation in all visual images, but he makes a more positive description by distinguishing in them the "factors" of definiteness, intention, and the consciousness of causality. Considered singly, thoughts are characterized by varying degrees of vividness, definiteness, and clarity. In addition to major thoughts there are all sorts of minor thoughts involved in connection with the subject. We understand a newly aroused thought by placing it into relation with already existent thoughts. For thoughts, just like ideas and images, are retained in the memory and can be reproduced at all times.

In America, too, several scholars reached similar conclusions. Thus, Woodworth determined the "Non-sensory

Elements of Space Perception"* by assuming "feelings of relation." Later, T. V. Moore studied the "Temporal Relations of Meaning and Imagery."** He accords to "meaning" a special rôle.

5. The studies of the Würzburg school did not extend only to mental experiences. The theories of feeling and will were also to be rid of their sensory dross. Orth discovered states similar to feelings which he called conscious attitudes (*Bewusstseinslagen*). Much attention was aroused by N. Ach in his experimental studies of the experience of will. The sensory associationists had denied that there was a special consciousness of will and had demonstrated that an act of will can be carried out without there being a special consciousness of will. When one presses a key upon a signal it can be done without a consciousness of will. But Ach proved in his experiments that while at the very instant of action no consciousness of will need appear, such a consciousness was none the less present as a "determining tendency" prior to the action and governing it. These "determining tendencies" were thus introduced into psychology as new mental facts and, like Bühler's "thoughts," have remained ever since.

Ach became interested in demonstrating the significance of these determining tendencies even in complicated cases. He introduced obstacles into his experiments which the subject could overcome only by special efforts of his will. In the repetition of nonsense syllables, for example, he demanded a change in the order in which they had been memorized. Or the subject had to compose a rhyme to one of these syllables. All this could not be done with the venerable laws of association, but only with "determining tendencies" which often worked directly counter to the laws of association. The stimulus syllable now received the name "reference idea" (*Bezugsvorstellung*) and the rhyme to be

*J. Phil. Psychol. and Sc. Meth., 1907.
**Psychol. Rev., 1915.

sought was called the "goal idea" (*Zielvorstellung*). In accordance with this Ach arrived at this definition: "Determining tendencies are special factors, derived from the goal idea and directed toward the reference idea, which influence the course of action with reference to the goal idea."

Georg E. Müller, as spokesman for the old associationists, skeptically remarked that "determining tendencies" was nothing but a new name for the phenomena which had long been known as "perseverations." Ach refuted this energetically, and claimed that the connotation of "intentionality" which distinguished determining tendencies was entirely missing in "perseverations."

6. If Ach's investigations introduced an active psychological factor, this factor became even more prominent in the studies of judgment, inference, and productive thought in the further studies that resulted from the Würzburg stimulation of the subject. Marbe (1901) had already started experimental studies on judgment in Würzburg.

Störring (1907) published his "Experimental Investigations of Simple Processes of Inference"* in which visual images were still markedly emphasized. O. Selz studied productive thought activity and regulated thought processes in detail. He admitted that in many cases the solution of mental problems seemingly occurs automatically; in other cases, however, the solution remitted from sustained mental effort, which could be explained solely by an intensification of will. Contrary to the views of associational psychology, Selz proved that it is not the intensity of association in a tentative attitude which distinguishes successful from unsuccessful movements, but a better correspondence with the schematic anticipation of the operation to be carried out. The new kinds of mental states originate not as a result of the meaningless play of associations, but always as a consequence of already formulated purposive

*Arch. Ges. Psych., XI.

operations. The personality as a totalitarian teleological structure emerges simultaneously as a background of single acts of thinking. With these experiments the psychology of thought consciously veers in the direction Dilthey had already indicated.

A series of studies, which were made independently of the Würzburg school, pointed in the same direction. The associationist psychology of thought had led to the close relation of thought processes to speech processes. The new research now studied also nonverbal thought processes. Erdmann distinguished between formulated and nonformulated thought which he separated into hypological thought and metalogical thought. In doing that, however, he still ascribed an important rôle to memories. Müller-Freienfels went farther and distinguished subverbal, nearverbal (for example, musical thought) and superverbal thought in which he, too, was led to the acceptance of non-sensory, totalitarian attitudes.

7. Sensory psychology, of course, did not accept the new discoveries without demur. It is an historical curiosity that the main opposition to the psychology of non-sensory mental life originated from Wundt and from Titchener, of all people! For, notwithstanding all discussions, the new school of investigation proceeded along those very paths which Wundt had opened. He had been the first opponent of sensory psychology; his "feelings" and "feeling relationships" were non-sensory elements of mental life; his "apperception" had been the first contradiction to the sole sovereignty of the laws of association. And it was no accident that Külpe, a pupil of Wundt, had instigated the whole new movement.

The most thorough criticism of the Würzburg school was made by Titchener in his book, *The Experimental Psychology of the Thought Processes* (1909). He denied bluntly that there is any such thing as a non-sensory thought. What were considered non-sensory thoughts were only interfused sensory elements which had simply not been recognized as such. The Würzburg experimental subjects had succumbed to "stimulus error," according to Titchener, because they had paid more attention to the proffered object than to their subjective processes. A few of Titchener's students, Okabe, Kakise, and Jacobson, confirmed their teacher's opinion by experimental research. They used the same problems posed by the Würzburgers but arrived at solutions in consonance with sensory psychology.

These experiments were open to criticism because the premise of the complete impartiality of the experimental subject was apparently not always complied with. Even if the subjects were unaware of the special aim, students belonging to a certain school were nevertheless liable to a certain degree of bias which was transferred to their descriptions. The subject of the experiment usually found what the conductor of the experiment desired and proposed. To this extent, experimentation did not bring perfect clarity into the matter.

8. No matter what one thinks of the value of the Würzburg experiments as regards detail, they succeeded, at any rate, in one thing. It was generally conceded that in thought there were no such pretty, visual projection pictures as the sensory psychologists claimed. Instead of these clear pictures there now appeared the sketchy thoughts which the Würzburgers had discovered or, more accurately, had readmitted into the realm of psychology, from which the sensory psychologists ever since Berkeley had banned them.

But the significance of this entire school of research does not lie merely in the introduction of a new type of psychological element. The sovereignty of the psychological laws of association, until then but little disputed, was shaken by those experiments. "Determining tendencies" could not be considered associative motives of consciousness. And could anyone still speak of "similarities" in such indeterminate phenomena of consciousness as the Bühler thoughts?

With "determining tendencies," moreover, a teleological factor was introduced into psychology which, according to the strict sensory psychology, had to explain everything solely in terms of cause and effect. A psychic activity which had always been forbidden by a passivistic sensory psychology was herewith accorded recognition. Then the union of the new schools of research with the Brentano-Husserl "act theory" was brought about. The Würzburg school, true to its original purpose, still remained technically entirely a psychology of consciousness; but actually it had already produced the knowledge that consciousness cannot be understood by means of consciousness alone, in a word, that an active mental structure is at work behind all consciousness. This, however, pointed more and more to a totalitarian conception of mental life.

THE DISCOVERY OF *GESTALT* IN CONSCIOUSNESS

1. The struggle against sensory atomism and the trend toward totality emerged much more distinctly in the school of modern psychology known today as "*Gestalt* psychology" than in the Würzburg school. To be sure, the discovery of "*Gestalt* qualities" came at the end of the nineteenth century, but the notion of "*Gestalt*" did not become a battle cry against "atomism" and "associationism" until 1912.

The notion of *Gestalt* is by no means new to psychology. Should one attempt to write a history of *Gestalt* psychology, one could begin with Plato and Aristotle just as in the history of the psychology of non-sensory consciousness. One might say that the Platonic concept of "idea" includes both; although it developed to include an abstract, non-sensory concept, the original meaning of the word is undoubtedly "image." "*Gestalt*" and the "idea" can also be "seen," as is evident in the *Symposium*.

In Aristotle "entelechy" is a *Gestalt*, although it is a *Gestalt* developing in time, which does not contradict the meaning *Gestalt* psychology gives it; for even a "melody" is a *Gestalt*. At any rate, the Romans translated the concept of entelechy by the word "forma," and all through scholasticism "formæ" play an important rôle; they are, indeed, just as in Plato and Aristotle, thoroughly objective data; yet there are also present in the subjective mind objective schemata through which we comprehend those external forms.

The "innate ideas" of Descartes and *"verités de raison"* of Leibniz are also formal capacities of the mind, and Kant, too, designates the categories as "forms" which we bring to the data of experience. It is obvious that it was usual for both rationalistic philosophy and psychology to accept mental "forms" or "schemata" by means of which sensations subsequently formed themselves into total experiences. On the other hand, the older sensory psychology and nominalism disputed the existence of such innate "forms," although both Hartley and J. S. Mill granted that there were mental experiences which were something more than the sum of their parts, analogic to the chemical molecule whose characteristics differed from those of its component atoms.

It is apparent that the problem of psychic *Gestalt* is ancient; and the controversy between psychologists who accept psychic *Gestalt* and those who want to construct it out of "elements" extends throughout the entire history of psychology.

2. The problem of *Gestalt* was introduced into modern psychology by the Austrian school of psychologists who followed E. Mach, a professor in Prague and Vienna. In the beginnings of modern psychology, the theory of *Gestalt* was not opposed to the doctrines of sensationalism and associationism because E. Mach, an extreme sensory psychologist, had already treated optical and acoustic problems in his *Analysis of Sensations*. He had raised the question concerning the reason why geometrically similar figures are also optically similar, but had at first aroused only mis-

understanding and ridicule. He showed that figures like
these

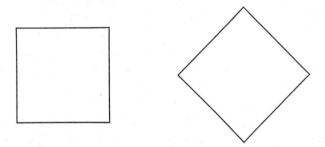

although geometrically identical, are physiologically, and
we may add also psychologically, quite different. By referring to the "intelligence" as a "helper," Mach, of course,
transgressed the bounds of "pure" sensory psychology.
But at any rate, he had already clearly formulated the
problem of *Gestalt*.

Later, the Brentano school took up the problem. One of
its members, C. von Ehrenfels, in 1890, had coined the
term *"Gestalt* quality" and introduced the term "transposability" as a criterion. A melody remains the same even
when it is transposed into a different key, even though no
single note of the original arrangement recurs. Ehrenfels
defined *"Gestalt* qualities" as "those positive image contents which are bound to the existence of image complexes
in consciousness which in themselves consist of separable
elements." That which remains similar in spite of the transposed elements is the *Gestalt* quality.

Witasek in 1898 drew attention to certain optic geometric illusions, and in some very thoroughgoing experimental studies V. Benussi also occupied himself with *Gestalt*
qualities. He studied spatial and temporal *Gestalt*, and, in
later works, tactual *Gestalt*. He added other criteria to
Ehrenfels' transposability: the dependence of *Gestalt* comprehension upon inner conditions, of attitude, and of volition; the independence from the sensory organ in so far

as the same *Gestalt* can often be comprehended through different senses, for example, the visual and tactual sense. With these experiments, the contrast between sensory psychology and passivisim was thrown into bolder relief.

3. It was a group of younger contemporary psychologists, however, who focused the attention of modern psychology on the problem of *Gestalt*. When we speak today of "*Gestalt* psychology" we think of Wertheimer, Wolfgang Köhler, Koffka, and their pupils. The centers of this school were the universities of Berlin and Frankfurt. Doubtless there were personal connections with the older *Gestalt* theorists of the Brentano school, since C. Stumpf himself, the teacher of the younger men mentioned above, came from the Brentano school. We shall not go into the controversy concerning the matter of priority which has arisen in *Gestalt* psychology.

The most characteristic sign of the latest *Gestalt* tendency is primarily a strongly emphasized contrast to the psychology of association; further, the attempt to revolutionize all psychology into terms of the problem of the totalitarian *Gestalt* experience; and lastly, a physiological theory of the concept of *Gestalt*. Köhler has even extended the problem into physics.

Let us first consider Wertheimer, who made the associationist theory ridiculous by dubbing it the "mosaic and bundle theory." This theory, according to Wertheimer, would be as follows: "The basis of all complexes is the sum of the given, juxtaposed, elementary components [sensations, and the like]." One is therefore dealing with an additive multiplicity of different components, a "bundle"; all the rest is constructed upon the addition of the elements; joined to sensations are the "residues" of previous perceptions, feelings, and factors like acts of attention, comprehension, will, and so forth. To this also belongs the associationist thesis: "If content A has often been together with content B, the occurrence of A will bring about the occurrence of B." The common fallacy of all such explanations (according to Wertheimer, whom we follow here) is the addition factor: the construction of the whole by the mechanical addition of pieces. While such things may occur, they happen but rarely.

In contrast to this is the central thesis of *Gestalt* psychology: "A given phenomenon is *per se* configured in '*Gestalt* form' to a greater or lesser degree; there exist more or less integrated, more or less well-defined wholes and 'processes of the whole,' frequently characterized by very concrete 'totality characteristics,' with inner causalities, distinctive totality tendencies, and with all parts conditionally bound to the wholes." "Pieces" are for the most part to be conceived of as "parts" in processes of the whole.

W. Köhler describes "group formation" in the *Psychologies of 1925* (W. Murchison) with the following example. He presents a diagram in which a series of lines is effortlessly arranged into "pairs" of two:

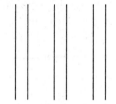

The attempt to arrange these lines into a different order cannot be made without special effort. Is distance the decisive factor which governs the formation of groups? Those lines which are closer together can be regarded "as a rather poor boundary inclosing space between them." But this figure can be changed by the addition of a few short horizontal lines. Then the wider space between the lines which are farther apart appears to be better inclosed.

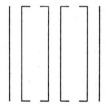

And besides, it now becomes easier to see the lines which are farther apart as pairs. Consequently, there appear to be two principles involved, that of distance, and that of "inclosing."

We take a further illustration of the concept of *Gestalt* from Koffka: When a bright object appears in the field of vision of a newborn child and its eyes and hands begin to move, this means that in the world in which the child was at peace, a new factor enters which destroys this peace. If one wishes to construct the phenomenological converse of this conduct, the circumstances must be considered as a whole. One will therefore not say that the child sees a bright spot, but that the child sees in the indifferent background a bright spot and feels an impulse at a certain place on his hand which otherwise lay quiescent; briefly and generally: out of the unlimited and indefinite background there arises a delimited and more definite phenomenon, a quality. The first phenomena of infantile experience would accordingly be qualities upon a background. "Such proximity of phenomena in which each part possesses its special character only through and with the others," Koffka calls "structures," which correspond essentially to Wertheimer's and Köhler's concepts of *Gestalt*.

The theory rejects the idea that there are extremely simple psychic factors such as the sensations, from which an ordered world is constructed. It also denies that primarily a chaos of light and color sensations exists. The *Gestalt* school emphasizes the fact that there is *a priori* a certain state of order in experience. It is incorrect to say that the child would be particularly impressed by particularly simple stimuli; it can be impressed by very complex images, for example, human faces which children can very soon not only perceive but also distinguish.

The comprehension of a melody is also considered by the latest psychology of *Gestalt* as an example of the totalitarian concept of *Gestalt* in contrast to the piecing-together-of-fragments theory. Such comprehension does not consist of possessing, let us say, the successive single sound contents, plus the single intervals, plus still further subordinate factors, or a quality of the complex of those contents; no, in all this a sound occurs *a priori* as part in its concrete function within the whole, within the dynamics of the whole.

It is the same with the seeing of figures, the hearing of a story, processes of thought, the conception of actions. The important advantage of this is that we can infer supplementations or make predictions because they are determined by the whole. "Experience," according to *Gestalt* psychology, does not consist in the frequent repetition of previously experienced pieced-together fragments and relations; experience only exists when the single fact is conceived as a part within a characteristic whole.

With this point of view in mind, W. Köhler undertook his well-known experiments in testing the intelligence of chimpanzees. The principle involved was the creation of a situation in which the direct path to a goal was blocked while an indirect path was left open. When the animal is placed in a situation which permits as complete a control as possible, it can demonstrate what type of conduct it is capable of, especially if it is capable of solving the problem along the indirect path. The decisive question is whether an animal chooses an indirect path spontaneously. Accidental solutions can be clearly distinguished from those which are based upon actual insight.

As a typical example we may choose the following: in front of the cage containing the animal a piece of fruit is lying beyond its reach; but in the cage there is a stick by means of which the fruit can be reached. When the animal makes use of the stick as a "tool" and this formerly irrelevant thing is drawn into the situation, then it acquires "functional value" for the situation; the entire field becomes restructuralized. If the solution is found, the situation is so changed for the animal that it too can be "solved." In the "solved" situation everything has its place conditioned by the total configuration. The concept of configuration (structure) thus expands beyond that of a simultaneous configuration to a totality, which is passing in time and has a beginning and an end.

It is of course not within our province to present the Köhler experiments in their entirety. I have attempted to show by this single example how these experiments test the existence of the capacity to perform acts which require insight and a sense of the total configuration of the problem.

We shall go into the physiological theories worked out by *Gestalt* psychologists to support their doctrines in another connection.

4. The sensory psychologists, seeing themselves so sorely pressed by *Gestalt* theoreticians, were not backward in their reply. In their vanguard, old G. E. Müller took up his pen in order to demonstrate to his opponents that the problem of *Gestalt* could also be solved from the standpoint of sensory psychology. He rejected the physiological theories of *Gestalt* (not yet discussed here) and came to the conclusion that "this view can in truth explain neither the uniformity of the *Gestalt* impression nor the fact that the effects of a *Gestalt* cannot be derived from the effects of the *Gestalt* components. It does not do justice to the influence of attention and experience upon *Gestalt* perception. It does not even maintain itself against the facts of the totalizing conception of *Gestalt* and *Gestalt* blindness."

In a more positive manner, Müller set up his theory of "complexes" against the theory of *Gestalt*. The formation of a complex occurs because of the fact that a group of images, whose objects stand in a definite space time and other relationships with one another, as a consequence of the collective concept which these objects partly become, achieves the capacity to evolve or experience mental effects as a uniform whole. The assumption of collective tendencies which cause the same collective conception to reënter at the recurrence of the same stimulus tendencies, is important for this explanation. Attention also plays an important rôle in the concept of complexes. We shall not go into the details of this very subtle doctrine. The main contrast simmers down to the fact that Müller leans toward empiricism, whereas the *Gestalt* theorists adopt aprioristic schemata. This is indeed a fundamental difference which cannot be decided on the basis of consciousness alone; for *Gestalt* consciousness permits various interpretations, and both groups, as a matter of fact, go back to physiological dispositions.

From the standpoint of consciousness as we deal with it here the *Gestalt* theorists have a better grasp of the matter than their opponents. For only in rare cases is a "collective conception" as such conscious: the notion of *Gestalt* has a certain directness, at times even a sudden "pyrotechnic" quality, for which reason the theory of *Gestalt* has been jokingly designated as the "psychology of sudden surprises," because the experimental subjects were shocked, often to their own surprise, into a rather sudden comprehension of the totalitarian situation.

Meanwhile *Gestalt* theorists have not only found opposition but also assistance. Sander, of the Leipzig school of psychology (which we shall meet later on) confirmed their theories to a broad extent. And there is a similar *entente cordiale* with the group of "phenomenologists."

5. In reviewing *Gestalt* psychology as far as it has been definitely formulated, one must recognize particular experiences of consciousness in *Gestalt*. Whether one thinks that these experiences are associatively combinable of sensations or not, one must admit that this combination or complex formation itself does not as a rule take place in the consciousness. A special mental act may be necessary in individual instances, as in the various conceptions of geometric optical illusions, but even then *Gestalt* is conceived as a totality. From the standpoint of an introspective psychology of consciousness, *Gestalt* forms are certainly

not combinations of elements but are conceived of *a priori* as totalities.

If this is admitted, then the whole theory of perception of sensory associationist psychology breaks down; for most of our perceptions take place in such a manner that no association or assimilation can be determined in our consciousness; on the contrary, we comprehend an object instantaneously as a totality. If I perceive a tree, I can possibly determine by subsequent analysis that there have gone into the perception complicated ideas of space, remembrance of former tactual experiences, and general concepts: but direct consciousness tells me nothing of all this. Perception appears in the consciousness as a completed whole. It is exactly so with images. If the image of "Rome" appears in my mind it does so as a complete whole. Only subsequently can I determine that there enter into it memories of my visit to the city, vague visual images of St. Peter's, the Palatine, and the Capitol.

Gestalt psychology in its contemporary form has not yet reached the stage of setting up an inclusive system of psychology. The psychology of totality has not yet treated the totality of psychology, but is essentially a new theory of perception which has been applied only to image and thought processes in single instances. The vast field of the psychology of feeling, emotion, and will has scarcely been touched by *Gestalt* psychologists.

Another question is whether *Gestalt* psychology stands in as extreme a contrast to the older analytical psychology as it would have us believe. Fundamentally, it isolates its "*Gestalt* forms" from the stream of consciousness no less than associationist psychology did its "perceptions" and "ideas." Only it does not pursue the analysis to such an extreme. The forms of *Gestalt* are "elements" even if elements of a higher level. Above all it is questionable whether *Gestalt* forms really deserve the name of "totalities." In fact, it is paradoxical to speak of "totality" in the plural.

This much is true: There is always a superimposed

totality in consciousness, even though it remains in the
background—and that is the ego. No matter what form of
Gestalt I comprehend as a totality, the comprehending self
with its general consciousness of the situation is always
operative in that consciousness. It is the subjective "con-
figurer" of the experience which totalizes it even when it
comprehends *Gestalt* forms as "objective." One might call
this "configuring" factor "apperception" in Wundt's sense,
but this leads to all the pitfalls this concept brings in its
wake, not to mention the fact that apperception occurs in
the consciousness as little as do associative relationships.

In all events, however, *Gestalt* psychology is historically
situated entirely within the line of evolution that leads
away from psychic atomization and associationism. It tends
toward totality; but since *Gestalt* is again essentially an
analysis of consciousness and takes into consideration only
cognitive mental life, it remains behind the evolutionary
trend which tends toward the study of unconscious mental
and emotional phenomena within their totality in the self.

THE DISCOVERY OF
"SENSORY VISUAL IMAGES"

1. The *Gestalt* psychologists were not the only ones who
discovered psychic "*Gestalten.*" The eidetic school followed
suit, using a Greek designation instead of a German word.
The word "εἶδος" is practically synonymous with "*Gestalt*"
or image, albeit the *Gestalt* forms or images discovered by
the eideticians were really something different from the
configurations of *Gestalt* psychology. The sensory visual
images (eidetic images) of the eidetic school were first
demonstrated in school children. The discovery of these
phenomena is one of the very rare instances in which experimental psychology really unearthed something new.
Formerly the experimentalists had occupied themselves
chiefly with the regimentation of facts already known to
introspective psychology and had contented themselves

with precise determinations, differentiations, and computations. Small wonder then that the fortunate discoverers imputed such importance to their discovery that they expected it to reform the entire field of psychology!

The eidetic facts, to be sure, had already been known a long time, but had been regarded as exceptional phenomena. As far back as 1907 "subjective optical visual images" had been pointed out by Urbantschitsch. E. R. Jaensch, however, demonstrated that the predisposition for such sensory visual images must be regarded as an entirely normal state common to the development of a great many people. Jaensch felt, moreover, that the eidetic phenomena were of considerable significance to the psychology of perception and concepts.

2. Eidetic images were discovered by E. R. Jaensch and his school, which was situated in the small university city of Marburg and therefore designated as the "Marburg school." Investigations in the elementary schools demonstrated that many children could describe pictures they had seen as distinctly as if they still had the picture in front of them. A picture was flashed onto a projection screen and then taken away. Even when the picture contained many figures and objects, the children could describe it in great detail after its disappearance. Indeed, it became apparent that they did not furnish these descriptions from memory, but that, so to speak, they actually read them off the projection screen as though the picture were still being flashed on the screen. Jaensch called such experiences of consciousness "sensory visual images." And the persons who experienced them were called eidetics.

The qualification of these eidetic images varies. Many of the subjects stated that they saw the images in more brilliant colors than the original picture had shown. Many confused their visual image with the perception of the original. Others saw the picture only in parts or in outlines. But its proportions were often so clear that they could be measured.

In spatial relations the visual image represents a mean between the afterimage and the eidetic image. Whereas the afterimage grows with distance, the eidetic image usually remains practically unchanged; it does not move if the head moves as does the memory image. Contrasting phenomena are strengthened in the afterimage. It requires no effort for the youthful eidetic to reproduce an eidetic image.

The eidetic predisposition should not be regarded as pathological. Subjective statements of the experimental subject are not to be wholly depended upon in determining eidetic predisposition. The observation of their outward conduct, their visual attitude, and the introduction of all sorts of distraction experiments are utilized to preclude the entry of mere suggestion. Eidetic experiences in contrast to "afterimages" possess a thorough character of reality. They are distinguished from hallucinations by the fact that an actual perception has preceded them.

Jaensch proceeded to study the individual characteristics which determine the eidetic predisposition. It was noticed that eidetics were apparently more common in the neighborhood of Marburg and in a few other regions of Germany than in other places. Walter Jaensch, a physician and a brother of the psychologist, studied the relation between eidetic disposition and the whole psychophysical constitution. This study revealed two different eidetic types which have a relationship to well-known clinical syndromes; tetany and Graves's (or toxic thyroid) disease. Graves's disease is called Basedow's disease in Germany. The Jaensch brothers distinguish a tetanoid type (T-type) and a Basedow type (B-type). The B-type, while not in itself pathological, is a miniature of Graves's disease, that is, an illness due to the overfunctioning of the thyroid gland. The T-type (also not pathological in itself) offers a miniature picture of tetany, an illness due to disfunction of the parathyroid glands.

Both types are externally different from one another. The B-type is characterized by large, sparkling, and vividly expressive eyes. These characteristics are but the partial manifestation of an intensified psychovegetative irritability whose other symptoms are rapid variations of the pulse, with variations of respiration and hyperactive skin reflexes. The T-type, on the other hand, presents an entirely different picture. The eyes are small, deep-set, and lackluster; there is a peculiarly "peaked" facial expression, and, in especially marked cases, an inclination toward depression and anancasm.

Both types display characteristic differences in respect to their eidetic predisposition. The B-type senses the eidetic images as something "belonging to the self, an intimate, dear possession that one would fain keep hold of." The eidetic images here resemble mental images (*Vorstellungen*), they are mobile and variable. Fixation of the actual object is not only not requisite but usually rather disturbing; interest aroused by the object is very helpful in the production of eidetic images. The representatives of the B-type prefer to make changes in the pictures seen, but these are rational changes in which the factual relations of what has been represented are emphasized without reference to their color.

The T-type comports itself quite differently. Its eidetic images are akin to afterimages, have only a slight relationship with the rest of the mental contents, and are dependent to a high degree upon physiological conditions of fixation and sharpness of outlines, but not upon the interest aroused by the object. Voluntary changes in the object cannot be made. The separation of the eidetic images from the rest of the mental content is indicated by the fact that individuals of this type sense them as disturbing foreign bodies.

Next to these "pure" types, which are comparatively rare, there exists an "alloy" of both: the B-T-type in which one or the other component predominates. The majority of youthful eidetics belongs to this B-T-type.

From a physiological point of view, it is interesting to note the effects of a high calcium diet. In the T-type eidetic images can be suppressed or actually extinguished by a high calcium diet, whereas the B-type does not respond to such a diet. In the B-T-type, the T characteristics are reduced by an increased calcium diet, with the result that only the B characteristics remain.

3. Jaensch and his school were not satisfied with the mere proof of eidetic images, but set themselves the task of proving the influence of sensory memory upon the rest of the mind, and reshaping traditional concepts in accordance with their discoveries.

Certain it is that the structure of the world of perception appears in a new light as a result of their experiments. Jaensch rejected the theory "that the similarity between the sensory and apperceptive structures and the structure of their images derives solely from the retroactive effects of the images originating in the primary or pure sensations originally present; and that, therefore, all empirical localization motives are secondary." On the other hand, he emphasized the fact that in the early phases of ontogenetic development at least, sensations and perceptions do not coincide at all with the schematic outline set up by traditional psychologists concerning primary visual phenomena; they diverge from this scheme in much the same direction and to much the same degree as the images. Jaensch found that it was only in the child's later development that something approaching traditional psychological notions occurred and even then it was never quite identical with psychological theory.

This means that pure sensation is not the beginning but an end product of these developments. The eidetic images are incipient, undifferentiated unities from which perceptions and images are later differentiated. In any event, the eidetic images are essential in the construction of the world of apperception. The eidetic images, moreover, are object bound (*objektadäquat*) and subject bound (*subjektadäquat*); the latter in as much as they represent a section of environment significant to the subject. In this manner, Jaensch sees the possibility of attaining a revival of Kantian apriorism through sensory psychology as a result of his eidetic studies.

Jaensch and his associates also attempted to apply eidetics to the theory of concepts. Whereas it was formerly accepted that general concepts arise in the manner of Galton's type photography, that is, by means of strengthening general characteristics and repression of individual ones, Jaensch distinguishes two other forms of synthesis which he discusses as "fluxion" and "rational composition." Fluxion is spoken of when pictures, which have been seen, appear in constant motion and organic change; an example of this is Goethe's famous description of his gift for creating animated pictures of rosettes and flowers when he closed his eyes. In "rational compositions" a choice of features according to their significance takes place. All these studies, however, have not yet been concluded.

An important innovation introduced into psychological research by eidetics is the theory of different "levels" of consciousness. In space perception as well as in thought and will there is not one form but an entire system of levels which are distributed among different individuals, but may also occur united in one individual and then work synergistically. Older, original levels of consciousness are preserved while newer, more differentiated ones are developed, so that even on a higher level of development the various means of solution, the older as well as the newer, can be alternately used according to whether one or the other level of consciousness is coördinated by corresponding mental "sets."

4. The discovery of eidetic experiences is interesting, but it is doubtful whether everything that is called eidetic consciousness is correctly conceived. The demarcation of hallucination and illusion from visual images is not sharp enough. Jaensch and his pupils immediately dub every famous man who writes something about visual experiences of imagination an eidetic, and they thus create an *élite* society at whose

head stands Goethe and to which many artists and writers belong. Whether these personages actually were eidetics in the technical sense allows neither of proof nor demonstration.

There is also considerable doubt whether the significance of eidetic images is as important with regard to perception and thought as Jaensch would have us believe. Everyone who does not have eidetic images would be at a great disadvantage, to say the very least. And besides, there are whole regions and racial stocks in Germany which seem to be alarmingly poor in eidetic types. No one, however, has ever shown that noneidetic persons and groups lag behind the elect eidetics in the rest of their mental life. This is the chief basis for the objection to the importance of eidetics in regard to the other aspects of mental life.

So far as the history of the psychology of consciousness is concerned it is interesting to note that the proponents of the eidetic psychology also ally themselves with the anti-associationists. Although Jaensch is a pupil of G. E. Müller, a confirmed sensory associationist, he nevertheless emphasizes the totality of eidetic experience. Indeed, he even diverges from sensualism in that he constructs a relationship between eidetics and Kantian apriorism. This divergence from empiricism and approach to apriorism, which eventually leads to the acceptance of an integrated mind instead of the *tabula rasa* mind of pure empiricism, we have already found in the Würzburg school and in the *Gestalt* psychologists, although they are all very cautious in drawing such conclusions. In the eidetic school, as in the *Gestalt* school, the tendency toward totalitarian observation is unmistakable, and the totality is not derived from experience but is regarded from the point of view of innateness and apriorism.

THE 1910 CRITICS OF THE PSYCHOLOGY OF CONSCIOUSNESS

1. The appearance of the three tendencies just discussed shows that the psychology of consciousness continued to flourish and to branch out in new directions despite the onslaughts of the great critics of 1890. Still, the new schools show traits that distinguish them from the old. They all reject the atomization and the mosaic-like synthesis of the older psychologists, although they themselves continue to discover new elements of consciousness; they all speak of totalitarian experiences although they advance with great caution toward a totality of the whole self. They are all empiricists in so far as they seek to demonstrate their newly discovered states of consciousness experimentally, but they are not empiricists in the epistemological sense because they do not derive their non-sensory thoughts, *Gestalt* forms, and eidetic images from sensory experience but accept the existence of innate, *"a priori"* structures. This fundamental difference places these three trends in a new historical generation.

Meanwhile an entirely new situation developed about the year 1910. The critics of 1890 had not denied the psychology of consciousness a right to existence; they simply criticized its atomizing methods; and the new schools of the psychology of consciousness continued in the same position. About 1910, however, a new, far more radical opposition to the psychology of consciousness assumed form. This time the investigation of consciousness was rejected *in toto* and new goals were set up for psychology. The psychologists of consciousness believed they were standing on the solid ground of all experience when they proceeded from the direct study of consciousness. The very extreme ones like Mach had declared that sensations were the sole realities in the world. Suddenly we come upon the astonishing reversal of this judgment with the declaration that all research of consciousness has been the investigation of a blind alley, and that all previous psychology was no more than a slavery to superficial phenomena.

Four main offensives were launched against the psychology of consciousness in the twentieth century, all of which assumed their first positions after 1900. We shall first consider only their critical orientation against the psychology of consciousness. We shall discuss their positive accomplishments later because each one of these four offensives divides into further subordinate groups, and each of their theories at the present time already has its own course of development and its own history.

The first of these offensives sees in consciousness nothing more than the manifestation of functions, capabilities, and other phenomena which are not in themselves conscious.

The second of these offensives completely discards consciousness as the subject matter of psychology and replaces it with "behavior."

The third offensive declares consciousness to be a deceptive mask, and strives to reveal the veritable motivating forces of mental life behind the conscious camouflage in the "unconscious."

The fourth offensive sees in consciousness only a product of social conditions.

We are concerned at this point only with the criticism directed against the psychology of consciousness by all these new tendencies. Their positive accomplishments leading to entirely new psychologies will be discussed later in greater detail.

2. Before we discuss these four offensives, let us recall a lonely critic of the psychology of consciousness who really belonged to the older generation: Eduard von Hartmann. This significant philosopher had the misfortune of becoming famous through a brilliant but immature work called *The Philosophy of the Unconscious* (1869). I say "misfortune" because this success prevented his later, really significant, and mature works from being properly appreciated. This is

true especially of his excellent *Theory of Categories* (1899); but it is also true of both his psychological works: *Modern Psychology* (1905) and *Outline of Psychology* (1908). In both he presents a very erudite criticism of the psychology of consciousness. He demonstrated step by step that an immanent science of consciousness is impossible by following previous research; that, on the contrary, the psychology of consciousness—and rightly so—always goes beyond the limits it prescribed for itself.

Von Hartmann spoke openly of the "bankruptcy of the standpoint of pure consciousness" in psychology. He insisted that a science of mental processes was possible only when it referred back to unconscious facts. The "unconscious" which he seeks is, however, not the material, physiological unconscious which physiopsychology investigated. Here, too, he points out the shortcomings step by step in a brilliant correlation of the facts. He emphasized that the psychological is, indeed, an indispensable condition of consciousness, but not its adequate cause. He disputed the theory that denied all psychic activity and attempted to recognize only physical activity. Thus far his criticism remained completely in the realm of empirical psychology.

Von Hartmann, however, went further and demanded that psychology probe into the preconscious and postconscious depths of the mind. And here begins his own theory, which is no longer pure psychology but metaphysics, or more exactly, vitalistic pantheism. Even in supposedly dead nature Von Hartmann recognized the operation of a psychic activity which is simultaneously Will and Reason. He named this cosmic psychological force the "absolute unconscious." From it he derived all the activities of consciousness; from it, too, he reinterpreted the relations between body and soul. We shall return to Von Hartmann's positive accomplishments in another connection.

3. Although such critics as Eduard von Hartmann may be ignored as rank outsiders from the standpoint of strict ex-

perimental psychology, it is not possible to ignore another offensive, the so-called Act or Functional Psychology, which took form at the beginning of the twentieth century. Its representatives, like Stumpf and W. Stern, had made significant contributions to the analysis of consciousness but had gradually turned in another direction which, eventually, compelled them to relinquish the study of pure consciousness. I am not yet concerned with the positive accomplishments of this school of research to which I shall devote an entire part of this book later on. I shall confine myself here only to its criticism of previous psychologies of consciousness.

Stumpf and a group of younger thinkers reproach older students of consciousness with having comprehended only that content of consciousness which had passed while ignoring the present consciousness which was being experienced, that is, the acts and functions of consciousness. These psychologists claimed that what had previously been regarded as "consciousness" was merely a passive thing, a superficial reflection of the external world, and not the really active internal world itself, whose inner structure made those "reflections" possible. For them a new consciousness appears beyond that consciousness which is but an epitome of what is known; this new consciousness is the knowing of what is known. Single acts or functions cannot be viewed isolatedly but can only be comprehended in terms of the totality of the "self," which is not itself conscious but which has consciousness.

These functional psychologists discovered a structure of the mind by means of theoretical conclusions. A practical method of proving it soon presented itself in the study of talents. Ebbinghaus, Cattell, and other American scholars had attempted to measure single "capacities" like memory or intelligence by means of the test method. Since Binet, the method of intelligence tests has been widely employed, and soon similar tests were also applied to other capacities and skills. Even though at first the aims were entirely practical, these experiments led away from the psychology of consciousness to a psychology of performance. But, as a theoretical background, here too capacities, skills, and talents emerged which, like functional psychology, bore a close resemblance to the supposedly long dead eighteenth-century "faculty" psychology of capacity; at any rate, this was something other than the analysis of consciousness.

A third school of research, the psychology of instinct, belongs in this category because it, too, led away from the one-sided study of consciousness. The newer animal and child psychology, that did not limit itself to the study of adult consciousness, had made a more precise study of the instincts which in the nineteenth century were considered purely mechanistic. McDougall pointed out that instincts are the bases of the emotions; to be sure, in addition to the factor of striving, he felt that they also have an emotional and cognitive aspect, but still they are rooted in bodily dispositions of behavior which are not conscious as such. Woodworth, too, in his *Dynamic Psychology* (1918), assumes a mass of "patterns," innate capacities, which are not clearly defined by nature.

All these researches, various as they are, are no longer pure analysis of consciousness. They attempt openly what the psychologists of consciousness had ventured somewhat shamefully and without definite avowal. All of them transgress the bounds of consciousness and seek for acts, capacities, instincts, and the like beyond consciousness. This tendency of research necessarily had to proceed beyond single acts, capacities, and instincts to the acceptance of a totalitarian self.

4. The combined offensive of the Russian psychoreflexologists and the American behaviorists was much more bitter in the condemnation of the psychology of consciousness than the attack of the functional psychologists. The functional psychologists had not completely denied consciousness; on the contrary, they had studied it very carefully,

albeit with the intention of revealing, by means of the contents of consciousness, the inner activity resulting in these contents which itself is no longer conscious in the same sense as the contents. Both the psychology of talents and of instincts started from consciousness in order to reveal contents or instincts which were not conscious as such.

The new tendency fundamentally eliminates consciousness and takes its point of departure from the observation of external conduct. In biology, German scientists in the nineteenth century had already taught a pure "objectivism." Similarly the Russian psychoreflexologists led by Bechterev and Pavlov attempted to explain mental life in terms of reflexes without including consciousness at all. "Conditioned reflexes" (Pavlov) were also supposed to explain satisfactorily the higher mental functions. The most radical procedure was that of the American John B. Watson, the founder of "behaviorism." In his polemics against the "introspectionists" like James and Titchener, who seemed rather inadequate to him, Watson rejected consciousness entirely as a subject for psychology. In place of it he defined psychology as the science of behavior. We shall not evaluate the positive accomplishments of behaviorism here but confine ourselves solely to its negative elimination of consciousness from psychology.

In all this, it is particularly interesting that Watson, much though his path diverges from that of other psychologists, still sharply emphasizes, in his way, a notion which had come to the fore even in the psychology of consciousness; the notion of totality. For, according to Watson, psychology is distinguished from physiology in that the latter studies single acts of behavior, whereas the former studies behavior as a whole.

5. If the psychoreflexologists and behaviorists had disposed of consciousness as a subordinate, irrelevant fact, an even worse reproach was made against it by the third group of the opposition; they declared consciousness to be false, un-

true, and deceptive. These psychologists cast, so to speak, moral aspersions on consciousness.

The most remarkable thing is that this attack upon consciousness occurred as early as 1880 and only the psychologist had left it unnoticed. The most significant champion of this movement had died in 1900 and his mind had ceased functioning even before his death. This was the philosopher, Friedrich Nietzsche, in whose works only the prophecy of the superman and certain scintillating moral paradoxes had attracted attention. The fact that he was also a brilliant psychologist was not discovered until the beginning of the twentieth century, even though in his last works he was wont to refer to himself as a "psychologist."

From the standpoint of the prevailing scientific psychology, to be sure, he was rather an "antipsychologist." The psychoanalysts, with Freud and Adler in the van, were the first to gather their weapons from Nietzsche's belligerent writings, and it was not until 1924 that a great, compendious work on Nietzsche's psychology appeared. It was written by Ludwig Klages, one of the most important representatives of the newer generation of German psychologists.

Nietzsche himself, in his attitude toward psychology, was in turn the pupil of Schopenhauer, who never grew tired of asserting that our understanding is only the advocate of our muffled, instinctive will. According to Schopenhauer, the understanding kindles a light for the will; according to Nietzsche, however, this light is deceptive. Consciousness only rarely tells us the truth, especially when it concerns our own self; it employs subtle means to deceive us about our true nature.

In general, Nietzsche's philosophic opinion of consciousness is that it does not have the task of informing us of the "true" knowledge of the external world or of our self; consciousness rather is a force in the service of life, that is, in the livery of the "Will to Power," and in this service it considers every useful deception permissible. Thus it falsifies the external world when a disguise suits its practical purposes; it also falsifies the image of the internal world if any advantage results from doing that.

This doctrine is clearly stated in Nietzsche's earliest writings. Thus he writes in 1873: "Man desires the pleasant, life-preserving consequences of truth; he is indifferent to pure inconsequential knowledge, and is even inimical to possibly damaging and destructive truths." "The intellect, that master of dissimulation, is free only so long as it can deceive without harming, and only then does it celebrate its saturnalia." For the emotional life, according to Nietzsche, two impulses hold sway: the Apollonian and the Dionysian, that is to say, the desire to dream and the desire to be intoxicated. Dream and intoxication, however, do not have much to do with truth.

But Nietzsche desires "truth"; he does not look for it in consciousness, but beyond consciousness, in its instinctive depths which he illuminated with cruel pleasure. There he discovered the Will to Power, which is also revealed in sexuality, resentment, cruelty, and other obscure instincts. He is indefatigable in discovering such chiefly amoral impulses in the depths of the mind and in disclosing the ideals of man as a camouflage designed to disguise these impulses. For what are ideals? "Sanctified lies!"

Nietzsche himself writes concerning his method, which, of course, he applied rather unmethodically: "If I possess an advantage above all other psychologists, it is that my eyes are sharpened to that most difficult and insidious kind of *a posteriori* conclusion [rationalization] by means of which most errors are committed; the conclusion from the work to its creator, from the deed to the doer, from the ideal to the one who has need of it, from every manner of thought and evaluation to the imperious necessity behind it." The psychologist must, therefore, describe not consciousness but that which lurks behind consciousness. But what is this? A great many passages in Nietzsche sound as though he simply meant the physiological structure of the body. He himself boasted of his knowledge of physiology and medicine and in his autobiography claimed to have studied nothing but physiology, medicine, and natural sciences, during the last decade of his life.

Literally speaking this is not true, although his own seriously ailing body constantly compelled him to observe his own physiological states. Because of this, he was led to detect pathological states everywhere; in other people, and in the great personages of history. When he speaks of physiology, however, it is not in the sense of traditional physiological psychology. Nietzsche visualized a vitalistic biology, although in this respect he pursued very few strictly scientific studies. He only permits aprioristic shafts of light to illuminate the depths of the impulse life and what he discovers there are things that until then had scarcely been noticed by science. He discloses no moral idyl, but a demoniacal, repugnant chaos, which is sustained by a profound meaning. All this is not conscious, although consciousness is regarded as a secret code, which must be deciphered if we are to get at the true meaning of life which is hidden beneath its cryptic text.

Again we are concerned only with the critical side of this doctrine. Although Nietzsche did not engage in any polemics with the scientific psychology of his time, which he scarcely knew, still his own system of psychology was fundamentally antagonistic to it, for it denied the principle that we can directly comprehend mental life in consciousness. The new task which he set for psychology was not description, but unmasking of consciousness!

In this direction Nietzsche prepared the way for psychoanalysis, one of the most influential movements that branched out from psychology in the twentieth century. Psychoanalysis, too, has very rarely expressed its opposition to the psychology of consciousness in direct criticism; and yet the entire system of psychoanalysis embodies a trenchant criticism of that psychology. For, according to Freud, consciousness can only be understood in connection with the unconscious. This leads to the realization that consciousness can only be understood metaphorically, as a masked process. In other words, consciousness is not to be described; it is to be interpreted.

Dreams in particular afford the psychoanalyst a glimpse into the depths of the soul. In addition, the true nature of mental life is betrayed by erroneously performed actions, slips of the tongue, errors in writing, forgetting, and the like. Consciousness exercises a "censorship" which suppresses a great deal that is essential, particularly sexuality, to which ordinary psychology had paid little attention and which now became the center of observation. We shall discuss the doctrines of Freud, Adler, and other psychoanalysts later. At this point we merely note that the appearance of psychoanalysis discredited the psychology of consciousness which became known as "superficial psychology," at least in the eyes of the public. Psychology now became primarily the study of the unconscious, and called itself "depth" psychology.

6. One final group of critics of the psychology of consciousness came from the newly arisen science of sociology and its related disciplines. These scholars completely ignored consciousness just as the behaviorists did. The same facts which the psychology of consciousness had explained from the point of view of individual consciousness, they described from the point of view of social conditions, as though the participating individuals had no consciousness at all. This group was known as the psychological sociologists. The Frenchman Durkheim was its typical representative.

Another group of sociologists took consciousness into consideration and accorded it an essential function in the creation of religions, customs, arts, and other social forms. But for this group, consciousness is not original in the individual, but is considered the product of social environment. Social environment gives consciousness a definite imprint by means of which it becomes fit for its creative task. Many scholars who entertain conflicting views are united within this group. In America, for example, John Dewey can be cited as a member. McDougall and his school also try to show not only the individual but also the social basis of consciousness in their theory of instinct. In France, scholars like Tarde and Le Bon pointed out the social dependence of states of consciousness and founded a school upon the basis of this concept. In Germany the theorists of race viewed consciousness as primarily dependent upon the biological and sociological factors of race. Many of the younger sociologists dispute the priority of consciousness and question the possibility of understanding the mind in its higher processes from the standpoint of individual consciousness.

7. In reviewing the manifold opposition to the psychology of consciousness which developed, in part from the ranks of the consciousness psychologists themselves, since the beginning of the nineteenth century, we observe that its temper is more radical than the critiques of the 1890 opposition. Bergson, James, and Dilthey insisted upon the inadequacy of the previous atomistic-associationist analysis of consciousness, but they had never claimed that the whole analysis of consciousness was a scientific fallacy. On the contrary, they had attempted to set an improved analysis of consciousness in place of the former one.

The new opponents went much further. They were united in attacking the whole method of pure analysis of the consciousness and in emphasizing that no science can be derived from the phenomena studied by previous methods of research. They claimed that even the inclusion of physiological facts and hypotheses, by means of which the older psychology had striven to support its knowledge and to fill in its gaps, was completely inadequate. In order to substantiate this claim the new critics invoked the evolution of psychology itself and simply demonstrated that psychology had long since passed the atomistic and mechanistic stage.

The critics of the psychology of consciousness agree in not searching for the causality of mental life within consciousness itself. To the extent that these critics do not entirely deny the significance of consciousness, as do the behaviorists, they conceive consciousness solely as a transitory stage beyond which research must probe for the true structure of the mind.

As a result of this, in the parts of this book dealing with newer research we shall have to pursue entirely different methods of investigation and descend into fields that are, to be sure, related to consciousness but are no longer consciousness as such.

The psychology of consciousness is by no means bankrupt in the present day. It is still energetically pursued. But it has long since ceased to be the psychology that it pretended to be at its inception.

Two periods can clearly be distinguished in the entire history of the psychology of consciousness. The first one, which attained its height in the second half of the nineteenth century, saw its chief aim in the isolation of psychic elements and in the synthesis of the higher mental processes from those elements. The second period began in the closing years of the nineteenth century and developed in the first decades of the twentieth. This period opposed the analysis of thought, will, perception, and the like, into elements, and emphasized their totalitarian nature.

In addition to this, our presentation has shown how new opponents have constantly arisen against the psychology of consciousness and have founded their own new schools. These opponents were able to ally themselves to certain fields of endeavor that had arisen within the psychology of consciousness itself, but that led beyond it. The new schools emphasized those very aspects of the study of consciousness that trespassed the limits of consciousness, and thus removed the focus of attention to a point outside the study of consciousness itself.

Psychologists of consciousness had always deliberately

sought the physiological parallels to processes of consciousness. Such parallel studies will be introduced in the next chapter to supplement those already discussed. The study of physiological parallels to mental acts will show that physiology, too, gradually emancipated itself from the construction of such parallels and eventually found independent solutions which led toward a totalitarian point of view.

We have shown that the psychology of consciousness could not help noticing the connection of consciousness with motor acts which are not merely parallel to consciousness. By making these motor responses a separate field of inquiry, new schools of psychology arose which, like functionalism, psychoreflexology, and behaviorism, were increasingly diverted from the study of consciousness.

But even without considering physiological and motor facts, psychology was increasingly inclined to accept the fact that certain capacities, predispositions and acts lay beyond consciousness. This led to a type of research which conceived consciousness merely as a transient way station, in order to fathom the structure of the mind and the totality of the self, which lay hidden beyond it.

The psychology of consciousness exceeded its limits because it was constantly obliged to assume the existence of interphenomena and auxiliary phenomena. By advancing along this line of inquiry, the psychology of consciousness became a psychology of the unconscious and other coexistential ruling factors of the mind. At this point psychoanalysis and the schools related to it entered the picture.

Moreover, when the psychologists of consciousness also observed the influence of superindividual factors upon individual consciousness, they began to occupy themselves with "racial psychology" or "social psychology." These tendencies of research necessarily led to the study of the superconscious, superindividual mental life.

Thus we can see how the new, differently orientated tendencies of research stem from the psychology of consciousness itself. The psychology of consciousness was the source of new psychological teachings which were destined to extend the field of psychology far beyond the pure analysis of consciousness.

PART TWO

PHYSIOPSYCHOLOGY AND
PSYCHOPHYSIOLOGY

CHANGING ASPECTS OF THE PROBLEM
OF PHYSIOPSYCHOLOGY

1. The newer psychology of 1880 had carefully delimited its field of study to include only "consciousness." However, its endeavor to be as exact a science as possible obliged it to ally itself to the sciences of the human body. Indeed, the representatives of this newer psychology took honest pains to provide the transitory, immaterial consciousness with a solid basis in physical reality, above all in the nervous system.

Their assumption, which soon turned into dogma, was that there must be a strict causal correlation between every single state of consciousness and some physiological act. Superficially, the effect of such an assumption was to create a mood of confidence; it hushed up somewhat the fact that, although a great deal was known about the body and about consciousness, still the central problem of the connection between consciousness and the body remained completely in the dark. The slogan of "psychophysical parallelism" drowned out all difficulties with its impressive resonance, but offered no real solution. Parallelism was only a working hypothesis, but it was often fallaciously regarded as an assured theory even by psychologists.

At this point we shall study the widely ramified field of investigation which attempted to clarify the physiological substructure of consciousness. This field of investigation by no means disclosed the causality which had at first been assumed, but led to increasingly difficult problems. The human body, which had at first been considered a transparent mechanism, proved itself, upon closer investigation, to be a very mysterious something, full of riddles and cryptic obscurities which no one had dreamed existed. Indeed, we shall witness the remarkable spectacle of psychology at first trying to rear itself upon biology and physiology only to find that with the advance of investigation, biology and physiology came to borrow more and more from psychology, so that physiological psychology gradually changed into psychological physiology and biology.

2. The new problem of the connection between consciousness and the body is very similar to the problem of consciousness. In reality this is a very ancient problem, the old question of the connection between soul and body, in a new dress. For the thinkers of former centuries, the soul as the "bearer" of consciousness always intruded itself between consciousness and the body. We shall have to show that this problem emerged again and again in modern psychology. To do this we shall summarize briefly the evolution of the older problem, which also throws light upon modern research.

Calling to mind the historical views of the soul discussed above, we can discern two divisions: the soul was either conceived of as substance or as power. (If some thinkers also used the word "form," they meant a formative power.) Of course, both of these conceptions coincide for the most part; "power" is either ascribed to the soul substance or the soul is "substantialized."

The primitive theory of substance, animism, operated mostly with analogies from the material world, that is, it identified the soul with "quasi-material" facts like breath, fire, shadow, and so forth. The effect of this is still evident in scientific psychology. We have also mentioned a number of the ancient theories of substance. The atomists and after them the Epicureans declared the soul to be substantial, even material. For to them the soul, like matter, consisted of atoms, albeit atoms that were particularly smooth, round, and mobile. Even the "pneuma" of the Stoics, literally "air," is a quasi-material concept.

The dynamic theory of the soul began with Plato, who considered the soul as the life principle and the origin of motion. This idea was further developed by Aristotle. The soul's contrast with matter, which had not been so marked in early Greek philosophers, became extremely prominent.

The purest dynamist was Leibniz, in whom the idea was reversed, for he considered the soul not in analogy with matter, but matter in analogy with the soul. This viewpoint was continued in Fichte and Hegel, and even in Schopenhauer; to them matter was no more than the manifestation or idea of a psychic world "force," which was alternately called "self," "idea," or "will."

Fundamentally, however, most of the older theories were dualistic. They separated soul and body, even when they strove toward monism; for every supposed monism has either a more materialistic and substantial aspect or a more dynamic and idealistic one. An unresolved portion always remains. The soul, in its incessant transmutations, can never be wholly reduced to matter, nor can matter be wholly reduced to soul. The necessity of reuniting the organic whole which has thus been split up produced the physiopsychic problem.

3. Older thinkers conceived this problem to be essentially spatial. They confined themselves mostly to the localization of the soul in some specific part of the body, without bothering in detail as to how the soul influenced the body from that particular part.

Even primitive psychology already saw the dwelling place of the soul not only in the body as a whole but in specific parts of the body. We have already mentioned that the brain, today considered the chief center of psychic activity, was then taken into account least of all. On the contrary, the organ of the soul was alternately considered to be in the blood, the kidneys, the heart, the diaphragm, the intestines, the genitals, and even in the saliva. These were not entirely far-fetched, ridiculous theories; indeed, we shall see that modern psychology occasionally reverts to such ideas, as, for instance, when the heart is placed in relation to emotions, when an influence upon mental life is ascribed to the blood and the endocrine secretions which enter it. Primitive man noticed very early that the heart begins to thump during a state of emotion or that a disorder of the liver causes a "bilious," irritable state of mind. Many primitive races even distinguished separate "soul organs" having special functions. These can be regarded as preliminary stages of the "faculties" of the mind which were adopted later.

Early philosophical psychology took over a great many of these prescientific assumptions. In Plato the body is not merely the dwelling place but the "prison" of the soul. The three parts of the soul which he distinguished were localized separately from each other. According to his *Timaios*, the reason dwells in the head, the thymoeides between the neck and the diaphragm, the epithymetikon between the diaphragm and the navel. In Aristotle, the heart is the central organ of sensation, whereas the brain is considered to be only a mechanism for cooling the blood. Since, however, the soul is not a substance to Aristotle but a life principle, the body was conceived as formed by the soul, and all body organs were permeated with the soul. To the Epicureans the entire body was pervaded with soul stuff. The Stoics, on the other hand, located the most important part of the soul, the *hegemonikón*, in the heart.

In modern times, Descartes fixed an exact spot for the soul in the brain. His choice fell upon the pineal gland. The reasons for this choice were purely speculative. As an unexpanded entity, the soul could touch the body at only one point; the *glans pinealis* must be the point sought for. According to Descartes, the soul cannot accomplish much in the bodily mechanism; it cannot create motion but can only change the direction of motion. The problem as to how the soul and body work together remained unsolved for a long time. The solutions offered were mostly transcendental and invoked the Divinity.

The modern English and French materialists finally chose the brain as the locus of psychic activities; for the most part, they simply identified the soul with the brain. However, more specialized localizations were soon attempted. Thus Bonnet placed the soul in the *corpus callosum*, Haller in the *pons Varolii*, Boerhaave in the *medulla oblongata*, Platner in the *corpora quadrigemina*, and Sömmering in the meningeal fluid. It is obvious that scientific imagination was not biased in locating the soul. There are very few parts of the body which have not at one time or another been regarded as its seat. But, by and large, the consensus of opinion increasingly converged upon the brain.

4. Since Fechner, the chief difference between the "new" psychology and almost all previous views concerning the relation of body and soul can be briefly formulated thus: the new psychology conceived the soul as consciousness. All substantial and dynamic notions of the concept of soul were expressly avoided. Consciousness was a phenomenon, a state. The matter can be put as follows: all theories of the soul as a substance were substantivistic, all dynamic theories verbal, and all theories of the new psychology are adjectivistic. Consciousness in its relation to the body is an attribute, a quality, an accessory phenomenon. The causal influence between soul and body, a problem that had been particularly annoying, is eliminated. It is assumed that consciousness as a mental phenomenon appears in the central nervous system, together with certain physiological occurrences. Causality was replaced by "parallelism."

Of course, this idea was not entirely new. It had already occurred to Spinoza. He denied the quality of substance to consciousness, or thought, as he preferred to say. He saw in consciousness, as well as in matter, only an attribute of the entire universal substance. For Spinoza there was no causality between consciousness and the body. The only cause of the individual bodies, as of the individual thoughts, is God, the total substance. The order and relation of ideas are the same as the order and relation of the body. The human mind recognizes its own body only in terms of the stimuli by which the body is aroused. The mind does not contain any adequate knowledge of the parts which compose the human body. Spinoza thus instituted psychophysical parallelism only as a metaphysical principle, without explaining in detail the relation between states of consciousness and physical stimuli. There was no precedent for such an explanation in the science of his time. Nevertheless, the main difficulty inherent in parallelism was already announced in Spinoza's assumption that the body is composed of innumerable single entities, whereas consciousness is a unity.

Fechner, like Spinoza, also started from metaphysical speculations in his psychophysics. It is an historical curiosity that Fechner's empiricism was ultimately rooted in metaphysical and mystical speculation; that in his microscopically exact experiments, there always lurked the tendency to prove the correctness of these cosmic speculations. Like Spinoza, he was convinced that the entire universe consists not merely of space and matter, but also of soul. Parallelism does not merely exist between the human body and its consciousness but there are psychic correlations to all events in the physical world. Fechner believed this so implicitly that he considered even the stars as animate.

According to Fechner, the physical and the mental are fundamentally identical; the distinction is only a matter of different aspects of the same data. Fechner's analogy of the body-soul relationship to a circle became famous, but it was largely overestimated in its factual significance. Just as a circle viewed from within is concave, and viewed from without is convex, so consciousness is the inner aspect and corporeality is the outer aspect. What is pain to me, is a prick of a needle to an external observer. What is a complicated process in the ether and in the ganglion cells from a physical viewpoint, is the sensation of color from a mental viewpoint.

This, of course, broadened the concept of parallelism to a questionable degree, for the physical occurrence is extremely complex, whereas the experience of consciousness amounts to a unity. Thus Fechner was obliged to make the following formulation: "The identical unity of consciousness is connected with a composite bodily system." By this formulation Fechner came into opposition with the monadological theory according to which single atoms must possess consciousness. His own "synechological" view, in contrast to the monadological theory, assumed that consciousness becomes real only within the causal unity of a system. All in all, Fechner's theory was not a solution to the problem but a delimitation of the solution which was still to be achieved.

Wundt, the other founder of the new psychology was not quite as extreme as Fechner in the matter of parallelism. Because Wundt viewed the will as the essence of mentality, his voluntarism approached a dynamism; indeed, he designated his psychology as "actualistic." Consciousness was not a passive attribute to Wundt but a form of activity, particularly in his theory of apperception. In spite of this, he still largely retained the notion of a psychophysical parallelism, even though he did not designate his theory as ascertained knowledge but rather as a "heuristic principle." For Wundt, parallelism was merely a postulate which enabled him to conceive an unbroken, causal continuity in the process of nature. The physical and the psychic form, each for itself, a closed causal continuity. Where the continuation of the causal series eludes our experience, it is permissible and necessary to go over to the other series to supplement the first. However, Wundt did not remain entirely consistent in his theory of parallelism and was severely attacked for it.

The third of the great pioneers of the new psychology, Herbert Spencer, was also a parallelist in a certain sense. For him, too, neural activity and psychological phenomena were the inner and outer aspects of one and the same change. He considered a direct proof of this impossible. But Spencer was satisfied, for the time being, that such an hypothesis coincided with the data of outer and inner experience. Spencer was more inclined to a theory of the soul as a substance, in so far as he assumed a single, inscrutable "substance" of the mind, by which he meant something which persists through all the changes of consciousness.

At any rate, a new problem existed at the beginning of the new psychology. The problem was to coördinate with the multifarious phenomena of consciousness equally isolable physiological processes, without the necessity of interposing a "soul." This determined the course of research until the end of the century.

THE LOCALIZATION OF SENSATIONS

1. Whereas the new psychology had begun its exact investigation with sensations, the new physiopsychology began with the physiological correlates of these sensations. The reasons were the same in both cases. The sensory organs are the easiest to observe and to experiment with. The organs can be anatomically dissected and their functions can be studied by themselves.

The discovery of "specific sense energies" is generally regarded as the beginning of modern physiopsychology. This discovery was made by Johannes Müller in the 1830's. According to his theory, the quality of sensations is conditioned by the special quality of the stimulated nerves. This is shown by the fact that every nerve responds to specific stimuli and even transforms indefinite, mechanical stimuli into its own specific sensation. As far back as Aristotle, it had been known that the eye responds immediately to sensations of light. But Johannes Müller was the first to formulate this in general terms. It is significant that this basic principle of empirical research, like so many others, did not come into being without the aid of philosophy, in this instance Kant's epistemology. Müller's theory was considered a confirmation of Kant's doctrine that in sensations we do not grasp the thing in itself (*das Ding an sich*), but only its effect upon the apperceptive self. On the other hand, the theory of specific sense energies seemed to confirm the fundamental postulate of parallelism that isolable acts of consciousness (in this case, sensations) and also isolable organs and processes correspond to specific nerve aptitudes.

Müller's very general theory was considerably clarified by Helmholtz, who tried to trace back to their nerve fibers not only the main types of sensation but also the more specific experiences of the separate senses. Thus he assumed the existence of specific receptor mechanisms for the separate colors and sounds in the peripheral organs as well as in the brain. We shall return to this later. Going on from where Helmholtz had left off, specific nerves were sought for in connection with all the senses; indeed the existence of certain nerves was hypothetically assumed in cases where anatomists could not find them.

Most physiologists allied themselves to the theory of specific sense energies but, of course, a great difficulty remained with Helmholtz' theory. It was necessary to assume a like number of innate physiological organs (whose existence could not be adequately demonstrated by anatomy) in order to account for the myriad qualities of sensation. Wundt tried to obviate this difficulty by setting up his "principle of the accommodation of sensory elements to stimuli." According to this principle, specific sense energy is not an innate fact but the product of an accommodation of the organism to stimuli. Wundt reached this conclusion by means of genetico-historical studies. Comparative physiology shows that most senses are only differentiations of the original and most general sense organ, the epidermis. Even in developed organisms the epidermis still has the functions of a general sense mechanism which unites in itself disparate qualities. This is still more clearly demonstrated in lower organisms in which the epidermis, even after the development of special senses, can still react to the already specialized stimuli.

According to Wundt, we must assume that the sense

organs need an adequate stimulus in order to develop. The frequent repetition of this stimulus causes changes in the nerves and in the central organs so that the latter react in a specific manner to every sufficiently strong stimulus. Every individual must have had sensations of light over a period of time before he can experience them. With congenitally blind or deaf persons, too, no optical or acoustical memory images can be attained by inadequate stimuli.

2. Whether the theory of specific sense energies can lay claim to universal validity is beside the point. The fact is that this theory has had a dominant effect upon the investigation of the physiological bases of the separate types of sensation. It particularly influenced the physiology of optical sensations. Thomas Young, who in 1807 had been the first to assume the existence of three basic colors, red, green, and violet, believed that there were three types of nerve fibers in the eye, each of which corresponded to one of the basic colors. The intermediate colors were supposed to originate through the increase of accompanying nerve stimulation, for example, yellow from red through an increasingly strong stimulation of the nerves for green.

This theory was adopted by Helmholtz about 1860 in his *Handbook of Physiological Optics.* Helmholtz sought the physiological bases for the three basic colors. At first he suspected that there were in the optic nerve three kinds of nerve fibers corresponding to the three basic colors. Later he assumed that there were in the brain and possibly in the retina three kinds of elements corresponding to red, green, and violet. Of course this was not a real explanation but merely a translation of psychological observation into the technical language of physiology. And besides, the difficulty remained that a mixture of the three types of nerve fibers or terminals had to be presupposed even upon the smallest surface of the retina.

A new epoch in the physiology of color vision was introduced by Hering's monograph of 1878 upon *A Theory of the Sense of Light.* Hering did not accept the theory of three basic colors, but started with the assumption of four colors. To this he united the theory of processes of assimilation and dissimilation alternately occurring within the living substance. This chemical change of katabolism and anabolism within the substances of the eye which are sensitive to light governs the origin of the contrasting colors: black white, red-green, blue-yellow. Particularly upon the basis of his study of color-blind people, Hering adopted three substances: the black-white, the red-green and the blue-yellow substance. Black, green, and blue were supposed to originate through assimilation; white, red, and yellow through dissimilation. In this way Hering evolved his theory of specific substances and processes as the physiological basis of color vision.

A significant discovery in the physiology of color vision was made by Von Kries in 1897. His theory of "duplicity" treated the eye as a dual mechanism. Daylight vision and twilight vision do not involve the same local organs of the eye. Twilight vision is not a function of the center of the retina but of its periphery where only the so-called "rods" of the retina are found. These rods are the organs of twilight vision while the "cones" of the retina are responsible for daylight vision. These zones were stratified behind one another and were supposed to have various functions. The zone theory united the three- and four-color theories in the following way: the peripheral functions were supposed to be integrated according to three components, whereas the central functions were supposed to be integrated in a manner corresponding to the four-color theory. On the whole, however, Von Kries was very cautious in coördinating psychological and physiological facts. He declared "that the physiology of the organ of vision and the psychology of the visual sensations are extremely different things, naturally not without many points of contact, but by no means as completely identical as has so often been assumed."

We shall not go into the numerous new studies of the physiology of vision. These studies agree that the processes of the visual organs are important preliminary factors in vision, but that physiologically vision cannot be exclusively coördinated with one of these processes; on the contrary, processes in the cerebral cortex must also be included. In a strict sense, this does not corroborate the theory of parallelism because extremely complicated processes in the various organs are bound up with the simple act of psychological vision.

3. In 1863 in a work entitled *The Theory of Sound Sensations*, Helmholtz developed his theories on sound which, like his theory of color vision, were influenced by Johannes Müller's theory of specific sense energies. To every sound, Helmholtz ascribed a specific end organ in the ear. He located these end organs in the basilar membrane of the cochlea. The basilar membrane is 2½ cm. long, very small, and is rolled up into a spiral. It increases somewhat in width from one end to the other. On the inside of the membrane there is a stratum of many thousand elastic, transverse fibers. Moreover, it is covered by several rows of cells upon which the nerve fibers end. Now, according to Helmholtz, the transverse fibers are each tuned to a specific sound just like the strings of a piano. (This is the origin of the term "cochlear keyboard.") These fibers are set into vibration and in turn stimulate the nerve endings which correspond to the particular fibers.

This theory has its advantages and its shortcomings. It coincides with the gradually widening shape of the basilar membrane and with the number of fibers which correspond approximately to the estimated number (13,400–24,000), of audible tones. The "piano theory" also coincides with the fact of tone gaps, that is, the deficiency of certain parts of the tonal series in many pathological cases.

On the other hand, objections to Helmholtz' theory have been raised. The theory does not satisfactorily explain tremolo, combinations of tones, or noise. Nevertheless, almost all suggestions for improvement resolve themselves into mere modifications of Helmholtz' theory. The idea of specific aptitudes of the auditory nerve fibers was not relinquished, but the assumption was made (Ebbinghaus) that several fibers could be stimulated at the same time. Wundt presupposed, as in vision, a gradual process of accommodation in audition and ascribed a certain latitude of receptivity to the single nerve fibers so that the same fibers could react to somewhat different sensations.

Whatever the further development of the Helmholtz theory may be, we have reasonable grounds to be sure that hearing is not confined to the auditory nerves but that parts of the cerebrum are also involved. Consequently, the same objections apply to a strict parallelism in the theory of sound as in the theory of vision.

4. Von Brunns located the organ for the olfactory sense in the *regio olfactoria* situated in the upper turbinated bones of the nose and in the neighboring section of the mucous membrane. The olfactory epithelium is somewhat smaller than a dime. Whereas Johannes Müller and others believed that odorous substances had to be dissolved first of all in the mucous covering of the *regio olfactoria*, Zwaardemaker, in 1895, advanced the hypothesis that the odorous molecules are already in a volatile form when they come into contact with the tiny vibrating cilia of the olfactory cells. In concordance with the theory of specific aptitudes, it is assumed that various kinds of olfactory sensations are produced by various olfactory nerves. The basis for this assumption is that many individuals who possess an otherwise well-developed sense of smell completely lack the power of detecting certain kinds of odors. Thus, there are people who cannot detect the odor of violets. Moreover, the olfactory organ is rapidly fatigued by certain specific odors whereas it retains its power with certain other odors.

In considering the sense of taste, the difficulty is to

separate from it what really belongs to the sense of smell. Lovén and Schwalbe discovered the terminal mechanisms of the gustatory nerves: the *circumvallate papillæ* or taste buds which are embedded in the epithelium of the mucous membrane of the tongue. The conductive gustatory nerve is partly located in the glossopharyngeal and partly in the trigeminus nerve; but the existence of other conductors is also assumed (Cassirer). Öhrwall's experiments have demonstrated that various types of taste qualities are yielded by various nerves, so that Johannes Müller's theory seems to be corroborated in this respect. Of course, with smell and with taste, too, the qualification must be made that the indicated nerves are receptors and conductors of the sensory stimuli, but are not the separate parallel organs of sensation.

5. The outer skin is the general organ for the psychologically different sensations of heat, touch, and pain, which are often summarily referred to as "the skin senses." But more specific organs for these different kinds of sensation have been found within the skin.

The fact that the opposite sensations of heat and cold are not felt at every spot of the skin and that, therefore, separated nerve endings are to be assumed, was shown by Blix in 1883, and independently of him, by Goldscheider in 1884. Subsequent research made the unequal distribution of heat nerves upon the skin a particular subject of investigation. Goldscheider worked out a very minute topography of the sense of heat which showed that there was a peculiar radiation of these sensations.

In the senses of pressure and touch we recognize not only pressure and touch but also the quality of the object touched. We distinguish whether the object is rough or smooth, sharp or dull, soft or firm. According to contemporary opinion, these distinctions do not originate from the tactile nerves alone but also from the coöperation of other nerves, particularly those related to the kinesthetic sense.

The distribution of tactile points was first determined by Blix. Von Frey showed that the stimulus hairs play an important rôle in this distribution. Since the researches of E. H. Weber, the "local indices" or local signs, that is, the ability to localize stimuli applied to the skin, have been determined; Weber demonstrated that these local signs vary considerably in different parts of the skin.

Pain is considered a special skin sensation. Older writers considered pain no more than an extraordinary intensification of ordinary centripetal nerve stimulation, but Von Frey in 1896 declared that specific pain nerves exist. Since that time there has been an intense research in the topography of the sense of pain.

6. The physiology of kinesthetic sensations has been a veritable battleground. C. Bell and E. H. Weber assumed the existence of sensory muscle nerves, Lotze and Schiff tried to confine the kinesthetic sense to the skin senses, and Lewinski sought for the kinesthetic sense in the articular and osseous nerves. Other authors like Leyden, Meynert, and Nothnagel assumed that there was a coöperation of several kinds of centripetal nerves. The anatomical proof of the existence of centripetal muscle nerves was advanced by Reichert, Kölliker, Odenius, and others. According to Goldscheider, the most important rôle in the sensation of passive motions is played by the centripetal nerves of the joints. In all events, a series of different nerves is involved in the perception of motion. A great deal of information has also resulted from the study of locomotor ataxia, a disorder which effects muscle coördination.

Special organs have also been assigned to the sense of balance. As far back as 1828, Flourens pointed out in a report the remarkable disturbances of balance which occurred in deaf individuals when the semicircular canals of their ears were destroyed. An experimental study was made of the effects of artificial stimulation of the semicircular canals by Goltz and Breuer in 1874, and later by

Ewald in 1892. This study revealed that the motion of the liquid in the semicircular canals tautens the cell hairs of the *crista acustica* and stimulates the corresponding nerve endings. Breuer, Mach, and Brown almost simultaneously determined the significance of the otoliths for the sense of balance.

There is still a great deal of groping in the dark with regard to the physiological phenomena which accompany the visceral sensations. Since these sensations are very indefinite in point of quality and locality, the attempt to discover their physiological correlates has been hampered by exceptional difficulties. Jodl bases this indefiniteness upon the fact that the sensory nerves of visceral sensation lead first of all to subordinate centers, particularly to the sympathetic system, from which they then radiate, thus making exact location difficult. To go into any further details in this connection would involve too wide a digression.

7. This short outline makes no pretension of offering a detailed presentation of the physiology of sensation and its various phenomena. As an outline, its only concern is to mark the chief stages in the development of research. We saw that the study of the physiology of the senses progressed at about the same rate as that of the psychology of the senses, and that very often the same investigators figured in both fields. Both of these studies were concluded to a certain degree in the second half of the nineteenth century. Everything accomplished after this was supplementary and consisted of minor improvements. Both of these studies led toward the discovery of specific end organs and afferent nerves in all the spheres of sensation; and the existence of such organs and nerves was an indispensable presupposition for the origin of sensations.

That there is a far-reaching separation of functions in the sense of Johannes Müller's theory of specific sense energies can be considered proven. This, however, as I have pointed out, does not greatly substantiate the hypothesis of physiopsychic parallelism. Specific sense nerves are, indeed, presuppositions for the origin of the consciousness of sensation, but they are only partial premises; in no case are they the complete substratum of sensation. As far as sensation can be localized at all, it does not seem to originate in end organs or in the afferent nerves but in definite areas of the cerebrum.

The contemporary opinion of physiology concerning specific sense energies is summed up by W. Nagel to the effect that the theory is, to be sure, not entirely demonstrable, but that its broader validity cannot be questioned. Side by side with this opinion, however, the nerves are regarded as mere conductors which transmit unspecified stimuli.

Thus the physiology of sensation, starting out from the theory of parallelism, contributed, as a whole, a great many valuable insights into the mechanism of nerves; but it has also shown that processes in the end organs and the afferent nerves are not the only correlates of sensation; the correlates of sensation must be sought in the brain. And, therefore, the physiology of sensory nerves requires the physiology of the cerebrum as its necessary complement.

THE LOCALIZATION OF THE "HIGHER" CONSCIOUSNESS

1. The successful accomplishments of sensory physiology which determined at least the peripheral physiological correlates of sensation encouraged the search for specific organs of the central psychic experiences. This search was conducted in two directions: on the one side, psychology was made the starting point for a descent into the physiological; on the other side, the starting points were anatomy and physiology, and psychology was consulted as an auxiliary science. Common to both these manners of investigation was the tendency to isolate single processes, and the dogmatic assumption that such isolation was necessarily possible. We shall designate the principle underlying these

investigations as the theory of localization because their main concern was to "localize" in the brain the states of consciousness which it was assumed could be isolated.

In order to understand these physiological investigations, one must realize that they cannot be pursued without the aid of psychology. To be sure, motor reactions resulting from specific stimuli are often revelatory in regard to the activity of single central regions, but the same motor reactions reveal precious little in regard to consciousness, especially as motor reactions can often occur without any consciousness at all. As soon as the question of consciousness is raised, a purely anatomical or physiological method becomes impossible, because only consciousness can determine anything about the presence of consciousness.

In the first half of the nineteenth century, physiologists still frequently alluded to the "investigation of the soul." Subsequent to this, however, they leaned very heavily upon the newly developing science of psychology. Since the new psychology, as we have noted, saw its main goal in the isolating of single phenomena of consciousness, this isolating tendency also conditioned the problems dealing with the physiology of the brain. In a manner of speaking, the theory of cerebral localization is the application of the theory of specific sense energies to the brain. Just as an exactly defined quality of consciousness is coördinated with the peripheral nerves, the parts of the brain were also supposed to have their separate functions and their specific energies, to which the elements of consciousness were supposed to correspond. For the time being, the ideal aim was to prove the existence of a single brain cell for every image or idea.

2. Like most other sciences, the theory of cerebral topography or localization evolved from a chaos of speculative mists. Its first impetus came from Franz Joseph Gall's system of phrenology which made certain inferences concerning mental aptitudes according to the shape of the outer skull. Since Gall was vigorously attacked in Germany, he made his way

to France, where he died in 1828. His first work, entitled
*Medico-philosophical Studies on Nature and Art in the Nor-
mal and Pathological States of Man,* appeared in German
in 1791. His later works, especially his *Recherches sur le
système nerveux,* done in collaboration with Spurzheim in
1809, were written in French. Gall's historical status is remarkable. Although his theories are today no longer considered scientific, nevertheless they stimulated science to
an extraordinary degree. Gall won over many serious disciples, but he also inspired many enemies. Indeed, the polemics directed against Gall's theories determined the direction of research for decades, since his opponents were
obliged to study phrenology in order to refute them.

Today Gall is more often quoted than read. But what
did he really teach? His psychology was just as primitive
as his physiology. He believed he could deduce from the
shape of the skull exactly what "inner senses" were located
under the phrenologist's "bumps." Gall distinguished no
less than twenty-seven such "inner senses" which are now
no longer regarded as indivisible unities. According to
Gall, there were supposed to exist a sense of locality, a
sense of speech, a sense of fact, a sense of comparison, and
the like. The existence of special organs was also assumed
for such varied capacities as poetic talent, the instinct of
propagation, the satirical spirit (*esprit caustique*), the metaphysical faculty (*esprit metaphysique*), and many others.

Although phrenology is ridiculed at the present time, it
must be given historical credit for having started the study
of cerebral topography and localization. One of the assumptions of phrenology even anticipated a subsequently significant discovery, the so-called speech center whose injury
results in aphasia. The connection between phrenology and
psychology is attested by historical evidence. In 1833
Thomas Hood described the first accurately observed case
of aphasia in the seventh volume of the *Phrenological Trans-
actions.* Moreover, Bouillaud, who later made a thorough
study of the topography of the speech center in the brain,

was a pupil of Gall. The very title of Bouillaud's chief work affirms this: *"Recherches cliniques propres à démontrer que la perte de la parole correspond à la lésion des lobules antérieurs du cerveau, et à confirmer l'opinion de M. Gall sur le siège de l'organe du langage articulé."**

These investigations were corroborated by Dax and his son, but their observations were objected to because of the suspicion of their phrenological bias. Among the objectors was a man named Broca who, therefore, created no little sensation when in 1861 he published a work in which he more exactly defined the Gall-Bouillaud theory. Broca's discovery is generally considered the foundation stone of the modern theory of cerebral localization, although in the interim also its correctness has been questioned.

3. Gall's primitive methods were supplanted by others which permitted the penetration of the solid covering of bone with which nature hides the brain from outside observation.

The oldest method was the anatomical method which, of course, can only be employed upon a dead subject. The brain is sliced into the thinnest possible sections. These are placed under the microscope and their structure is revealed by special tissue-staining processes. An important advance was the comparative anatomical method which was developed at the end of the century. The particularly marked development of certain parts of the brain was inferentially connected to certain functions which were exercised with particular frequency, and in this way certain extremely interesting developments, which we shall discuss later, were discovered.

The clinical anatomical method consists in the determination of the connection between the pathological disorders of certain parts of the brain and the simultaneous loss of certain mental functions.

*Arch. de Méd., 1825.

A great deal of our knowledge is based upon the method of extirpation, in which parts of the brain of animals are experimentally destroyed. Supplementing this is the stimulus method introduced by Hitzig and Fritsch in 1870. In this method, specific parts of the brain are stimulated by a current of electricity and the resulting responses are observed. Toward the end of the century, Flechsig introduced the myelinization method. A temporal sequence in the development of certain parts of the brain in early childhood can be determined by studying the gradual sheathing of the axis cylinders of nerves with myelin matter.

These methods, which were usually applied in combination, gradually resulted in giving us a picture of the evolution of the brain. Of course, in the first joy of discovery, there was a tendency to draw overhasty conclusions, and subsequent generations often had to retract what had previously been proclaimed as certain knowledge. Thus the development of cerebral topography sometimes occurred in periods which inclined toward a strictly mechanistic conception of cerebral activity, and sometimes in periods which favored a totalitarian conception.

4. An important attack on Gall's speculative theory of cerebral localization was delivered by Flourens, who looked upon the cerebrum as an essentially homogeneous organ. In the meanwhile, however, several discoveries had been made at the beginning and middle of the nineteenth century that cast doubt upon Flourens' dominant view. Broca's speech center was already being discussed. Andral, moreover, had shown that certain clearly defined injuries of the cerebrum govern the loss of power over the limbs. Meynert, in an address before the Vienna Academy of Medicine in 1869, expressed himself as favoring a localization of the psychic functions on the basis of his knowledge of the structure of the brain. The decade between 1870 and 1880 brought with it important discoveries, at least in regard to the cerebral localization of sensory impressions and simple motor acts.

The problem was attacked experimentally by Edward Hitzig, who accidentally discovered that the eyes are set in motion when an electric current is allowed to flow through the back of the head. Hitzig pursued the matter further, and by subsequent experiment discovered that electrical stimulation of specific parts of the brain results in coördinated muscle contractions of opposite sides of the body.

Fritsch and Hitzig presented the results of their experiments on dogs in 1870 in a work entitled *On the Electrical Sensitivity of the Cerebral Cortex*. Further results were contributed by Hitzig's investigations from 1873 to 1876. Briefly, these investigations ascertained that there are areas in the cerebrum that are directly related to bodily movements. On the other hand, Hitzig discovered other areas in which there was no such relationship. The extirpation of certain tiny centers in the parietal lobe of the forebrain cortex changes the nature of certain limb movements, such as those of the foreleg. Upon the basis of this, Hitzig assumed that there must be a loss of the nerve end connecting the muscle to the brain, that is to say, a loss of the "muscle sense." As a result of such extirpations, the operated animals have a deficient awareness of the limb in question and can only form incomplete images of it. These investigations strongly stimulated subsequent research, although Hitzig remained either uncritical or indecisive in the question of the influence of the "soul" upon physical functions. He knew for a certainty that a few mental functions could be definitely located in the cerebral cortex, but he believed that it was possible that all mental functions might be located there.

5. Hitzig's own line of research was followed even farther by Herman Munk. What Hitzig had regarded as only an hypothesis, Munk accepted as an established fact. Munk's contention was that "we know that the cerebral cortex is the seat of perceptions and images."

Munk applied this principle to the separate fields of sensation, mostly on the basis of extirpation experiments. Thus he ascribed the *gyrus hippocampi* cortex to taste; the cortex of the temporal lobe to hearing, and the cortex of the occipital lobe to vision. He localized the remaining senses in the cortex of the frontal lobe and the parietal lobe. We cannot enter into the detail of the experiments by which Munk supported his assertions. But upon the basis of his investigations, central cerebral areas have been determined as the loci of the most important fields of sensation. Of course, posterity has modified and developed Munk's findings to a great extent, but in the meantime a certain degree of possibility in localizing the sensations is admitted even by unfavorable critics, who only add that in the consciousness of sensation still other parts of the brain are coöperatively involved.

This point of view changed the significance of the notion of "brain areas." Whereas at first the brain was merely considered the place where sensory stimuli reach consciousness, it was gradually realized that this would be only a duplicate or a central substitute of the peripheral organs. The idea of a brain "center," however, presupposes the idea that this center connects several functions to each other. The connection between sensations and their more or less related motor responses became particularly important. Thus the location of sensory and motor areas was arrived at, a distinction which was, to be sure, only of relative significance. Today, these areas are no longer regarded as the absolute "seat" or sole place of origin of isolable acts of consciousness or motion.

6. Encouraged by Munk's results, cerebral physiology rapidly began to localize all the higher mental experiences. The cerebral physiology of the 1880's presented a picture surprisingly similar to that of the contemporary psychology of consciousness. The psychology of consciousness had also been very exact in the study of sensation; but as soon as it had developed the results of this study into a sensory

theory of all the higher mental acts, it left the firm ground upon which it had been standing and embarked upon theoretical speculation. The physiology of the brain did exactly the same thing. After sensory areas had been determined, the scientists wanted to find separate areas for the various images, feelings, acts of thought and will. The brain was divided into areas, much as a real-estate office subdivides a new suburban development. And this division was often made upon an hypothetical basis. Every isolable act of consciousness was assigned to the area which was named after it.

A special topography of the brain was developed which yielded nothing to Gall's phrenology in point of boldness, even if it passed itself off as more scientific. Of course, there were some sort of clinical observations behind all this; but the observations were generalized in an uncritical way. Single ideas were even ascribed to their own cells in which they were supposed to be "deposited." Or, more precisely, since most ideas were divided into partial ideas, a special cell was assumed for each partial idea. Thus, Ziehen, for example, described the idea of a rose as consisting of many partial images; a visual image, which he localized in the visual area; an olfactory image in the olfactory area; a tactile image localized in the area of touch. To these were added the residues of the act of speech and the acoustical impression of the word. The stimulation of one partial image-cell was supposed to arouse simultaneously all the other cells. All this, of course, is not an empirical explanation, but scarcely more than a translation of psychological hypotheses into physiological terminology.

The matter was not clarified by sharp warnings that the "deposition" of ideas in the separate brain cells was not to be conceived of materially. Such warnings did not prevent many psychologists from computing from the number of existent brain cells the possible number of ideas that a normal person could form. More recent investigators arranged the central areas into an ascending hierarchical order. They distinguished primary areas, whose injury suspends sensations and simple motor reactions, while above these were the secondary areas dominating the perceptive and conduct reactions. The mnesic or ideational areas belonged to the tertiary hierarchy.

7. We shall not present the various forms of the speculative theories of cerebral localization, since their chief value lies in their being curiosities. Let us discuss only a few of the main investigations because they acted as incentives in a pioneer field, although they contributed no ultimate results to modern science.

The difficulties that existed can be imagined if we attack only the controversial question of whether ideas arise in the sensory areas corresponding to them, or whether separate ideational areas must be assumed. Opinions on this immediate problem were widely dissenting.

The theory of identity assumes that both the sensation and the idea are located in the same sensory cortical area. Only the special kind of stimulus determines whether the response is a sensation or an idea; sensations originate from the stimulation of an external sense organ; ideas, on the other hand, are centrally stimulated. It is not necessary to think of the area of an idea as delimited and insular; on the contrary, the newer proponents of the theory of identity, like Ebbinghaus, emphasize that an image is not deposited in one or a few cortical cells, but that the elements of an idea can be localized in different parts of the brain.

Opposed to the theory of identity is another theory which assumes separate areas for sensations and thoughts. Thus, Wilbrand, one of the chief representatives of this theory, pointed out cases of cortical blindness in which the patients had no visual perceptions but were able to form visual images in their dreams. On the other hand, cases have also been shown in which perception is intact but the power to form visual images is lacking.

Today most scholars contradict the assumption of separate memory areas. The basis of this contradiction is the theory of association which compounds a perception from sensations and images. There are sound reasons for rejecting this sensory assumption, but such a rejection undermines the whole theory. We are confronted here with another example of a doctrine palming itself off as physiological when it is merely masking a psychological theory behind physiological concepts.

8. The most important principles governing the central localization of the higher processes of consciousness were unquestionably provided by cerebral pathology and by modern investigations into the various forms of aphasia. But, as we shall see, these discoveries can be interpreted variously from a psychological viewpoint.

Broca's discovery in 1861 is celebrated as a heroic feat of cerebral localization research. Broca demonstrated that the destruction of the posterior third of the third left frontal lobe and also the neighboring portion of the operculum of the front central lobe caused motor aphasia in right-handed persons. This part of the brain has been known ever since as the "Broca area." Although the intellect of such persons is unimpaired, they can no longer speak and often lack the power to write and read.

This discovery was immediately adopted as completely proven, and was followed by a multitude of studies on aphasia that formed a basis for the localization of the higher mental processes.

At first, two main types of aphasia were distinguished: motor and sensory aphasia. Motor aphasia or word dumbness is present when the patient distinctly knows what he wants to say but cannot utter the words he seeks in spite of the fact that his external speech mechanism is intact. Motor aphasia is not to be confused with anarthria in which the peripheral speech mechanism is defective. Only the ability to find word sounds is disturbed in motor aphasia, where the mastery over the free production of sound is lost.

In sensory aphasia or word deafness, the patient understands words spoken to him as little as though they were in an incomprehensible language, even though hearing and intellect are unimpaired. Sometimes the patient can still understand written words, or some of the words spoken to him. Paraphasia also occurs, that is, the patient can speak but say only incomprehensible, disconnected words. The problem of aphasia has been studied by a great many scientists including Broca, Wernicke, Ribot, Pick, Ballet, Gutzmann, Liepmann, Gowers, Von Monakow, and others.*

At the present time we are interested only in the value of these studies in relation to the question of localization. For a long time Broca's discovery was believed to be absolutely certain, but in 1905 Pierre Marie shook this belief with the proof that the Broca area can be destroyed without the occurrence of aphasia. And according to Monakow, the Broca area is an area in which the nerves important for speech can very easily be put out of commission; but this does not make the Broca area the only speech area. Wernicke located the area of sensory aphasia in the first left temporal lobe (the Wernickean region). But Monakow's investigations, although confirming the importance of certain parts of the cortex for speech comprehension, did not localize speech comprehension as a whole within insular areas.

9. A corroboration of the theories of localization was believed to be provided by certain forms of amnesia, the pathological loss of memory or memory material.

And now, what were the psychological facts? Charcot in 1883 discovered so-called mental blindness. He had a merchant under observation who had formerly possessed an excellent visual memory, but had completely lost it after an illness. Persons and buildings with which he had been formerly closely acquainted appeared entirely strange to this

*Translator's Note. The best English text is Sir Henry Head's *Studies in Aphasia*.

patient. We mentioned previously that this case led to the setting up of ideation types. But it was also important in cerebral localization.

In mental deafness acoustic images disappear. Corresponding disturbances of the tactual sense are also observed.

These forms of perceptive amnesia are collectively referred to as "agnosia," according to Liepmann. In addition to these, there is also motor amnesia or apraxia. In apraxia there is a loss of motor memory. Although the patient's mind is sound, his motor organs are no longer capable of performing such simple functions as eating, washing, and the like. Liepmann described such a case with great precision. He concluded that the innervation from the preceding mental part of the action had been cut. In hysterical paralysis, which superficially resembles apraxia, there is no physiological destruction of central areas.

We have mentioned only a few of the salient facts upon which the theory of higher mental life is based. Scholars vary widely in their interpretation of these data. A great deal of information about the brain and its functions was derived from the numerous cases of head injury during the War, which were studied by Poppelreuter, Goldstein, Isserlin, and others. Such studies are beset with serious difficulties. When a brain center is destroyed and there is a simultaneous loss of certain states of consciousness, it is almost impossible to determine whether the "seat" of these states of consciousness has been destroyed, or whether only "conductor" paths have been destroyed. The puzzling phenomena of the gradual restoration of the functions of a destroyed brain area add to the difficulties of research. The theory of "vicarious substitution" was developed to explain these phenomena.

10. Next to the localization of the separate states of consciousness in the brain, the physiological aspect of association became one of the focal problems of physiological psychology. The reason for this was that the psychologists of

sensory consciousness considered association the fundamental principle of all changes in consciousness. Cerebral physiology applied the term "association fibers" to those nerve fibers which interconnect the single cells and cell areas of either side of the cerebrum. Such a connective function, however, has not been definitely proven.

Paul Flechsig's theory of "association centers" was presented to the Psychological Congress of 1897. Flechsig separated the centers of association from the sensory areas. He made a genetic study of the fetus and of newborn children in order to clarify the interrelations of the connecting nerve tracts. According to Flechsig, the nerves of bodily feeling are the first to develop. These serve as conductors for general feelings like hunger and thirst, and the senses of position and touch. The olfactory nerves are developed at about the same time, to be followed by the visual, and finally the auditory nerve tracts. All these sensory areas together comprise the "bodily feeling area," making up about a third of the cerebral cortex. According to Flechsig, the most remarkable thing is that the separate sensory areas in the newborn child exist at first entirely without interconnecting neurones. Thus, the newborn child probably possesses the senses of sight, hearing, and touch, but is incapable of coördinating them. In other words, the newborn child possesses separate spheres of consciousness.

Among the areas of the child's brain there are certain still undeveloped areas of the cortex comparable to the oceans that lie between continents. Since no proof can be advanced that these undeveloped surfaces later develop into sensory areas, Flechsig ascribed the function of connecting the separate sensory areas to them. In other words, the centers of association, which are considered the basis of higher mental activity, are formed several months after the birth of the child. Centers of association can no longer be structurally distinguished from sensory centers in adults.

Flechsig distinguished three such centers of association: first, the large, occipital center of association which is bounded by the tactual, visual, and auditory areas. An injury to this center causes partial or entire loss of the ability to relate ideas to their corresponding written or spoken words. Second, the frontal center of association whose injury unfavorably effects certain higher feelings bound up with judgment and with the personality as a whole. And third, the middle center of association which coincides with the so-called insula. Meynert suspected that this center is intimately related to the mechanism of articulate speech. According to Flechsig the brain is primarily an organ of association into which sensory conductors lead, and from which motor impulses radiate.

Although Flechsig employed the anatomical method in his investigations, there were also attempts to interpret association functionally, in a mechanistic sense. Ribot had already assumed that there is a change in the composition of nerves with every act of memory or thought. He visualized the process somewhat after the analogy of a photographic plate upon which certain lines can come into existence as a result of an external change.

Semon introduced a new term with his notion of "engrams." His theory of the "stratification" of these engrams was too insufficiently elaborated to be of any real aid. Ziehen developed his "elimination or reduction hypothesis" and A. Lehmann his "facilitation or channel theory" to explain the evocation (or "ekphoration," as Semon says) of latent residues in association. "Inhibition" was made the polar quality of "facilitation" in association, and all sorts of analogies were borrowed from the material world. As brilliant as these theories were, they were all based only in small part upon actual, established physiological data. These theories are really only attempts to illustrate mental functions by means of figures of speech borrowed from the mechanical world.

11. Whereas most of the efforts at localization were essentially based upon associationist psychology, the repre-

sentatives of other psychological tendencies tried to place the mental processes which they had discovered on a physiological basis. This was especially true of Wundt, who conformed to the associationists in the matter of sensations and ideas, but, nevertheless, as we have seen above, introduced the idea of apperception as a special mental process. In accordance with the principle of localization, Wundt also tried to localize apperception, and discovered a "center of apperception." From Meynert, Hitzig, Ferrier, Flechsig, and others, Wundt adopted the demonstrated fact that the frontal lobe bears an intimate relationship to intelligence.

But Wundt discarded the concept of intelligence as too vague, and replaced it with the notion of an apperceptive process, which he explained physiologically in terms of inhibitory phenomena. Since apperception represses certain concomitant stimuli, it puts other uninhibited stimuli in an advantageous position. This explains the psychological process in which an apperceived sensation achieves greater clarity. There is no intensification of the contents of the sensation, but the stimuli are shunted to superimposed centers where the connection of sensory contents to more complex products takes place. According to Wundt, the theory that this process takes place in the frontal brain is corroborated by the fact that injuries in the region of the frontal brain often occur without any disturbance of the motor and sensory functions, whereas disturbances of the mental functions and loss of the powers of concentration and will almost always occur. For the most part, however, Wundt himself characterizes his physiological theory of apperception as entirely hypothetical.

12. An attempt was also made to provide *Gestalt* psychology with a physiological foundation. The problem had been raised by Mach long before the appearance of "*Gestalt* psychology" in its narrower sense. Mach attempted a solution in terms of accompanying motor phenomena. Von Kries, on

the other hand, evolved a "channel theory" based upon the "facilitation theory" of the associationists.

In contrast to all explanations of this sort stand the totalitarian theories of the newer *Gestalt* psychologists, Wertheimer and Köhler, who have likewise founded their doctrines upon physiology. According to Wertheimer and Köhler, the experience of *Gestalt* does not depend on the mere stimulation of a brain center plus association, but on total processes comprising total characteristics. The arousal of stimulated cells is supposed to develop into a total process by means of the nerve impulses which radiate from these cells. We shall not pursue the details of this as yet incomplete theory. It interests us here only in so far as it attempts to replace the view of functional localization with totalitarian viewpoints, thus indicating a path which the pioneers of the newer physiology of the brain had already discovered.

13. In summing up what can today be considered the scientific store of definite knowledge in regard to the problem of localization, we can say that there are today few serious proponents of the minute topography of the brain which was so boldly proposed at the end of the nineteenth century. The absolute theorists of localization imagined the brain to be like the famous "organ" of Peter the Great, which consisted of a platoon of soldiers each one of whom had been trained to sing a single note at a designated signal. Whether the esthetic enjoyment of such an instrument was very great can be doubted; and at any rate, a choirmaster was necessary to unite the multiplicity of voices. It can also be doubted whether connected thinking would ever be possible if separate cells containing atomized consciousness had to work together without any unifying supervision. The bold attempt to divide the brain into insular regions is today considered impossible. Only a few localizations have been physiologically and clinically proven, namely, the auditory center, and the motor centers for the head and the limbs.

Even in these instances, opinions vary widely if the question is asked what it actually is that can be localized in these centers beyond mere anatomical localization. We know that these centers are involved in the functions summarily ascribed to them. But that these centers fulfill their ascribed functions alone can today no longer be maintained.

Nor can we naïvely speak of "parallelism" in the old-fashioned sense. The idea of "parallelism" is rendered impossible by the fact that psychological experiences, that is to say, states of consciousness, are relatively simple and unified, whereas their physiological components are extremely complex and can only spring into existence through the coöperation of the most widely separated brain areas. The sensory perceptions of adults, which are so simple psychologically, presuppose an extraordinarily complicated phylogenetic and ontogenetic history, and contain innumerable functional elements to which introspective consciousness gives us no clue. For this reason, the critics of anatomical localization, such as Von Monakow, whose argument we follow here, demand that the sensory perceptions and motor functions gradually acquired since the fetal stage be divided into more precise physiological units before they are located within circumscribed cortical areas. And this applies in an even greater degree to ideas, speech, and so-called intelligence.

Today we can, therefore, hardly speak of the localization of single phenomena of consciousness. Close scrutiny of the theories of localization discloses that they do not localize single states of consciousness, but complex "capacities" or "functions." Such complex localization prematurely directed physiology into a field which psychology did not enter until after 1900, when it began to seek for "acts" and "capacities" which in themselves were not "conscious" in the same sense that the "contents" of consciousness were conscious. But this was tantamount to an advance beyond the theory of parallelism which sought for parallels only between states of consciousness and physiological phenomena. And once again out of the background emerged the structuralized "soul" that possesses consciousness, but is not conscious itself. We shall become acquainted with corresponding psychological investigations in the following section.

THE OPPONENTS
OF ISOLATIVE LOCALIZATION

1. There are many empirical and philosophical barriers obstructing all attempts to localize mental functions in specific parts of the brain. Theories of localization were very much inclined to lead to materialism, since they relegated the mind to a complete dependence upon physical functions. Above all, however, such theories endangered the unity of the soul, which was a necessary premise of immortality in religious doctrine. This consideration had already figured in Descartes, Leibniz, and many of the older philosophers, and still lingered on in Flourens, Lotze, and other modern scholars.

As we have already seen, the first opposition to theories of localization arose in criticism of Gall's phrenology. A prominent antagonist was Leuret, who criticized Gall on the basis of studies in comparative anatomy. There was also Magendie, who proceeded in a strictly empirical fashion in his *Leçons sur les fonctions et les maladies du système nerveux*, published in 1839. The most important investigator of this period, however, was Flourens, who experimentally refuted Gall in 1842 in his *Examen de la phrénologie*. Flourens had published in 1842 in his *Recherches expérimentales sur les propriétés et sur les fonctions du système nerveux dans les animaux vertébrés*, the results of his experiments on chickens and pigeons from which he had removed portions of the cerebrum. On the basis of these experiments, he determined that the *medulla oblongata* is the center for cardiac and respiratory activity; the *corpora quadrigemina* are the central organs for the visual sense; the cerebellum coördinates the voluntary motions; the cerebral lobes are the seats of "intelligence" and "will."

According to Flourens, the higher central organs were supposed to perform their functions in a totalitarian manner, much as the lungs perform the respiratory function. "There are no separate centers either for the various capacities or for the various perceptions. The capacity to perceive, judge, and will one thing is situated in the same place as the capacity to perceive, judge, and will some other thing. Consequently, this essentially uniform capacity is situated within one and the same organ."

Flourens also observed cases which were later utilized in undermining the theory of localization, that is, those cases in which lost cerebral functions were restored. But he still spoke of the "soul," and not only believed that the cerebrum was the exclusive seat of the soul, but also that the soul was indivisibly situated in every point of the cerebrum. This points to the likelihood of a Descartian influence in Flourens.

Although experimental, Flourens' studies were not purely empirical; they still showed the influence of the metaphysical question concerning the "seat of the soul." The same metaphysical influence was evident in the work of Eduard Pflüger, who, in 1853, published his now famous monograph on "The Sensory Functions of the Spinal Cord in Vertebrates." In this work, Pflüger endeavored to refute the error that the brain is the only sensory center. He maintained, on the contrary, that sensory functions are rooted within the entire cerebro-spinal system. Pflüger experimented with amputated eel and lizard tails, which offered him proof of the "sensational and volitional activity of the cerebro-spinal system in its entire extent." In the same way, Pflüger believed he had proved the existence of "sense receptive and volitional animal fragments" in his experiments on decerebrated frogs whose legs still jerked toward stimulated spots on their skin. This led to the further assumption of a "spinal soul."

During this entire period, it was the "soul" and not the physiological locality of phenomena of consciousness which men were seeking. This same trend was also evident in the works of Hermann Lotze, the most important theoretician of the time in Germany. Lotze, to be sure, conceived the body as a mechanism, but he set up a monad-like soul to direct it; for the unity of the self is at the same time a proof of the existence of a soul. The scholars enumerated above did not adopt the notion of parallelism, which isolates the phenomena of consciousness and searches for their physiological correlates.

2. Problems of parallelism did not arise until the 1860's and 1870's. These problems resulted from the advance of the experimental research discussed above in connection with the discoveries of Broca, Hitzig, Munk, and others. The question of the mind as a totality receded into the background. Most of the interest centered about the localization of single phenomena of consciousness, which, in the early joy of discovery, were placed in isolated parts of the brain the way a quartermaster quarters his troops upon a civilian population. The important thing is that the troops be assigned to quarters. Whether they can manage to get along with their hosts is an irrelevant question.

A reaction against this piecemeal localization followed very swiftly. In psychology the reaction did not come until 1890 when the criticism against atomism set in. But before this, about 1880, an opponent of isolationist physiology arose in the person of Friedrich Goltz, who became involved in a long feud with Munk, among others.

Goltz took his point of departure, like Flourens, from the cerebral functional restoration and compensation phenomena. He wanted to know whether all losses of cerebral functions induced by injuries to the cerebrum were really restored. With this in view, he tried to distinguish the type of movements which could still be made when a specific part of the brain was injured. Carl Hauptmann formulated these distinctions more precisely as follows:

a. Qualitative disturbances, which indicate the loss of specific sense aptitudes.

b. Structural disturbances, which have to do with the combination forms of normally existent specific sense energies.

c. Quantitative disturbances, which have to do only with the degree of muscular action.

Concerning qualitative disturbances, Goltz determined that there is no section of the cerebral cortex that we can call exclusively the circumscribed seat of vision, hearing, smell, or any other sense; because no matter which disturbances he instituted in the course of his animal experiments, the loss of function was always temporary. He concluded from this that the same section of gray matter serves various psychic functions, and that there are no isolable sections of the cortex comprising either sensory or motor functions. On the contrary, every section of the cortex, independently of other sections, can be connected with all the voluntary muscles and all the sensory nerves of the body.

Goltz's investigations also disclosed that the cerebrum is of unequal value, from a structural point of view. Not the qualitative, but the structural (formal) functions are permanently destroyed by injuries of the cerebrum. From this, Goltz concluded that every part of the cerebrum possesses not a qualitative but a formal significance which cannot be assumed by other parts of the brain. Purely quantitative disturbances, on the other hand, can be qualitatively and formally remedied by hyperfunction of other parts of the brain.

Thus we have in place of the strictly isolating theory of localization only a relative localization of functions, according to Wundt's expression, supposedly proved by substitution and by functional restoration and compensation. According to Wundt only the elements that make up the complex functions and not the functions themselves were localized. Yet even these elementary functions can still undergo many transpositions. This theory is, in a manner of speaking, a compromise between the older theory of totality and the theory of localization.

3. New perspectives in physiopsychology were opened up by the investigations of Jacques Loeb, who exploited the field of comparative physiology of the brain for the purposes of psychology. Loeb gained an interesting insight into the mental life of man by his exhaustive studies of the behavior of invertebrates.

A great deal of attention was aroused by Loeb's doctrine of tropisms which caused a complete revolution in the theory of the mechanism of reflex action. It had formerly been assumed that all reflexes were bound up with the ganglion cells. But Loeb brought out the fact that the effect of light upon lower animals coincides completely with the heliotropic effects of light upon plants that have no nerves. He concluded that heliotropism is not based on specific characteristics of the central nervous system.

Loeb disposed of the objection that the destruction of the ganglion cells disrupted reflex action with the explanation that only the stimulus connection between cutaneous surfaces and the muscles was broken. However, he rejected the notion that nerves possess functions which are entirely missing in simple protoplasm. The specific importance of the ganglion cells as the sole bearers of reflex mechanisms was considered an inadequate explanation. Loeb considered the ganglion cells to be cells that were merely more easily irritable and better conductors, a fact which really does make them very valuable to animals. Speaking in general terms, the doctrine of tropisms represented a totalized theory. Loeb thought that the most rudimentary reactions of the organism were borne by the protoplasm from which the nerves developed as the specific organs of a general functional activity characteristic of all living substance.

Loeb did not venture to say that all lower forms of life

possess consciousness. He felt that consciousness was entirely bound up with associative memory activity. By "associative memory" Loeb meant the influence by which a stimulus-cause produces not only effects corresponding to its nature and to the specific structure of the stimulated being, but also stimulus effects of other causes that had previously impinged on the organism simultaneously or almost simultaneously with the original stimulus. However, consciousness, that is, "associative memory" in Loeb's terminology, is bound up with the existence of a cerebrum.

Although Loeb apparently identified himself with the current theories of physiopsychology in his conception of associative memory, he was in reality much more cautious than other investigators. He claimed that the cerebrum of vertebrates was indispensable to the processes of associative memory and consciousness, but he did not claim that the cerebrum was the sole organ of consciousness. On the contrary, he said that the entire central nervous system might be considered an organ of consciousness as long as it was connected with the cerebrum, the cerebrum being but an indispensable part of a whole in an act of memory association. Once again we perceive here a reversion to totality as opposed to isolative theories.

Loeb's attitude is even more clearly evident in his "segmental theory," which he advanced in place of the theory of brain centers. While he by no means assailed the topographical method of diagnosis in brain disturbances, Loeb pointed out that mere anatomical localization should not lead to conclusions contradictory to fact with regard to the physiological significance of localization. The segmental theory was substituted for the center theory with the intention of leaving topographical diagnosis of the brain untouched.

Loeb does not speak of centers but of "segments." Such segments of the central nervous system are the protoplasmic conductor connections between the stimulable cutaneous surfaces, the voluntary musculature, glands, and the like.

The peripheral structural relationships of segments primarily determine the success of a stimulus-cause. According to the center theory, every specific reaction has its specific part of the central nervous system which has to do only with this specific reaction or function. This specific part of the central nervous system is called the "center" of the corresponding function. According to the segment theory the segmental ganglion only plays the part of a protoplasmic conductor. In reality, reactions are determined by various stimuli, for example, the sense organs of peripheral structures, and the arrangement of the muscles. A great deal of what we today designate as cerebral functions should be considered as functions of peripheral structures. Only such matters as the arrangement and orientation of neural elements and associative memory activity come into consideration as specific qualities of the central nervous system.

Loeb illustrated the difference between the center and segment theories through an analogy with the retina: "The optical perception of objects is based upon the fact that the single retinal components determine various space sensations, each according to its position on the retina. The same retinal component can thus serve in the formation of a great many different images. In much the same way, we must imagine the rôle of the central nervous system, from a segmental viewpoint, in which the various components or ganglia take the place of the retinal components in the perception of objects. The same components (ganglia) take part in a great many functions, and each component (ganglion) determines the successful completion of the sensation only according to its segmental position, orientation, and other general and particular qualities. If, however, we should try to realize the conception of space vision which we should have to formulate in analogy with the center theory of the central nervous system, we would arrive at the monstrous notion that every retinal component of perception serves a special image, and we can see as many different images as we have retinal components. I do not consider this analogy an injustice to the modern center theory. Consistent representatives of the center theory actually assume that each memory image is deposited within a separate cell, and that the number of brain cells determines the number of possible memory images."

As sharply as the segment theory veered away from the center theory, Loeb still adhered to a mechanistic view of life. In his work entitled *The Mechanistic Conception of Life*, published in 1912, he decisively stresses that our entire inner life is ultimately reducible to physiochemical data. "Our wishes and hopes, disappointments and sufferings, have their source in instincts which are comparable to the light instinct of the heliotropic animals."

4. Loeb's significance is not based solely on his tropism and segment theory. Valuable physiopsychological conclusions also resulted from his comparative anatomy of the brain. Older cerebral physiology had drawn chiefly upon adults or mature higher animals for its investigations, and had thus evolved theories which today must be considered false. Loeb succeeded in focusing his interest on the lower animals and on the early stages in the development of the higher animals and human beings. As we have already noted, it became evident in phylogenetics that functions taken over by the brain in later stages of development are carried out by entirely different organs in earlier stages. This exploded the prejudice that the brain or the nervous system is the only seat of mental functions. Phylogenetics proved that the brain itself is a gradually developing special organ. Functions formerly ascribed with great certainty to specific brain areas were really taken care of by one organ after another during the course of their phylogenetic development, and the constant direction of this shifting of functions was toward the head (and brain) end of the organism.

Without going into the innumerable investigations in the field of comparative anatomy and physiology, we shall briefly summarize their results according to Von Monakow.

The most rudimentary nervous system is composed of a few sensory and ganglion cells which are connected to the muscles and organs by means of nerve fibers and fibril bands. The first impulse toward the development of a central nervous system originates from the ectoderm, the outer germinal layer, and particularly from the visceral nerve cells. This is the beginning of a separation of functions. Special body organs and a muscular system are developed. Subsequently, more and more finely developed sensory organs and parts of the body come into existence, together with new forms of perception and movement.

During this process, early phylogenetic functions shift in continual stages from old to newly developed structures in a direction leading toward the brain. These functions pass through quite typical forms of organization before they reach the next highest stage. Finally they attain the form of the integrated brain of vertebrates.

The earliest structure of the central nervous system in mollusks and insects is in the form of loosely joined ganglion pairs which are coördinated with single organs and limbs. These ganglion pairs exercise directive functions, and the front pair takes the lead.

At the lowest vertebrate stage (amphioxus), the ganglia are supplanted by a metameric system which develops at the expense of the old ganglion system. The old ganglion system now provides only the nerve plexus for the intestines. On a lower level, the metameric system is formed by means of the spinal and cervical cords. The impulse toward movement and space orientation is taken over by a button-shaped knob which contains the parts of the brain embryo.

In the case of fish, we find a quinquepartite brain without a cortex. Meanwhile the roof of the mid-brain becomes increasingly larger and develops into the organ for vision and space orientation (the mid-brain system).

In the amphibia and reptiles, the sensory organs are then perfected. With the development of the extremities more complex movements appear. Not only a considerable in-

crease in size of the entire brain, but also the typical formation of a nexus of cerebral parts, which is superimposed on
the metameric and mid-brain system, corresponds to the
development of these movements. The most important
component of this formation is the stratified cortex, especially
the cortical areas that control vision and the extremities.

The fundamental innovation at this stage of development
is found in the division of labor between the brain elements.
The higher functions are taken over by this cortico-somatic
system, although the ganglionic, metameric, and mid-brain
systems still retain important functions. The cerebral cortex, however, not only exercises supervision over the whole
but also takes over the more specialized, subsequently acquired components of the older systems.

In the higher animals (mammals), the cortico-somatic
system develops into cortical fields of association spreading
out over the entire cerebral cortex, which then acquires
more and more convolutions. These fields of association
take care of the functions involved in individually developed
experiences and practical activity. This development finds
its crowning achievement in man. In man, the old and new
functional systems are simultaneously and coöperatively
activated in a most remarkable way. Each separate nerve
conductor controls extremely multiplex nerve paths and
centers which supplement each other and function at entirely different times.

This interesting genetic history of the brain clearly
shows that functions are by no means always bound to the
same organ. Von Monakow illustrated this by the example
of the visual sense. The centers of vision and the movements
of the eyes, originally situated in the mid-brain, shift toward the cerebral cortex. In the cerebral cortex they come
into connection with the other senses and become the basis
for space images. Thus, there is a transition from mid-brain
vision to cortical vision.

These phylogenetic data were supplemented by ontogenetic studies of the human fetus and the newborn child. We

have already mentioned Flechsig's observation to the effect that the stimulation of the parts, particularly the formation of the medullary sheaths, runs parallel to the gradual development of functions.

All these anatomical discoveries were certainly interesting but essentially negative in connection with the theory of localization. We have discussed them only because they were so positively antagonistic toward the notion of absolute localization of mental capacities. But we must emphasize the fact that anatomy alone can give us no positive insight into even the most simple neural processes, not to mention consciousness. The biological inference is that the data reviewed above do not make for a mechanistic interpretation of life, but for a totalitarian and vitalistic view. We shall discuss this later.

5. Charles S. Sherrington attempted a totalitarian theory of the nervous system in his chief contribution which bears the illuminating title of *The Integrative Action of the Nervous System* (1906). Sherrington proposed the theory that it was primarily the nervous system that integrates a multicellular animal into a unit organism. This theory was in marked contrast to the theory of the autonomous existence of the nerve cells championed by Verworn, as it was also opposed to the contemporary theory that the nerves were no more than stimulus conductors. And yet it was built up on the findings of both these theories. Sherrington's theory explains that the origin of the unit organism derives from the juxtaposition of various organs and organ systems on the basis of this integrative action of the central nervous system. Since every reflex is an integrative action, the reflex is considered the "unit reaction" of all integration. Sherrington considered the "simple" reflex an abstract fiction, because a multiplex interaction always exists between the isolated simple reflexes which combine with each other simultaneously or successively. It was his opinion that reflexes are adaptive reactions, and he considered the

brain the chief integrative organ since it effects the integration of "distant receptors" with precurrent reactions.

6. Among the newer physiologists of the brain, C. von
Monakow of Zürich has probably achieved the greatest
reputation. He can by no means be called an antagonist of
localization; on the contrary, he accords the widest recognition to cerebro-anatomical discoveries. He merely notes
that such discoveries hardly clarify the problem of functions.
Whereas cerebral anatomists investigated spatial aspects
for the most part, Von Monakow laid great emphasis upon
the temporal factor, for functions are not only active in
space but also in time, that is, sequentially.

Von Monakow raised the question of time relationships,
particularly in the case of cerebral injuries and restorations.
He examined the often neglected fact that most local symptoms last for only a short time. Even in cases of serious
lesions, losses are often very rapidly restored. Indeed, Von
Monakow emphatically denied that there is a lasting loss of
"ideas." He therefore makes the following precise distinctions:

a. Lasting or residual symptoms. These must appear
when the seat of the injury is definite. Such symptoms are
the results of definite anatomical lesion.

b. Temporary symptoms. While they may often accompany residual symptoms, they may also occur by themselves.
These symptoms disappear according to the location and
the extent of the primary lesion, and according to whether
this lesion affected a sound or an already injured brain.

Von Monakow rejected the old explanation that neighboring parts of the brain vicariously assume the cerebral
functions destroyed at the focus of a lesion. The fact that
the power of speech, for instance, is often quickly restored
after the destruction of the hypothetical speech center, cannot be explained by substitution when we consider how
long it takes to acquire the power of speech. Like Goltz and
Loeb, therefore, Von Monakow discarded reacquisition and

functional readaptation as an explanation. He believed, rather, that there is a temporary functional cessation (passive inhibition) which gradually disappears. Such functional cessation is remedied by way of those nerve cells which have remained sound, or by way of nerve cell complexes which are connected to the lesion focus by nerve fibers.

This view is especially based upon facts designated as "shock." Shocks are those temporary functional disturbances that are caused by an acute physiological or psychical concussion; histological injury to the organ which has ceased functioning may but need not occur. There are three recognized types of shock. First, the psychic shock caused by violent mental agitation. Second, wound stupor in which vital brain centers cease functioning as the result of a peripheral injury. Third, the apoplectic stroke in which the entire nexus of cerebral activity is disrupted by a vascular accident in the brain. In the case of shock, spatial and temporal orientation, as well as all consciousness, is suspended (coma).

To these known types of shock Von Monakow added diaschisis, the splitting of a function due to the loss of one of its directive elements. This is caused by injury to the brain, but such injuries are small, narrowly defined, and can be precisely located anatomically. Irregular lesions of the nerve tracts are also present. Diaschisis is distinguished from the apoplectic stroke by its closely connected and spatially delimited central lesions, and also by the manner of its distribution, which is determined by the direction in which the fiber tracts radiate from the focal lesion. Von Monakow cites the loss of the patellar reflex which sometimes occurs after epileptic fits, the temporary suspension of the pupillary reflex, or the loss of speech, as examples of the effects of diaschisis. When these phenomena recede, Von Monakow does not assume that there has been a vicarious or readaptive restoration of function in other parts of the brain, but rather that the neural elements bearing the function have been liberated from the diaschisis.

According to Von Monakow, diaschisis is extraordinarily

illuminating in the question of cerebral localization. Diaschisis bridges the gap between lesions that are accessible and those that remain inaccessible for the purposes of localization. It represents the disintegration of the subtly organized activity of the brain structures, a collapse which takes place in the anatomically uninjured nerve cells outside the focal lesion. This collapse generates a struggle for the maintenance of the function, a struggle which terminates with the victory or defeat of the elements or collective combinations involved.

As the result of countless single investigations, Von Monakow arrived at the following total view of the problem of localization. He granted the existence of anatomical processes, which can even be determined with minute exactitude. He grouped the reflexes primarily in this category. Yet even in the simplest reflexes several neurone arrangements are coöperatively involved. The cerebral cortex also participates in reflexes, because in local injuries of the cortex, reflex action is impaired without any restoration. Nevertheless, reflexes can be distinctly localized according to the time elapsed and according to their purpose.

The more complex functions of the nervous system are distinguished from reflexes by their increasingly complex chronological structure. The more complex a reflex is, the more we must assume the existence of a wider reflex arc which includes the most various cortical fields and nerve tracts. Still, even here we can topographically isolate many motor and sensory components. The principle involved is that of sequential localization.

In the highest functions, in speech, in temporal and spatial orientation, and in conduct, localization can be made only "transitorily," in the sense of developmental or reconstructive phases. Yet here, too, the sensory and motor centers distinctly localized in the child furnish definite points of departure and a bond of union.

If we accept Von Monakow's doctrines as typical of the contemporary study of the brain, it is obvious that the problem of localization has become extremely complicated. The chief center of interest is no longer spatial topography; the problems of time, of genetic relations and temporal aspects of processes intrude themselves in every instance. A great many fascinating discoveries have been made, but the number of problems has also grown.

7. In this presentation we are not intent upon furnishing a detailed history of the physiology of the brain. We have merely attempted to show the degree of success attained in working out the assumption of newer psychology that isolated states of consciousness are coördinated with equally isolated organs and processes. After the first apparent successes, it became obvious that this assumption grew more and more problematical. A simple parallel process for single experiences of consciousness could nowhere be proved, since even the most simple experiences of consciousness have extremely complicated physiological components. Nor could any isolable centers for the single groups of experiences of consciousness be proved with any certainty. The only thing that is certain is that connections exist between experiences of consciousness and processes in the nervous system; but the existence of such connections cannot be called "parallelism."

Instead of parallelism between consciousness and cerebral processes, an interesting historical parallelism became evident between psychological and physiological investigation, both of which were forced more and more into the acceptance of a totalitarian point of view. Indeed, physiology arrived at a totalitarian stage even before psychology. Physiology first conceived the brain as a totality but was obliged to include the other parts of the nervous system as well. And then the tendency arose to consider this expanded "totality" only as a system composed of parts. We need not wonder, therefore, that these studies were pursued further. Soon, neither the brain nor the entire nervous system came to be considered the sole bearers of mental life; the total organism was included. Physiology of the brain developed into the new research in human constitution.

An even wider perspective is disclosed as soon as we begin to ponder the essence of this mental totality. Since mental totality brings about manifold transmutations and restorations of physiological organs, we can hardly imagine it as being purely physical. Any mechanism that autonomically restores itself can no longer be a mechanism, from a totalitarian viewpoint. If we were to follow out the implications of this idea, we would arrive at a vitalism which, as a matter of fact, is implicit in many of the newer physiological doctrines.

PSYCHOLOGY AND RESEARCH
IN HUMAN CONSTITUTION

1. Most of the psychologists we have discussed heretofore went about their investigations with the presupposition that mental life on the whole is essentially related to the nervous system in general and to the brain in particular. If we were nevertheless able to observe an increasing drift toward the notion of totality, this drift was merely intended to demonstrate the totalitarian participation of the nervous system or of the whole brain in mental acts. Meanwhile, other psychologists appeared who gave the concept of totality a much wider connotation. Not merely the nerves and the brain but also the remaining organs were discovered to be significant in the life of the mind. The whole human "constitution" was considered to be involved in mental acts. Thus, in addition to research in the brain, the widely ramified and much more encompassing research in human constitution became an accessory science of psychology.

There is no agreement on the definition of the concept of constitution. There is, however, the common idea of regarding the organism as a totality united, as regards structure and function. The concept of constitution was first brought into currency by physicians who, in the treatment of diseases apparently localized within single organs, could not help observing connections with the total organism. A sort of predecessor of the concept of constitution was that of "susceptibility" or "predisposition," by which was meant the total reaction of the organism, mostly with regard to specific diseases.

Thus it is said that a person is "predisposed" to tuberculosis or "susceptible" to colds, and by this is meant the greater or lesser resistance of the total organism. The idea of constitution, however, is defined as that quality which governs the specific reaction of the organism to stimuli. The central field of interest for modern research in constitution is the study of the formerly neglected endocrine glands, whose connection with the aggregate of mental and physical life has become increasingly important.

In the matter of the influence of physical organs not belonging to the central nervous system, there was less concern with the sensations, ideas, thoughts, and acts, emphasized so one-sidedly by the psychology of consciousness, than there was with emotional states of consciousness. And once again we are confronted with the astonishing fact that prescientific and preëxperimental psychology knew or suspected a great deal that modern psychology left uninvestigated at first. We have already mentioned that the psychology of primitive races did not identify the soul with the brain, but with the heart, the blood, the liver, the intestines, the genitalia, the diaphragm, and other inner organs. Was such an identification entirely wrong?

In science, too, the connection of mental data with chemical matters, particularly with the composition of the blood, was not a completely new thing. Hippocrates traced the "four temperaments" to the predominance of one of the four bodily humors. Our very language is the witness of this correlation. The sanguine temperament takes its name from the blood, the phlegmatic temperament from the phlegm, the choleric temperament from the bile, and the melancholic temperament from the black bile. These inaccurate theories were completely discountenanced for the last few centuries until suddenly, toward the end of the nineteenth century, they emerged in a new light in connection with the research in the endocrine secretions.

The historical stage for the study of the glands was set by Harvey's discovery of the circulation of the blood. But a long time elapsed before the complete significance of this discovery was realized. In the second half of the eighteenth century, Bordeu traced the physical phenomena following on the removal of the sex organs back to the cessation of the gonadal glandular secretions. By way of experiment, A. A. Berthold (1849) determined the influence which an organ can exert upon the blood stream of the entire organism. He transplanted the testes of roosters to other parts of their bodies and observed that such roosters "still retain their masculinity as regards voice, the instinct of propagation, pugnacity, the growth of the comb and wattles." Berthold concluded from this that the testes exert an influence upon the blood and upon the entire organism. For the time being, however, Berthold's discovery remained unnoticed.

Claude Bernard is designated as the discoverer of the "*sécrétion interne.*" In 1855 he taught that all organs of the animal body govern the body's nature by the products which they discharge into the blood stream. He demonstrated glycogenesis as an instance of internal secretion in the liver, demonstrating the accumulation of glycogen and its consequent passage into the blood stream. Brown-Séquard in 1869 expressed the theory in an even more general way when he announced that all glands secrete useful or necessary substances into the blood, and a deficiency of these substances could bring about pathological deficiency phenomena.

The birthday of the doctrine of inner secretions was the convention of the Parisian Société de Biologie which took place on the first of June, 1889. At this convention Brown-Séquard, who was then seventy-two years old, reported upon injections of testicular secretion which he had tried on himself. The results were a surprising increase of physical vigor and mental acuity. Soon thereafter a small volume was published containing the principles of the Brown-Séquard method of organotherapy.

The discovery that the nervous system is not unique in its function, coördinating the bodily activities, but that there is also a chemical correlation which effects a mutually adapted activity of the parts of the entire body, constituted an amazing innovation in sharp contrast to traditional views. Every organ, every tissue, and every cell exercises a definite influence upon the other parts of the organism by means of its own chemical nature and by means of its own products of secretion, through the medium of blood circulation. Thus the secretion produced in the epithelial cells of the intestinal mucous membrane causes a secretion of the pancreatic juice, an increase in the bile production in the liver, and the formation of the *succus intericus* in the glands of the intestinal wall, via the blood stream. Bayliss and Starling gave the name of hormone (from the Greek ὁρμᾶν, to arouse) to those substances which serve as chemical messengers in the blood stream between various parts of the body. The organs producing these hormones were termed endocrine organs and their function is spoken of as "inner secretion" (endocrinology).

2. We are naturally not concerned with an exhaustive study of the physiology of endocrine glands, but only with their effects upon the working mind. We shall, therefore, present only a brief summary of the most important endocrine glands, to the study of which an entire generation of scientists of every nationality has devoted itself. These are:

a. thyroid and parathyroid glands (*glandula thyreoidea, glandulæ parathyreoideæ*).

b. thymus gland.

c. adrenal glands (interrenal and adrenal glands).

d. pituitary gland.

e. pineal gland.

f. gonads (generative glands).

g. pancreas.

h. mucous membrane of the stomach and the intestines.
i. kidneys.

Just as pathological cases yielded most of the information in studies on the psychological significance of brain areas, so disorders of the endocrine glands were investigated in order to discover the physical and mental significance of these glands. Here, as in cerebral physiology, extirpation and other surgical experiments were a great aid in studying the mental effects of the glands.

The most important studies were those on the function of the thyroid gland. For a long time the significance of the thyroid was a matter of doubt. Today, as a result of extirpation experiments, we have a fairly clear conception of the rôle which the thyroid gland plays in the organism. Deficiency of the thyroid leads to the syndromes of myxedema (Reverdin) or *cachexia thyreopriva* (Kocher). Hypertrophy of the thyroid gland results in Graves's disease, also known as Basedow's disease (1840). The manifestations of these diseases are diametrically opposed from both a physical and mental point of view; this may be shown in the antithetical description of A. Kocher:

Atrophy of the Thyroid Gland	*Hypertrophy of the Thyroid Gland*
Slow, small, regular pulse	Rapid, strong, occasionally irregular pulse
Poor circulation, cold skin	Easily disturbed vascular nervous system
Apathetic, calm eyes, expressionless and lifeless	Anxious, shifting eyes, angry expression when observed
Retarded digestion and excretion, poor appetite, little demand for food	Abundant excretion, mostly abnormal appetite, increased demand for food
Thick, opaque, wrinkled, dry skin	Thin, transparent, moist skin
Sleepiness and desire for sleep	Sleeplessness and restless sleep
Retarded sensation, apperception, and action	Intensified sensation, apperception, and action
Sluggish mind, indifference and callousness, unemotionality	Racing thoughts, mental agitation to the point of hallucination, mania, and melancholy
Awkwardness and dullness	Constant uneasiness and haste
Retardation of osseous growth, short, thick bones	Tall skeletal structure, occasional soft and thin bones
Constant feeling of cold	Unbearable feeling of heat
Slowing of respiration	Superficial rapid respiration
Gain of weight	Loss of weight
Aged appearance even in young patients	Youthful and ample bodily development, at least in the initial stages

The above table of contrasts shows clearly that there is also a contrasting symptomatic picture of mental states, according to the hypofunctioning or hyperfunctioning of the thyroid gland, thus proving the influence of the thyroid upon mental life.

At this juncture, we should like to recall our previous discussion of eidetic psychology. You will remember that Jaensch distinguished a Basedow's disease (B) type and a tetany (T) type among his "eidetics." Such a classification correlates the particular type of eidetic capacity to the functions of the thyroid gland. Walter Jaensch, a brother of the psychologist, continued the study of such relationships in a work entitled *Physiological and Clinical Principles of the Psychophysical Personality*, published in 1926. He pointed out particularly the effects of increased or decreased calcium diet (parathyroid glands) upon the eidetic capacity. Here, too, interesting perspectives are unfolded in the psychophysical problem which will perhaps lead us still further in our study of personality.

The significance of the adrenal system in the organism was fundamentally recognized by the description of a disease resulting from the destruction of the adrenal glands, and named after Thomas Addison (*morbus Addisonii* or Addison's disease). Addison described this disease in 1855. The symptoms are anemia accompanied by general weakness and apathy; the digestion and the functioning of the nervous system are upset; a bronze-hued pigmentation of the skin and the mucous membranes makes its appearance. Modern research has isolated adrenalin as the essential product of the adrenal glands. The exact formula of this chemical substance is known and it can be produced artificially. It is usually marketed as "adrenalin" or "suprarenin." As the internal secretion of the adrenal glands, adrenalin passes into the blood stream and acts as a specific stimulant to the sympathetic nervous system. It accelerates the heart beat, constricts most of the blood vessels and raises the blood pressure; it temporarily stops peristaltic movements in the stomach and intestines. All this, of course, has a strong effect upon the mind.

The relationship of glands and organic function does not depend entirely upon the physical constitution. Mental disturbances can affect the functioning of the glands. Cannon, the American physiologist, for example, contributed the information that in dogs and cats that have been aroused to anger there is a profuse secretion of adrenalin accompanied by a rise of blood pressure and the production of glycogen in the liver.

The pituitary gland or hypophysis, so-called because of its proximity to the brain, was formerly believed to be an organ supplying the brain with nutrition. Ernst Liégeois in 1860 recognized the fact that the pituitary gland is one of the endocrine glands. Marie, in 1886, discovered that acromegaly or gigantism was related to tumors of the pituitary, and soon thereafter other illnesses, like pathological obesity, were related to irregular pituitary functioning. The pituitary gland is a vital organ; its extirpation in animals generally results in death. The pituitary is closely related to the thyroid gland and particularly to the gonads. It affects growth and the metabolism of fat, among other functions.

While the pineal gland is today no longer regarded from the Descartian viewpoint as the seat of the soul, its essential significance in physical and mental development and the state of nutrition is recognized. E. von Cyon was the first to engage in physiological experiments with extracts of the pineal gland. According to these experiments, the pineal gland primarily affects the heart action, a view which, incidentally, is disputed by some authors. Disturbances of function in the pineal gland cause, particularly in boys under the age of seven, an abnormal growth in height, unusual hirsute growth, premature sexual development, and mental precocity. The pineal gland is believed to have an inhibitory influence on the development of the gonads, and a secondary influence on mental development.

That the gonads or sexual glands affect not only the physical but also the mental development of individuals was already known among the ancients, who had abundant opportunity to observe the effects of religious or other forms of castration. A great many physicians were formerly of the opinion that differences in the sexual glands governed the entire difference of the physical and mental sexual character between men and women. Virchow wrote: "Woman is woman because of her generative glands. All the idiosyncrasies of her body and mind—in short, everything that we admire and revere in a real woman, is merely dependent upon her ovaries." On the other hand, other authorities pointed out the fact that sex and sexuality were already determined in human beings before the development of the sexual glands, so that the specific development of the sexual organs is not a cause but a symptom of specific sexual variation. In any event, we can only say at the present time that the factors determining sex variation are not definitely ascertainable. Many authorities assume the existence of an original hermaphroditic predisposition.

No matter how much scientific opinions differ, we know that the entire physical and mental sexual character is dependent upon the sex glands. This is corroborated by cases in which a decided change in the sex glands during the course of life causes a change in certain secondary sexual characteristics, or even in the entire sexual nature. It is questionable whether the so-called secondary sexual characteristics are dependent upon the gonadal glands when they make their first appearance. But the complete maturation of these secondary sexual characteristics does not occur without the influence of the generative cells.

That puberty has decided effects upon the body and the mind is known beyond all peradventure; these effects are traced to the secretions of the gonads. Of late, experiments in the transplantation of the reproductive glands upon individuals of the opposite sex attest to the influence of the sexual hormone. Steinach's attempts at artificial rejuvenation by means of the inoculation of gonadal extracts have brought a rather dubious popularity to endocrinology.

The significance of the pancreas was first recognized in 1889 by Von Mering and Minkowski, and approximately at the same time by De Dominicis. The cause of diabetes was also discovered at this time, because the extirpation of the pancreas causes not only digestive disturbances but also a permanent secretion of sugar in the urine.

At the present time, when research in human constitution is still in the midst of its task, it has already completely altered the psychophysical problem. The nervous system can no longer be regarded as the sole correlating and coördinating unit between the mind and the body. On the other hand, we must not pin our hopes too strongly on the notion that personality and character are nothing more than a matter of chemistry, and that it is sufficient for every person to find out his "individual gland formula" in order to determine his character and predict his actions. We do know, however, that not only his brain processes but also his whole body is bound up in man's mental life.

3. The relationship between mind and constitution was impressively illustrated by Kretschmer in his studies on *Physique and Character*. These studies dealt with facts which everyone knew and no one had previously been able to explain. How often have you noticed that fat people frequently have a comfortable, easy-going disposition whereas very thin people are often irritable? People with literary inclinations at least were familiar with the saying of Shakespeare's *Julius Cæsar:*

> Let me have men about me that are fat;
> Sleek-headed men and such as sleep o' nights;
> Yon Cassius has a lean and hungry look:
> He thinks too much . . .

No casting director would ever think of letting a fat actor play the part of Mephistopheles; and an underfed Falstaff would be impossible. But what is the origin of this correlation between types of character and types of physique? Kretschmer's book promised the answer to this question which had previously never even been broached by science.

E. Kretschmer is an alienist by profession. He observed, like so many physicians before him, that certain mental diseases can be recognized from the external appearance of the patient. The cretin, the acromegalic, and the eunuch bear a physical imprint. Kretschmer discovered, furthermore, that two chief forms of mental disease—schizophrenic and manic-depressive psychoses—are frequently accompanied by certain physical appearances. By methodically studying these phenomena, Kretschmer arrived at three basic bodily types, which he named asthenic (leptosomic in later editions), pyknic, and athletic. We shall first describe these three types externally.

The asthenic type displays impaired growth in height and slight lateral growth. This proportion of growth applies to all parts of the body; the face, neck, torso, limbs, bones, muscles, and the vascular system. The skin is dry and bloodless. Thin arms append from narrow shoulders. The ribs can be counted upon the narrow, flat chest. The abdomen is thin, and body weight bears a low correlation to height. Kretschmer tried to avoid the evaluative connotation of weakness and sickliness implied in the word "asthenic" by replacing it with the term "leptosomic."

The athletic type possesses a powerful, erect head, borne upon a flexible neck. Stout chest, broad shoulders, and a torso tapering down toward the hips mark the athlete. The joints and hands have a thick bony structure. The muscles and skin are well developed. Body size is above the average.

The third basic type is that of the pyknic, the "stocky" or "thick-set" individual. This type is usually of medium height and solidly built. A soft broad face surmounts a short, massive neck. A fat abdomen is situated under a deep chest. The limbs are formed with very little muscular and bony relief and are often shapely. The hands are soft and inclined to be short and broad. The shoulders are not as broad as the athlete's, but are rather small and drawn up. The head often sinks down so that it almost hides the neck; the skin is soft and smooth.

In addition to these three basic types, Kretschmer also recorded a number of special types which he included under the name of dysplastics. He included such types as the eunuchoid giants, the eunuchoid and polyglandular forms of obesity, and others in this category.

Kretschmer correlated the three basic types, not always sharply distinguishable from one another in real life, with basic types of mental disease. In the manic-depressive he discovered a strong predominance of pyknic types, while asthenic, athletic, and dysplastic types predominated among the schizophrenic.

Facts determined from the type as a whole were studied in detail. According to Kretschmer, there are no irrelevant factors of physique from the psychiatrist's point of view. Not a single hair of the head nor a variant in the shape of the nose tip is irrelevant. There is no such thing as an "accidental" individual variety. Every centimeter of hand size and every degree of jaw angle may figure in the constitutional formula of the person under examination. Of course, all this must be done with the reservation that such details are to be viewed within the frame of typical pictures.

The shape of the face is especially interesting. In the asthenic schizophrenic, an angular profile, long nose, and wide oval-shaped face predominate. Athletic schizophrenics usually have steep oval faces and coarse "high heads." In the pyknic manic-depressive, a flat, pentagonal type of face is the rule.

Hair growth is also important in the study of these types, since it is related to endocrine data. The texture and color of the skin are important characteristics as well. The facial hue of persons afflicted with cyclic insanity is predominantly reddish; those suffering from schizophrenia are predominantly pale.

Of course the problem of endocrine secretions is particularly important in these cases. But no very marked correlations have as yet been determined. Our information extends with comparative certainty only to the significance of the sex glands. In schizophrenia there is often a hypofunction or disfunction of the gonads. A rather ambiguous and aimless sex life is probably related to this, whereas in the manic-depressive the sex life is usually normal. On these questions, however, Kretschmer is noncommittal.

4. We have confined ourselves so far to psychiatry in the study of types. In general psychology the problem does not assume importance until we inquire what the study of types has to offer us as an aid in judging normal individuals. Kretschmer broadened his investigations to include this field as well.

Kretschmer uses the terms cycloid and schizoid to designate those types of personality that represent a transitional stage between the abnormal and the normal. These two types can often be found among close relatives of abnormal types; but the abnormal types themselves often display cycloid and schizoid traits before their affliction is definitely manifested.

The cycloid type is described by Kretschmer as distinguished by three groups of characteristics:

a. sociable, kind-hearted, friendly, genial.

b. cheerful, humorous, lively, passionate.

c. quiet, calm, grave, soft.

The first group embraces those qualities that exist independently of both extremes of mood. The second group appears in the hypomanic phase of mental disorder. And the third group is characteristic of the depressive phase. As a whole, cycloid types are sociable, placid, uncomplicated individuals whose characters are frankly revealed.

Schizoid individuals are much more difficult to fathom. The depth of their nature does not correspond to its outward signs. They dissimulate their inner feelings. One can never tell how they feel; and very often they, themselves, do not know how they feel, or they are very uncertain about their own feelings. Bleuler, who was the first to present a lucid description of schizophrenia, speaks of "autism," because the people concerned are entirely absorbed in themselves.

Kretschmer classifies the characteristics of schizoid types in groups analogous to those of the cycloid types:

a. unsociable, quiet, reserved, serious, humorless, cranks.

b. bashful, shy, delicate, sensitive, nervous, excitable, book-loving and nature-loving.

c. amenable, good-natured, docile, even-tempered, dull, stupid.

The relationship of these three groups of characteristics is quite different from that of the cycloid types. The first group contains those characteristics that occur most frequently in the schizoid personality. The second group consists of characteristics of hypersensitivity. The third group comprises characteristics of insensitivity. Schizoid temperaments are situated between the polar extremes of sensitivity and dullness, while cycloid temperaments lie between the extremes of cheerfulness and sadness. But the schizoid individual does not vacillate between the two poles as does the cycloid individual. The key to the understanding of schizoid types is the realization that such types are hypersensitive and cool at the same time, and display these characteristics in varying proportions.

From the social angle, schizoids are either absolutely unsociable or very exclusive, or superficially sociable without any rapport to their environment. They never mingle with their milieu, and feel themselves strictly isolated from the external world. At the same time they are capable of sacrificing themselves to abstract ideals like socialism or temperance. There are splendid characters and a high nobility of purpose among schizoid types, even though they never achieve the warm-heartedness of the cycloid personality.

5. Both of these contrasting types and their interesting

variants also occur among normal people in less accentuated although distinguishable forms. Once we have learned to differentiate both groups in their pathological extremes, we can very easily classify our acquaintances in accordance with them. Kretschmer uses the name cyclothymic for those normal individuals corresponding to the cycloid type, and schizothymic for normal individuals corresponding to the schizoid type.

The subdivisions of the cyclothymic type are: talkative, cheerful people; people with a pleasant humor; quiet, moody persons; complacent, pleasure-loving people; active, practical people. The subdivisions of the schizothymic type are: dignified, sensitive persons; unworldly, idealistic people; calm, masterful persons; egoists, and dull persons.

We cannot here enumerate all the details of Kretschmer's typology, yet from what we have already noted we can see what interesting conclusions may result from the correlation of physique and mental make-up. Indeed, for a while this typology was so popular that it became a parlor game in certain circles.

Recently, however, the experimental method has been applied to the research of physiopsychic types. Characteristic differences of the Kretschmer types were discovered in the realms of sensation and thought. According to the results of such inquiry, it appears that pyknic individuals have greater color sensitivity, while leptosomic persons are more sensitive to form. Pyknic types have emotional associations while the associations of leptosomic types are more intuitive. Pyknics prefer detailed and objective descriptions; leptosomics are more subjective. In short, experimentally as well as in life, leptosomics are more intensive, more abstract, and tenaciously persistent; they have a few eccentric notions, are subjective and are apt to conduct themselves emotionally. On the other hand, pyknic individuals are more expansive, objective, constructive, easy to speak to and to persuade, and emotionally naïve. Leptosomics are artistic, whereas pyknics are realists.

In a book entitled *The Psychology of Men of Genius*, Kretschmer made a thorough study of genius. Since Lombroso, psychiatrists have shown great, if not always flattering, interest in the genius. Now Kretschmer correlated men of genius with his types.

6. The end result of Kretschmer's studies was a theory of temperament anchored in the biological. To Kretschmer, the notion of temperament included both the sensory, cerebral, and motor mechanisms, and temperament "in the narrower sense." The physical representative of this latter form of temperament is the cerebro-glandular apparatus. Temperament affects the mechanism of the mind in an inhibitory as well as in an accelerating manner. It exercises an influence over psychesthesia, that is, the hypersensitivity or insensitivity to mental stimuli; it also influences mood, that is, the pleasure-displeasure tone of mental contents. Temperament affects the hastening or retardation of mental action and influences psychomotility with regard to tempo and timber. Eidetic and ideational types are also related to the two forms of temperament.

So far as the physiological principles supporting the theory of temperament are concerned, the following may be noted: the brain is at the very least an end organ of response in which all factors determining temperament, even those originating in the chemism of the blood, find their focus. Kretschmer did not say how far beyond this extent the brain influences mood and psychic tempo. But he energetically contradicted that psychophysiological school which proposed to subsume ultimately everything mental within brain centers. Kretschmer, on the contrary, emphasized the significance of the endocrine glands and confidently declared that the endocrine system exercises an essential influence on the mind and especially on the qualities of temperament. His point of view is strikingly illustrated by pathological cases such as cretins and eunuchs. The differences between cyclothymics and schizothymics in normal temperaments, too, are related to the entire chemism of the blood. In this connection, we must also include the intestinal glands, and, ultimately, the influence of all bodily tissues.

7. We shall not enumerate all the details of glandular influence, some of which Kretschmer himself admitted were purely hypothetical. But I should like to emphasize his whole attitude to the problem of psychophysics. In place of the one-sided parallelism of brain and mind, Kretschmer deliberately instituted a parallelism between the somatic and the psychic. He was impelled to this by the fact that despite painstaking research, cerebro-anatomical data were insignificant in the explanation of the chief forms of mental disease, and wholly negative in regard to the manic-depressive psychoses. For this reason the latest medical theory of today inclines toward a constitutional endocrine theory of causation of manic-depressive insanity. Psychology, too, cannot ignore these facts.

The correctness of Kretschmer's studies in point of detail, and the question of whether his typology even approximately encompasses the vast plenitude of human character, are both immaterial: the relation between character and physique is indisputable. Furthermore, it is noteworthy that "consciousness" still plays only a minor rôle, and that character, temperament, and the like, signify subconscious mental dispositions which have an effect upon consciousness but are not conscious themselves. At this point Kretschmer's investigations went off on the tangent of structural psychology which will be discussed later.

An attempt to outline a totalitarian medical theory of the personality by utilizing the entire research in human constitution and many other specialized fields was made by F. Kraus, then Professor of Internal Medicine in Berlin, in a work entitled *General and Special Pathology of the Personality*. We shall merely touch upon a few of his ideas, in so far as they fall within our province. To Kraus, the antithesis of mind-body is only of secondary interest. Personality characteristics are never exclusively mental or physical. Both are organically intertwined. Mental life must be understood through the life of the individual as an organic whole. The original whole of any member of the species is the genotypical constitution. The concept of personality, however, is a phenotypical concept. The principle of individualization is only one of the many principles of organization. According to Kraus, research in human constitution is vitally important. But the abundant material in his book is as yet unintegrated.

This is partially due to the fact that the extensive research of modern biology has also delved into the problem of psychophysiology, and has also thrown new light on the relation between body and mind. We shall, therefore, turn our attention to biology, which grasps the concept of "totality" in a new sense.

PSYCHOLOGY AND VITALISTIC BIOLOGY

1. Since the beginning of the twentieth century, a new tendency has arisen in biology. Discoveries which intruded to a great extent upon the working sphere of psychology began to appear at this time. And, since even strict analysts of consciousness were little concerned with the boundary lines drawn by psychology, biologists also displayed the same lack of concern and appropriated consciousness as an additional subject for their investigations. They constructed completely novel theories regarding the relation between the mental and the physical, and these theories were destined to have a revolutionary effect in the realm of psychology.

Biology, at the close of the nineteenth century, like its sister science psychology, was predominantly mechanistic. The human body was essentially conceived as a mechanism, and all its functions were explained as far as possible according to physico-chemical laws. As far as consciousness was investigated by biology, it was integrated with this mechanism, that is to say, it was completely despoiled of its essential nature. Psychology was inclined to affirm this view, inasmuch as it, too, apprehended consciousness as an associative or reflex mechanism. We have already noted above the difficulties attendant upon the advance of this line of research.

In 1900 or thereabout, psychologists and biologists began to be aware of certain facts which directly contradicted the mechanistic interpretation of life, and which gradually led to the development of a nonmechanistic, vitalistic biology. The living body was no longer considered a machine, but an organism governed by supermechanical laws. A teleological view came more and more to replace the view of pure causality. To this extent the development of biology proceeded in approximately the same direction as that of psychology in which, as we saw, the teleological as well as the totalitarian point of view had assumed increasing prominence.

The facts primarily responsible for this reversal of view were first of all instances of restitution, that is, the healing and restoration of destroyed organs resulting from the autonomic activity of these organs. This was difficult to explain in a purely mechanistic fashion. Could the total process of formation of the organism be a mechanical one? And furthermore, could inheritance be explained in mechanistic analogies? These questions could not be dismissed. A totalitarian factor was needed to operate within the organism in a vital, formative way. This factor, however, could not be conceived as material and mechanistic save in analogy to those functions which had formerly been eliminated from the study of biology because they were "psychic." Thus, science reverted to vitalism, that venerable doctrine which the nineteenth century had presumably buried for all time.

2. Historically, the problem of the process of formation was first posed by Plato, if we disregard his lesser-known predecessors. Plato saw in all perceptible things the operation

of "ideas," literally "forms" (*Gestalten*). To be sure, Plato was rather ambiguous as to how these forms, existing, moreover, as absolutes, become operative in the empirical world. Aristotle was much more plastic in relating "ideas" to empirical entities, and in grasping these ideas not merely by philosophical speculation but also by concrete observation. The remarkable thing is that Aristotle placed the natural process of formation upon an equal plane with the artificial one, as, for example, when he wrote, "In everything produced by nature or art something that exists as a possibility (δυναμει ὀν) arises by means of something that exists in reality (ἐντελεχεια ὀν)." Aristotle's equalization of these two processes can only be understood if we assume that he conceived "something that exists in reality" as an "idea," as a mental or intellectual principle. In organisms, Aristotle recognized the significance of the germ plasm which makes the body grow, and this significance was based upon a vitalistic principle, because for Aristotle the life principle was identical with the soul. The soul is the "entelechy," the operative and formative principle in animate being. Aristotle's vitalism is, to be sure, no elaborate and factually established system of natural science, but it is nevertheless an hypothesis which has had credence even in modern times.

Aristotelian vitalism dominated the Middle Ages and also the Renaissance. Harvey, the discoverer of the circulation of the blood, was the first to assert his independence of Aristotle, although still accepting the germs of an Aristotelian principle, a *"primordium vegetale"* which changes into form. But Harvey rejected Aristotle's comparison between organisms and works of art; that is to say, he sharply distinguished between unconscious and conscious formation. In doing this Harvey granted capacities exceeding consciousness to his principle of the unconscious.

Vitalism achieved a new interpretation through the efforts of G. E. Stahl (1660–1734), who is chiefly known in the history of science as the originator of the "phlogiston theory." For Stahl, the conscious soul was once again the first principle of life, an *"ens activum movens et intelligens."* But Stahl denied that there existed in addition to the *"anima rationalis"* an *"anima sensitiva"* and an *"anima vegetativa"* as Aristotle had taught.

At the close of the seventeenth and the eighteenth centuries, science was involved in a controversy regarding the formational process of life. The question was whether the resultant form was "preformed" in the then newly discovered spermatazoa, or whether it developed through "new formation" (epigenesis). Whereas the "preformists" were inclined toward a mechanistic viewpoint, most of the "epigeneticists" were vitalists. To be sure, Buffon was still a preformist in reference to the entire development of the organism, but he was an epigeneticist in reference to embryonic development, inasmuch as he denied that all future germinal elements were already present in the embryo. Caspar Friedrich Wolff (1733–94) was a pure epigeneticist who ranged himself with the vitalists by assuming the cause of the process of organic formation to be a *"vis essentialis."*

Kant stands at the threshold of the nineteenth century. In his *Critique of Judgment* (1790), he made a circumspect conceptual division between the formation of mechanistic and teleological concepts. Subsequently, the flourishing vitalistic speculation in German natural philosophy earned for vitalism an undeserving disrepute. As a consequence, the mechanists had no difficulty in the middle of the century in critically annihilating vitalism. But it was only mythological vitalism and not vitalism in general which Claude Bernard, Lotze, and many other scholars disposed of so neatly. These men were able to refute the arguments of their contemporaries, but they could not refute the facts which led a later generation to accept the doctrine of vitalism.

Indeed, in the second half of the nineteenth century vitalism amounted to a dead superstition. Just as it was impossible to refer to a substantial soul in psychology, it was also impossible in biology to speak of a vital force or an organic entelechy. Just as in psychology all mental functions were reduced to mechanisms of consciousness, so in biology too all vital functions were reduced to mechanical processes. It was as essential for the modern savants of that time to believe in the dogma of mechanism as it was for a pious Catholic to believe in the Trinity.

The few men who dared to raise their voices against the mechanistic dogma were not even heard, although men of importance were among them. In the ranks of natural scientists there were the Germans C. E. von Baer, J. von Haustein, and the American Edmund Montgomery. Among philosophers only Eduard von Hartmann, whom we have already met as a critic of mechanistic psychology, valued vitalism highly. In his principle of the "unconscious," which simultaneously includes will and reason, Hartmann explained the process of formation, the instincts, and the relation of the mental and the physical. Since this "unconscious" is conceived as a cosmic force in analogy with mental data, Hartmann was an outspoken vitalist. He advanced a particularly brilliant criticism of Darwinian mechanism and mechanistic psychology.

The reason for this abbreviated outline of the history of vitalism, which is really a biological matter, is that biology and psychology constantly overlap in the theory of vitalism. The older form of vitalism, as embodied in Aristotle, Stahl, and many later philosophers, endeavored to explain vital force or entelechy in terms of the conscious soul by the forcible imputation of more or less conscious "purposes," or the interpretation of vital force as "psychic" in analogy to the soul. The newer form of vitalism regards vital force as unconsciously operative, but cannot dispense with the problem of the relation of consciousness or the conscious soul to vital force. The radical division which modern science makes between biology and psychology is unquestionably arbitrary, for at the very least, the life of higher animals cannot be understood without including unconscious vital functions.

3. Undoubtedly the most important of the neovitalists was Hans Driesch who began under the influence of the "evolutionary mechanist" Roux, and then advocated a "mechanistic teleology" before he arrived at vitalism by way of the problem of conduct. In 1899, Driesch published a work entitled *The Localization of Morphogenetic Functions: A Demonstration of Vitalistic Action*. This was quickly followed by a series of other works, such as *Organic Regulation* in 1901 and *The Mind as an Elementary Factor of Nature* in 1903. The year 1905 saw the publication of *The History and Theory of Vitalism*, and the years 1907–8, after Driesch had been converted from natural science to philosophy, saw the publication of his *Science and Philosophy of the Organism*, which first appeared as the Gifford Lectures in Aberdeen.

It must be emphasized, however, that Driesch found the decisive turning point in the course of his studies not as a speculative philosopher but as an experimenter in biology. Like his teacher, Roux, the founder of evolutionary mechanics, Driesch experimented with ova. But while Roux had only been able to rear the right half and the left half of an embryo from a dissected frog's egg, Driesch, while in Trieste, succeeded in 1891 in rearing not half but whole embryos from the dissected eggs of sea urchins. In the following years, he continued his experiments in the aquarium at Naples, and there he succeeded in raising stunted but whole larvæ from quarter and three-quarter embryos, and even from embryos in which the mutual position of nuclei and cell plasm had been deranged.

The surprising thing about these experiments was that they demonstrated the complete inadequacy of every preformational theory and every mechanistic interpretation. In a flash, as he tells us, Driesch realized the necessity of insisting upon the "autonomy of life." And in order to achieve this, he collected material from all fields of biology, out of which he constructed four proofs of vitalism.

The first of these proofs is based upon morphogenetic considerations, or more precisely, upon the question whether the process of formation can be reduced to a series of formative acts each of which occurs upon a basis of "prospective potentialities" and with the aid of "media." If this were so, then the organism would be a "machine" not merely in respect to its functioning but also in respect to its origin. Upon the basis of his experiments Driesch reached a point at which he was obliged to answer this question in the negative.

He found a solution in the concept of a harmonic equipotential system. By this Driesch meant such cell totalities as appear either in embryos or in the restoration of disturbed organisms, for whose organizational accomplishment it is immaterial whether any of their parts are removed or displaced. Thus it is obvious that the process of formation cannot be explained solely through the localization of parts, as had been assumed by previous research. The one act which each part performs in each instance is indeed one act; still the potentiality of each part is not one, but includes the possibility of many single acts. In all systems many single potentialities operate during the process of development, but the sum of that which issues in every instance from the aggregate of single cell acts is not merely a "sum," but a total unit. Apparently there is a sort of "harmony" among the actual end products of the system. The organism is, consequently, not a machine, for we can conceive of no machine which, like sea urchins, can be cut into pieces which then independently develop other machines. The development and the renewal of organic forms are non-mechanistic occurrences.

Driesch evolved a second proof of the autonomy of life from the facts of inheritance. Here, too, it would be absurd to designate as a machine something which is divisible a great many times and which always returns to totality. On the contrary, an elementary factor of nature which brings about the individual process of formation in the succeeding generation must be assumed. This factor, which is also responsible for the restoration of organic systems, Driesch calls "entelechy." Entelechy is in itself an unspatial multiplicity. It does not operate in space. But entelechy belongs to nature; it is a factor of nature. The operation of entelechy divides organic from inorganic nature in which everything comes to pass in accordance with mechanical laws.

The discussion so far has been confined to pure biology, so that the question of what all this has to do with psychology is in order, especially since we have defined psychology as the study of consciousness. However, we begin to approach psychology when we consider Driesch's third proof of the "autonomy of life," which he derives from the analysis of organic movements, particularly "action."

Action has been defined as every animal movement whose especial quality cannot be explained in terms of the actual stimulus, but which must rather be explained in terms of the life history of its performer. In this instance, Driesch speaks of the "criterion of historical reaction basis," but to this must be added a second criterion, that of the "individuality of coördination between stimulus and response." Every action of a human being at a given point in his life is conditioned by a stimulus. Stimulus and response are "individualities," that is, composite totalities which are correlated with each other totally and not additively. The matter at issue here is, therefore, the evaluative utilization of past experience, a fact that cannot be demonstrated in any machine. This is an additional proof of the autonomy of life, since a machine that reacts like an individual and varies its reaction upon the basis of previous experience is inconceivable.

What is this Something which causes nonmechanical actions? The temptation is to speak of entelechy in this instance, too, but Driesch was, at least for the time being, intent upon distinguishing the agency which forms the body from the agency which directs it. For this reason he designated the agency of action as the "psychoid," and thereby distinguished it from the psyche or mind; because there can be no mind in the sphere of spatiality within which action is considered to take place. The psychoid is not the "mind," but it can only be discussed in analogy to the mind.

After Driesch had portrayed action purely as a process of nature upon the basis of external observation, he made use of introspection, that is, the viewpoint of the psychology of consciousness, and thus gained a fourth proof of vitalism. To the factor which he had named the historical reaction basis, he ascribed memory as the capacity for future experience unconditioned by sensory stimuli. To the factor with which we have become acquainted as the individualizing evaluation of past experience, he ascribed the capacity of new creation, as revealed in all so-called higher mental activities.

While these correlated functions are inadequately understood in connection with human conduct from a physical standpoint, a psychological scrutiny reveals their laws very distinctly. These functions include the knowledge concerning causal relationships and logical inference. Only through them can human conduct be understood.

Such data soon take us outside the sphere of "nature." We must classify states of consciousness according to quite different principles. And this classification leads to the concept of "mind" or "soul." In order to attain this concept Driesch started from a fundamental statement: "I am conscious of Something organized," or "I know Something (organized)." Whereas logic has to do with the "Something," psychology asks to what extent I am conscious of the "Something." Many of the Somethings that I am conscious of are oppositely ranged in time, between a "then" and a "now." Analogously there is a difference in meaning between the "I" that was conscious *then* and the "I" that is conscious *now*. To distinguish the two, Driesch calls the first the "self" and the latter the "I."

This self, however, is projected into the continuity of time as something variable within a constant. The self in its noncontinuous existence must have a constant basis, and Driesch calls this basis "my mind or soul." "My soul" is therefore my "constantly apprehended self." Or, in other words: my self, completed by unconscious (but not physical) being and having, is "my soul." This soul is an unconscious, that is to say, a not I-conscious, invisible organism possessing immanent laws of activity. On the one hand it is a retainer (memory) and on the other hand an organizer. The soul is, consequently, a special realm of being that we conceive as an object which behaves as though it existed independently.

From the dual point of departure of external observation and introspection, Driesch arrived at two separated realms, "nature" and "conscious experience." But these two realms must be correlated. Driesch decisively rejected the older parallelism which considered "physical" the same as "mechanical." A good part of his writings were concerned with the refutation of this point. In the analysis of such human conduct as belongs to "nature," we arrive at nonmechanistic natural phenomena, that is, the "psychoid"; on the other hand, in the analysis of consciousness we arrive at the "soul," an unconscious independent realm of being. Driesch united both these concepts, the soul and the nonmechanical nature factor. The result was a triple parallel that has nothing to do with psychomechanical parallelism. What actually exists is a parallel between the processes in my conscious experience, in my soul, and in my psychoid. Together these form the "mind-pervaded body" or the "psychophysical personality." Metaphysically, one real entity appears in three forms, of which the first is a variable experience and the other two are conceived as constants. In place of the psychomechanical we have a "psycho-entelechal" parallelism.

In reviewing Driesch's very complicated system which we have outlined here with regard to the psychophysiological problem, we note that the entire problem has changed in a remarkable way. Most of the cerebral anatomists and physiologists had accepted the body and the brain as definite, given facts, primarily as a well-constructed mechanism which incidentally produces consciousness. Their chief problem had been to determine how single acts of consciousness are related to physiological processes that take place in the brain. Vitalism goes back much further and questions how this supposedly mechanical body came into being. Vitalism thus determined that the body is no machine at all, but that in its development a special, nonphysical agency is coöperatively involved, an agency which Hartmann called the unconscious and Driesch called entelechy, but which can also be called "life." This agency does not merely develop the body; it also maintains it, and within certain limits even restores it when one of its parts is injured. The physical functions of the body are also governed by this vital agency.

The problem is, therefore, not the relation of consciousness to physico-mechanical processes, but its relation to the vital processes which have developed the body and which pervade it. The point at issue is not the relationship between consciousness and the body, but the relation between consciousness and life, between consciousness and entelechy, to which Driesch added the further concepts of "soul" and "psychoid."

It does not devolve upon us to investigate whether Driesch's theory is an ultimate truth. The theory has undergone many changes even in Driesch's own mind, and its acceptance presupposes the acceptance of Driesch's logico-metaphysical system. The essential thing for our purposes is the change of problems.

For Driesch's vitalism did not stand alone. In later chapters we shall become acquainted with other vitalistic doctrines distinguished from those of Driesch by the prominence they give to morphology. Since these doctrines are derived even more than Driesch's from mental premises, they are usually called psychovitalistic. We shall discuss them in connection with psychomotor research.

CONCLUSION

IN this chapter we have epitomized the work of several generations of scholars in several sciences: psychology, physiology, comparative anatomy, and biology. Each science from its own particular angle endeavored to solve the relationship between physical and psychic data. Although none of them evolved an ultimate solution, they embarked upon a specific direction of research, the continuation of which may perhaps result in a final solution. This hope is strengthened by the fact that the paths of physiology and biology lead in the same direction which the study of consciousness has been forced to take independently of them.

These paths, in both instances, led away from atomizing mechanism toward a totalitarian point of view. Atomic psychology certainly found no corroboration in the fact that all its attempts at finding physiological parallels to match its "elements of consciousness" proved invalid and impossible. Instead of a circumscribed localization, a highly complicated coöperation of numerous cerebral processes and of other physical organs was discovered, all of which could be understood only from totalitarian viewpoints. And just as in psychology not merely the totality of consciousness but also a totality operating beyond consciousness, although not itself conscious, became the focus of attention, so also, the sciences of the human body were impelled to accept a totality which, in itself is not purely physical. The problem of a "soul" organically governing consciousness and physical life, which at first had been set aside almost disdainfully, now came into its own.

Today, of course, we do not regard such a view dogmatically but merely as a working hypothesis which is indispensable in the solution of the physiopsychic problem. This manner of envisioning the problem was reached by rigorously methodical labor to which innumerable scientists of all countries devoted their lives, and which cost the lives of millions of laboratory animals. The result is, as we have said, not yet the bright sun of knowledge, but at most, a nebulous halo from which a clear light may develop.

We are justified in this hope not only because the research tendencies which we have discussed converge toward it but because a third tendency seems to point in the same direction. This third research group, which tries to apprehend mental life not through consciousness or through the structure of the body but through action, shall occupy us next.

PART THREE

THE PSYCHOLOGY OF ACTION
AND CONDUCT

1. So far we have studied two possible approaches to the inner world of man. We have either relied upon introspection to probe consciousness, or we have studied the structure and functions of those organs which were regarded as the substratum of consciousness. But there is still a third possibility: we can also confine our attention to the perceptible actions of the body which are unquestionably related to the life of consciousness, and which project it externally and render it effective. Even the pure psychology of consciousness, inasmuch as it endeavored to treat consciousness as a world in itself, could not help recognizing such relationships.

Because of the great significance of action, we can easily understand why the soul was long considered as the motor center of the body. What distinguishes the dead from the living is the cessation of action, so that death was interpreted to mean that the soul, the instigator of action, had departed from the body. In the primitive concept of soul, action was probably more important than consciousness, the conception of which presupposes a considerable degree of abstract thought. The essential nature of the souls or demons imputed to things was not so much a form of consciousness as it was a form of activity. The magic power issuing from demonic forces was a form of action; the extent to which this action was conscious was a moot question.

This conception of the soul as an activating force remained dominant for a long time until science turned to the problem of the soul. In Greek psychology, the soul was primarily an activating force, and only secondarily a sensitive or thinking agency. The atomists, the Pythagoreans, Anaxagoras, and others (according to Aristotle) defined the soul as an activating or self-activating entity. Only in a corollary sense was the soul also designated as reason, that is, consciousness. The most profound analysis of the problem of action in relation to the soul was made by Aristotle. Aristotle distinguished four types of action: locomotion, metamorphosis, reduction, and growth. He denied that action inherently appertained to the soul; he considered the soul the active principle of life, the entelechy, the form-giving power, which is not always entirely active but always potentially present.

In the psychology of modern Western civilization, mental life also became connected with action. In particular, all materialistically inclined thinkers strove to reduce consciousness to action, when they did not go so far as simply to define thought as action. Thus Hobbes, for example, reduced sensation to motion which is transmitted as a sort of pressure to the brain and to the heart from which the reciprocal motion (*conatus*) then issues. Similar notions dominated most materialistic philosophers of the following centuries, whereas the idealists rather avoided than pursued the problem, presumably because of the fear of succumbing to materialism. And to this very day, every psychologist who subordinates the mind to action brings down upon his head the onus of materialism and mechanism, often very unjustifiably, as we shall see.

2. The newer school of exact psychomotor research is distinguished by the stress it lays upon reflex action, that is, a motor reaction which takes place without consciousness and is regarded as the primary form of all complex action. As a rule, Descartes is considered the founder of the study of reflex, but long before him Galen knew of the pupillary reflex. The term "reflex" seems to have occurred for the first time in the works of Astruc in 1736. In 1781 Whytt published further observations on reflex actions. The present-day distinction between reflex and voluntary action appeared in 1833 in the publications of a Scotch physician residing in London by the name of Marshall Hall and in the publications of Johannes Müller. Hall distinguished four types of action, among which reflex action was fourth. The

reflex originates in the spinal cord and is independent of the brain or consciousness. Recognizing Hall's priority, Müller, in the second edition of his *Handbook*, also presented an exposition of reflex action, although he assumed the participation of the brain as well as the spinal cord. From that time on, psychology occupied itself more and more with the problem of the reflex, and evolved the theory of the reflex arc according to which all human actions ultimately go back to reflexes that are modified only through the intercession of the brain and of memory.

3. The founder of modern motor psychology was Alexander Bain who formulated the principle of the primacy of action in a manner which, with certain reservations, is still acceptable today. Although Bain remained under the influence of associationist psychology, he did not regard action as merely subservient to idea but introduced it into psychology as an independent factor. Action amounts to a simple, elementary capacity of the organism, and although at first independent of external stimuli, later forms an essential part of all sensations. We become aware of spontaneous action by means of the muscle senses. Spontaneous action originates in the impulses which the nerve centers transmit to the muscles. Activity and force are therefore inherent in all mental phenomena. Spontaneous actions are originally aimless and indefinite; experience directs them toward definite goals. As a consequence of the constant connection between sensations and actions our belief in an objective world comes into being.

Bain's chief works were *The Senses and the Intellect* (1855) and *The Emotions and the Will* (1859). His permanent significance is due to his having emphasized the importance of "visceral sensations," although his assumption of a special nerve sensation was later discarded. Viewed from the historical perspective, Bain must be recognized as a potent stimulator of all motor psychology. Both French and American psychologists, especially William James, were influenced by Bain in this respect, but he was scarcely noticed by German psychologists.

4. Among the forerunners of modern motor psychology was Charles Darwin. Darwin was the first to make a systematic study of *The Expression of the Emotions in Man and Animals* (1872). He was of the opinion that expressive actions were innate and inherited. Upon the basis of a wide observation of animals, children, and insane people, Darwin set up three principles. The first was the principle of purposive, associated habits. According to this principle, apparently aimless expressions of action, like the gnashing of teeth in anger, were to be traced back to originally purposive action, such as biting. These actions were supposed to be inherited even when they were performed only symbolically. The second principle, that of contrast, endeavored to explain those actions which could not be derived from the purposive principle. According to Darwin, there is a tendency for contrasting actions to parallel contrasting emotions. The third principle was that of the direct activity of the nervous system, according to which a mental stimulus is transmitted to the motor organs without the intercession of will. This principle explains shivering or perspiring with fear. Darwin's theories have had a great and stimulating effect even though modern criticism has picked them to pieces.

Valuable as all this psychomotor research was, it had only a peripheral significance for psychology. Not until the end of the nineteenth century did the psychomotor principle really influence psychology.

WILLIAM JAMES AS THE FOUNDER OF A PSYCHOMOTOR PSYCHOLOGY

1. The first pioneering system of psychology in which action and movement were evaluated in their full significance was that of William James whose theories were disseminated

throughout the world in the two substantial volumes of his *Principles of Psychology* (1890–92). Of course it has been customary among the more radical "psychomotorists," especially the behaviorists, to treat James as an "introspectionist," but this is unjust, as we shall endeavor to show. To be sure, James tried to apprehend consciousness through introspection, and incidentally became a predominant critic of the atomizing analysis of consciousness, as we have shown in the first part of this book. However, we do not touch upon James's positive, creative accomplishment in psychology until we realize his emphasis upon the relationship of mind to physical action. Here he actually discovered new territory, even though he had been influenced by Bain, Fouillée, and others.

It is highly significant that James's name first came to the notice of the international world when, in 1884, in *Mind*, he asked the question, "What is an emotion?" His answer was that an emotion is the becoming aware of visceral phenomena. His originality is undiminished by the fact that at almost the same time a Dane by the name of Carl Lange presented a similar theory in his book *Om Sindsbevoegelser* (*Concerning Emotions*) (1885), which appeared in Germany in 1887 but was not published in English until 1922, when it was included with the James theory under the single format of *The Emotions*. James did not explain merely the emotions from an essentially motor viewpoint, but also included habits, instinct, and will; yet he never went so far as to eliminate consciousness completely.

From this point of view, the main thesis of James's system was embodied in his sentence: "All consciousness is motor." This thesis was further elaborated by the statement "that every possible feeling produces a movement, and that the movement is a movement of the entire organism, and of each and all of its parts." This conception is as "totalitarian" as anything can possibly be, not only in a psychological but also in a physiological sense. Physiologically, James regarded the organism as a machine whose function it was to transpose stimuli into responses. The conscious part of our life represents the middle or central part of these mechanical processes, inasmuch as it serves to adapt the response to the situation. Consciousness is bound up with processes of the cerebral hemispheres in which the important factor of memory is localized. This may sound mechanistic, but James's psychology, as we shall see, was certainly not a mechanistic system.

At first James confined himself entirely to the mechanistic principle, a proof of his desire for strict exactitude. He recognized the significance of habits which he described as automatisms, "due to pathways through the nerve centers," although he added that they were not dependent upon ob-served sensations. However, habits reduce conscious atten-tion and simplify movements, and are thus agencies of economy. The fact that James dwelt upon the ethical and pedagogical significance of habit was a procedure far re-moved from that of the psychologists of pure consciousness. He recommended making valuable conduct as automatic as possible in order to have the body as an ally and not as an enemy.

Although this has a fairly behavioristic sound, James did not deny the influence of consciousness upon actions. On the contrary, he estimated this influence much higher than any other theorist of consciousness. He wrote that every process occurring anywhere in the central spheres radiates in all directions and in some manner affects the whole organism by increasing or diminishing its activity.

James distinguished three kinds of centrally aroused actions:

   a. expression of emotions.
   b. instinctive actions.
   c. voluntary actions.

2. James's motor theory of the emotions is extremely original and controversial. Strangely enough he separated emotions from instincts even though he was distinctly

aware of their relationship, since they are both closely allied to physical movements. James defined an emotion as a response confined to the body of the individual, whereas an instinctive response goes further and strives to enter into a practical relationship with the stimulating object. Postponing our criticism of this definition, we continue with our exposition of James's version of the emotions.

From the standpoint of introspection, emotions present themselves in infinite multiplicity and profusion. Viewed through consciousness they are scarcely to be classified. We must therefore select another criterion and view emotions in their external manifestations, in so-called "expressive gestures." The popular conception is that the perception of some fact arouses an emotional state of consciousness and that this emotional state of consciousness in turn gives rise to the expressive gesture. Contrary to this, James insisted that the sequence was to be conceived in quite a different fashion: physical actions follow directly upon perception, and emotional states of consciousness are only the concomitants of these actions. Indulging his inclination for paradoxes, James wrote: "We do not weep because we are sad, but we are sad because we weep." This particular phrase contributed to the misunderstanding of his theory, because "weeping" was considered to be only the secretion of tears, whereas James rightly took into account the abundance of inner physical occurrences which are also part of "weeping."

Emotion is, therefore, the becoming aware of a bodily state and is based upon a purely bodily cause. "Our whole cubic capacity is sensibly alive; and each morsel of it contributes its pulsations of feeling, dim or sharp, pleasant, painful or dubious, to that sense of personality that every one of us unfailingly carries with him." The infinite number of components is what makes it so difficult to describe exhaustively the complete expression of an emotion. There are not merely the muscles and the neural impulses which activate them, but also the skin, the glands, the heart, and other visceral organs. Therefore emotions are so extremely diverse, even in a single individual, because their physiological components depend upon the entire constitution.

William James's psychomotor theory of the emotions attracted the attention of the entire world of science. Psychologists of pure consciousness were in a furor. In their favorite way, they first made their own distorted caricature of the "peripheral" theory of emotion and then blasted it to pieces. Among the sharpest critics of the Jamesian theory was Wundt, who took decided issue with the motor theory of emotions. Wundt raised three objections: first, emotions can arise which are perfectly clear in regard to direction and quality while their concomitant gestures are only in an incipient stage. Second, thoroughly different emotions have closely coinciding expressive symptoms. And third, certain expressive gestures can be produced experimentally without the appearance of the corresponding emotions.

These arguments are a gross distortion of James's theory. In the first place, the externally visible gestures "in an incipient stage" do not at all have determinant significance for the emotion. Emotion, according to James, is conditioned by visceral and circulatory action. For this reason alone, the name of "peripheral" theory of emotion would be fallacious. Peripheral action is often not at all determinant but rather derivative with reference to the emotion.

James himself, unfortunately, did not draw this distinction. External weeping, for example, does not merely determine pain but often eases it. This, however, does not preclude the possibility of inner action, which is scarcely perceptible on the surface and which precedes the secretion of tears, from having an emotional significance. More than anything else, one marvels at Wundt's contention that such diverse emotions as exultant joy, excitement, and anger, "have closely coinciding expressive symptoms." This is indicative of such deficient observation that it is useless wasting time over it beyond noting that such coincidence merely includes a few external symptoms and does not at all take into consideration the innumerable inner processes.

The argument that experimentally aroused gestures do not bring on an emotion is invalid because in experiment only a part of the whole motor system can be aroused. And, furthermore, the inner movements which are so very decisive are scarcely accessible to experiment. Naturally, the Jamesian theory of emotion was not ultimately perfected and underwent a great many improvements; but we must accord James the honor of having been the first to recognize the significance of action with respect to emotion.

3. James defined instincts as the capacity for performing purposive actions without any foresight of the purpose. In contrast to the doctrine of the immutability of instincts as regards their previous conditioning, James granted a certain modifiability of instincts through experience. Of course, such modification comes about through the interplay of several instincts, because the instincts stand in a certain contrast so that they can reciprocally retard or advance each other. Instincts can also be modified through habit. James laid particular stress upon his law of the transitoriness of instincts. According to this law, instincts mature to a certain point and then disappear again if they have not been transposed into fixed habits. Contrary to a frequently made assumption, man possesses not fewer but more instincts than animals. It is the task of education to change innate reactions so that they become more adaptable or are replaced by other kinds of reactions. A supplementary task is to effect the transition of instinctive actions into voluntary ones.

4. This brings us to the psychology of will which is also a brilliant chapter in James's work. Here, too, he vigorously emphasized the essential importance of action, even if he did term voluntary actions "secondary" in contrast to "primary" reflexes, instincts, and acts of expression. He rigorously denied the existence of a specific capacity of will

without whose fiat no action would be possible. On the contrary, every state of consciousness, whether it be an idea, perception, or feeling, has its "motor cue," that is, the tendency to discharge itself into a motor effect. There need not always be an outward action; an inner reaction may follow just as well; indeed, James claimed that the tendency of all states of consciousness to express themselves in outward or inward action is one of the most fundamental tenets of modern psychology.

If there is but a single content in the consciousness, the ideomotor action follows directly. Should there be several ideas in play together, a conflict between impulses and inhibitions sets in. Voluntary action is always a resultant of the antagonistic struggle between impulses and inhibitions. Should the impulses predominate, the result is an uninhibited (precipitate) will; should the inhibitions predominate, we have an inhibited (obstructed) will. The former, in extreme cases, is indicative of mania, and the latter, of melancholia.

It was only an apparent contradiction of his motor theory of will for James to designate attention and thought as the secret of will. The act of decision was supposed to consist in fixing upon a single one of the conflicting ideas by means of attention. With this supposition James broke with his former straight-laced mechanism and made a modest contribution to the doctrine of free will, a contribution that later was to be of the greatest significance. As he himself said, it is sufficient for the chain of causal determination to be broken at only one tiny link to make it ever after impossible to speak of the absolute determination of mental phenomena. It goes without saying that this was the very point at which James's mechanistic opponents took their departure from him.

5. Although James, in his theory of perception and thought, did not carry out the motor interpretation as energetically as many of his successors, still his "pragmatism" can only

be understood within the context of his motor psychology. With this epistemological theory, James, at the beginning of the twentieth century, agitated the scientific world no less than he had previously done with his psychology of the emotions. "Pragmatism," which James diffidently called "a new name for some old ways of thinking," consists, in brief, in seeking the truth of a doctrine in its practical corroboration; that is to say, neither formal logical criteria nor intuitive consciousness of truth, but only action determines what is true. However, as all action is in some way related to motion, the relation of pragmatism to psychomotor psychology is obvious.

It appears that James himself was not entirely aware of this relationship. By seeking the essence of "truth" not in the coincidence of consciousness and reality but in its practical verification, James transplanted the problem (as he had done in his psychology) from the sphere of consciousness to the sphere of action, that is, useful action. The practical utility of an idea alone determines its truth. Pragmatism is, so to speak, a philosophy of the working hypothesis. Truth consists in the possibility of working with a theory in the most economical fashion. In any event, James's struggle against rationalistic epistemology takes place on the same plane as his struggle against the one-sided doctrine of consciousness in psychology.

6. An evaluation of James's psychology as a whole is difficult because, in spite of its remarkable presentation, it was not a complete whole. There were many gaps. For example, he never devoted a complete treatment to the simple feelings of pleasure and unpleasure. And his psychology was not free from contradictions. Of course McDougall was too summary in saying that there were two Jameses: "James the physiologist and sensationist psychologist, and James the author of the purposive psychology which was the root of his pragmatic philosophy." There were many more Jameses than that!

James fought against "mosaic" psychology as a psychologist of totality, but for all that still remained at times within the confines of associationism. In his chief work the unconscious played no essential rôle, and was not accorded complete recognition until James turned to the psychology of religion. There were many other such contradictions in James. Although we have here emphasized the psycho-motor aspect of his psychology, we are aware that this does not exhaust his entire system. It is this particular side, however, that exercised the greatest influence upon his contemporaries and successors.

Even the extremely motoristic behaviorists who fought against James can trace their origin to him, for compared to the psychologists of pure consciousness, he was a decided behaviorist, although, of course, not a theorist of purely mechanical conduct. In his *Varieties of Religious Experience* he even conceived religion as a kind of conduct, conduct toward the whole universe. What appears to us to be contradictory in his system was essentially due to the fact that he readily assimilated English, German, French, and American influences which he united into original and daring combinations. For all that, however, there was at bottom only one William James, a vital, fascinating personality standing back of every contradiction and expressing itself in every phrase. James, who strove to envisage a pluralistic universe, was himself a pluralistic personality enabled to view things from the most diverse points of vantage; but no matter which standpoint he adopted, it was always backed up by his whole living individuality.

AMERICAN FUNCTIONALISM

1. In William James's multifarious system were hidden the germs of many new tendencies. To be sure, James founded no school like Wundt or Titchener. He was in no respect a schoolmaster, and his greatest asset, his original personality, could not be taught to anyone. But inspiration

radiated from him in all directions, and the most disparate groups were alternately able to invoke him as their sworn ally or to take umbrage at him. We shall first discuss a few psychologists and psychological groups who were inspired by James in a positive way.

The tendencies toward an individualistic conception of mental life were fostered by M. W. Calkins and others. The further development of psychomotor psychology is especially interesting for us here. The first to be mentioned is James's colleague, H. Münsterberg of Harvard University, who did not dedicate his *Principles of Psychology* to William James merely as a casual gesture. Münsterberg was called from Germany to America in 1892 after he had published a book on *Voluntary Action* (1889), which was still strictly mechanistic in its temper..In his chief work on psychology, however, the strong influence of his system of philosophy, a sort of neo-Fichtean theory of values, was already noticeable. We cannot, at this juncture, go into the exhaustive discussion of his psychological principles and his distinction between the physical and the psychological worlds. Negatively, according to Münsterberg, the physical is distinguished from the mental in that the former is spatial while the latter is nonspatial. The positive distinction lies in the fact that the physical is universally distributed while the mental is individually distributed.

Here we are concerned only with Münsterberg's "actionistic psychology," which further developed the realm of psychomotor ideas. Münsterberg had no desire to discard the sensory psychology of consciousness, but merely to expand it by emphasizing the significance of motor phenomena. The quality of a sensation, Münsterberg claimed, depends upon a specific nerve stimulus, and its intensity upon the quantitative aspect of the stimulus; but the sensation's vividness is dependent upon the induced motor response. No sensation can occur without causing a variation in our complex of action and tension, even if it be only a glance, a verbal impulse, the momentary paralysis of the vocal cords, or the bending of a finger. This internal motor complex presents itself as an antagonistic interplay of intensification and inhibition which decides whether a sensation goes over into consciousness or not. The sensation's shade of value depends upon the motor response.

It is obvious that Münsterberg, going beyond James in this point, attempted to explain perception, too, from the psychomotor point of view. Unfortunately, he allowed his chief psychological work to end with the publication of the first volume, so that we have no complete picture of his entire doctrine. However, it is quite probable that his subsequent interest in psychotechnical problems was also bound up with his fundamentally psychomotor point of view.

2. The American school of functional psychology was inspired by James, although not founded by him. (That this school is not to be confused with German functional or actional psychology has already been mentioned.) To the American functionalists, function is a biopsychological concept. Functionalism developed as a countermovement against Titchener's "structuralism." (Structuralism, too, is different from German structural psychology which is somewhat similar to German functional psychology!) In this chapter we shall use the terms in their American sense, while in the following chapter we shall adhere to German usage.

American functionalism was founded by John Dewey, who is also prominent as a philosopher and pedagogue, his philosophy being significantly similar to pragmatism. Dewey (born 1859) had already published psychological works in the '80's. But as a functionalist, he did not attain prominence until 1896, when his essay on" The Reflex Arc Concept in Psychology" appeared in the *Psychological Review*. In this essay, Dewey not only attacked atomistic psychology in general, but he also denied that the reflex arc could be neatly divided into stimulus and response. Furthermore, he insisted that totalitarian actions must not be broken up into reflex arcs, and that it is impossible to separate whole combinations from their past and future. In short, Dewey completely adopted the standpoint of a totalitarian psychologist. As such, he further disputed the notion of dualism and viewed man always within the context of a given situation toward which he maintains a purposive attitude.

Dewey studied the physiopsychic organism in its vital, teleological relation to environment. The presumptive coordination of stimulus and response is an organization of means with reference to some comprehensible end. What is separated out as a stimulus is in reality dependent upon the motor response, for the stimulus is not a stimulus until the motor response lets it become one. In this contention, Dewey showed a point of resemblance to Münsterberg.

Dewey's totalitarian attitude caused him to view the individual not as segregated from other individuals but within a social context. And so he was necessarily impelled toward a system of social psychology which he did not elaborate until later, and which we shall not discuss until we come to the evolution of social psychology.

3. J. R. Angell (born 1869) was another member of the functionalist group. Much more distinctly than in his popular textbook of psychology, Angell championed the principles of functionalism in his address on "The Province of Functional Psychology" delivered in 1906. Here he presented three conceptions of functional psychology. Functionalism can first of all be understood as the "psychology of mental operations in contrast to the psychology of mental elements" wherein we not only ask about the "what" but also question the "why." Secondly, functionalism is that branch of psychology which searches for the "fundamental utilities of consciousness" in which the mind intermediates between the environment and the requirements of the organism; for the function of consciousness is that of adaptation to what is new. Whereas these definitions limit functionalism to consciousness, there is a third possible definition which includes

the whole psychophysical organism with its unconscious habits. This triple separation is a matter of theory to Angell. In practice, the different forms of functionalism always intermingle.

Functionalistic features are also discernible in other psychologists who do not belong to the school itself. Thus, G. T. Ladd was related to the functionalists in his emphasis upon the biological, teleological, and personal aspects of consciousness. In the meanwhile, functionalism was replaced as the cynosure of interest in America by a much more radical tendency, behaviorism.

BEHAVIORISM

1. As far back as William James, the relation of consciousness to action, which had been an absolute first principle of consciousness in associationist psychology, was altered greatly in favor of action. As often happens in such developments, there was a tendency to go to extremes. And thus the progression of James, Münsterberg, and Dewey was continued in the school of "behaviorism." The central thesis of behaviorism is that only movements or "conduct" are the subject matter of psychology, but not consciousness which is, so to speak, a superfluous fantasm. This is a highly remarkable reversal of facts. Whereas the older sensationalists and introspectionists regarded consciousness as the only certainty, and declared all cognition of objects and even of one's own body to be derivative, the behaviorists contend that consciousness is a much too uncertain foundation upon which to construct a science. Indeed, many behaviorists ignore consciousness entirely. They regard the human being as a mere automaton. The behaviorists do not engage merely in the study of a psychology without a soul, as did the associationists; theirs is also a psychology without consciousness.

We shall first trace these curious developments historically. To begin with, behaviorism originated in the evolution of experimental psychology. Experimental psychology had tried to eliminate introspection in favor of experiment, but in practice it had been to all intents and purposes only introspectively experimental, as with Wundt and his contemporaries. Most of these "experiments" consisted in creating some sort of artificial stimulus and having the experiment subject tell what kind of state of consciousness he subsequently experienced.

This procedure gradually changed until the emphasis of the experiment was shifted to "performance." The introspectively reported experiment was replaced by a performance experiment. The method of testing no longer concerned itself with the states of consciousness produced by these tests; it merely took the tests as objective data, compared these data, and tabulated them. If any inferences were made concerning mental data, the tendency was not to include pure states of consciousness but only dispositions, talents, and skills, which are at least not wholly conscious. Experiment had changed its center of interest from subjectivity to objectivity. Behaviorism is the continuation of this tendency. It deliberately shuns the data of subjectivity.

A second historical trend leading toward behaviorism was found in child and animal psychology. No one expected children or animals to report on their inner states, and thus it became necessary to observe their external conduct. Animal psychology particularly was studied in America by Thorndike, Yerkes, Margaret F. Washburn, and others. With animals and children the introspective method was completely inadequate. Prebehavioristic psychology interpreted conduct in subjective terms: behaviorism rejected this method as unscientific. We must certainly admit that in the practical conduct of life, which we know as the understanding of human nature, objective observation of others is a necessary procedure. Our understanding of other human beings has always been governed by our appreciation of their conduct. Behaviorism raised this prescientific procedure into a scientific method, in the course of which it precluded all subjectivistic "interpretation."

A third tendency leading toward behaviorism was of a philosophical nature. We have witnessed how psychology gradually developed into an exact science from the vague chaos of theological and metaphysical speculation. According to behaviorism, this development was never completed. Watson is of the opinion that modern introspective psychologists have never rid themselves of religious metaphysics and are still just as much dualists as the primitive medicine men, even if, like Wundt, they use the term "consciousness" instead of "soul." But just as a great many atheists make atheism an exceedingly bigoted religion and dogma, so, Watson, too, is oblivious of the fact that his case against religion and metaphysics derives from a very dogmatic philosophy. Watson is the dogmatic champion of a fanatical ultra-pragmatism.

2. The following is a condensed presentation of behaviorism according to the system of J. B. Watson.

The point of departure is observation of conduct, of all that the human being does and says. For "saying" is also a kind of "doing," and is therefore a kind of conduct. Speaking out loud or talking to oneself (thinking) is just as objective a form of conduct as playing football.

With respect to such conduct, the behaviorist asks whether conduct is to be regarded as stimulus or as response. The stimulus can originate from some external object or from changes in the physiological conditions of the living being. The response is everything that the living being does. One of the central problems of behaviorism is the study of the constantly growing field of stimuli to which the individual reacts. Whether a stimulus becomes effective, however, depends upon the organism's ability to react. Responses are either internal or external, learned or unlearned. They can also be classified according to the sense organs, as visual, kinesthetic, and the like. The chief aim

of behavioristic psychology is to predict which response
follows upon a given stimulus or, in the perception of a
response, to determine which stimulus induced this response.

This is sufficient to show the essentially practical attitude
of the behaviorists. They are not concerned with theoretical
insights but with practical purposes. That is why the behaviorists are not satisfied with the observation of responses;
they must also create and transform these responses.

The behaviorist also studies what are known as the
"higher mental processes." Thus, he considers the instincts,
for example; but only in order to discard them as academic
and irrelevant. To the behaviorist, instincts are the unlearned, innate paraphernalia of man. Behaviorism asks
whether all types of the species *homo sapiens* respond with
the same reactions to the same stimuli. On this question,
Watson admits that there are individual differences in the
structure of human beings, but he traces them back to habit
impressions which begin in embryonic life. Habit impressions continue to play an important rôle in young children;
this leads Watson to the assumption that older views concerning inherited and learned conduct must be definitely
discarded. In the old conflict between nativists and empiricists, Watson thus decides in favor of a thoroughgoing
empiricism.

Watson also incorporates the emotions into his system,
or more correctly, he disposes of them as he disposes of the
instincts as special mental processes. Emotions are reducible
to movements of the eyes, arms, legs, and the torso, and
especially to visceral and glandular functions. The "cold
sweat" of fear, the thumping heart of the lover, and similar
data are not literary phrases but actual observations.
Whereas James assumed the coexistence of states of consciousness, Watson disposes of the idea as an "introverted
standpoint." The opinion that such responses are congenital
is rejected as undemonstrable in much the same fashion as
Watson treated the instincts. On the contrary, he claims

emotional responses develop through habituation to external conditions. It is because of the cryptic inaccessibility of visceral phenomena that society has not yet found the means to improve them. Notwithstanding this, behaviorism purports to educate emotional responses. Examples are cited and the reader may therefore hope that in the future all people will be reared as moral beings through the readjustment of their endocrine glands and their inner visceral functions.

One might expect that thinking would present insuperable obstacles to the behaviorists. For centuries philosophers have accustomed us to regard thinking as something entirely nonphysical. But J. B. Watson does not let such considerations disturb him. He declares bluntly that what psychologists have until now called thinking is nothing else than speaking to oneself. The term "thinking" must synoptically include all verbal conduct even if this is performed subvocally. The creation of poems and brilliant essays is accomplished by the manipulation of words in ever changing combinations that finally result in a new form. Speech habits are only a partial factor within more complex forms of motor conduct. Memory is defined as the function of the verbal part of a habit whole; for whenever an individual thinks, his entire physical organization is also involved. It would therefore be impossible to think without words in any form, be it manual or visceral. According to Watson, this motor explanation practically dissolves the "fiction" of a mental life.

Since thinking as a mental act has thus been exorcised out of existence, there is not the slightest difficulty in representing man as an "organically-bound, tuned-up machine." (Even the logical contradiction of such a definition of terms is compatible with Watson's theory of thinking.) Personality is defined as the sum of activities revealed by constant observation of conduct over a sufficiently long period of time. Personality is therefore only the end product of our habit systems. The method of behavioristic study of the personality consists in presenting a cross section of the "stream of activity" (Watson's version of the Jamesian "stream of consciousness"). The particular situation in which we happen to be always dominates us and serves to mobilize one or another of our dominant habit systems. The dominance of one of our powerful habit systems is called "attention." The only way to change the personality is to change the environment in such a manner that new habits are formed. Some day, when behaviorism has come into its own, there will be hospitals of plastic surgery for the personality. The behavioristic treatment of personality will then hold the same rank as medicine and surgery.

Thus, behaviorism shows us the way to a paradise on earth, for it offers us a basis for a more wholesome existence. Prophetically Watson exclaims: "I should like to be able to show you the rich and splendid individual that we could make out of every healthy child if we would let it grow by itself and then place it in an environment favorable to its development—an environment free of legendary folk tales about events thousands of years old, uninhibited by shameful political history, and unhampered by senseless customs and traditions. The world will change when it rears its children not in a licentious freedom but in the freedom of behaviorism!"

3. I have given a thoroughly behavioristic exposition of the ideological trend of behaviorism, for the most part in Watson's own words. And I have done this without irony, something which the behaviorist, incidentally, has scarcely any right to understand, according to his own principle; for in irony speaking and thinking are not identical but are antagonistic. At any rate, it is obvious that behaviorism, in spite of all its eloquent scientific pretensions, ultimately resolves itself into a matter of prophecy. Of all the paradises promised us by clerics and philosophers, the utopia of behaviorism impresses me as the most boring, because it transforms the universe into a machine shop. Conscious-

ness does not exist, neither does pain nor fear, but there is also no joy, and no hope.

It is our task, however, to portray behaviorism not as a prophecy but as a psychology. Watson himself is firmly convinced of the strictly scientific nature of his accomplishment. He himself raised a dangerous question when he asked: "Does the behavioristic point of view overlook anything psychological?" Watson answered his own question with a categorical "no!" Should we try to retort that there are such experiences as happiness, sadness, memories and hopes, dreams and moods, all of which can be apprehended (imperfectly to be sure) through the portrayal of demonstrable, physical, concomitant phenomena, Watson would counter with the charge that we ourselves do not know what we mean by these terms. He would accuse us of having accepted them uncritically as part of our social and literary tradition. But Watson is not very convincing, and more important yet in this connection, he is not even very scientific, nor behavioristic. In the first place, science must recognize the facts which exist. Even Watson will admit that he has upon some occasion become conscious of a toothache; else why should he visit the dentist? He might tell us that we do not know what we are talking about; then, of course, he would be admitting that knowing and talking do not always coincide and that one can think something different from what one says.

However, it is almost too much of a temptation to belabor the dogmas and vagaries of behaviorism, and so we shall dispense with any further negative criticism. From the historical point of view, we must decide the extent of behaviorism's positive accomplishment and its place in the development of modern psychology.

As a positive gain, let us consider the energetic observation of external conduct which, as a matter of fact, had been woefully neglected by the psychology of pure consciousness. The extreme associationists have no grounds for despising the behaviorists, because it is doubtful whether their portrayal of man as an associational mechanism is either better or more useful than the behavioristic portrayal of man as a mechanism of conduct. But the behaviorists are barking up the wrong tree when they attack William James, because it was he more than anyone else before him who had emphasized the importance of the study of psychomotor data. William James was a forerunner of behaviorism, although he never fell into its one-sided dogmatism. There is only one historically important fact more strongly emphasized by behaviorism than by James, and that is the totalitarian nature of every motor reaction. From the historical point of view, it is this emphasis which permits us to see in behaviorism a modern movement and not merely a retrogression to primitive mechanistic magic.

Just as the psychology of consciousness, since the turn of the century, progressed from the isolating anatomy of consciousness toward a totalitarian conception of mental life, so also behaviorism found itself on the road toward totality in contrast to the isolating psychoreflexology of the nineteenth century. Watson dwells upon this totalitarian conception with admirable clarity: "If you consult a physiological or anatomical textbook you will find that the human body has been thoroughly studied in every part, the digestive apparatus, the circulation of the blood, the respiratory system, the nervous system, and the like. The physiologist is obliged to work experimentally first upon one part of the body and then upon another. The student of behaviorism, on the contrary, works with the entire living body. It would be quite possible for him to pursue his studies entirely without a knowledge of the separate parts."

Through this emphasis on the totalitarian nature of every physical reaction, and the condemnation of the one-sided preference of the central nervous system exhibited by other psychologists, behaviorism has made several important contributions. Unfortunately, it detracts from the value of its totalitarian standpoint by its radical exclusion of all conscious experience from its studies.

Watson's thesis was first developed in 1913 in his work *Psychology as the Behaviorist Views It.* In 1914 appeared *Behavior, an Introduction to Comparative Psychology* and, in 1919, *Psychology from the Standpoint of a Behaviorist.* But Watson did not remain alone. He found allies in A. P. Weiss, E. B. Holt, E. C. Tolman, W. S. Hunter, Lashley, and others, who either defended the new school against the functionalists, structuralists, *Gestalt* psychologists, psychoanalysts, and others, or applied behavioristic methods to animal psychology, child psychology, psychopathology, and other fields. But opponents also arose, as, for example, McDougall and Roback.

RUSSIAN PSYCHOREFLEXOLOGY

1. Unquestionably the development of motor psychology originated chiefly in England and America. Because of this, attempts were very soon made to determine the relation between Anglo-Saxon racial traits and the motor school of psychology. It was claimed that the utilitarian character of the Englishman and the American impelled the savants of these races to seek out the motor processes of mental life. There is probably some degree of truth in this. However, one hesitates to accept it entirely in view of the fact that a very similar motor psychology, which also strove to eliminate consciousness, arose in Russia. This is particularly puzzling because the custom has been to characterize Russians, in contrast to Anglo-Saxons, as passive, indolent, and profoundly subjective emotionally. Of course there is the explanatory fact that the newest development in Russia, Bolshevism, is motivated by a thoroughly materialistic and mechanistic philosophy that regards all mental life in terms of cerebral acts. A symbol of this philosophy is the historic

fact that Lenin himself ordered his brain to be dissected for scientific purposes after his death. But we must also remember that the objective psychology of V. M. Bechterev dates back to long before the Bolshevist Revolution, and that I. P. Pavlov, the chief contemporary representative of Russian psychology, is by no means an absolute sympathizer with the Soviets.

2. I shall outline briefly the system of *Objective Psychology* (German translation, 1913) which V. M. Bechterev, Professor at St. Petersburg, presented under the name of "psychoreflexology." In a manner closely related to behaviorism, Bechterev set forth his aims: "We do not analyze consciousness with its inner experiences and its extensive flight of ideas which bear the human spirit upward toward the loftiest heights. Free from endeavors to penetrate the subjective world of dreams and fantasies, psychology offers prose instead of poetry. For psychology views neuropsychic functions exclusively from their external side and reduces them to associational reflexes of various descriptions. Notwithstanding all this, it seems to me that psychoreflexology holds the key to those functions which we have since time immemorial called 'mental' and which are surrounded by the halo of the immaterial or 'spiritual,' but which are now explained as reflex activities of the organism which have gradually and hereditarily evolved from the contractile movements of cellular protoplasm. This broadens our horizon much more than the farthest flight of subjective fancy, and correlates facts that until now have appeared to be isolated and contradictory."

No wonder the behaviorists hailed the psychoreflexologists as comrades in arms. The psychoreflexological view annihilated the pure psychology of consciousness. Although psychologists of consciousness had also aspired to elevate psychology to the status of an exact natural science, psychoreflexology consigned their work to limbo with the derisive epithets of poetry and fantasy. According to Bechterev, it is only in the form of psychoreflexology that psychology has the right to align itself with chemistry and physics. However, Bechterev did not entirely discard the study of consciousness. Far from that, he designated psychoreflexology as the link that bridges the gulf between objectively observed facts and the subjective world. Bechterev believed that future experiment would determine the relations between psychoreflexology and subjective experiences, with the elimination of all the fancies of the obsolete psychology of consciousness.

The standpoint of consciousness psychology was thus rejected by Bechterev: "The task of psychology consists in the recognition of all psychic occurrences in the broadest sense of the word, that is, both conscious and unconscious expressions of psychic activity." By "psychic" Bechterev did not merely mean the subjective, but also the objective and material functions of the brain which always accompany mental processes; he meant the "neuropsyche." The neuropsyche is the subject matter of the new science of psychoreflexology, which fundamentally eliminated all methods of introspection.

Consciousness is, therefore, no longer a criterion of the mental; the criterion is experience, that is, the conditioning of conduct upon the basis of previous experiences. (The question whether experience is possible without consciousness is not discussed.) The neuropsychic process is, therefore, distinguished from the simple reflex in that the former is based upon individual experience and the latter upon hereditary experience. Neuropsychic processes are reflexes whose arc includes the higher centers of the nervous system. Old channels are renewed and influence the new reaction. Thus each neuropsychic process consists of the following trisection:

a. the centripetal conductor.

b. cellular stimulation in the central organs (brain).

c. the centrifugal conductor.

The entire field of psychoreflexology is classified in the

following subdivisions of the type of reflex to be studied: first come simple reflexes and automatisms; then concentrative reflexes, then symbolic reflexes, and finally personal reflexes.

This is not the place to enumerate all the details of psychoreflexology. Bechterev takes into consideration all the ascertained data of the study of consciousness but translates them into the technical terms of physiology. What subjective psychology termed "attention," for example, Bechterev describes as "concentrative reflexes" comprising external and internal concentration. "Symbolic reflexes" are also involved with these. Symbolic reflexes consist of expressive gestures and speech, among other things. Just as the associationists explained speech comprehension by means of ideational complexes, psychoreflexology traced the comprehension of speech back to physiological "channels." In place of the ideational complex, we have the "channel complex."

What has been designated as thought, as analysis or synthesis, is based upon the related association of channels. Symbolization enables us to operate with combinations of impressions far removed from reality. The totality of the channels of organic associational reflexes represents the "personal sphere" about which a part of the externally stimulated reflexes is associatively grouped. The personality consists of two intimately related channel systems, one of which is closely linked to the organic sphere and the other to the social sphere. The higher the development of the neuropsyche, the more important becomes the participation of the social sphere of personality in the responses of the individual. Personality is the conditioning factor in deeds and actions.

In this fashion, psychoreflexology purports to show the strictly causal evolution of complex neuropsychic phenomena from simple reflexes. In man, this evolution is based on the systematic education of associational reflexes by means of life experience. Personal experience is nothing other than the aggregate of channels of bygone and partly inhibited association reflexes.

3. Next to Bechterev, the most important Russian reflexologist is I. P. Pavlov (born 1849) who, since 1903, has experimented extensively with animals, and who published the results of his work together with that of his assistants in *Conditioned Reflexes: an Investigation of the Physiological Activity of the Cerebral Cortex* (1927); and *Lectures on Conditioned Reflexes* (1928). The central theme of Pavlov's research is the "conditioned reflex," which might also be called the temporary or individual reflex in contrast to the ordinary fixed reflexes. The conditioned reflex consists of the creation of a connection or dependency between a specific external stimulus and a specific physiological activity which did not previously exist. Pavlov made a special study of the conditioned reflex with respect to the activity of the salivary glands in dogs. When a stimulus (say the pouring of acid into the dog's mouth) coincides in time with the feeding of a dog, after several such coincidences, the stimulus alone is sufficient to cause secretion of saliva. Even sound stimuli of a very specialized kind can influence the secretion of saliva to such a degree that the response does not follow when the sound is changed even slightly.

In such "conditioned reflexes" Pavlov sees the possibility of examining the entire activity of the cerebral hemispheres. Conditioned reflexes are brought about by the coöperation of responses and inhibitions. There are three types of inhibition: sleep inhibition, external, and internal inhibition. The chief aim of research is to determine the paths along which the neural process spreads or concentrates.

At this point we must consider Pavlov's attitude toward psychology. It is completely negative. There would be no point in stating that Pavlov stressed only physiological investigations were it not for the fact that he claimed that he could replace psychology with something better. Yet

Pavlov declares psychology to be utterly hopeless as a science of subjective states of consciousness. He believes, on the contrary, that all psychological problems can be solved with the methods of natural science. Meanwhile natural science itself ventured into new paths which brought it closer to psychology.

THE PSYCHOLOGY OF INSTINCT
IN AMERICA

1. Toward the end of the nineteenth century, the problem of instinct became more and more prominent in natural science. Zoölogists had observed such remarkable forms of conduct among the various animals that the description of these forms of conduct as innate reflex patterns became increasingly unsatisfactory. But even if conduct did consist of innate reflex patterns, the problem of their origin intruded itself, unless one assumed the existence of a Divine Clockmaker who had fitted these supposed mechanisms so perfectly together. To be sure, the evolutionists had endeavored to ascribe the origin of instincts to previous generations, but neo-Darwinism opposed this view with its proofs that acquired characteristics are not inherited. There were also those instances in which certain insects lay their eggs in a certain pierced larva but always die before they can even experience the results of their action. From the standpoint of the theory of evolution the fixed, purposively adapted instincts were very mysterious.

Lloyd Morgan's investigations in the '90's contributed new material to the problem of instinct, material which indicated that the instincts could no longer be considered as they had been heretofore. Morgan proved, for instance, that even the baby chick must learn to pick at grains of corn. And in the same manner, Loeb and Jennings contributed proofs of "learning" in lower animals.

Psychology at this time was very little concerned with the instincts. There were textbooks in which the word did not even occur! Since the field of psychology had been delimited to consciousness, and the instincts were by definition "unconscious," there really was no place for them in psychology. Motor psychology was not only able but was obliged to take up the problem of instincts in order to adhere to its own principles. We have already seen how William James devoted exhaustive discussions to the instincts, even though his line of demarcation between instincts and emotional actions was rather blurred. We have also seen how behaviorism denied the innateness of instincts.

2. McDougall, an Englishman who came to America, was the first to make instincts the focus of all psychological investigation. He did this in his *Introduction to Social Psychology* (1908). Subsequently, McDougall elaborated and refined his theory of instinct to a further extent. In 1923 appeared *An Outline of Psychology* in which all psychology was interpreted in terms of the problem of instinct.

A cursory glance at McDougall's chief work might lead one to consider him a behaviorist, because several of his opening chapters treat of "conduct," from that of the lower animals up to the behavior of primitive man. But his introductory definition of "conduct" is distinctly antibehavioristic. The distinctive traits of conduct are enumerated as: duration of activity independent of the stimulus; change of direction in durative actions; cessation of action as soon as a specific change of situation is reached; preparation for the new situation toward the attainment of which the action is directed; and finally, improvement in conduct when repeated under similar circumstances. All these taken together comprise the "purposiveness" of conduct, which in turn includes foresight. The basic datum of psychology is, therefore, "purposive action." This must be sharply distinguished from mechanistic reflexes. It is not an isolated process but (and this is the ultimate trait of action) the coöperation of vital energies in the whole organism.

McDougall's contrast with behaviorism is obvious. The

basic subject matter of psychology is not mechanical reflexes. McDougall denies that it is possible to grasp the notion of a higher mental life by means of mechanistic thinking. He brings the instincts prominently to the fore, instincts which he defines as innate capacities for purposive action. Intelligence, on the other hand, is the ability to vary innate impulses according to what individual experience has been in similar situations. The psychology of instinct refuses to make the strict separation of instinct from intelligence that Bergson required. Instinct and intelligence are indissolubly connected. Such a view is strengthened by observations on the lives of insects in which instinctive conduct predominates as a general rule, but is occasionally varied in an intelligent manner.

In vertebrates, the capacity for "learning" is of course much greater than in insects. Motor mechanisms are not instincts themselves but instruments of the instincts; for every instinctive impulse can employ several motor mechanisms. Thus an instinct cannot be defined by the kind of actions in which it is expressed, but by the kind of changes of situation of the animal which tends toward these actions and toward the ultimate goal, irrespective of which actions are involved.

Consequently, it is impossible to speak of a "play instinct" or an "imitative instinct" because they lack purposiveness. The real instincts are: the parental instinct, the fighting instinct, curiosity, self-preservation, repulsion, the instinct of escape, the gregarious instinct, primitive sympathy, the instinct of self-assertion, the instinct of subjugation, the mating instinct, the instinct of gain, the constructive instinct, the instinct of appeal, and several others. One of McDougall's main theses is that these instincts are either singly or collectively the motivators of all human activity. Even the faintest and calmest thought is ultimately rooted in instinct. The most complicated intellectual functions serve the gratification of instincts, and the pleasure-pain principle serves only in a minor capacity. Without instincts the organism would be an inert, lifeless mass. Instincts are the motivators and shapers of all individual and social life; in them dwells the central mystery of life, of mind, and of will.

The other fields of mental life are elucidated in accordance with this main thesis. Perception is a process of choosing from among the stimuli converging upon us, and indicates the presence of an object in the form of symbols. These stimuli are revised according to qualitative, spatial, and temporal patterns. Perception does not merely consist of sensations and other states of consciousness; its essential component is the "cognitive disposition."

All mental life is a process, an activity. It can, therefore, not be described by static concepts like "image," or "idea," but should be described by dynamic expressions, by verbs. Attention and interest are traceable to instincts. They are, therefore, not reducible to ideas or other intellectual data but to a union of strivings concentrated upon a single object.

Imagination on the one hand is a form of anticipation and on the other a form of remembering. But images are not the most important factors in imagination. What is known as remembering is only a mental act in which the relation to the past, inherent in all mental activity, emerges more distinctly. A good memory is equivalent to a well-organized mind. Memory, too, is based upon conations; for these are the motive forces of memory just as desire lends wings to the imagination.

McDougall also reduced the emotions to instincts. What appears as instinctive, physical conduct to external observation is accompanied by states of consciousness known as emotions. Thus, self-preservation corresponds to the escape instinct, fear or anger to the fighting instinct, sexual emotion or "love" to the mating instinct, and so forth.

Those emotions which can clearly be related directly to an instinct McDougall calls "primary emotions." But there are a great many emotions, such as joy, worry, disappointment, surprise, remorse, hope, and despair, which cannot be related to instincts without some difficulty. In order to distinguish these from the primary emotions, McDougall calls them "derived emotions." They are not closely linked to separate instincts but may be manifested during the course of any conation, and are independent both of the effect of the tendency and of new attitudes toward the object. These emotions are not original forces but derivative intermediate states.

With reference to the cognitive structure of the intellect, McDougall opposed the ideas of sensory psychology which portrayed the process of mental development as the evolution of special perceptions into more general ideas. According to McDougall, the opposite is true. Mental development begins with the recognition of a few fairly general objects and only develops gradually to the point of apprehending more concrete objects and their special qualities.

The processes of development may be classified in three types: discrimination, apperception, and association. The first two govern the logical structure of the mind in so far as it reflects things and qualities, differences and similarities. The temporal order between objects is effected by means of association which unites the dispositions of the logical structure by means of a system of "cross connections." The capacity of reasoning consists, psychologically speaking, of the conditioning of a judgment or of a new belief by older beliefs. The system of beliefs is never completely uniform in anyone, since different aspects of life require different systems of belief.

The conclusion of McDougall's psychology is a presentation of the development of sentiments and the organization of character. Character is a system of "conative tendencies." The "units" of character are "sentiments" or complexes. Sentiments, according to McDougall, are all acquired conative tendencies, whereas complexes are those sentiments which are somehow pathological. Every sentiment includes the individual tendency to experience certain feelings and wishes in regard to a specific object. Such sentiments are: hate, love, contempt, respect, friendship, "the tender passion," self-esteem, and moral sentiments. The ideal of character is an harmonious system of moral sentiments. Conscience is the moral character. Will is not a separate capacity but the "character in action."

Obviously, it is only with reservations that we can speak of McDougall's instinct psychology as a psychomotor system. In the first place, he often includes consciousness in his discussion; and in the second place, the organic coöperation of instincts points toward an unconscious but not purely material unity. A new and rising school of psychology uses the old, long-condemned name of "soul" to designate this unity. Thus, McDougall can be said to belong, in some measure, to the school of "egopsychologists."

McDougall's instinct psychology was by no means accepted without opposition. Knight Dunlap, in the *Journal of Abnormal and Social Psychology* (1919), asked: "Are There Any Instincts?" and J. Kuo, in the *Journal of Philosophy* (1921), spoke even more decidedly of "Giving up Instincts in Psychology." Tolmann's rebuttal followed in the *Journal of Abnormal and Social Psychology* (1922).

3. After the appearance of McDougall's *Social Psychology* but before the publication of his *Outlines*, Thorndike, the famous animal psychologist, drew up in 1913 a system of instinct psychology which is closely related to behaviorism. This system is incorporated as the first part of his *Educational Psychology* under the title of *The Original Nature of Man*. Thorndike's premise is that human beings, disregarding all education, are provided with "tendencies" to feel and to act under certain circumstances. These unacquired tendencies are called reflexes, instincts, or capacities, according to their degree of definiteness. Of course, most situations in life are not simple enough to release only one reaction; tendencies operate together in manifold combinations. Like McDougall, Thorndike drew up a classification of the human instincts and capacities. Since his chief concern was pedagogical, Thorndike devoted most of his dis-

cussion to the psychology of learning, the details of which we shall not go into here. Suffice it to say that the course of Thorndike's argument led him to the consideration of individual differences. Thus, like McDougall, he embarked upon a problem that is no longer within the sphere of conduct psychology but which points toward a permanent structure of the mind.

4. Still closer to this problem is the *Dynamic Psychology* of R. S. Woodworth, published in 1918, in which a distinction is made between "drives" and "mechanisms." The "mechanism" is the manner in which we do something; the "drive" is the impulse which causes us to do something. This is illustrated by the example of machine in which the motive power corresponds to the "drive" which sets the mechanism in motion. In mental life, however, the drive cannot always be separated from the mechanism; the drive is an already stimulated mechanism and can thus become the stimulus for other mechanisms.

Woodworth examined the innate "equipment" of man and distinguished it from his acquired equipment. In contradistinction to McDougall, Woodworth emphasized the view that the objective environment has greater significance in the specialization of conduct. Nevertheless, personality is not regarded as a "collection of tendencies with no organization and no control. A well integrated personality is organized about its master motives, these acting as selective agencies with respect to other tendencies."

5. An historical examination of instinct psychology, as construed by its most eminent representative, McDougall, is most illuminating if we compare its tenets to behaviorism. As a matter of fact, McDougall frequently crossed critical blades with Watson. Both of these psychologists resemble each other in that they adopt psychomotor data as their point of departure, but they are radically different in the further development of their systems. Their differences are

the age-old differences of viewpoint recurring anew in the new field of motor psychology.

The first difference involved is the contradiction between mechanism and teleology. Behaviorism is, of course, radically mechanistic, whereas instinct psychology lays stress upon the factor of "purposiveness." A further difference is the ancient and much disputed contradiction between "empiricism" and "nativism." The behaviorists and psychoreflexologists emphasize the importance of experience and endeavor to limit the field of innate capacities as far as possible. Instinct psychology, on the other hand, positively recognizes an innate structure of the soul. Notwithstanding these fundamental differences, there are still elements in common which mark these two movements as children of the twentieth century; they regard conduct not isolatively but from a totalitarian point of view. Behaviorism, to be sure, is inclined to regard this totality as an innate mechanism, while instinct psychology attempts to penetrate the façade of conduct to find an innate central factor formerly (and now once again) called the "soul." Even though this inference was not explicitly mentioned by instinct psychology, McDougall and his school were at least headed in a direction with which we shall become acquainted later under the name of "the psychology with a soul."

PSYCHOMOTOR PSYCHOLOGY IN FRANCE

1. So far we have traced the development of psychomotor psychology in America where it was cultivated more than anywhere else. But in the meanwhile this line of research was not neglected in Europe. We shall begin with France where psychomotor research went its own individual way.

The distinctive characteristic of French psychology is that it has pursued its research chiefly in close relation with psychiatry. French psychology was given to the exact observation of physiological processes. Such observation was intensively conducted by Charcot, the most famous of

French psychiatrists, who made a special study of the peculiar lapses of motor capacity in hysteria, and who enriched normal psychology by his description of a special motor type of personality. Charcot's inspiration was passed on to Janet. Theodule Ribot (1839–1916) was another of his disciples.

Ribot had from the very beginning recommended an objective method in psychology to supplement the subjective one. In his earlier works he had already stressed the significance of motor processes as, for example, in his *Psychologie de l'attention* (1888), where he stressed the motor factors of attention. In his later period, introduced by his *Psychologie des sentiments* (1896), he eagerly availed himself of the influence of William James and his doctrine of the motor basis of emotions. In all emotional states, Ribot distinguished two elements: the motor processes, which are primary, and the phenomena of consciousness, which are secondary. With this as a premise, Ribot outlined a system of emotional life which, in his opinion, conditioned all mental life.

Ribot was an opponent of pure intellectualism and it was his belief that feelings and instincts govern the entire mental conduct of man. Even the creative imagination of artists and scholars, which he studied in his *Essai sur l'imagination créatrice* (1900), is of an essentially motor emotional nature. Every creation of fancy has a motor origin. Imagination in the mental sphere is the same as will in the motor sphere because both are subjective, personal, and teleological.

2. The most original theory of French psychomotor psychology and instinct psychology was advanced by the philosopher Henri Bergson, whom we have already encountered as one of the three great critics of the older psychology of consciousness. Bergson contradicted the atomizing and spatializing of consciousness and stressed the temporal character of conscious states arranged in an or-

ganic whole in *"durée."* According to Bergson, memory operates beyond these conscious states as an immaterial metaphysical entity.

We are not concerned here with Bergson's metaphysics but with his psychology which is, to be sure, drenched through and through with metaphysics. His psychology is, just as in the case of his friend William James, essentially a psychomotor system. Bergson is an avowed dualist, since he correlates memory (*la mémoire pure*), as a metaphysical datum with the body, which he conceives essentially as a motor apparatus. "My body, destined to move objects, is a center of action which in itself cannot generate an idea. The objects surrounding my body reflect the possible actions which my body can exercise upon them." These possibilities of action, that is to say, motor acts, also govern perception, because perception is primarily an act of choice conditioned by the body's motor set toward objects. Anything that does not release an action is eliminated. Feelings, like pain, can be traced back to internal movements and actions. The subjectivity of feelings is due to their internal nature; the objectivity of perceptions is due to their external nature.

Meanwhile we have not yet reached the realm of the spirit in treating "pure perceptions," but are still in the realm of matter. We do not approach the mind until we include memory which preserves the past and extends it into the present within the individual consciousness. The question is now whether memory is a function of the brain and whether it merely yields a difference in intensity between perception and remembrance, or whether memory is something entirely different from a cerebral process, and whether there is an essential difference between perception and remembrance. Bergson sides with the second possibility.

Bergson's theory of instinct had an even greater vogue than his theory of memory. His theory of instinct derives from his biological views, but it also fruitfully influenced psychomotor theory. Just as he had shown the stark antithesis of perception and memory in his book *Matière et mémoire* (1896), Bergson developed a somewhat similar antithesis between intelligence and instinct in his greatest work, *L'Évolution créatrice* (1907). Intelligence and instinct are not different in degree but in kind. They are not, however, abstract capacities of consciousness, but stand in relation to action, albeit in entirely different ways. Intelligence serves in revising dead matter; it is the capacity to manufacture artificial objects, especially tools. Man should be called not *homo sapiens* but *homo faber* in order to emphasize clearly his difference from animals. Instinct, on the other hand, pertains to life which man apprehends through sympathy. Intelligence apprehends only the form; instinct penetrates to the core. The former is a mechanizing agency; the latter is organic.

We leave Bergson's metaphysics aside and pass on to his psychology, and yet even as a psychologist he belongs in our context only with reservations. His metaphysical dualism again asserts itself in his psychology, for he conceives of memory primarily as a metaphysical datum and only partially as a psychological one. Bergson nevertheless made important contributions to psychology in its psychomotor aspect. Both in perception and in conceptual thinking he ascribes especial significance to motor processes as, for example, when he views concepts merely as schemata whose function it is to serve practical action. Our whole body is a center of action and not of ideas. Our nervous system receives and gives out movements and actions and nothing else.

In spite of this emphasis upon motor activity, Bergson is by no manner of means a mechanist but distinctly a vitalist. This is especially evident in his theory of instinct. Whereas instincts, for the most part, had formerly been characterized as innate mechanisms, in Bergson instincts evolve from the *"élan vital"* and are directed toward life. Notwithstanding his rejection of mechanism, Bergson is not a finalist in the ordinary sense. He rejects the traditional doctrine of final causes as an inverse mechanism. Life is creative and indeterminate.

An interesting glimpse into Bergson's psychology is afforded by his brochure entitled *Le Rire*, which is not a purely psychological work in spite of its psychological theme. Together with the social factor in laughter, the motor factor is strongly emphasized. The comic is primarily revealed in actions, above all in mechanized actions; the mechanistic comprises the ridiculous and is thereby diametrically opposed to the organic. "The postures, gestures, and movements of the human body are ridiculous in proportion as the body reminds us of a machine." Thus, Bergson indirectly attacks mechanism in this work.

3. Our justification in referring to Bergson as a psychologist is based on his influence on psychology. This influence is revealed, for example, in the works of G. Dwelshauvers, who, in conjunction with Bergson, emphasized the totality and the organic connection of the mental life with the individual subject who experiences it. In his book entitled *La Synthèse mentale* (1908), he stated that there are no such things as psychic elements but that these elements only occur in synthesis. Roustan, too, in his *Leçons de psychologie* (1911), attacked psychophysical parallelism, sensationalism, and atomism, in an idiom closely related to Bergson's. In the field of psychopathology, C. Blondel in *La Conscience morbide* (1914) further propagated Bergsonian ideas.

G. Finnbogason, a native of Iceland, who in 1913 published a book entitled *L'Intelligence sympathique*, was a pupil of Bergson. Finnbogason utilized psychomotor psychology in a singular way to explain mutual understanding among humans. We understand the mental state of other persons only in the degree that we imitate their actions. Such imitation usually occurs unconsciously. Understanding lies not in thinking but in mimetic coexperiencing. Consequently, individual matters can be understood only through the *"intelligence sympathique"* and not through generalizing logic.

4. Although most French psychologists take psychomotor psychology into extensive consideration while doing full justice to consciousness (even to the extent of separating it from everything physical), there is no lack of investigators who demand a purely objective psychology and thus veer toward behaviorism. The leader of this group is Henri Piéron, the present Director of the Laboratory for Physiological Psychology at the Sorbonne.

Piéron's doctoral thesis treated *Le Problème physiologique du sommeil* (1913). In this thesis, sleep is explained as the interruption of sensorimotor functions which effects the disappearance of independent activity. It is typical of Piéron to have started with a study of sleep, that is, with a state of suspended consciousness. In his later works which deal with states ordinarily designated as "conscious," Piéron treats them as though consciousness played no rôle in them. He even maintains that he does not know what consciousness is.

Piéron rejects Bergson's theory of the pure, psychic essence of memory. He sees in memory only the intensification and relaxation of neural influence along specific channels. He even speaks of the memory of inorganic bodies and considers adaptation the essence of organism. Memory is a general process of nature. Human associative memory is distinguished from lower forms of memory only in degree, but can also develop into social memory. Like the reflexologists, Piéron stresses his pure, natural science standpoint, particularly in his work entitled *Thought and the Brain* (1923).

Although the French psychologists were not in intimate contact with America, it is obvious that in France, too, similar psychological tendencies and counter-tendencies recur. These contrasting tendencies are: mechanism and vitalism, instinct psychology and reflex psychology, atomistic psychology and organic psychology.

PSYCHOVITALISM IN GERMANY

1. For a long time German psychologists did not even broach the psychomotor problem. The fact that Germans feel more at home in the sphere of "pure" consciousness than in those spheres in which consciousness establishes contact with the external world is traceable to the abstract nature of the German character. The Wundt and Brentano schools and their modern offshoots in particular paid scant attention to the significance of motor phenomena in mental life.

The biologists, on the contrary, attacked the problem all the more energetically. In most universities a doctrine that regarded the instincts as rigid mechanisms predominated for a long time. However, toward the end of the century, a school of neo-Lamarckism arose which gradually evolved into a school of psycho-Lamarckism or psychovitalism. In contrast to Driesch's morphological vitalism, which primarily studied form structure and reduced it to psychoid but not psychic factors, psychovitalism begins with vital functions in which direct psychic factors, such as memory and even judgment, are operative. Form structure is explained secondarily in terms of function.

Lamarckism stands in contrast to Darwinism, which interprets apparent purposiveness mechanistically, by means of natural selection. Lamarckism, on the other hand, grants the existence of a certain teleology and interprets the metamorphosis of species by means of the hereditary effect of use and disuse of organs. Lamarckism is, therefore, a theory of functional adaptation; but we must keep in mind the fact that Lamarckism in its modern dress has very little to do with the teachings of Lamarck.

Modern biology has shown us many instances of an adaptation of functions followed by the consequent metamorphosis of organs. But Darwin's mechanistic interpretations do not suffice to explain them. Hence, psycho-Lamarckism invokes mental categories. The older psycho-Lamarckists were particularly bold in their use of psychological concepts.

Thus G. von Bunge in his textbook of *Physiological and Pathological Chemistry* (1876) remarked that even amœbæ exercise a choice among stimuli, which must be regarded as intelligent action. Bunge also assumed the existence of choice on the part of intestinal cells in the higher animals, a choice between the assimilable and the nonassimilable food elements. This factor of choice is not mechanistic but must be interpreted in analogy to mental life.

A. Pauly, in his *Darwinism and Lamarckism*, published in 1905, went even further. He endowed cells with a primary capacity of judgment on the strength of which they can utilize available means to counteract disturbances of vital equilibrium.

In recent times greater caution has been the rule. E. Becher, who can be considered a typical representative of psychovitalism, lays claim only to memory as a psychic aid. He begins with the analysis of simple actions in rudimentary forms of life. These actions are at first haphazard trials from which purposive actions are retained.

Pioneer work in this field was performed by the experimental studies of Herbert Jennings, the American biologist who investigated the conduct of the elementary forms of life with respect to stimuli to which they react. As opposed to J. Loeb's theory of tropisms, Jennings found that such conduct is fairly variable providing one does not merely look to the final result. Jennings showed that the simple reflex is not the most primary motor response, but that "trial actions" precede it. In several cases a kind of conduct is evinced that Jennings designated as "trial and error," because primary organisms cease to perform useless reactions and also appear to learn from experience.

Although psychovitalism includes memory, in other words, a psychic factor, we must not think of it only as conscious memory. When psychovitalism speaks of memory, it means a general function of organic substance. This notion was first formulated in an address delivered in 1870 before the Vienna Academy of Science by the great physiologist,

E. Hering. Hering propounded the thesis that memory is not really a faculty of consciousness but of the unconscious. Our experiences endure not as conscious images but as unconscious dispositions and become conscious only at times. Memory is the unconscious bond of unity connecting sporadic thoughts and concepts. But there is also a body memory and a muscle memory; indeed, all muscle growth is only an effect of frequently reproduced performances. Memory even persists beyond the limits of individual life; for what we call heredity is at bottom nothing other than a reproduction of something that has been learned before. "Thus, every organic being of the present ultimately stands before us as a product of the unconscious memory of organic matter, which, becoming ever more richly variegated with the passage of time, ever growing and dividing, ever assimilating new matter and returning other matter to the inorganic world, ever incorporates the new into its memory in order to reproduce it over and over again."

From this point of view, the entire evolutionary history of a more highly organized animal forms a continuous chain of memories linked to the evolutionary history of that long series of living entities whose culminating point is that animal. Together with the inner and outer formation of the body, of the organs, and of the cells, their functions are also reproduced. Instincts are expressions of memory and are to be understood only as such. What occurs in animals as instinct, occurs in humans in a freer form as innate predisposition. To be sure, concepts are not hereditary, but the capacity to think conceptually is a heritage or memory of the species. Hering's theory of memory was later further elaborated by H. Semon as the theory of the "mneme" in an essentially mechanistic sense.

Psychovitalism continued the same theory in a different direction. It speaks of "trial and error" and "learning" even in reference to unicellular life. It does the same with cells and cell groups incorporated within multicellular organisms. Psychovitalism even refers to the "trial and error" learning of glands when these adapt their responses to certain stimuli. This is not as paradoxical as it sounds because the glandular cells are thereby endowed with no other capacities than those generally accorded unicellular organisms.

In many instances, however, the purposive reaction is already inherited. When that is the case, Lamarckism assumes that trial and retention have taken place in the ancestor; these were then stabilized and inherited.

The above theory, which we have sketched in gross outline, is Lamarckistic because it assumes a direct adaptation to external stimuli. It is also psycho-Lamarckistic because it includes the coöperation of mental factors.

Our concern is not whether Lamarckism is tenable as a biological theory but only whether it has any significant bearing on psychology. Psycho-Lamarckism extends into the field of psychology by including mental factors in the explanation of purposive conduct.

By tracing purposive adaptation, reproduction, and heredity back to "memory," a factor is introduced which is primarily apprehensible through the consciousness and which is, consequently, a mental factor. In point of fact, a great part of our conscious actions are also based upon "trial and error" and retention, even if the trial movements are often not actually performed but are only anticipated in imagination and appropriately rejected or affirmed. In principle, most mental performances are also based on trial and learning.

Psychovitalism thus injects the mental factor as a distinct component of reality into the whole of reality composed of both the physical and the mental. Psychology is essentially concerned with the reciprocal conduct of the mental and the physical within man, that is, with the body-soul problem.

In consonance with its fundamental view, psychovitalism tends toward a theory of reciprocal interaction. This theory was very much current in prescientific thought, for the naïve person believes it to be a matter of direct experience that he can move his body about by means of his ideas and will, just as he conversely notices at every juncture that physical facts influence his consciousness. He accepts this uncritically without inquiring about the how and why of it all. When science approaches these questions it must investigate the problem thoroughly, and in all detail.

Of course, we must admit that the psychovitalists, in rejecting parallelism and inclining toward an interaction between the physical and the mental, are in no position whatsoever to offer us a conclusive theory—but neither are their opponents. Their argumentation is predominantly negative when they endeavor to disarm certain objections leveled against them. One grave objection is that the theory of interaction cannot be made to harmonize with the law of the conservation of energy.

Recent studies by Rubner, Laulanie, Atwater, and others have confirmed the application of the law of energy to the human organism. How can the operation of vital influences be made compatible with this law? An attempt to solve this question was made by E. Becher in a book which appeared in 1911 entitled *Brain and Mind*. Becher maintained that vital forces engage "directively" in the physiochemical activity of the organism without themselves performing any work or causing any change in the existent amount of energy.

2. Jakob von Üxküll does not belong to the psychovitalists but to the vitalists. He is one of the most excellent observers of animal conduct and is well known for his fascinating book entitled *Environment and Inner Life of Animals* (1909) and his *Theoretical Biology* (1920). Üxküll's portrayal of his scientific point of view almost gives one the impression that he is a behaviorist. He rejects all analogical inferences in regard to animal consciousness. He is content with determining, as an external observer, the influence of the external world upon animals and the influence which animals in turn exert upon the external world. Yet Üxküll does not arrive at a mechanistic view by way of this procedure.

Let us first consider what observation can tell us about the conduct of animals. Every animal is the pivotal center of an environment toward which it reacts as an independent agent. But environment is not identical with mere external surroundings. On the contrary, all animals live among the same surroundings, but each lives in his own particular environment: the earthworm lives in an earthworm environment; the mosquito in a mosquito environment, and man in a human environment. And in the earthworm environment there are only earthworm things. It is a genuine delight to have Üxküll transport us into the environment of the lower animals: amœbæ, polypi, sea urchins, and the like. This is how he portrays the environment of the medusa or jelly fish:

"Looking down from the deck upon a shimmering expanse of blue sea, we behold the mute bells of the medusa hovering about like wondrous flowers in a magic garden, and an involuntary quiver of envy runs through us. To be privileged to float about in all this colorful splendor, abandoned and fancy free, borne by sonorous waves through the radiant day and the resplendent, moonlit night, must be a glorious destiny. But the medusa is oblivious to it all. The entire world about us is a locked door to her. The only content of her inner life is the regular, self-generated stir of energy ebbing and flowing with monotonous change within her nervous system. Thus, this wonderful organism is built to comply with merest necessity. Its structure assures the animal of nourishment and necessary motion without involving any stimuli of the external world. An environment that fills the nervous system with a wealth of stimulation does not exist for rhizostoma, but only an environment from which its stomach can derive nourishment."

The environment of every animal can be divided into a world of observation and a world of function, both of which are united into a whole by the inner world of the body. Only inchoate qualities of things enter into the animal's world of observation on the one hand, and its world of function on the other. But the carriers of observation and function coincide within the same object. To the human observer, the sensations of animals are always unknown; he can recognize the phenomena which affect animals only as qualities of his own world of phenomena. Every animal carries its specific environment about with it all its life, like an impenetrable shell. It is endowed with this environment by the particular organization of its nature, which is in harmonious accord with that very section of the external world which is to become its specific environment. There is no such thing as absolute space or absolute time common to all living things. Every living thing experiences only its own environment in its own fashion, both in the way of observing and of functioning.

Üxküll goes so far in his organic view that he does not merely conceive the organism as a totality but, in a manner of speaking, conceives the organism plus environment as a totality in which both components are in harmonious accord. Nevertheless, he does not, like most theoreticians of milieu, consider functions and organs as predominantly conditioned by external stimuli, but assumes an endogenous, formational factor which he calls the immaterial "plan." He sees such a "plan" in crystal formation and, in a much more complex form, in living organisms.

We must leave Üxküll's biological theories, his "formational plans" that develop the organism, and confine ourselves to the portion of his work dealing with problems of psychomotor psychology. In this connection his theory of "schemata" is extremely original. Observational signs are schematically arranged into "space plans" by means of which environment is classified for animals. Functional signs also fall into schemata which Üxküll calls "performance plans." By means of their "performance plans" organisms are enabled to vary fixed spatial forms. Man, in particular, has such performance plans at his disposal; only to him (but not to animals) a table is a table because the table enters only into human performance plans as something

upon which to place something else. The choice of which
performance plan is to be applied depends upon the totalitarian "set" which is conditioned by inner organic data.
Single performance plans are in turn arranged into a total
plan which governs the organisms, and this is in turn
governed by a universal purposiveness.

Thus, Üxküll, without touching the question of consciousness, arrives by way of biology at a philosophy bearing an astonishing resemblance to that of Leibniz. He does
not use the term "monads," but, as a matter of fact, each of
his organisms is a monad which experiences the total world
by observing and functioning in its own particular way,
finally reshaping the total world into its own particular
environment. Üxküll explains this vitalistically. "Physical
Weltanschauung boasts of having exposed and annihilated
all qualities as subjective illusions, and of having replaced
them with quantities as the only true factors of nature.
Biological *Weltanschauung* derides these sacred quantities,
which are basically nothing else than objectified, subjective
qualities of order whose only meaning is to supply the
frame for qualities of content."

We may well subscribe to this quotation, yet the question
remains whether it actually embodies only a biological
Weltanschauung and not also a psychological one. Although
Üxküll, on methodological grounds, confines himself to an
objective description of the conduct of living things, he
would certainly not deny that performance plans are carried
out consciously, at least in human beings. If this is granted,
then vitalism does become psychovitalism after all.

GERMAN PSYCHOMOTOR PSYCHOLOGY

1. In the twentieth century, the German psychologists also
approached the problem of psychomotor psychology, after
having left it at first solely within the province of biology.

Among the foremost German scholars belonging to the
psychomotor school was Karl Groos. In 1892 he had already

hit upon the idea that the essence of artistic appreciation was an "inner imitation." He later correlated this theory with motor psychology in a book entitled *Esthetic Enjoyment*, published in 1902. In the interim he developed a theory of play and an essentially motor theory of conduct in two books entitled *The Play of Animals* (1896) and *The Play of Man* (1899).

Groos demonstrated in his investigations that impulses and instincts are manifest in most types of play. The youthful individual tries to gain mastery over his own psychophysical organism by means of his play activity. Thus, a teleological viewpoint was brought into the investigation and the purely mechanistic theory of instincts turned out to be totally inadequate. Groos classified the instincts into those of the first order and those of the second order. Instincts of the second order are differentiated from those of the first in that they regulate the conduct of the individual toward other individuals. Groos adhered to the biological point of view in all of his later works, as, for example, in his studies on the mental life of the child.

2. Studies in esthetics were especially instrumental in leading to the understanding of physical actions and modes of conduct in Germany. For a time, the theories of O. Rutz were held in great repute. Rutz distinguished three types of posture among singers. Each of these three types is supposed to endow vocal delivery with a specific timbre. The first type protrudes the abdomen and thus gives the voice a hollow, smooth resonance. The second type keeps the abdomen in and the chest out; this results in a clear, mellifluous resonance. A third type stretches the body and pushes the muscles of the torso downwards; this yields a clear and sharp resonance. These observations were subsequently elaborated by Rutz into a typological classification of musicians which was later applied to speech and poetry by the philologist Eduard Sievers. In the course of time, an attempt was made to explain the whole of esthetics

in terms of specific posture. Of late, the problem of posture. is no longer viewed in such an isolated fashion but rather in connection with the totalitarian psychophysical attitude of the ego.

3. Richard Müller-Freienfels also entered psychology from the field of esthetics. In his *Psychology of Art*, published in 1912, he laid stress upon the significance of motor factors in esthetic experience. Later, he developed his own system of psychology, which he named "Vital Psychology" in order to emphasize its contrast to the pure study of consciousness and at the same time to point out its fundamentally vitalistic temper. This system was first published in 1916 under the title of *Principles of Vital Psychology*, and later revised and issued in two volumes in 1923 and 1925.

Müller-Freienfels was greatly influenced by William James but goes even further in his emphasis on organic totality. He points out that the entire self is involved in every mental act, a fact borne out by language which says: *I* sense, *I* think, and the like. All mental experiences are "attitudes" of the totalitarian self. These attitudes are of a fundamentally motor nature. They are rooted in instincts which are involved in all intellectual life. What atomistic psychology designates as independent "elements," that is, feelings, sensations, ideas, and so forth, are to be conceived only as fractional phenomena of the organic attitudes of the self, in which bodily movements play a decisive rôle. Every perception, every act of thought or will is not merely an experience of consciousness; the total psychophysical self in such acts adopts a simultaneously active and sensitive attitude toward a real or imagined object. Categories like reality are grounded upon such attitudes of the self, upon readiness for action, which decisively modify the experience of consciousness.

The "idea" is likewise not a pure experience of consciousness but a totalitarian psychophysical "attitude" toward some content, and need not, therefore, be visual (*anschaulich*). Thought, too, is not a mere experience of consciousness but evolves from impulses and motor acts that are involved in all acts of thinking in the most diverse forms, among which speech is the most essential. Behind all apparently separate acts, however, stands the totality of the self, whose structure conditions not only separate acts but one's whole *Weltanschauung*.

Another book by Müller-Freienfels entitled *Personality and Philosophy* (1919) shows how the artistic style and the religious or philosophical world of ideas of every person is dependent upon the specific structure of his "self." With this, however, Müller-Freienfels diverges into "structural psychology," which will be discussed in a later section. Müller-Freienfels' system of psychology, especially in its treatment of instinct, is very close to McDougall's system, with which he did not become acquainted, however, until after the completion of his own.

4. Undoubtedly the most individual contributions to the psychomotor problem in Germany have been made by Ludwig Klages, a thinker outside of the academic pale, who began as a creative writer and finally arrived at a metaphysical system by way of characterology and graphology. We must be careful in calling him a psychologist because he is decidedly derogatory in referring to contemporary psychology and prefers to call the object of his endeavors characterology. His contributions to psychology are, nevertheless, extremely valuable.

Klages began his life work with graphological studies. He applied himself to the task of reclaiming graphology from an intuitive procedure and raising it to the status of a rigorous science. In doing so, he was able to join his efforts to various former works. Among his predecessors were a German named A. Henze, a Frenchman, J. H. Michon, who had written a *Système de graphologie* (1875), and his pupil Crépieux-Jamin. W. Preyer, in his work *The Psychology of Writing* (1895), had likewise occupied himself with these

problems. The best treatment before Klages was Georg
Meyer's *The Scientific Principles of Graphology* (1901).

Science is unjustified in viewing graphology as a quasi-
mystical practice. Graphology, studied with circumspection,
is another form of experimental psychology, or at least of
test methodology. Writing is by no means a form of
stereotyped mechanics but embodies cardinal traits of character. The fact that it includes utilitarian and conventional
factors renders psychological interpretation difficult but not
impossible.

Klages labored very conscientiously over a period of
years and distinguished innumerable single forms of writing
which he tested for their correlation to the mental traits of
the writer. Among the characteristic signs found in handwriting which were distinguished by Klages are regularity
and evenness, distribution, speed and heaviness, breadth,
angle of incidence, "pastiness," consistency, connectedness,
variety and tendency, initial stress, crossing-out and dynamic
distribution. But Klages is far from ascribing fixed, isolated
traits of character to these separate graphological signs.
He constantly takes into consideration the organic whole.
In this connection, his concept of "form level" (*Form-
Niveau*) is particularly important although it is not amenable to scientific so much as to intuitive demonstration. The
most complete among Klages' numerous publications is his
Handwriting and Character, first issued in 1916 and later
reprinted several times.

For our purposes, the general psychology of expression
which Klages derived from his empirical analyses of writing
is more important than his practice of graphology. This
psychology is summarized in his *Expressive Action and
Creative Power* (1913). Klages' standpoint is strictly totalitarian; he opposes all atomizing and isolating tendencies.
Every action, according to Klages, discloses the vital unity
of the agent. Personal forms of expression are contained
within every voluntary gesture. All knowledge that we
have of another's individual mental life is based directly

upon our understanding of his gestures or facial expressions. This sounds behavioristic but is not at all intended to be so. Klages stresses that in the understanding of another's mental life, the rôle of the physical, which yields that understanding, is by no means conscious, but that the mental life of another has to be grasped directly.

Every expressive bodily movement concretizes an experienced impulse, a feeling not necessarily confined to that of pleasure or pain. In every expressive gesture or facial expression, we can read the form, duration, and sequence of tendencies in the mental impulses. Of course, expressive action must be sharply distinguished from voluntary action: expressive action follows the stimulus of an impression while voluntary action aims at a set goal. Expressive movements are symbols of action. The expression of terror is the symbolic enactment of motions performed as though one were escaping from something which arouses terror. In entertaining this notion, Klages does not endorse Darwin's theory of emotions which literally interprets all expressive actions as the rudiments of earlier purposive actions. Klages rejects such an idea as "rationalization" and "mechanism" and, contrary to Darwin, maintains that expressive actions derive from the subjectivity of their origin; for the living organism does not respond to the same stimulus with the same reactions but responds to similar impressions with similar reactions. Instinct adapts itself only to species which are similar. Individuation does not take place until after the advent of judgment and will.

The theory of will developed by Klages is more amazing than any of his others. Will, according to Klages, is not rooted in the feelings but is opposed to them as a general inhibitive agency. The energy of will is a quantum of motor drive which has become nonqualitative and is intended for the harnessing of life in subservience to a goal. Voluntary action does not spring directly from life but is bound to a causality set up by the mind. The regulation of voluntary action is entirely different from that of expressive actions.

Voluntary actions are molded by the expectations of their success. Every person unconsciously carries a personal idea, an unconscious mask, before him, which he seeks to represent at all times.

Since every impulse is blocked by certain inhibitions, Klages arrives at an important law: the "dual significance of expression"; that is, every act of expression must be understood in terms of the total personality. Should one, for example, witness a person performing a very violent action, this action may be due either to the special attractive power of the goal, or to the individual's lack of inner inhibitions. A domineering will may indicate strength of will, but also embittered feeling. Sensitiveness may be traceable to delicacy, but also to irritability. Thus, in all such judgments, the decisive factor is the total intuition of the personality.

The problem is not to search for states of qualities, but for "essences," because ultimately any individual form of action cannot be analyzed. Hence, the search for essences is not at all a form of purely objective recognition but a form of evaluation. Yet we need not lapse into pure subjectivism, for values are not grasped as entities independent of consciousness, but are experienced as realities. The acceptance of values is a self-abandonment to reality which is serially graduated according to its vital content:

"According to the being in whom it occurs, each pulsation evokes another and yet another vital content, be it a faint stirring of the soul or the frenzy of passion; the raging of one person may be more paltry and shallow than the mere breathing of another. He who can observe this, and build up an understanding on the basis of his observation, so that he can differentiate the true personality from a precipitate of its psychic activity, such as would be found, for example, in handwriting, has perceived the agency through which form or function alternately expresses a psychological 'minus' or 'plus.' He can, therefore, decide from instance to instance whether it is the strength of a vital impulse or the weakness of an antagonistic inhibition which is manifested in objective traits." The vital content of which Klages speaks here is revealed in the organic character of expression called the "form level" (*Form-Niveau*).

Formational or creative power, which is the capacity for unusual intensification of expression, derives from natural expression. The evolution of culture, according to Klages, is a gloomy pageant in which the natural power of expression recedes in favor of a soulless predominance of will, which is made manifest finally in the state. Ultimately, however, expression and creative power are rooted in the totalitarian structure of character. Klages' elaborate characterology will be discussed separately in the following section.

5. Among the newer German psychologists who have especially devoted themselves to psychomotor phenomena, E. Kretschmer must be included. In the beginning, as we have seen, he studied the correlation between physique and character. In his *Medical Psychology* of 1922, he included not only studies of static form but also of dynamic conduct. He treated "imagery processes" (*Abbildungsvorgänge*), that is, sensation, perception, and imagination. From the viewpoint of psychiatry, Kretschmer threw interesting light upon such little observed data as image agglutination, stylization, and image projection. But he was even more engrossed by psychomotor phenomena.

In the development of expressive processes, Kretschmer distinguishes first "vegetative actions," which usually are rhythmic; secondly, "trial actions," which are governed by the law of formula-like condensation in frequently repeated acts. A third stage comprises the expression of will and emotionality, which are not yet distinguishable from one another in lower stages of development. Instinctive actions are distinguished from calculated actions in that the former are predominantly constant while the latter are variable. Kretschmer's proof that in certain pathological cases conduct reverts to the lower stages of development is particularly valuable.

Kretschmer does not stop with the portrayal of partial aspects of conduct but views conduct as an organic whole. He distinguishes personalities and reaction types and thus reverts to views that he had already attained in portraying types of physique. Personality is not an isolated datum but must be viewed within its complex psychic milieu. On the basis of how one subjectively revises experience, various types can be distinguished that are conditioned by the structure of the personality. Thus, Kretschmer also arrives at the problem of "structure," to which we shall later devote a special section of this book.

CONCLUSION

In reviewing the development of motor and conduct psychology as a whole, we are struck by its remarkable parallel to the development of the study of consciousness and of psychophysiology. Just as these had commenced with the investigation of isolated states of consciousness or isolated cerebral processes, and had been subjected to the increasing constraint of a totalitarian view, motor psychology, too, began with the description of separate types of conduct, and was increasingly impelled to study conduct in its totality.

A second parallel is found in the fact that at first motor psychology, the psychology of consciousness, and physio-psychology were mechanistically biased, and carried this bias to the point of absurdity; but the newer schools were under the increasing compulsion of recognizing the factor of purposiveness, and shifted from mechanism to vitalism.

The general procedure of these schools of research varied. Some of them endeavored to treat consciousness, and others motor actions, as separate data and carried their procedure to such lengths that on the one hand consciousness, and on the other, motor actions were treated as entirely nonexistent. Notwithstanding this, in the newer schools of psychology, both of these tendencies joined forces and realized that consciousness cannot be understood without physical action and vice versa.

Into this latter point of view, also, the problem of totality obtruded itself; for, whatever totality per se may be, totality in general simultaneously includes consciousness and physical action. However, as soon as we ask ourselves, "What is the nature of this totality?" the same problem of "soul" that we have witnessed asserting itself in physiopsychology and biopsychology emerges from the chaos of disparate manifestations of consciousness or separated motor acts.

Try as they would to pursue their researches "without soul," the psychology of consciousness and psychomotor psychology were compelled to capitulate in the long run. Hence we need not be astonished that a new school of research emerged from these two schools of thought and energetically applied itself to the very problem of finding out what the "soul" was. We are now confronted with a school of research which states explicitly that "psychology with a soul" is the goal of its studies.

PART FOUR

THE PSYCHOLOGY WITH "SOUL"

1. Physiopsychology and psychomotor psychology both started with essentially unconscious data: the one concerned itself with cerebral processes and the other with bodily movements. Both these schools of psychology attempted to correlate their data with the processes of consciousness only to become increasingly estranged from consciousness in the end.

Simultaneously, a new approach to psychological data originated in the study of consciousness. For a long time the "consciousness psychologists" were unaware that they had completely relinquished the principle of consciousness in working with concepts which their school had until then contemptuously ignored as "faculties."

This new group at first attained exceedingly variable empirical results through experimental research in the reactions, image reproduction, and concept formation in different individuals. Were these variations caused by new facts in the conscious, or could they be traced back to unconscious data? Without being entirely clear on this point in theory, in practice these new experimenters employed concepts taken from daily life: memory, imagination, reason, temperament, and the like. That they thereby overstepped the analysis of pure consciousness worried them as little as it had the representatives of the psychology of consciousness, who had selected these very concepts without clearly realizing that, although the separate contents of memory, imagination, and reason were conscious; memory, fantasy, and reason—in other words, the acts which produce those contents—were not conscious in themselves. Then, of course, consciousness became structuralized upon "capacities," "*Anlagen*," and "dispositions," all of which were at bottom merely different words for what preëxperimental psychology had called "faculties." In practice, the psychology of innate capacities went about the experimental testing, comparison, and measurement of intelligence and other capacities without burdening itself with theoretical considerations. In doing this, the boundaries inclosing the field of operations of consciousness psychology were neatly trespassed. The day of a new "faculty psychology" had dawned, only it was neither recognized nor named as such.

Another lively trend in the newer research soon reached the same point. It was known as evolutionary psychology and comprised the various branches of child psychology, animal psychology, and the psychology of primitive man. The child, the animal, and primitive man are not distinguished from the civilized adult merely by the contents of their perceptions, images, and thoughts, which are little known at best; they do not only perceive, mentally reproduce, think, and feel different contents of consciousness; they also experience the world in an entirely different manner.

The contents of consciousness are secondarily conditioned by capacities and dispositions, primary faculties which are formed during the course of the individual's evolution. In a similar way, it was discovered that the imagery and thinking of primitive man deviate from those of civilized man not only in their contents but also in their entire disposition. Manifold changes in mental capacities occurring during the phylogenetic evolution of animals forced themselves to the attention. All this was not consciousness psychology, but a study of the premises underlying consciousness, a research of the psychic "faculties," or ultimately of the "structure of the soul."

The newer psychopathology worked along in the same direction. We have already seen, in our discussion of cerebral physiology, which was to a large extent cerebral pathology, that research not only sought to localize sensations and ideas as isolated conscious data, but also attempted to localize the complex faculties of sensation and imagination. Thus, psychopathologists, in treating their patients, diagnosed them as illogically associating separate chains of thought, and also claimed that their faculty of thought, or reason, was destroyed. These pathologists did not care a jot for isolated contents of consciousness; they were interested solely in the mental faculties which produced them. In short, they, too, employed the concepts of "faculty" and "soul structure."

All this grew out of actual practice and thus was more closely related to everyday psychology than to the strict theoretical psychology of consciousness.

2. After the psychology of talents and capacities, as well as child psychology, had developed to a fairly advanced stage, theoretical psychology also began to open its eyes to the presence of a problem which was no longer an analysis of consciousness in the old sense. At least, the concept of "consciousness" now received an entirely different meaning. We shall try to define as concisely as possible the dual connotation of the word "conscious," which is used so loosely in colloquial speech. We can say on the one hand: "An image or a thought is conscious to me." This can mean: the image or thought is known, is passively conscious, or consciously had. On the other hand, we often say: "I am conscious," or "I consciously experience." In this case, "conscious" means knowing, actively conscious, or consciously having. English and French words ending in "ion" and German words ending in "ung" are indiscriminately used in this dual sense. Perception signifies on the one hand "that which is perceived," and on the other, "that which is perceiving." Imagination signifies both "that which is imagined" and "that which is imagining," that is, passive as well as active image consciousness.

Science must institute sharp distinctions in such instances. We have already seen that sensory psychology and its related tendencies viewed consciousness as essentially passive, both as qualities or attributes, which were often erroneously substantiated. An "image" became a sort of "picture," a passive datum which appeared and disappeared according to the mechanism which lured it out or caused it to disappear. Gradually, however, the realization dawned upon psychology that consciousness is something active; that not merely passive pictures emerge, but that an active imagination is at work. Psychologists began to think gerundively. This, however, brings us to an active consciousness. In place of consciousness known, we have consciousness knowing.

This knowing consciousness, that is, this active perceiving, imagining, thinking, feeling consciousness does not exhaust itself in an accidental, single experience. It is a continuous capacity which remains constant while its contents change. "Seeing" is something constant, whereas that which is "seen" varies. And thus we arrive at a capacity, a "faculty."

Theoretical psychology timorously avoids the word "faculty." It speaks of "acts" or "functions," or the "capacity" of sensing or imagining, and the like, to which it opposes as "contents" that which is "sensed" or "imagined."

At this juncture we are interested solely in finding a point of view in order to envisage the problem correctly. We shall discuss the attempts toward its solution later. The sensationalists tried to explain these acts or functions merely as physiological capacities. Such an explanation is impossible; for, even though sensing, thinking, and feeling may have physiological correlates, as acts or capacities they are not merely physical but psychic data, although they are not, like their contents, passively conscious; they are knowingly and actively conscious.

The older psychology classified different contents of the same faculty together, but contented itself with external classifications. The procedure of the older psychologists was similar to that of the older botanists, who placed similar plants in "classes" according to their external resemblances. The factors governing those resemblances, the specific, formational forces operative behind every single genus, remained unfathomed. Older psychology confined itself to the "formed" and not to the "forming." The newer biology, however, tries to grasp the "forming," that is, the "type," not merely as "acted" but as "acting." We must view the endeavors of modern structural psychology analogously: it, too, does not desire to fathom that which has been enacted but that which is acting, not the thought alone, but the thinking faculty.

Having advanced thus far, a new problem arises, that of the correlation of the separate faculties and the inner unity and totality of psychic life. The associational psychologists viewed the "soul" only as consciousness in the sense that it was the sum of all conscious contents, and they thereby ran into a blind maze whose exit they could not find.

Modern structural psychology, however, is curious to learn just what it is that makes that sum into an organic unity; it would like to know the nature of the knowing subject which knows those known contents. Thus, once again, the problem of the unified "soul," whose structure is constituted by the "faculties," presents itself. The "soul" therefore amounts to consciousness, not as a sum of what is "known," but as the totality of the "knowing" faculties of consciousness.

Modern psychology's position in regard to the problem of soul faculties and, ultimately, the soul, is the same as that of modern biology in regard to the problem of vital energy and vitalism. Once again, it is no accident that both problems, after a period of exile, were revived at approximately the same time, in 1900. In both sciences, atomic–mechanistic research had reached a dead impasse; in both sciences, the problem of totality obtruded itself, since the categories of mechanism were inadequate. However, it is not merely an historical parallel which emerges in these two sciences; both problems are also related in content, just as they had been inseparable in antiquity when "psyche" meant both "soul" and "life." We have already seen in our study of vitalism, particularly of psychovitalism, how intimately related these problems are.

At the present time, we are obliged to say that older

psychology was at fault in seeing a solution in the concept of "faculty," whereas this concept really presents us with a problem. Such, at any rate, is the position of the contemporary psychology of the "I" in regard to the matter. Undoubtedly, Locke was right in derisively pointing out that one might just as well speak of a singing or dancing faculty as of a faculty of the soul. But it is just as erroneous to believe that there is any sort of explanation embodied in such words as it was for Molière's doctor to be satisfied with knowing that opium had a *"vis dormitiva."* Such a phrase is certainly no solution, but rather accentuates a problem that is as little solved through ridicule as through superstition. This problem is the problem of the soul and its structure. (Let me observe once again that in this chapter the word "structure" is not used in the sense in which the American structuralists use it. The term "structural" or "tectonic psychology" is used throughout in the German sense, in order to include the unconscious substructure of consciousness.)

3. As novel as this problem appears at first sight, it is not completely new, for it is but a new approach to the problem that once was called the dissection of the soul or the "classification of soul faculties." In general, the psychology of previous centuries considered the existence of a soul as axiomatic. Even when the existence of several souls was assumed (as in Aristotle), a connective hierarchy was believed to exist among them, since the uppermost soul ruled the lower ones or, as some authorities claimed, the superior parts of the soul ruled the inferior ones. Thus it was merely a verbal distinction to speak of a unified hierarchy of several souls, or of an hierarchally integrated single soul. The number of soul parts varied; instead of the tripartite soul favored by Plato and Aristotle, the Stoics assumed eight soul faculties by viewing, in addition to the five senses, fertility, speech, and thought, as faculties of the pneuma, among which thought, as *hegemonikón*, dominated the others.

In the Middle Ages, the main procedure consisted in varying the Platonic-Aristotelian classification.

In the psychology of the sixteenth and seventeenth centuries, with Descartes, Leibniz, and Locke, the question of
soul faculties receded into the background or was disguised
by other modes of expression.

The father of the widespread "faculty" psychology in
the eighteenth century, especially in Germany, was Christian Wolff. His classification of the "faculties," however,
was not entirely uniform. And his very concept of "faculties" vacillated. At first he termed the faculties "*nudae
agendi possibilitates*," but later he compared these capacities
to the organs of the body. Among such faculties the cognitive and appetent faculties are opposed to reason and sensation. Each of these faculties was supposed to behave
independently to a certain degree, although an occasional
coördination between them was admitted.

Among Wolff's successors, the number of the faculties
was either increased or an attempt was made to explain
complex mental performances through the amalgamation
of several basic faculties. Thus the poetic faculty was supposed to originate from the union of imagination and understanding, and the union of imagination and reason was
supposed to yield the faculty of prognostication.

In place of Wolff's dual classification, Tetens instituted
a tripartition of the basic faculties by classifying feeling,
together with reason and will, as original faculties of the
soul. Kant's psychology was also a psychology of faculties.
He adopted Tetens' triad of reason, will, and feeling; but,
like Wolff, divided the cognitive faculty into sensation and
understanding.

In general, Herbart's criticism can be said to mark the
end of German faculty psychology, whose later variants we
need not trace. Herbart saw in the faculties only classifica-
tory concepts, which might be justified in terms of consciousness but were not independent, basic forces of the
soul. Besides, they were—so Herbart argued—undemon-

strable in inner experience. We experience only single thoughts and feelings but not a thought faculty or a thought feeling. Instead of faculty, Herbart preferred the term "force." By means of this terminological distinction, he desired to eliminate the arbitrariness of traditional faculties, and to express the necessary occurrence of an action under certain circumstances. In place of the formerly accepted spontaneity of the soul as regards faculties, Herbart introduced the passive mechanism so characteristic of all associationist psychology.

Of course, the question remains whether Herbart's criticism really disposed of the psychology of mental faculties for all time, as was assumed in the second half of the nineteenth century. Temporarily it surely did, because for a long time it was just as compromising to speak of faculties in psychology as it was to speak of vital force in biology. Meanwhile, however, even though the word "faculty" disappeared from scientific books, certain concepts were employed which, when closely observed, turn out to be synonymous with "faculty" after all.

The concepts employed were memory, thought, and will, which by no means signified momentary states of consciousness, but faculties that produce states of consciousness. Moreover, the extrascientific psychology of everyday life was not at all impressed with Herbart's verdict against the "faculties." In real life, people nonchalantly ascribed to themselves and to their neighbors a greater or lesser reason, a stronger or weaker will power, and so forth; all of which was precisely equivalent to the dispossessed "faculties."

Although modern structural psychology troubles itself very little with the old psychology of mental faculties, and flatly denies any sort of relationship to it, as historians we are obliged to asseverate that structural psychology moves in the same rut which faculty psychology formerly occupied. And it is probably no accident that modern structural psychology is predominantly cultivated in Germany, just where the old faculty psychology saw its prime!

The difference between modern scientific psychology and the old psychology, as often happens, lies in the change of approach. In previous centuries, a totalitarian soul was postulated, which was divided into faculties or parts in order to cover the explanation of separate functions. Modern research begins with the description of states of consciousness and their separate manifestations; it then classifies them and emphasizes their general laws. This leads in turn to the question concerning the faculties which perform these separate functions. Having advanced thus far, it is impossible to ignore the question concerning the unity and totality operative behind these faculties. In short, whether we wish to or not, we come up against the problem of the soul; and this problem suffers little change should we supplant the word "soul" with "self," or "subject," or "personality," in order to safeguard ourselves from the taint of animism.

THE PSYCHOLOGY OF TALENT AS A PRELIMINARY STAGE OF STRUCTURAL PSYCHOLOGY

1. No mystical speculation but experimental practice compelled scientists to proceed to investigate the dispositional structure of the soul.

We have already seen above how experimental psychology, once it began to direct its attention to individual differences, went beyond the sphere of consciousness to the determination of talents, capacities, and dispositions. Thus a vast field of research grew up, which devoted itself very little to theoretical questions, but proceeded first of all to develop an extremely complicated method designed to determine the "facts." This was thoroughly justified and resulted in the widely ramified practice of intelligence and capacity testing in connection with the study of capacity and personality. This movement is often collectively referred to by the name of "psychotechnics."

Historically, the inception of the exact study of mental capacities was dependent upon the introduction of measurement in connection with mental performance, although it was a fairly long time before measurement was employed not merely from the standpoint of averages but also from that of individual differences. Individual differences were regarded as secondary matters in the beginning and treated as such. Not until the beginning of the '90's was there a shift in this view. Psychologists systematically began to compare the performances of different individuals, to plot individual curves, and to compute coefficients of capacity.

2. This quantitative measurement of capacities was first tried in mnemonic experiments. Naturally, the results of these experiments showed that "memory" is not a uniform capacity but includes several subcapacities. Thus Ribot distinguished retention, renewal, and localization. W. Stern distinguished learning capacity, memory retention, and accuracy. Meumann redivided learning into three types: discriminative learning, rote learning, and learning for the purpose of recalling essentials. Of late, the problem has grown increasingly involved, so that at present we must say that the study of memory has by no means confined itself to memory, and now includes other capacities, that is, imagination, thinking, sensitivity, attention, and the like.

The first experiments in memory were made around 1880 by Ebbinghaus. He used himself as a subject and exercised heroic patience in his daily repeated experiments. G. E. Müller, in conjunction with a complete staff of assistants, later carried out such experiments on a large scale and with more refined methods. In America, Cattell was the first to make similar experiments. France contributed its inspiration by way of its three image types: visual, auditory, and motor. Meumann and others studied memory performance in these types, but the result of their studies showed the advisability of distinguishing a factual and a verbal memory. A prodigious diligence was expended upon such investigations in every civilized country.

We need not question the practical worth of these experiments, which has been variously evaluated at this point. We should merely like to make clear that they all started from the psychology of consciousness but soon trespassed beyond it; for whenever types of memory or gradationally different qualities of memory were distinguished, not only did consciousness enter into the discussion, but also psychic dispositions and capacities. Opinions differed as to whether these capacities were traceable to innate brain capacities or to the exercise of other acquired factors such as adaptation. Before they realized it, the psychologists virtually found themselves in the midst of a psychology of capacities, in which the number of "special capacities" increased from year to year.

3. The most intensively cultivated field in the psychology of capacities, next to memory, was in all likelihood the "measurement of intelligence." With the concept of intelligence, a faculty was admitted into psychology for which one looks in vain in older textbooks. Here, too, Ebbinghaus was one of the first to open up new vistas by his method of *Completion Tests*, published in 1898. Ebbinghaus laid before school children passages in which certain words were omitted. The gaps had to be filled in so as to complete the sense. The number of successes and failures offered a possibility of exact comparison, so that at least the capacity of "completing" the meaning of sentences could be numerically determined. Here, too, the question remained whether such procedure enabled one to estimate "general intelligence," or very different special capacities working together in various ways.

The test method of measuring intelligence has been particularly elaborated in America and in other countries. Cattell and his coworkers were pioneers in this field. Kirkpatrick, Kelly, Norsworthy, and others, preëminently

298 The Evolution of Modern Psychology

in educational psychology, undertook intelligence test experiments on a large scale in the first decade of the twentieth century.

Intelligence tests were first strictly systematized by A. Binet. Binet had already begun such experiments in 1895, but did not publish his first test until 1908, on the basis of extensive examinations conducted in schools under the auspices of the French Ministry. Together with his co-worker, Simon, Binet issued a revised form of his scale in 1911. Hence, the current usage of the expression: Binet-Simon method. The method consists of providing a scale of normal tests for various age groups of school children. On the basis of these tests, one can rapidly determine whether a child is normal, or whether it is advanced or retarded in relation to schoolmates of the same age level.

The Binet-Simon method was soon introduced in other countries and improved. In America, it was first applied by Goddard in 1910. After Healy and Fernald had worked out further tests, and Terman and Childs had set up their "Stanford Revision Scale," intelligence tests became widespread in the United States. During the World War, in connection with recruiting, psychology was accorded military honor in being consulted as to the placement of recruits.

In Sweden, the method was introduced by Jaederholm; in Germany, by Bobertag; and soon there was no longer any country in which intelligence was not being measured and evaluated.

Of course there was no lack of criticism. Objections were raised that Binet's tests jumbled together different types of subcapacities. In answer to these objections the capacity of "general intelligence" was split up into subcapacities, according to which special types were distinguished. Binet had already distinguished several such types: the descriptive, observant, emotional, and scholarly types. Meumann differentiated between productive and reproductive types. Spearman pointed out that two factors must be distinguished in every mental performance: a general factor and a specific one. The participation of the "G-factor" and of the "S-factor" would be entirely different in different performances.

4. The testing of skills is an accessory field in the psychology of talents and capacities. The testing of skill grew out of reaction experiments in which the influences of concentration, distraction, fatigue, and exercise could be studied. A widely ramified "psychology of performances" was the result. A. Lehmann, Höfler, Kraepelin, Hillgruber, Foucault, and others were pioneers in this field. The performances studied consisted of adding columns of numbers, proofreading, and the like. In America particularly, the procedure was enlarged to include specific skills in the most diverse occupational tasks. Thus, Bryan and Harter studied skills in telegraphic sending and receiving. Book investigated skills in typewriting. And Thorndike also applied the method to animal psychology.

In these experiments, too, the realization arose that performance and skill are not unit concepts, but that very different factors are involved even in apparently simple performances. Many of these factors are of a general nature, like exercise, adaptation, and fatigue. But more special capacities like attention, memory, and intelligence with its subdivisions, are also involved. The performance curves which were plotted did not always yield sufficient information as to the specific factors back of good or bad performances. Cattell, in 1899, had already evolved his principle of "higher units," according to which the perception of elements is not always necessary in more complex perceptive performances. Similarly, it became evident in later experiments that a more complex performance could often be not more, but less, difficult than an apparently simple one. The influence of "interference" and of performance variation was also studied, especially by Conrad.

We need not trace the evolution of psychotechnics and its immensely expanded research any further. It is sufficient to observe that here, too, the concepts of performance and skill can be divided into innumerable single factors which are by no means data of consciousness. Rather, they are to be viewed as the unconscious premises of performance; and many of them can also be viewed as "dispositions" or "capacities."

5. A branch of the study of capacities evolved from the measurement of correlation. This branch proposed to determine a specific computable correlation between different mental performances or capacities. As far back as 1893, Gilbert had determined correlations between intelligence and the capacity to make distinctions; and further, between intelligence and reaction speed. Ebbinghaus discovered the correlations between learning, adding, and combining. Through Pearson, Spearman, Betz, Jaederholm, and others, the study of correlation was developed into an involved mathematical method.

The basic goal that the study of correlation aims at is the determination of the degree of probability according to which a good result in one series leads us to expect good results in other series. In order to measure such correspondences an attempt is made to find the coefficient of correlation which expresses the total ratio of proportion between two types of characteristics rather than general determinants of how much larger or smaller a specific number may be. The factor of probable error must also be calculated.

It is not within our province to analyze the subtle methods and multifold achievements of the study of correlation. Our interest is essentially in the aim of such study. This aim is undoubtedly directed toward a numerical determination of the organic causality governing separate capacities.

The limitations of quantitative statistics soon revealed themselves. As a result more qualitative "psychograms" were developed, by means of which psychology strove to apprehend individual traits and coördinate them into types.

A typology of the most involved nature came into existence, in which exceedingly disparate principles held sway.

At any rate, the psychology of capacities developed more and more into a complicated study of personality as a result of the increasing realization that single capacities were dependent upon some organic whole. The attempt to derive the total personality from a study of its separate capacities seemed the chief goal of this research, a procedure which, of late, has been vigorously assailed by students of intuitive characterology. Whether intuition is the way in which the goal is to be attained is immaterial. Here, too, the problem is to conceive personality as a totality. Hence the problem presented is, at least implicitly, that of the structuralized or tectonic soul.

EVOLUTIONARY PSYCHOLOGY AS A PRELIMINARY STAGE OF STRUCTURAL PSYCHOLOGY

1. In addition to the experimental study of capacities, another well-trodden path of modern psychology led to an inquiry concerning dispositions, capacities, and, lastly, the structure of the soul which determined experiences of consciousness. Evolutionary psychology was its name, and its chief branches were child psychology, the psychology of primitive man, and animal psychology. The concept of evolution had become a central problem during the nineteenth century, especially in biology. Psychology could not escape the implications of this problem. Evolutionary research was first pursued in England in both instances.

The first issue raised was that of consciousness, but the problem led merely to unwarranted anthropomorphisms. Hypotheses were drawn up concerning thinking and feeling in babies, infusoria, and Australian Bushmen; but to be honest with themselves, investigators were obliged to realize that the resulting data were more in the nature of supposition than of established fact. One of the results of this state of affairs was the behavioristic theory that claimed that nothing whatever could be said definitely concerning the mental life of babies and animals, positing instead the claim that the study of their external conduct was the only valid field of research.

Most of the evolutionary psychologists, however, were not content to resign themselves to such limitations, and still hoped to gain insights into the mental life of babies and animals. They went about this by describing and experimentally studying, so far as possible, the evolution of mental capacities and dispositions. Capacities and dispositions are problematical, however, when one is interested in the consciousness involved with them. To avoid such uncertainty, interest was shifted more and more in the direction of the organismic interaction of these capacities. The result is that we are again confronted with the problem of a "consciousness-possessing soul" rather than a "soul" of which we have been conscious.

At first research proceeded along separate ways, as child psychology, as the psychology of primitive man, and as animal psychology; the bold speculations which were hazarded soon overlapped into related fields. It was not until recent years that these widely disparate aspects have been collectively referred to as "evolutionary psychology."

2. Of all the various stages of individual life, the age of childhood first aroused the interest of science, although thousands of years of history elapsed before childhood came to be studied with any degree of exactitude. In previous times, as far as there was any concern with children, they were regarded as diminutive and, as yet, undeveloped adults. The first systems of pedagogy had no inkling of a specific structure of the child soul. Rousseau's *Emile* had a soul conceived at the writing desk. When the romantic poets finally discovered the child, its soul was poeticized and romanticized.

Science did not discover the child until the nineteenth century, but it was not until the nineteenth century was almost over that the branch of child psychology separated itself from general psychology. Child psychology, to be sure, had a lone forerunner in the eighteenth century in Tiedemann's *Observations on the Development of Mental Capacities in Children* (1787). This was followed in the middle of the nineteenth century by Sigismund's *Child and World* (1856), and Kussmaul's *Studies Concerning the Mental Life of Newborn Children* (1859).

The foundations of modern child psychology, however, were first laid in 1882 by Wilhelm Preyer in a work entitled *The Soul of the Child*. The author was a physiologist by profession and, as a consequence, primarily interested in physiological data. But he also studied the development of mental capacities: the senses, speech, space perception, memory, and the like. The subject of his experiments was the scientist's own son. Thus Preyer initiated a procedure which soon led to the publishing of innumerable "diaries" of the development of various children.

Similar investigations arose in rapid succession in many different countries: in France, namely, Perez, Egger, Cramoussel; in Bulgaria, Gheorgow; in Anglo-Saxon countries, Miss Shinn, Moore, Major, Chamberlain, and others. Compendious works on the subject also made their appearance: in England, Sully; in France, Compayré; in America, Tracy; in Russia, Sikorski; in Italy, Paola Lombroso; in Switzerland, Claparède. In Germany, research in child psychology did not set in again until the twentieth century, and was due largely to the collaboration of married couples, for example, Clara and William Stern, Karl and Charlotte Bühler, David and Rosa Katz. In addition, the names of Meumann, Stumpf, Ament, Groos, and Dyroff deserve mention.

Science next turned its attention toward the study of adolescence. The first step in this direction was Stanley Hall's two-volume work, *Adolescence*, published in 1904. In

Germany the study of adolescence was not taken up until recently. A work which received extremely favorable notice was Spranger's *The Mental Life of Adolescents* (1925), which directly advocated a structural approach in the spirit of the Dilthey school. In addition, mention may be made of Charlotte Bühler's *Childhood and Youth* (1928), and further, the works of Tumlirz, W. Hoffmann, Kroh, Katz, and others. The interest in the adolescent phenomena stimulated by psychoanalysis was largely responsible for the extensive demand for the above-named works.

The later age levels in human development were studied far less intensively than the early stages, chiefly because the adult was considered the human "norm," and because everything that can be broadly included under the name of psychology is, at bottom, adult psychology. Only extreme age was honored with special studies, foremost among which was Stanley Hall's *Senescence,* published in 1922. Of late, Spranger and others have published their views on this subject and it is to be expected that other evolutionary psychologists, upon attaining old age, will also devote themselves to the scientific study of senescence. The first compendious psychology of the entire course of human life in all its stages was essayed by Charlotte Bühler in 1933, although a pioneer effort in this direction dates back as far as 1808, when F. A. Carus took up the problem in his *Psychologie.*

For our purposes, a summary of the achievements of evolutionary psychology would be superfluous. We are more interested in the basic principles of mental life which can be derived from evolutionary psychology. The first of these principles is the realization that evolutionary psychology cannot be derived solely from the contents of consciousness; evolution consists in the variations of the inner structure of the "soul." Unquestionably, certain single capacities emerge sooner than others; and undoubtedly the relationship between capacities varies. The evolution of consciousness must be referred to the evolution of a knowing consciousness, that is, to the structure of the soul and its capacities.

The cardinal subject of research, in the early stages of evolutionary psychology, was the knowing consciousness. An attempt was made to determine at what age the separate senses begin to function, what contents the memory retains, when speech expression first appears, the size of the vocabulary at various age levels, when abstract concepts appear, the sequence in which instincts and emotions announce themselves, and other such similar problems. Comprehensive studies of the growth in the range of ideas in children exist today as a result of these studies.

Important as these studies are, they can no longer be considered as exact as they were formerly considered to be. Does the use of a word prove beyond all question of a doubt what meaning the child ascribes to it? Such studies are based upon inferences. Indeed, very few psychologists are content with the mere establishment of facts concerning known consciousness, but seek to fathom the knowing consciousness active behind it. The dispositions and capacities of the soul are more important than the content of consciousness. But even these are not to be considered isolatedly; for, in reality, capacities do not develop separately; it is the entire personality which develops. This fact is often overlooked. Hence, the psychoanalysts, for example, try to interpret the transition from childhood to adolescence from the angle of sexual development. But the fact is that the child does not become an adolescent because of the onset of puberty; no, it is because the child, as an organic totality, reaches adolescence that puberty follows. A symptom should not be confused with its cause. The cause, in the present instance, lies in the organic character of the development of the "self," and not in the appearance of segregated capacities. Thus, evolutionary psychology does not merely lead to a psychology of capacities, but to a psychology of the total soul appearing simultaneously with the capacities as a temporal continuum.

3. At the same time as the study of the early stages of individual life, there appeared on the psychological stage a lively interest in the early stages of ethnic evolution. The Romantic Era not only discovered primitive man, but also romanticized him. Poetic conceptions of the paradisiacal existence of aborigines were dominant until late in the nineteenth century. Not until then did an exact science of ethnology and anthropology observe and accurately describe the real life of aborigines. Psychological interpretations followed in due course. What was then known as "racial psychology" was to all intents and purposes a psychology of primitive man.

It is not our intention to enumerate all the works which attempted to take an "inventory," that is, tried to determine the content of consciousness, so to speak, of the primitive soul. Almost all civilized countries made their contributions. Germany produced the great works of Waitz-Gerland, Wundt, and Preuss. In America, F. Boas and, in France, Lévy-Brühl were pioneers in the field. Whereas the above-named scholars usually availed themselves of the material gathered by others, younger scholars struck out independently, established field bases for research, and subjected the aborigines to systematic investigation. Thurnwald investigated the South Sea Islanders; Frobenius studied Negroid strains; Preuss observed the Cora Indians; while Myers lived with the natives of Torres Strait.

From the extremely interesting results of this research, we select only what is significant for the problem of soul structure. It immediately became evident that the mental life of savages was not only conceptually but also functionally different from that of adult Europeans. These differences plumb the most fundamental categories. In the primitive mind, the subjective and the objective are not separated as in ours, while the category of reality is easily and uncritically transferred to the figments of imagination and fantasy. Events are not ordered with strict causality, but "magical"

interpretation and practice are adduced everywhere. Even
the logical principle of identity does not exist, for the savage
encounters no difficulty in thinking that a man is simultaneously also a wolf. In short, the primitive mind not only
experiences different things from those which our minds
experience, but does its experiencing differently. The
structure of the primitive mind is entirely different from ours.

In all this, the question may still remain whether such
thinking is really primitive, if by the word "primitive" we
mean "simple." On the contrary, primitive thinking is exceedingly complex, and mingles ideas and emotional states
which we carefully separate. Neither is it satisfactory,
without further qualification, to draw a parallel between the
mental life of primitive man and that of the child, as was
done for a while on the basis of the "fundamental law of
biogenetics."

Similarities exist, to be sure, but there are also great
differences. Separate capacities are differently developed in
aborigines than in civilized man, but these separate capacities, for all their separateness, still form a completely
interlocked whole; so that we have to refer to it unqualifiedly
as a different structure of the soul. Whether this structure
is innate or is developed by social conditions is beyond the
present scope of our investigation.

4. The third field that offers insight into structural differences is animal psychology. For centuries animals were
viewed anthropomorphically and endowed with human
thoughts and feelings. Subsequently men lapsed into the
opposite error of considering animals as purely reflex
mechanisms completely devoid of consciousness. We have
already discussed the studies of animal reflexes and instincts.

When experimental psychology turned its attention to
animals, it primarily investigated their responses to sensory
stimuli: color sensation was tested in bees, hens, and other
animals, and the outcome was that distinct differences were
found in animal as compared to human responses. In

America, Yerkes, Thorndike, and others conducted experiments on a large scale. The French investigators, such as Espinas, Forel, and J. H. Fabre, occupied themselves largely with the "communal" insects. The Germans tested animals chiefly for their ability to distinguish *"Gestalt"* experiences; Volkelt worked with spiders, while Köhler tested chimpanzees on the Island of Teneriffe.

We have named only a few typical representatives of modern animal psychology in order to apply their achievements to our central problem. Today, it is unanimously admitted that there is not solely a difference of degree between animal and human mental life, as would be the case if animals were merely more stupid and possessed somewhat less developed souls whose structure was otherwise similar to that of man's soul. Yet neither are animals any longer considered as mere reflex mechanisms. To a certain extent, animals are capable of performances which humans cannot emulate. Yet the question concerned is not one of plus or minus, but one of quality. This qualitative difference, however, does not merely extend to single performances, but primarily to the totalitarian structure. This totalitarian structure is so ordered that animals, in their own environment, are able to perform what is necessary for their preservation with an harmonious coördination which often impresses us as "uncanny." So far as animal psychology is concerned, it is evident that psychologists must study more than mere separate mental "capacities." The total structure of mental life confronts us with problems that not only suggest the existence of a unitary soul but actually compel us to assume its existence.

Does all this entail speculation and metaphysics, as the behaviorists contend? By no means. Most evolutionary psychologists would spurn such an imputation, and rightly so. They would retort that the mere tabulation of external data is no science, least of all a science of psychology. Every science is not only justified but is also duty bound to draw inferences from given data. We are doing nothing more than this when we infer the existence of an orientational faculty from a child's adjustment to its environment; nor does such an inference preclude further divisions of this faculty. Just what is to be understood as a disposition or a capacity in the above, we have not discussed. In spite of this, it seemed necessary to wade through these separate capacities in order to reach a totality, without which these capacities could not be understood. And, undoubtedly, the totality attained was more than the sum of its separate capacities.

5. We are justified in aligning psychopathology with evolutionary psychology at this point, because mental disorders often represent cases of regressive evolution or degeneration. Of course, we have no desire to relegate all mental illnesses to this formula. However, it is essential for our purposes to realize that practical psychiatry has scarcely ever confined itself to a strict psychology of consciousness, but views the delusions and obsessions of the insane only as manifestations of abnormal variations of mental capacities. In so doing, psychiatry does not stop at symptoms or syndromes, but strives to discover the total pictures.

Let us take Karl Jaspers' *General Psychopathology*, published in 1913, as a typical example; it is the best German book in this field. Jaspers starts with the subjective phenomena of the pathological mind and continues with a study of single objective performances; but as yet he treats these only as symptoms of dispositional disturbances. From then on, however, he begins to consider the "connections of mental life." Among these, he distinguishes the "cognitive" connections, which are "understood," and the "causal" connections, which are "explained." Understanding psychopathology has two tasks: it tries to extend our understanding of extraordinary connections, such as sexual perversion or instinctive cruelty; and it tries to recognize states, conditioned by abnormal mechanisms, like the hysterical reactions. Explaining psychopathology, on the contrary, investigates the exogenous or endogenous causes of such phenomena and arranges them in typical courses. Jaspers then goes on to mental life as a whole, that is, to intelligence and personality. Under the heading of personality, he groups "all psychic phenomena indicative of an individual and thoroughly understandable connection which an individual experiences with the consciousness of his particular self."

We do not pursue the details of Jaspers' work further. Our only intent was to let Jaspers serve as an illustration of how psychopathology, too, was necessarily compelled to discover an ultimate unitary totality behind the isolated states of consciousness and their manifestations.

"PHENOMENOLOGY"

1. B. Brentano, with whom we became acquainted as a representative of pure consciousness in psychology, was a forerunner of the theoretical research in intrapsychic activity and of the structure of the soul. He was a pioneer in a very real way. The germs of a new tendency were latent within his system of psychology, as is evidenced by the fact that several chief representatives of the new tendency, pre-eminently Husserl and Stumpf, were originally disciples of the Brentano school. In Brentano, the concept of the mental "act," and the distinction that we, in our terminology, have called a distinction between the "known" and the "knowing" consciousness, both figure prominently. With reference to ideas, Brentano separated "content" from the "ideation" of that content, without, however, drawing the inferences which his pupils attained. Brentano's mental "act" was by no means a "faculty" and cannot even be called an "activity," except in a limited sense.

2. The concept of the "act" did not become the focus of interest until the beginning of the twentieth century, when a new science called "phenomenology" developed. Phenom-

enology does not purport to be a psychology, but was none
the less, at least in its initial stages, a descriptive psychology.
In its later development, of course, it became a sort of intuitive logic and finally devolved into speculative metaphysics. As such, it does not concern us. We are interested
in phenomenology only in so far as it treats psychological
problems. To be sure, phenomenology did not treat these
problems for their own sake, but for the sake of establishing
a system of pure logic. Its founder, Edmund Husserl, Professor of Philosophy, first at Göttingen and later at Freiburg,
was a thoroughly confirmed logician. His first great opus,
Studies in Logic, was published in 1900 and revised in 1913.
Husserl made his debut with all the pathos of a pioneer and
a reformer. He gathered about himself a large body of
students, some of whom later deserted him.

What is the aim of phenomenology? Husserl, in his early
period (the only one pertinent to our discussion), explained
it thus: "In its pure and intuitive procedure, phenomenology
analyzes and describes with essential generality—especially
with regard to the phenomenology of thought and insight
—the experiences of ideation, judgment, and cognition,
which are conceived empirically as classes of real phenomena
related to animal reality. Phenomenology subjects psychology to a scientific empirical scrutiny. From another approach,
phenomenology reveals the 'sources' from which the
fundamental concepts and ideal laws of pure logic originate,
the same sources to which these concepts and laws must
again be traced back."

Disregarding the second approach, phenomenology appears to be merely a descriptive psychology, or even a pure
analysis of consciousness. But Husserl differed from the
previously discussed psychologists in his more critical grasp
of the concept of "consciousness." To these psychologists,
consciousness had merely been the sum of its contents, that
is, "known consciousness." To Husserl, such an interpretation was only one of three possibilities. His version of
this latter interpretation was that consciousness amounts to

"the total, real phenomenological estate of the empirical self; or to the intermingling of psychic experiences in the uniform stream of experience." This "known" or, as Husserl wrote, "experienced" consciousness is rigorously conceived by the phenomenologist as devoid of all relation to empirical existence, as, for example, to man as a natural being.

Husserl's second interpretation is that of consciousness "as the inner realization of one's own psychic experiences." This concept of consciousness, according to Husserl, is the prior one.

In conclusion there is the third concept of consciousness "as a collective designation for every manner of mental act or intuitive experience."

It is obvious that Husserl, in this third definition, leans heavily upon Brentano, even if he often corrected his predecessor in the matter of distinctions. In using the concept of the "act," Husserl desired to exclude absolutely every connotation of "activity."

In every act, there are separate distinctions of quality and matter, to which is added a third distinction, the "object itself." When we designate an experience as a judgment, we mean that which it has in common with all other judgments. This is the quality of judgment. However, that which differentiates a judgment from all other judgments is its matter, that is, its specific meaning content. Quality in this sense remains constant, whereas matter is variable. (This corresponds somewhat to Stumpf's distinction between function and manifestation.)

Most of Husserl's extremely subtle distinctions (which we shall not attempt to enumerate here) were drawn in reference to epistemology and logic, and are of secondary importance to psychology. We shall consider only the ideas related to our main psychological thesis, that is, the relation of single acts to the whole self. This, too, was of secondary significance to Husserl; moreover, he changed his views in the interim between the first and second edition of his main work. And even in the second edition, these views are not presented in any systematic form.

In the first edition, Husserl declared: "That which I myself am able to perceive is the empirical 'I' plus its relation to those personal experiences or external objects which at a given moment have become the objects of special attention." Husserl thus eliminated the "bodily I" which appeared as a physical thing just like other physical things. He merely considered the "mental I" that appeared to belong to the "bodily I." Phenomenologically viewed, Husserl's "I" is a nexus of cognitively apprehensible experiences. This nexus is related to its analogous "mental I" the way the perceived aspect of an external thing is related to the thing as a whole. Such perception of one's own "I" (to which belong the "bodily I," the "mental I," and thus the whole empirical "subjective I"), need not be commensurately visual; it is, as in external perception, only a conceptual realization of the "I." However, the "I" is nevertheless "perceived" in the sense of being aware of its own physical presence.

In the second edition, Husserl also recognized a "pure I," somewhat in the sense of neo-Kantianism, but failed to substantiate it with particulars.

The relation of the "I" to the separate acts is explained in such a manner that the "I" appears as the known member of an incomplete equation whose unknown member is some external object. The "I" as a cardinal and equi-identical unit of the equation can be substituted for every act. But in many acts, especially when we are utterly absorbed in an object, the "I" fades out entirely as an equational member of the completed acts.

Taken as a whole, Husserl's psychology is essentially an analysis of consciousness; but its approach and its results are quite different from those of the sensationists and their reproductions; that is to say, it was not merely "known" consciousness. On the contrary, Husserl viewed consciousness as a nexus of "acts," inestimably more involved than the "contents" comprising the sole interest of sensationist

psychology. And behind consciousness, Husserl divined the
"I," though in a nebulous way.

The paradox of Husserl's scientific influence is accentuated by the fact that, although he greatly stimulated
psychology, yet personally, he treated psychological problems only "parenthetically," as he said. Deep down in his
soul Husserl loathed psychology and coined the word
"psychologian" (*Psychologisten*), for all those who correlated problems of logic with psychology. The word "psychologian," enjoyed an extended vogue in German science
at one time as a term of opprobrium.

THEODORE LIPPS'S PSYCHOLOGY OF THE "I"

1. Theodore Lipps (died 1914), late professor at Munich,
was, next to Husserl, among the pioneers of modern
structural psychology. Like Husserl, Lipps was an avowed
logician and proclaimed his kinship with Husserl by championing his cause while he was still comparatively unknown.
Indeed, a group of Lipps's students openly announced their
conversion to phenomenology. However, Lipps, unlike
Husserl, was not only secondarily a psychologist, but was
convinced that psychology was the backbone of most philosophical disciplines. Lipps developed this conviction particularly in his studies in esthetics.

For all the peculiar and even arbitrary temper of his
thought, Lipps possessed an extraordinarily versatile mind.
In his earlier writings, such as *The Basic Data of Mental
Life* (1883), he was still very closely related to associationist psychology. But later on he openly advocated a psychology of the soul; he viewed the task of psychology not
merely as the description of consciousness, but also as the
construction of consciousness upon the basis of a "soul,"
and the understanding of the laws that govern consciousness. In consequence, Lipps engaged in many a combat with
his colleagues of the experimental school, and was a rather
isolated figure in his time. The acuity of his mind corre-

sponded to a certain caustic temper in debate. Whenever he lectured from his podium in Munich, usually without recourse to notes, while investing all his thoughts with an aura of novelty, his students probably had the impression that they were being addressed dictatorially by criticism incarnate.

We shall confine ourselves chiefly to Lipps's later works, and, as occasion demands, to the last editions of his earlier works, since we should like to consider Lipps's psychology in the form in which he finally meant it to appear. Lipps's writings hardly make for easy reading; they require intensive concentration and dialectic interest. There is no single psychological concept that Lipps did not split up into several subconcepts, which he then juggled about like a prestidigitator.

2. Like William James, Lipps saw in consciousness a continuous stream, even though its continuity was represented by a frequently broken line, whose interruptions were conditioned by external impulses registered through the senses, if they did not issue from previous experiences of consciousness. Lipps was also akin to James in relating all single contents of consciousness to an "I," the primary or direct "I," the "consciousness self."

This direct "I," however, is not synonymous with the "soul." The "soul" is the real premise imputed to the "I" and is metaphorically designated as the "substratum" or "carrier" of consciousness. Neither is the "brain" identical with the direct "I," but it is a complex of physical phenomena which, in themselves, are perhaps identical with the brain, but are just as unknown to us as the soul. The direct "I" can be neither defined nor described, but everyone experiences it; indeed, it is the only absolutely certain existence. The unity of individual consciousness consists in consciousness itself being coexperienced with every experience of consciousness. Consciousness is a point of reference, but it can be extended into a line leading to some terminal point, and this line is often identical with the newly attained terminal point. Notwithstanding such identity, consciousness is in a state of constant qualitative change; for example, I, who was sad yesterday, can be happy today; indeed, I can hardly understand my sadness of yesterday.

From this stream of consciousness, manifold tendencies, activities, and acts detach themselves, though they are not experienced isolatedly, but are experienced as "issuing from" other experiences. We experience this "issuing" not merely as a chronological sequence, but as a correlation, which we also characterize as "definiteness," "conditionality," "dependency," and the like. Now all this is rooted in the experience of "I"; that is, "I" feel my activity conditioned by an event, "I" find myself dependent upon a fact. In no event, however, must we identify these experienced references to "I" with the causal references which we determine, or, more precisely, infer in the external world. The expression "motivation" is much more appropriate for the directly experienced unity of consciousness. Motivation, in this sense, designates the living "joints," so to speak, between the breaks in inner activity. Motivation, of course, is only a chronological category, not a causal one. Causality does not lie in the consciousness but in the "soul."

According to Lipps, psychology as an "interpretative" science (this term is not to be confused with Dilthey's use of the word) is pledged to the task of basing a directly experienced correlation of consciousness upon a causal correlation; for all interpretation entails causal correlation. This task of psychology runs parallel to the task of natural science which also creates a cognitive basis for its discovered data by the subsumption of molecules, atoms, and the like. The difference between psychology and natural science is that the latter conceives its basis in the terminology of sense phenomena, particularly in spatial terms; whereas psychology creates its own terminology, which must be derived from the experiences of consciousness.

The substratum that psychology primarily needs to

bring causal order into the life of consciousness is the "soul." The soul, however, is not identical with consciousness, as the psychology of consciousness used to claim, but is a reality postulated in order to make consciousness understandable. The soul is the real "I" in contradistinction to the experienced "I." It can even be designated as substance if, in so doing, we do not think of the material essence of things which we impute to the objects of sense perception. Thus, psychology is not the science of the facts of consciousness, but it is the science of the soul and of soul "phenomena."

Conceptually, the soul is wholly different from the brain, even though the soul is probably identical with the brain per se. The soul and the brain per se are the same unknown quantity. But the soul is a psychological concept. There is just as much sense in saying of the brain that it thinks or desires as there might be in asking how many grains the soul weighs, or what kind of cells the soul is composed of. It is equally senseless to ask where the soul is situated.

3. Lipps departed from the pure psychology of consciousness in his methodology just as he did in his conception of the "soul" as the substratum supporting consciousness. He designated his method self-examination or analysis. Yet he did not conceive this simply as the record of what is experienced, but the interpretation of experiences. He also spoke in this connection of experiments, but distinguished inner experiments from outer or psychophysical experiments. Lipps did not confuse psychology with physical or biological concepts but advocated specific psychological observation and interpretation.

As a result psychology now feels it incumbent upon itself to create its own fundamental concepts. To be sure, Lipps, apparently like the sensationalists, made sensation his point of departure; but in the Lippsian psychology sensations are not stimulations of the senses but of the "soul," that is to say, of the real "I" underlying consciousness. Therefore, the real sensation is not identical with the experience of consciousness as such. In a similar way, the "idea" to which Lipps referred is not merely a phenomenon of consciousness but a "soul" phenomenon upon which the phenomenon of consciousness is based. Hence, psychology is concerned with the determination of these sensory and ideational phenomena, with their nature and causality, with their relations to one another and to the soul. Sensations and ideas are the "elements" of the soul phenomena.

Thinking is no new category beyond sensations and images, but it is an interpretation of what is already contained in these pictures. "Objects" are seen in terms of sensations and images in the "mind's eye." Thinking is therefore the having of images upon a higher level. A still higher level is the apperception of objects about which we think.

Feelings and tendencies are not special mental occurrences but are explained as the reflection, within consciousness, of the action of sensory and ideational phenomena, and of their relations to one another and to their substratum, the "soul."

One might possibly be tempted to place Lipps among the sensationists because he termed sensations and ideas "elements." But this would be doing him an injustice, because he clearly distinguished the objective from the subjective content of such phenomena; in other words, that-which-is-sensed from that-which-senses. Thus, he belongs in the ranks of the "act" psychologists, even though he, himself, never used the term.

Attention is one of the subjective traits that appears in conjunction with "content." In order to clarify this concept, Lipps introduced the terms of psychic "force" and psychic "energy," which are not to be confused with the same terms customarily used in physics. Psychic force is that which makes it at all possible for phenomena to originate within the soul. Psychic energy is the possibility immanent within these phenomena themselves which enables them to realize this psychic force inherent in themselves. Such realization, however, is conditioned both by the energy of the phenomenon and the phenomenon's relation to the total soul plus other competitive phenomena, because in the soul everything is related to everything else. Isolation must always be supplemented by unitary interrelationships.

We shall not enumerate here the particulars of Lipps's psychology. Like all dialectitians he was indefatigable in the matter of classifications and distinctions. No matter what he discussed, apperception, judgment, feelings, or will, he constantly split his concepts up into a host of special subconcepts, all of which he defined with great acumen. It is distinctly questionable whether all these distinctions are fruitful for the further development of psychology. Lipps's studies were haunted by a sense of the abstract and were hardly ever enlivened by concrete examples. Perhaps that is the reason why his teachings inspired only a narrow circle of his personal students.

Let us, however, discuss one definite and particularly noteworthy contribution of the Lippsian psychology. This was his theory of "empathy" (*Einfühlung*), upon which he constructed his system of esthetics. Whereas in ordinary insight, judgment, and tendency, the "I" experiences its object as standing "opposite," there is also such a thing as an experience within the object. The "I" projects itself into the object with which it becomes identified. This gives rise to a special and peculiar form of consciousness which divines the inner life of objects and is of utmost significance in the most varied walks of life. While there is a certain violation of fact in the manner in which "empathy" is explained, it has unquestionably become one of the most fruitful ideas of Lipps's psychology.

It is difficult to fix Lipps's position in the history of science, since he hardly ever cited other authorities in his writings. He undoubtedly had something in common with Herbart, Lotze, Wundt, and James. Lurking in the background, however, is the spirit of Leibniz to whose psychology of the soul not only Lipps's theories but also those of the other structural psychologists are indebted, even if they are unaware of the fact. For the real "I" of Lipps, which is substance in the dynamic sense, is intimately related to the monad of Leibniz.

THE FURTHER DEVELOPMENT OF THEORETICAL STRUCTURAL PSYCHOLOGY

1. The ideas stimulated by Brentano, Husserl, and Lipps took root in many younger scholars, most of whom felt themselves unequivocally opposed to associationist psychology. We have already mentioned the fact that the Würzburg school of "thought" psychology had certain connections with phenomenology. A. Messer developed the contrast between "act" psychology and passivistic sensationism in a book entitled *Sensation and Thought*, while the *Gestalt* psychologists like Wertheimer, also confessed a certain kinship with phenomenology.

The psychologist who most clearly and also most circumspectly developed the distinction between the known consciousness and the knowing consciousness was Karl Stumpf. In an academic address in 1907, Stumpf elucidated this contradistinction by the terms of "phenomena" and "psychic functions." Phenomena, he held, are the contents of sensations and their reproductions; psychic functions are the becoming aware of phenomena plus their relations, the combining of phenomena into complexes, the forming of concepts, understanding and judging, emotions, desire, and will. The concept of function (synonymous with act, state, or experience) is understood as an activity in much the same way that heart action in systole and diastole is understood as an organic function. The main proof of Stumpf's investigations is directed toward the logical separability of both groups. That they are logically separable is evidenced by the fact that, on the one side, psychic functions can change without an accompanying change in phenomena. This is analogous to the manner in which we may detect a single note in a chord, without any attendant change in the chord itself as a phenomenon. And on the other side, changes can occur in the phenomena without a change of function. The illustration for this, among others, is offered by such cases in which something actually changes in the field of vision without being noticed.

In the sphere of emotional life, Stumpf also tried to prove the separability of phenomena and functions. With regard to the question whether a substance, in other words, a substantial soul, might be assumed beyond functions, Stumpf preferred to suspend judgment. "If we were to believe ourselves justified in imputing an unknown constant to that sum of psychic functions and dispositions which we name the soul, or, if we were to consider the soul as a known but in itself impalpable part of that sum, the soul would still remain only an inference which is not directly known. . . . The consciousness of psychic functions is not without further qualification the consciousness of a substance behind the functions." Stumpf expressly rejected the identification of functional psychology with the psychology of the "I."

It is obvious that the representatives of the older generation, to which Stumpf belonged, had qualms about introducing a unified soul or an "I"; because to have done so in a psychological laboratory would have been just as much anathema as speaking of God at an atheist meeting.

2. Nevertheless, the introduction of the soul was inevitable. T. K. Österreich, a young scholar who had been influenced by Lipps and Husserl and who was one of Stumpf's school, dared the first step. In his book, *The Phenomenology of the "I"* (1911), whose very title betrayed the influence of Husserl, Österreich investigated those experiences of consciousness that could rightly be ascribed to the "I." For the purposes of this investigation, he quoted interesting pathological cases in which the consciousness of the "I" had either been obliterated or split; in other words, he dealt with those cases that are generally called "depersonalization."

Österreich arrived at the conclusion that the "contents"

of perception, imagery, and thought are "objective" but that their respective "functions," that is, functions of the "I," are subjective, like feeling and volition. In all phenomena, such as perceiving, judging, feeling, and willing, we cannot evade the question: Who is perceiving, who is judging? And the only answer can be: Some "I" is perceiving. The subjective factor, because of its very nature, is inseparable from all these phenomena. The "I" is a dependent factor in psychic phenomena, but is never lacking in any person. It cannot be constructed sensorially out of sensations, that is, from inner bodily sensations; nor can it be based upon memory. The "I" in every person remains permanently identical with that person's self. Neither states of depersonalization nor the simultaneous or successive splitting of the "I" signify the suspension of this identity. Such pathological phenomena are either alternating states of the same "I," which remains identical in every change of its emotions; or else they are abnormal processes which, though forcing themselves to the surface, do not permanently displace this unity. A nonsubjective psychology cannot explain these states. It is necessary, rather, to return to a monadological conception of the "I." The notion of parallelism is inadmissible. It is only as an interaction that we can understand the relation of the "I" to the body.

Österreich soon advanced so far in his conception of the "I," that he overshot the bounds of science. In his latest book, *Problems of the Unity and Splitting of Personality*, he considers the phenomena of split personality in reference to mediumistic "psychic" phenomena. "If we grant that the organism is constructed by the psyche, then spirit materialization is simply the organism newly constructed by the split-off 'I.' " Together with split personality, Österreich also discusses the fused personality, but his monadological theory of the 'I' " is subjected to forceful and recondite application, and soon dissipates entirely into the metaphysical.

3. We must also include Driesch in this discussion on the

strength of his book entitled *Fundamental Problems of Psychology*. Driesch differentiates a materialogy of mental life from a dynamics of mental life. He rejects the term "activity" of consciousness but emphasizes that "sense" and "meaning" must have their place among elementary psychic objects. Driesch recognizes directive agencies in the service of order as the most important unconscious mental factors. He also devotes an exhaustive investigation to those modifications appearing as the walking, dreaming, or hypnotic "I," or in the various forms of the split "I," all of which seem to indicate that the structure of the soul can be split into parts. Driesch also recognizes the special importance of parapsychological research, and is even of the opinion that the psychology of the future will be based upon such research.

4. Max Scheler (died 1928), the philosopher, was far more intimately related to phenomenology than Österreich, at least during the middle period of his eventful career. Scheler was one of the most inspired and inspiring thinkers among the younger Germans. Even though he was primarily a philosopher, he was none the less an excellent psychologist who preferred to call himself a phenomenologist. He began as an idealist, and was tremendously inspired by Nietzsche and Bergson before going over to Lipps and especially to Husserl. There are a number of his essays dating from this period that are occupied essentially with psychological problems of the feelings and of the "I," the very problems which Husserl had relegated to "parenthetical" importance.

Scheler pursued the study of psychology chiefly with an eye to ethics and the philosophy of religion. In an essay on "Resentment in the Development of Morals," he elaborated upon an inspiring idea derived from Nietzsche, who had been the first to stress the significance of "resentment." In an extensive essay on "The Idols of Self-understanding," Scheler sought to destroy the fallacious notion that insight is undeceptive, and thereby energetically advocated the standpoint of the psychology of the "I." What we call experiences are, according to Scheler, not parts of the "I," but abstract symbols of it from which we reconstruct a unified totality for the purpose of social understanding.

Scheler devoted himself most intensively to his *Phenomenology and Theory of the Feelings of Sympathy, Love and Hate*, published in 1913. The second edition, which appeared in 1921 under the title of *The Nature and Forms of Sympathy*, was supposed to inaugurate a series of works on emotional life which was never completed. In this critical treatise, Scheler assailed all the "naturalistic" theories which derive love and hate from the instincts, or try to combine them from simple feelings. He defined love as an "action" in which every object bearing value attains to its highest possible value or to its ideal value essence. Hate is the counterposed action.

Scheler's compendious work on ethics, *Formalism in Ethics* (1913), also contains an abundance of valuable analyses of emotional states classified according to their respective value. In his last period, of course, Scheler turned away from phenomenology and ascribed great significance to the instincts which he had formerly rejected. His main interest was latterly concentrated upon the distinction between "soul" and "spirit."

5. There is another school, also traceable to Wundt, that tends toward an organic structural psychology in conjunction with the research in evolutionary psychology. Its founder is Felix Krüger, Wundt's successor in Leipzig. H. Volkelt, H. Werner, and F. Sander also belong to this group, and their teachings are closely related to *Gestalt* psychology. These scholars stress the fact that genetically the total quality is prior to the partial qualities, and that *Gestalt* experience develops from indeterminate experience. An additional trait peculiar to this school is its emphasis on the feelings and on complex feeling qualities to such a degree that it even speaks of an experiential and functional

primacy of feeling. In the Krüger school, pluralism of feeling is brought out even more prominently than in Wundt, and "depth" of feeling is introduced as a special quality.

The Krüger school does not merely confine itself to the analysis of consciousness. It is far more concerned with the unexperienced psychic phenomena. This factor has an organic composition which is not to be conceived in the least mechanistically. Among the types of such compositions, Krüger emphasizes "structures," in which his school is mainly interested.

Another characteristic of this school is its evolutionary psychological approach. Since its interest is primarily directed toward complex emotional totalities, the early stages of development are especially fruitful for its particular type of research. Krüger's school speaks of "emotional prime totals" out of which more definite forms of mental life issue through differentiation and development. Krüger refers to the gradual setting in of "de-emotionalization," inasmuch as genetically earlier stages are more strongly emphasized emotionally than later ones. In addition great stress is laid upon the fact that psychic phenomena are regularly dominated by the after-effects of previous experiences.

In corroboration of our claim that the new Leipzig school originated in Wundt we have, on the one hand, its emphasis on feeling and, on the other, the fact that it strives as much as possible to substantiate its conclusions experimentally, a trait not at all prominent in the other psychologists mentioned in this section. But it is not the Wundt of physiological psychology, it is the Wundt of the "racial psychology" whose spirit and influence marches with the younger Leipzig school. This younger school criticizes Wundt because it does not wish to emulate him in constructing racial psychology upon general psychology, but insists that a "general" psychology is impossible without preliminary research in racial psychology.

WILLIAM STERN AND "PERSONALISM"

1. William Stern, in the meantime, essayed the task of fathoming the structure of the soul, or of the "personality," as he prefers to call it, without being very much touched by the research trends we have just discussed. Stern encompassed the totality of psychic phenomena to an even further extent than Lipps, who based such phenomena merely upon a somewhat abstract soul which he subsequently tried to connect with the brain. Stern also includes the body as a matter of course, and christens the indivisible body-soul unity with the name of "personality," always emphasizing that all personal experiences are entirely "psychophysically neutral." For the same reason he prefers to call his psychology "personalism," so that, from the very outset, it proclaims its dissociation from all mere analysis of consciousness, and from all systems of psychology which, having determined an experience introspectively, strive to find some cerebral process to correspond with it. Stern's concept of psychophysical neutrality is intended, if not ultimately to solve, at least to replace the body-soul problem with an improved working hypothesis.

Stern does not divide the entire universe into the traditional duality of "spirit" and "matter," which no philosophical ingenuity has ever been able to reunite; instead of these, he institutes two other basic categories: "person" and "thing," which are diametrically antithetic to the traditional views. Now Stern finds this antithesis in the entire cosmos; and so his science of "personalistics" only comprises part of an inclusive metaphysical system which he calls "personalism." The entire world, according to Stern, can be considered from two sides: "from above" and "from below," metaphorically understood, of course. If we consider the world "from below," for example, man is a sum of chemical substances; seen "from above," he is a personality.

If one approaches Stern's personalistics from the metaphysical side, one might easily fear that he had evolved his entire psychological theory by pure speculation. But such a fear is groundless. Stern merely fitted his theory into a metaphysical frame after he had fought his way through the myriad details of painstaking laboratory research. He began as a pupil of Ebbinghaus and thoroughly mastered differential psychology and child psychology, the two research fields which we have designated as the necessary preliminary stages of structural psychology.

2. Stern presented all he had garnered from his inductive detail work in his system of personalistics, which comprises the second part of a work in three parts entitled *Person and Thing*. The second part bears the title of *The Human Personality*, and its first edition appeared in 1918.

The human personality, like all other "personalities," is introduced as a self-determining, purposive, meaningful totality. It occupies itself with self-preservation and self-development. Beyond this, of course, the personality also subordinates itself to suprapersonal aims transmitted to it by means of "introception." That is to say, the teleology of the human being is not purely individual but simultaneously supraindividual, since it also enters into the service of its fellow men and of humanity. The independence of the personality is not to be understood as though it were completely independent of its environment. Rather, the environment is necessary to the personality. Personality and environment are "convergently" related to each other.

Stern is primarily concerned with the inner structure of the personality. As we have seen, the personality develops in "convergence" with the environment and by means of the "introception" of supraindividual goals; but the individual brings his personality into the world in the form of tendencies or dispositions. In the beginning, these tendencies are present only in vague form as "dispositions" (*Anlagen*). However, in the course of existence, these dispositions shape themselves, in convergence with the environment, into more definite "characteristics." The personality is, therefore, not literally but figuratively determined. It is plastic and, as a result, can be educated, of course, within such limits as are set by the dispositions. The dispositions are not to be understood as antithetically pigeonholed "faculties" in the sense of the older psychology of faculties —but as partial radiations of the unitary total personality which dominates and interpenetrates every separate disposition. For the whole antedates the parts and is more real than the parts.

For this reason Stern rejects every attempt at an atomization of the personality into elements. To be sure, he admits that it is scientifically necessary to study the separate dispositions isolatedly; but he insists that such studies always be made within the frame of an organic point of view. The personality is *"unitas multiplex."* It is no doubt divided into integral parts of various order: organs, functions, purposive tendencies, spheres of performance, experiences, and the like, but all these integral parts are intercorrelated in a greater or lesser interpenetration, and in a greater or lesser dominance or subordination of their factors.

Every separate disposition is simultaneously "directed" toward some goal (conative) and purposefully "equipped." The so-called instinct of imitation, for example, contains, on the one hand, the tendency toward imitation; and on the other hand, the capacity to imitate. Depending upon the predominance of either the direction (conation) or the equipment (capacity), we can distinguish directional and equipmental dispositions. The directional dispositions (conations) comprise that which is known as character; character is the unity of a person's directional (conative) dispositions. The equipmental dispositions, on the other hand, comprise a person's gifts; they include the capacities and skills necessary for the fulfilment of his life tasks.

The relation of the partial structure to the whole is designated by Stern with the concepts of "incorporation"

(*Einbettung*) and "detachment" (*Abhebung*). In the most diverse levels of experience, a single experience can detach itself from the whole, but, at the same time, it constantly remains incorporated in the whole. The detachment may be vague or may have definite form. In perception, for instance, "forms" are sharply detached but constantly remain embedded in the whole personality. In contradistinction to *Gestalt* psychology, which treats forms (*Gestalten*) as something objective, Stern coins the phrase: "No form without a former." And this "former" is none other than the totalitarian personality.

The life of personality thus presents itself, as regards detail, in a dual aspect: as expression and impression. Everything bodily is expression; everything psychic is impression. Experience occurs as an expression, or as expressive action; but, as consciousness, it is simultaneously an impression. Expression and impression are two forms of the same experience. But their relationship is not to be understood in a parallelistic sense, as if every fragment of bodily function corresponded precisely to some fragment of conscious function. On the contrary, both expression and impression enter into the most diverse combinations of purpose and meaning because of their attachment to the unit totality of the personality.

According to Stern, consciousness arises only in the event of a conflict. Only when external or internal dissonances, obstructions, or contradictions arise does a spark of consciousness fly out of the resulting friction. That is why consciousness does not mirror all of life but only the conflicting aspects of the "I," that is, of our inner conflicts; in objective consciousness, we become aware of that part of the world which must be conquered or repulsed.

PSYCHOLOGY IN THE CULTURAL SCIENCES

1. We now return to Wilhelm Dilthey (died 1911), a philosopher with whom we became acquainted in the first

part of this book as one of the critics of the psychology of consciousness in the 1890 decade. We recall that he disparaged the associationists in a program demanding the organic description of the teleological "structure" of the soul, and inveighed against its hypothetical dissolution into elements. He had already indicated, at that time, that individual differences were not merely accidental deviations from the norm, but were to be "interpreted" in terms of the totalitarian structure of the soul.

As we have stated, Dilthey never succeeded in developing his psychology into a system, however much such a system existed latently in his numerous separate essays, some of which were not published until after his death. Since Dilthey's interests were preëminently historical, his labors consisted chiefly in rendering historical personalities comprehensible. To this end, he availed himself not only of an individualizing but also of a typifying method in which he classified historical personalities according to certain typical mental attitudes. The most famous of all his later writings was his essay, "The Nature of Philosophy," which first appeared in 1907 in Hinneberg's *Kultur der Gegenwart* (Vol. I). In this essay, Dilthey gave a brief presentation of his psychological leanings and, at the same time, outlined a typology of philosophic attitudes which was designed to embrace the realms of religion, art, and philosophy.

We shall postpone for later discussion Dilthey's integration of the individual into a purposive, socially conditioned, supraindividual nexus. But in every individual there also operates a teleological structural nexus. For, whenever the mental unity experiences anything valuable to it in pleasure or pain, it responds by attention, by the choice and revision of impressions, by conations, by acts of will, by a choice of goals, and by casting about for the means to achieve its ends. This purposive tendency is directed in the first instance toward the objective mastery of reality; secondly, toward the determination of the values of life; and thirdly, toward practical aims. All this crystallizes by gradual development into definite forms, which, taken as a whole, represent the individual's *Weltanschauung*.

Dilthey applies his typology of *Weltanschauungen* and the personalities which evolve them most intensively in the field of formal philosophy. Here he distinguished three fundamental types which recur in the history of the philosophy of all peoples and epochs. Materialism and scientifically grounded positivism fall into the first category. The representatives of this type are Democritus, Lucretius, Epicurus, Hobbes, the Encyclopedists, Comte, and Avenarius. For this type the understanding of reality is the main issue, while such concepts as value and purpose recede into the background.

The objective idealists form the second group. Here everything is viewed from the standpoint of value; reality is conceived as the expression of an inner, an either unconsciously or consciously operative psychic whole. To this type belong Heraclitus, the Stoics, Spinoza, Leibniz, Shaftesbury, Goethe, Schelling, Schleiermacher, and Hegel.

The third group comprises the idealists of freedom. They affirm the independence of the mind from nature. They project their volition into the universe and thus derive such notions as divine personality, creation, and sovereignty of the subjective self in the universal flux. To this group belong Plato, Cicero, the Christian philosophers, Kant, Fichte, Carlyle.

We need not determine whether this typology is exhaustive or not. It serves, however, to illuminate Dilthey's psychological procedure of deriving an inclusive philosophy of life from the totalitarian behavior of specific types. If we may reproach the atomistic psychologists with having confined themselves too much to elements, we might reproach Dilthey with not having gone into sufficient detail; we might object that his psychology is based upon intuition and is, therefore, not quite strictly a science. As a psychologist Dilthey, nevertheless, exerted an uncommonly inspiring influence despite the fact that he never developed an exact psychological system; and every history of psychology must of necessity accord him a position of distinction.

2. Of all Dilthey's many students Eduard Spranger (born 1882) is most highly regarded as a psychologist. He became the formal successor to Dilthey when he was appointed to the latter's chair at the University of Berlin. In addition to Dilthey's inspiration, Spranger also learned a great deal from the philosophy of Rickert; but as a psychologist, he follows, for the most part, in Dilthey's footsteps, independently developing his teacher's ideas. Since Spranger's writings were much more readable and concrete than those of his teacher, he was destined to enjoy a much more popular success, particularly in the field of pedagogy. His principal works are *Types of Men: the Psychology and Ethics of Personality*, the first edition of which appeared in 1914, and the second, completely revised, in 1919; and the *Psychology of Adolescence*, which appeared in 1924.

Spranger defined his psychology (in open contradistinction to the "scientific" school), by calling it a "psychology from the standpoint of the cultural sciences," even more sharply than Dilthey did. This distinction between the natural (physical) and cultural sciences (also called mental sciences, that is, *"Geisteswissenschaften"*) has been an exceedingly controversial problem in modern German philosophy since the days of Windelband, with the final result that the natural (physical) sciences were robbed of their previously generally recognized claim to be the only "scientific sciences." The subject matter, aims, and methods peculiar to the cultural sciences, which include the historical sciences, were systematically defined as a result of this controversy.

Like Dilthey, Spranger does not wish to relegate psychology to the status of a physical science, but desires to treat it as a cultural science. As a cultural science, psychology takes the inner phenomenon as a meaningful whole belonging to a psychic situational whole. Whereas Dilthey spoke of the purposive nexus, Spranger prefers to speak of the meaningful nexus. Meaning, he defines as always having a reference to value. Unlike Dilthey, Spranger stresses the fact that the teleological structure is not merely centered in the "I," but yields to normative laws of value corresponding to the various valuational classes. Herein Spranger displays the influence of Rickert's neo-Kantianism. Now psychology is not concerned with the norms themselves but with their deviations, that is, so-called "subjective evaluations." For psychology is not a normative but a descriptive science, the aim of which is understanding; its *a priori* mission is the understanding of mental objectifications. In the mental life, objective and subjective "meanings" are often contradictory. Spranger calls the realization of that which is of objective value "performance." Consequently, the structure of the soul is a nexus of performances.

Within the total structure of the soul, however, partial structures are meaningfully embedded; such as the structure of insight, of technical labor, of religious consciousness. In addition to these, Spranger also speaks of "acts," by which he means the activities of the "I" structurally interwoven of various functions. By means of these "acts" the "I" can produce mental performances of supraindividual meaning. "Experience" is receptive meaningful conduct; it corresponds to "act," which is spontaneous conduct producing meaning. In experience we grasp the supraindividual meaning implicit in historical forms of the intellect, in works of art, and the like. Acts and experiences cannot always be sharply separated. Both occur in time, and both realize values. Mental "understanding" means tracing temporal phenomena of the mind back to their timeless, genetic nexus.

Although Spranger distinguishes different acts and experiences, his manner of doing so is totalistic throughout. "Every total act which produces meaning simultaneously includes all the basic forms of acts which produce meaning, and the totality of the spirit interpenetrates every single act."

The basic forms of acts producing meaning are:

a. economic.

b. theoretical.

c. esthetic.

d. religious.

These forms, of course, are constantly intermingling, but can be logically separated. Besides these, Spranger also distinguishes social acts, which embrace experiences of dependence and sympathy, and political acts, which aim at power.

3. From these general premises, Spranger derives a practical psychology in the form of a typology. Spranger's typology differs from Dilthey's; it classifies not only *Weltanschauungen* but also "types of men" (*Lebensformen*); and is, consequently, broader and more comprehensive. Spranger's types are differentiated according to which of the above-mentioned acts (or attitudes) predominate in the meaningful acts of the individual. Upon this basis, there are the following types:

a. The theoretic man. Cognition is the basic performance of his mental life. It is directed toward objectivity and toward objective causality. The theoretic man craves the possession of the total value of the world through a comprehensive cognition of existence. Hence he subordinates all other values to cognition.

b. The economic man aims at the practical and the utilitarian. For him everything resolves itself into means of preserving life and of making life pleasant. Knowledge, beauty, and all other values are subordinated to economic values.

c. The esthetic man. For him esthetic values are superlative. At times he abandons himself to the appreciation of external impressions (impressionist); at times he transfers all external impressions into expression (expressionist). Sometimes the esthetic individual strives for the union of impression and expression in harmonious form (classicist).

d. The social man. The social attitude becomes the organizing principle of his mental life. This attitude has its highest development in love. The social individual considers the aiding of other individuals to be the highest value.

e. The political man subordinates all the values of life to his will for power. Knowledge is power to him. He views economic and esthetic values as means to power. His goal is personal dominance and the establishment of his values as the only values.

f. The religious man subordinates his entire life to the quest for the highest values of existence, whether they lie in an absolute affirmation of life, or in an extreme negation embracing some transcendental philosophy of values. Most religious persons, however, combine both of these forms of life. Yet they completely subject knowledge, beauty, love, and riches to religious ideology.

Such are, according to Spranger, the basic types of man's mental attitudes. Naturally, they are presented as ideal types that never occur entirely "pure" in real life. In most real individuals "mixtures" of several of these attitudes are found. At any rate, Spranger's typology offers a method of differentiating and understanding the multitude of human individualities.

Spranger's psychology as a cultural science is bent upon "understanding" and not "explaining," like the so-called "scientific" psychology. Understanding, unlike explanation, seeks no basic causality, but a nexus of "meaning" relationships. Understanding is that complex, theoretical act in which (with an attempt at objectivity) we grasp the inner, meaningful nexus in the life and actions of an individual. To understand means to penetrate into the specific system of values of a mental nexus. We can do so on the basis of objectifications, which always have a physical and a mental side. In so far as we deal with life forms different from ours, understanding becomes in part a process of assimilation and in part a process of contrast.

In all probability the goal of complete objectivity will never be attained. Yet from the conception of psychology as a cultural science, and as a result of the historical and valuational approach a new Something arises, a Something that is an intellectual medium of supraindividual significance. And in this triply determined medium the mind creates itself. What we have here is, therefore, a self-understanding of the mind which is a broad, common medium encompassing the individual and the objectifications arising from the summation, interaction, and stratification of innumerable other individuals. Thus, psychology as a cultural science arrives at the problem of a supraindividual superconsciousness to which the last part of the present work is devoted.

All in all, psychology as a cultural science presents us with a picture that differs vastly from that of most other psychological systems. It does not even touch upon their bitterly disputed problems, such as the relation between soul and body. Neither does it offer us an analysis of consciousness, because the "structures" and "acts" that it studies are at most partly conscious, although by no means unconscious in the behavioristic sense. Here, the dynamics of psychic life dominate its "statics." Psychology as a cultural science has unquestionably achieved new insights that "scientific" psychology cannot afford to ignore.

CHARACTEROLOGY

1. While bitter theoretical controversies were waged concerning the existence of a structuralized "I" or "soul" beyond the phenomena of consciousness, actual daily practice introduced the concept of "character" into the discussion. The lay world demanded neither subtle disquisitions on states of consciousness nor cerebral localizations from psychology. What the layman wanted was a practical insight into his neighbor's character that would enable him to achieve some clarity in his personal and social relationships, and in the end better govern his own conduct. Such a practical study of character has always accompanied theoretical

psychology since the dawn of science in antiquity. This practical psychology did not take the form of scientific treatises but appeared usually in the form of typical "character sketches" or aphorisms.

Such character sketches had already been made by Theophrastus, one of Aristotle's pupils; and La Bruyère continued the practice. Typical characters like the "miser" or the "sycophant" were portrayed with full descriptions of all their various foibles. A practical understanding of human nature in the form of aphorisms was also attempted by other Frenchmen like Montaigne, La Rochefoucauld, Vauvenargues, and later by the German Lichtenberg; penetrating observations which, however, were never rounded out into a scientific system. Even the most profound of these aphorists, Friedrich Nietzsche, never achieved a comprehensive system, although his writings contain such vast stores of material for a deeply penetrating characterology that they have not been exhausted to this day. Julius Bahnsen, a philosopher who began as a disciple of Schopenhauer, outlined a system in his *Contributions to Characterology* (1867), but his work had no subsequent influence.

The modern psychology of consciousness at first paid scant attention to the problem of character. There were many psychological works in which the word "character" did not even occur. Of course, the reason for this was that no matter how we may define character, it certainly is not a phenomenon of consciousness. On the contrary, most people are rather hazy concerning their own characters; and when they are not, their opinion is very likely to be self-deceptive. Nor is there any less deception in what most people think of their neighbor's characters. Nevertheless, the desire for a scientific insight into character remained very much alive. As a result a plethora of pseudosciences such as palmistry and astrology came into vogue. The test method discussed above developed very gradually, and it suffered from the basic defect of attempting to piece the total character together from separate constituent character traits. The one thing these test experiments proved indisputably was that character is more than a sum of component and isolated traits; it is a living totality within which the same expressions may have different meanings.

2. One of the few professional psychologists who interested himself in the problem of character was Frédéric Paulhan, a Frenchman. He studied character in terms of its "elements," his chief aim being to find the important psychic elements that constitute the structure of a personality. In his work, *Les Caractères* (1894), Paulhan listed these elements as dominant tendencies, fixed ideas, and prevalent wishes. He grouped characters according to mental laws formulated by himself. When the law of association predominates, we have characters who are at one with themselves and possess psychic balance and poise. When the law of inhibition predominates, we have characters who are capable of self-control and deliberation. Association through contrast dominates in the characters of restless, nervous, and quarrelsome individuals. When the elements of the mind are independent of one another, impulsive, disorganized, and complicated characters result. The predominance of vital tendencies results in gluttonous, temperate, sexually active, or frigid characters. In a similar fashion, mental and social dispositions also determine distinguishable characters.

3. The most elaborate system of characterology of recent times is that of L. Klages who has given us not merely a classification of characters but a fundamental insight into the structure of character. We have already become acquainted with his system of graphology and his psychology of expression which were the sources of his characterology. As a psychologist Klages began as a pupil of Lipps; he was influenced to an even greater degree by Nietzsche, whose attainments in psychology he critically systematized (1927) in a special volume. In addition to the previously quoted

works of Klages, those which concern us here are *Principles of Characterology* (1910), which in its widely revised, later editions is entitled *Fundamentals of Characterology*; and *Personality* (1927).

In order to eliminate the moral evaluations which obtrude themselves into all character sketches, Klages worked out his own concepts and terminology. In every character he distinguishes: material (*Stoff*), structure (*Gefuege*), quality (*Artung*), tectonics (*Aufbau*), and attitudes (*Haltungsanlagen*).

Material includes all capacities such as memory, conceptual thinking, acumen, strength of will, sensitivity, etc. The very variety of these capacities reveals the fallacy of the *"tabula rasa* theory." Material, in this sense, consists of compound characteristics whose degree can be expressed numerically. These characteristics or capacities are a store of possessions, the working capital, so to speak, which the human being has at his disposal for the purpose of development and exploitation.

Under the heading of structure, Klages lists such characteristics as temperamental or untemperamental, mobile or immobile, impressionable or unimpressionable. These characteristics refer to the function of inner organs. They can always be determined, in contradistinction to innate capacities, from the quotient of correlation between intensity of impulsion and intensity of resistance.

Quality includes dispositions of feeling and will, the instinctual drives (*Triebfedern*) and interests. In so far as they have specific direction, the instinctual drives are also directional characteristics; for example, ambition and acquisitiveness are directed toward wholly different objects.

Tectonics comprise the mutual correlation of all the characteristics of the previously named groups. Under tectonics, Klages considers uniformity, equilibrium, disorganization, dependability, and similar characteristics.

The attitudes or attitudinal dispositions include those traits that, like boldness, garrulousness, shyness, boisterousness, are evidenced in external conduct, but must be traced back to their essential basis. Popular typology which characterizes the gentleman, the army officer, or the clergyman bases its judgments primarily upon such attitudes.

All those traits are important for characterology, but according to Klages, the most fundamental ones are those of quality: the capacities of feeling and will. Consequently, Klages found it most important to establish a system of motives according to a principle based upon the antithesis: self-submission and self-assertion. We cannot here enter into the minutiæ of Klages' extremely subtle and involved system; nor can we dwell upon the other fine distinctions he draws between memory and the capacity of recall, and between impression capacity and conceptual tendencies.

Unquestionably, Klages' characterology belongs in the category of the psychology with "soul," despite the fact that he does not ascribe to the "soul" all that an earlier psychology had designated as "psychic." On the contrary, one of his basic theses, upon which he constructed his entire philosophical system, is the differentiation between "soul" and "mind." Klages views "consciousness" only as the "capacity to take cognizance of something," that is, the capacity of judgment and understanding. Sensation and feeling are separated from consciousness as "experience." Things are conceived by reason but are not "experienced." The disposition for such conceiving is identical in all carriers of consciousness and is called "mind." As long as the mind is connected to the experiencing "I," the mind is called "I" and is bound to reality. The "soul," on the other hand, is the premise of experience. Soul and body are not related to each other as cause to effect, but as a symbol is related to that which it symbolizes. The soul is the meaning of the body.

We shall not enter upon a minute discussion of these problems which can only be understood within the context of Klages' highly complicated system of philosophy. Klages is not merely one of the most able psychologists, but also one of the most significant philosophers of modern Germany. While his characterology demands intensive study, it opens up amazing perspectives which lead the student far beyond the confines of experimental psychology.

CONCLUSION

A COMPARISON of the psychological systems summarized in this section with those of the "new" psychology, which professed (in 1880) to have laid a solid foundation for the future, discloses that psychology as a cultural science has rejected almost everything that was taught by that "new" psychology.

The first ideal to be exploded was the hope of making psychology into a natural science. The contrary is now stressed. Mental life does not belong to nature. The mind is a realm fundamentally different from the realm of physico-chemical data. The methods borrowed from the natural sciences, especially the experimental method, were also rejected. The importance of the experimental method with regard to the determination of certain data in the spheres of sensation and imagery is not disputed, but the belief that the essential nature of perceptions and ideas can ever be fathomed experimentally, is denied. These phenomena occur only as functions of the "I," of the soul. Consequently, it is necessary to know the soul first before one can understand subsequent details. The soul is not a sum or conglomeration of its experiences. By no means. The soul is a whole which exists before its parts; and it is only when the whole is known that the parts can be understood. In this, structural psychology concurs with vitalistic biology which also placed the whole before its parts.

Since psychology is not a natural science, the categories which it borrowed from the natural sciences in the 1880 era must be eliminated. It is forbidden to speak of mechanisms, or of elements and combinations as in chemistry. Psychology must create its own purely psychological categories. These alone, of course, do not yet constitute a unity. Many modern psychologists, nevertheless, agree in their usage of fundamental concepts such as totality, structure, and conation or purposive tendency. To be sure, the category of consciousness is still employed but in an entirely different sense; it no longer denotes the known, passive consciousness but the knowing, active consciousness that in itself is not "known" but is the "carrier" or "substratum" of known consciousness. In consequence, the very word is frequently avoided and instead of consciousness, psychologists prefer to use the word "I," "personality," or "soul." In short, the soul, once pronounced dead, has proven its immortality, although not in a religious, transcendental sense.

As diametrically opposed to the older psychology of consciousness, to physiopsychology, and to psychomotor psychology as the new "psychology with soul" may appear to be at a first glance, it is possible to demonstrate that the evolution even of those earlier tendencies of research converged upon the necessity of demanding a totalitarian soul. One must admit that this totalitarian soul is not yet known with complete clarity. But today we can no longer dispute the fact that there is some totality beyond disparate psychic phenomena. This belief is confirmed, moreover, by those recent investigations that penetrate beyond consciousness and its manifestations into the realm of the unconscious. The unconscious, however, frequently extends into the realm of consciousness, and must be considered, therefore, as part and parcel of the soul. To these investigations we shall now direct our studies.

PART FIVE

THE PSYCHOLOGY OF THE
UNCONSCIOUS

THE "UNCONSCIOUS" AS A SOURCE
OF PSYCHOLOGICAL KNOWLEDGE

1. As a general rule, psychology has regarded the study of normal mental life as the "King's highway" of its research. But toward the end of the nineteenth century there appeared a school of psychological research that sought to gain an insight into the essence of the soul by studying mental abnormalities as found in certain mental diseases. As we have already seen in our presentation of cerebral physiology, a similar procedure was successfully applied to the physical substrata of mental life, in the course of which valuable information was also derived for purely psychological research. Thus a reciprocal relation grew, the psychiatrists borrowing psychological terminology in order to describe their patients' symptoms, while the psychologists, in turn, derived a considerable enrichment of their knowledge covering normal mental states by virtue of the remarkable instances of hyper-intensification, inhibition, variation, and disproportionality proffered by the mentally deranged.

A more precise examination disclosed that the boundary between the normal and abnormal mentality could not be drawn to a hair's breadth; indeed, it was exceedingly difficult to determine at all. The greatest difficulty was found in the determination of the point at which a definite mental state begins to be pathological. In general, a pathological state is defined as one which endangers an individual's self-preservation. But this is by no means the case in all psychic abnormalities, especially when they occur only transitorily or to a faint degree.

As a matter of fact even in the otherwise normal mentality temporary states very similar to those of insanity occur under certain circumstances. The emotions of pain, love, hate, and the like may be intensified temporarily to such a degree that they virtually upset the mental balance. When a normal individual is under severe stress, moreover, he may suffer from illusions, hallucinations, daydreaming, obsessions, and completely illogical behavior. Such phenomena impress the objective observer as insanity even though the individual in question becomes wholly "normal" again after he has calmed down. Artificial means, such as alcohol, hasheesh, mescal, and the like, can also induce temporary states of intoxication during which the subject behaves quite abnormally.

At any rate we can safely say that even the most bizarre pathological phenomena are not wholly different from manifestations of normal mental life but are either quantitative or qualitative variants of what are considered to be "normal" states. This enables us to understand mental abnormalities to a certain extent. In turn, hyper-intensities, subnormalities, and other abnormal variants shed interesting light upon normal cases. Pathological states are often distortions of normal experience in which certain normal features appear in an exaggerated form, or in sharper focus. Thus pathological melancholia is the profound intensification of "the blues," which are still considered normal, while the "fixed ideas" of mental patients correspond to the "single-track" associations of otherwise normal people.

2. We have just given a biological definition of the pathological correlating of mental phenomena with the process of self-preservation. Any attempt at a psychological definition of the "normal" immediately confronts us with the problem of the dual connotation of the word "norm." On the one hand, "normal" connotes the average or the general viewed as existing in the present; on the other hand, it also refers to that which should be, that which is exemplary and corresponds to a future idea. Both of these connotations are involved in the concept of normal consciousness; in perception, the normal is that which all of us perceive in the same way; in thinking, it is that which is commensurate with the laws of logic.

Now there is no need to believe that everything that

does not convey one of the two connotations of the word "normal" must be chaotic simply for that reason. Even among so-called abnormalities there exist certain typical phenomena possessing a fairly well-defined regularity. Obsessional neuroses for example, or the behavior of the hysteric or psychasthenic, display thoroughly typical features. These cannot be explained on the basis of consciousness alone; but even a physiological explanation often fails, since no anatomical basis for the above symptoms is discoverable. On the other hand, in the case of traumatic neuroses, it is possible to demonstrate psychic causes whose after-effects continue in the unconscious. Consequently, in order to explain such abnormalities, the concept of the unconscious "complex" was created. This subsequently led to the assumption of a subconscious, that is, a psychic substructure of the normal superconscious. The subconscious is not directly accessible from the superconscious but influences it profoundly.

Even the most extreme champions of consciousness psychology could not manage to interpret human conduct without the interpolation of unconscious phenomena. When associationist psychologists spoke of unconsciousness, they simultaneously admitted the existence of a systematized subconsciousness. The "complexes" of which the psychopathologists speak are precisely those "constellations" that can be inferred from consciousness only very indirectly, albeit they influence consciousness to deviate from its ordinary course in a manner which at first appears incomprehensible to the uninitiated observer. When King Lear connects the most impossible incidents with his ungrateful daughters, his particular complex influences his associations.

Psychopathology, therefore, was fully warranted in attempting a systematic investigation of the unconscious or subconscious, as a result of which the secret depths of consciousness today have been penetrated and explored. The psychology of the unconscious is today one of the most important branches of the whole science of psychology.

Physiopsychology, psychomotor psychology, and even structural psychology, to be sure, do not confine themselves to data that are "conscious" in terms of the old associationist psychology. We are dealing with something entirely different in the present discussion. It is even doubtful whether the terms "unconscious" and "subconscious," which are used almost interchangeably, are a very happy choice. It might be better to use the terms "near-consciousness" or "split-consciousness." However, we must confine ourselves in our historical presentation to the terminology used by the various authorities despite the fact that they differ among themselves.

The fact of greatest importance, however, is that the influence of the unconscious, at first observed in so-called abnormal cases, also contributed very interesting information to normal psychology.

THE CHANGING GOALS
OF PSYCHOLOGICAL RESEARCH

1. Man's interest in mental abnormalities is age old. As a matter of historical record there has always been a rather remarkable dual evaluation of such abnormalities. The insane have either been regarded as supernormal or, also in the moral sense, as subnormal individuals. Sometimes they were revered as holy and often it was believed they had the power of clairvoyance and wizardry; but they were also regarded as criminals possessed of the devil, with the result that they were frequently executed under the most revolting circumstances.

The actual conception of abnormal individuals as being mentally "sick" is of comparatively recent origin. Only after thousands of the insane had been burned at the stake as witches in medieval times, and only after countless others had been imprisoned as dangerous criminals, did a more humane treatment become prevalent in the eighteenth century. St. Luke's Hospital in London was probably the first insane asylum devoted exclusively to the cure of the insane. Founded in 1751, it became the model for other institutions, after Burton in his *Anatomy of Melancholy* (1621) and Sydenham in his *Processus Integri* (1692) approached insanity with scientific insight.

A pioneer in this new development of psychiatry was Pinel who, in 1792, became the director of the "Bicêtre," an institution for the insane in Paris. Since then, all civilized states have considered it their duty to establish institutions for the shelter and care of the insane. Such institutions in the course of time have naturally become centers for scientific research in mental abnormalities.

2. Parallel to the atomizing tendencies of psychology, toward the end of the nineteenth century psychopathology first studied the abnormal phenomena of single states of consciousness. The basis for this study was the classification of mental processes offered by associationist and apperceptionist psychology.

We cannot even begin to discuss the vast material uncovered in connection with this research. We shall only differentiate the main fields of research, and mention the most important anomalies that were studied. Psychologists and psychiatrists supplemented each other's work in this research.

In the field of the sensations abnormal differences of intensity, such as hypersensitivity and hyposensitivity, were discovered. Abnormalities of quality were also found. We have already mentioned the color-blind, the unmusical, and other similar cases. Among the insane, however, certain colors are sometimes mistaken for other colors, or everything is seen in but one color tone. In synesthesia we have the peculiarity of sounds being "seen" or colors "heard," a faculty which, while it also occurs among normal persons, is evinced to a far greater degree among the insane.

In the field of perception, the favorite subject of study was that of the illusions, instances in which a given datum is erroneously interpreted. Illusions, to be sure, may also occur in the normal mind, especially when a person is under great stress. Hallucinations and pseudo-hallucinations are phenomena chiefly peculiar to the insane. In the latter, in contrast to actual hallucinations, the hallucinating individual is aware of a sense of unreality in his experience, as Kandinsky has so well described. Disturbances of space perception were frequently present. A subject of intense interest was the phenomenon of the *"déjà vu,"* the state of paramnesia in which a new experience appears with the halo of having already been experienced.

We have already learned about ideational anomalies in our discussion of the various phases of amnesia and related phenomena. Ribot's work on the diseases of memory was a first summation of the subject. We may mention false memories, compulsions, delusions as ideational anomalies, in which, at times, a consciousness of the pathological is clearly present. Investigation has disclosed an emotional gamut extending from complete apathy to pathological elation, together with the existence of completely unmotivated emotions ranging from unwarranted worry to equally unwarranted happiness which might on occasion rise to the ecstatic consciousness of beatitude.

So far as volition is concerned, these researches demonstrated every variation from abulia, or the complete absence of will, to the other extreme, hyper-intensified impulsiveness. The compulsory impulsions and inhibitions in which patients conceive of themselves as automatons acting under some foreign influence have been a special subject of study. The patients carry out their actions against their own will. There also exist states of complete volitional impotence.

This brief summary· of the disorders to which single psychic states and functions are subject has been presented not only for its own sake but also in order to demonstrate that most of these isolated anomalies cannot be understood in any such atomizing terms. They all imply totalitarian constellations that are necessary for the understanding of the component manifestations. There are anomalies, to be sure, like color-blindness for example, that are directly traceable to local organic disturbances; but most apparently isolable anomalies are indicative of causes which do not lie within themselves nor within their physiological correlates.

Thus, most deviations of sensation, perception, and ideation occur simultaneously with profound alterations in mental life which always show a higher degree of unitary organization than any of the disparate acts of objective consciousness. On the other hand, primary anomalies of the emotions and of volition coinduce secondary anomalies in the ideational sphere. Only in the rarest of instances are the causes of disturbances "conscious." Consequently, the organic totality which we are seeking must reckon with unconscious causes.

3. The totalitarian character of mental abnormalities, although in itself essentially unconscious, is none the less revealed in most cases by the fact that the patients themselves experience their total consciousness as being abnormal. This of course does not mean that the altered "I consciousness" represents a correct knowledge of the actual disease of the "I." Such disturbances in the "I consciousness" are nevertheless of extreme interest.

The French scholars, Ribot, Janet, and their pupils, focused the general interest on these states. They used the term depersonalization for the state in which single experiences appear strange to the "I consciousness." States also occur in which the "I" no longer experiences itself as a unity but as a dual being. In such instances, a distinction is made between a simultaneous and a successive splitting of the ego. In psychiatric literature we have the detailed description of such cases. Scholars differ in their interpretation of them. The sensationists tried to solve the problem in terms of organ sensations, but their solution was inadequate. The rôle of the emotions is much more important in this connection, yet even these are not isolable but are enmeshed within the totality of the "I." Interesting problems are also posed by the phenomenon of "being possessed," in which a strange soul takes possession of some body. Österreich comprehensively investigated such states.

States of religious conversion and cases of spiritual "rebirth," in which a new person awakes within the old, are closely related to the phenomena of the "splitting of the personality," although they are not unqualifiedly pathological. Such cases have been studied in America by Starbuck, Coe, Leuba, James, and others. French psychologists, too, have described such states, primarily the experiences of mysticism, which also involve a fundamental change in the "I consciousness." Among these psychologists we may mention Delacroix, Maréchal, Blondel, Flournoy, Baruzi, and others, who usually selected historical religious personalities as the subjects for their studies.

4. The attempts to organize the manifold phenomena of mental aberration into disease entities have been many and various, and the last chapter has by no means been written even today. Symptoms are so kaleidoscopic that some scholars believe that the sharp differentiation of clear and distinct disease entities is an impossibility. They suggested the theory of a single unit psychosis whose variations are infinite. Another group of scholars, by contrast, sought to discover natural disease entities with specific symptomatology, etiology, development, and physical findings. These scholars, also, have attained no certain results. According to Jaspers, we can distinguish approximately four stages in the development of psychiatric research in quest of synthetic mental disease entities.

In the days of associationist psychology, the earlier attempts to establish the unity of a symptom complex or syndrome made consciousness their point of departure. Symptom complexes were studied such as melancholia, delirium, derangement, imbecility, and the like. Or else single striking symptoms were selected and described as a unitary disease and then provided with some sonorous name, usually derived from the Greek. Thus an illimitable series of diseases was arrived at—kleptomania, pyromania, dipsomania, agoraphobia, triskaidekaphobia, and others, all corresponding to the patient's inclination for stealing, committing arson, imbibing alcohol, or his fear of crowds, or of the number thirteen. A more profound approach was realized in the attempt of Meynert and Wernicke to ascertain the "basic structure" of mental diseases with the aid of associationist psychology and the localization of brain functions. But these attempts collapsed when the bankruptcy of their theoretical premises was established.

Another tendency of research pioneered by the Frenchmen Morel and Magnan did not start from a psychological approach but sought the causes of disease in order to find a "natural" unit therein. In this quest the significance of heredity became apparent. The psychiatrists of this movement established degenerative insanity as the most important type of mental disease. However, it soon became obvious that the concept of degenerative insanity was merely a combination of many different disease types and, consequently, inadequate.

A third basis for the classification of mental diseases was established on the findings of anatomy. Here characteristic changes were actually found in the brain, such as multiple sclerosis, cerebral lues, brain tumor, and the like, and these were regarded as the causes of insanity. In these studies, general paresis became the most prominent focus of research, especially when its physical symptoms were discovered by Bayle and Calmeil, while Nissl and Alzheimer discovered characteristic microscopic lesions in the cerebral cortex. To be sure, general paresis is at most an anatomical unity and not a unit disease so far as its psychological symptoms are concerned. On the contrary, in similar morphological disturbances wholly different mental phenomena appear. General paresis today is considered solely an anatomical concept and not a psychiatric symptom complex. Psychological determinants have nothing to do with the production of general paresis. For that reason it is an irrelevant disease so far as the aims of psychology are concerned, since it does not yield a psychological unity.

Here, too, the totalitarian approach represents a counter-movement to the theoretical attempts to derive mental disease types from the single track point of view proffered by psychological observation, etiology, or pathological anatomy. Kahlbaum was the first to demand a totalitarian approach, in 1874; but it was actually put into effect for the first time by Kraepelin. Kraepelin described two chief groups of mental diseases: the manic-depressive psychoses and dementia precox. These are the chief types which are today distinguished as cycloid insanity and schizophrenia, according to Bleuler's terminology. We have already encountered them in our discussion of Kretschmer's types of physique.

At present we are concerned solely with the theoretical principles that governed Kraepelin in his formulation of these groups. His endeavor was to observe the total aspect and the total development of mental diseases, and in this way he enriched our knowledge concerning their psychological structure. Kraepelin's successors then studied the forms of development in the perspective of whole life developments and thus worked out subordinate groups of psychoses. The hope of finding distinctive anatomical conditions corresponding to Bleuler's chief groups of psychoses has not been realized to this day.

The most admirably delineated psychosis at the present time is the one that Kraepelin designated as "dementia precox" and Bleuler as "schizophrenia." Bleuler elaborated his designation in a work published in 1911 and entitled *Dementia Precox or the Schizophrenia Group*. The name is derived from the "splitting" of the personality, especially the "splitting away" from unpleasant reality. The patient excludes all reality; he dwells in a delusional inner world which he values more highly than objectivity. Hence, Bleuler speaks of "autism." A complete apathy of the mind frequently sets in; action is often entirely eliminated or is expressed in negativism. The causes of schizophrenia are as yet unexplained.

Psychoanalysis, which has discovered new methods of penetrating into the depths of the soul, might be considered as a further stage in the development of psychiatry. However, we shall postpone the discussion of psychoanalysis to the separate chapter reserved for it.

5. Certain abnormalities, such as hysteria and psychasthenia, while not actually mental diseases, have become important foci of psychological research. These disorders in extreme cases can exclude the patient from human society. However, they frequently occur in such mild forms that the persons afflicted with them are not considered diseased. Yet both of these disorders present us with phenomena that have become exceedingly illuminating in our attempts to understand many of the functions and data of the normal mind.

This is especially true of those manifestations which we vaguely catalogue under the name of hysteria. Since this disorder occurs with particular frequency among women, it has been regarded ever since the days of antiquity as a specific disorder of the female organs. Indeed, the name itself is derived from "hystera," the womb. Its first well-documented description was the work of a Frenchman named Briquet (1859). Briquet compared the symptoms of hysteria with the emotional reactions of normal persons and spoke of the intensified sensitivity of the brain areas serving the emotions. In the '70's, Charcot made hysteria the central theme of his studies. He placed hysteria in a now obsolete correlation with hypnotic manifestation. Charcot considered hysteria as a disease of the nervous system. The psychic origin of hysteria was first proven by Charcot's pupil, Janet, and in Germany by Möbius.

Viewed as a psychic phenomenon, it is impossible either to delineate sharply the clinical aspects of hysteria or to determine its causes in a completely uniform fashion. According to Janet, the nature of the hysterical person possesses, on the one hand, a hypersensitivity, inasmuch as all ideas emerge with hallucinatory intensity and are easily transposed into deeds, while on the other hand, there is also a dulling of sensitivity to the point of anesthesia. Entire parts of the body lose their sensitivity to pain. In compensation, we have an intensification of emotionality. The patient's self-importance expresses itself very forcefully and he tyrannizes over the persons about him.

Another type of mental anomaly is represented by what Janet terms psychasthenia. Formerly, the terms mania and phobia were employed. Janet, however, in his *Les Obsessions et la psychasthénie* (1903) outlined a uniform picture which he very effectually contrasted with hysteria. In contrast to the wild abandon of hysterical persons, everything is inhibited in the psychasthenic person; such persons are indecisive, full of anxiety, and suffer from obsessions of all sorts, but, and this is the essential difference from hysteria, they are aware of the splitting of their consciousness, whereas the hysterical person represses all such awareness from his consciousness. Thus the French refer to psychasthenia as *"folie consciente."*

In Germany, Kraepelin distinguished the pictures of obsessional neurosis and impulsive insanity. In the former, Kraepelin assumed an emotional cause which creates a permanent state of unease. The patient consequently does not feel himself equal to any of his tasks. Frequently, his qualms may be of a religious nature. Impulsive insanity, on the contrary, results in apparently meaningless and purposeless actions such as the mixture of poisons or the committing of robbery. Here, Kraepelin assumes the existence of a discord among the impulses, the suspension of important inhibitions that ordinarily block such proclivities when they emerge in normal people.

6. A review of psychopathological research during the past half century shows us that abnormalities are certainly not merely a matter of disturbances in the realm of consciousness. Most disorders of consciousness are accompanied by disturbances of the motor functions. A physiological cause, moreover, has been anatomically proven in some mental diseases without, however, making it possible to explain all the existing psychological phenomena in terms of such physiological defects. The extent to which disturbances in the structure of the "soul" are to be assumed cannot be determined as yet through this field of research.

A new method of interpretation, however, has come into prominence, at least in certain disorders, which, although it assumes consciousness as its starting point, leads down to the subconscious. We know that the waking consciousness or superconsciousness does not encompass the whole of mental life. This is already evident in the normal person who retains within his memory a host of impressions which condition the course of consciousness without always becoming completely conscious themselves. In normal instances the super- and subconsciousness work harmoniously together. But in many psychoses this harmony seems to be disturbed. The subconscious goes its own ways and often conflicts with the superconscious. A separate system of the subconscious is formed, which frequently penetrates into the superconscious and superimposes itself upon the latter as a dual personality. Many disturbances of the "I consciousness," particularly in schizophrenia, hysteria, and psychasthenia, can be explained only by the assumption of subconscious complexes occurring parallel to the superconscious, and exerting a disturbing influence upon it.

Modern psychiatry, at any rate, was unable to manage without the assumption of detached complexes, even if it did not share in all the conclusions which were to be drawn later by psychoanalysis.

HYPNOSIS AND SUGGESTION

1. That states extraordinarily similar to pathological ones can be superinduced in normal persons through artificial means has been common knowledge among all peoples since antiquity. Primitive religions, through ritual dances, music, and the performance of magic, were able artificially to produce states of ecstasy in which normal consciousness either partially or wholly disappeared. Most of the practices of primitive medicine men must today be designated as suggestional or autosuggestional therapy; and there are sceptics in good number who believe that in the modern science of medicine, too, suggestion often plays a more important part than the chemical effects of medicine.

The practice of yoga among the Hindus is also a form of suggestional influence. Indian fakirs are capable of transporting themselves and their audience into the most peculiar mental states. An abundance of material covering this theme has been gathered by O. Stoll in a work entitled *Suggestion and Hypnosis in Racial Psychology.*

2. The rather obscure field which we designate today as suggestion and hypnosis was first brought into the proximity of science by Friedrich Anton Mesmer (1733–1815), the discoverer of "animal magnetism" or "mesmerism." The story of Mesmer's life represents a remarkable parallel to that of Gall, the phrenologist. Like Gall, Mesmer came to Paris from Austria and achieved a great fame that soon disappeared because of the antagonism of scientists. But Mesmer, like Gall, nevertheless, exerted an exceedingly stimulating influence on science; and his errors (or charlataneries) proved themselves fruitful to future scholars, not only because of the facts on which they were based, but also because of the criticism they aroused in scientific circles.

In the beginning, Mesmer must have firmly believed his own theories. He put his patients into extraordinary mental states, partly by means of manual stroking and partly by the employment of a tube filled with magnetized iron. Since he was able to effect successful cures, the French Government desired to purchase his secret for 20,000 livres. But through private subscription, he received 240,000 livres, although he did not entirely reveal his method even for this sum. However, he was unable to hold his own against a forum of physicians and natural scientists, and so was forced to leave Paris as an imposter.

Mesmer's theory assumes the existence of an invisible "fluidum" which penetrates the body and imparts something foreign to it. This something may be an insight into nature or other living beings. Mesmer named his fluidum "animal magnetism" since it seemed to issue from the body itself, particularly from that of the *"magnétiseur."* Today, this theory is considered completely disproven.

3. In a scientific form, the phenomena of suggestion were first treated by Braid in his *Neurypnology* in 1843. This was followed by Liébeault's work, *On Sleep and Analogous States*, published in 1866 in the city of Nancy. Braid coined the term "hypnotism"; the word "suggestion" in this particular connotation was introduced by Liébeault. The scene of Liébeault's activities was Nancy as was H. Bernheim's, the most famous investigator of this entire group of phenomena.

The Nancy school voiced the opinion that hypnotic states could be induced in most people by the production of corresponding states in the imagination. According to Liébeault, the ability to lapse into hypnotic states was proportional to a person's power of imagination. We can be certain, he wrote, that a person who directs his attention upon some idea, let us say the idea of being touched, and experiences this idea as if it were real, is extremely susceptible to hypnosis. If a person convinces himself of something, we refer to such a procedure, as did Bernheim, as "autosuggestion." Bernheim also demonstrated the existence of unconscious suggestion. Here the idea in question appears so momentarily and so faintly in the mirror of the super-conscious that it fades entirely from memory, yet nevertheless has a powerful suggestional after-effect. The mechanism of suggestion, that is, the way in which the audible word of the hypnotist brings about the actual hypnosis, always remains unknown to the superconscious.

4. A third theory of hypnosis, whose exponents continually fulminated against the Nancy school, was the so-called "somatic theory." This theory was championed by Charcot and his followers in Paris and struck a mean between the theory of animal magnetism and that of the Nancy scholars. Charcot invoked no "fluidum" and no spirits but he did attempt to trace hypnotic phenomena back to known elemental forces without the intermediation of psychic activity. The effects of peripheral stimuli transmitted by metallic substances to neural end organs were accorded great importance. Charcot believed that he could induce typically different types of hypnosis by means of different mechanical stimuli. Thus fixation of the eyes was supposed to cause catalepsy; lifting of the lids would also produce it, stroking of the forehead would result in somnambulism with specific sensory and motor reactions (the so-called "*hyperexcitabilité neuromusculaire*"). A fact worthy of comment is that Charcot believed only hysterical persons susceptible to hypnotism. He also held that hypnotized subjects are totally unconscious and cannot be influenced by suggestion.

Charcot's theory, however, was definitively disproved by Bernheim who showed that the experiments which Charcot had demonstrated on hysterical subjects in the Salpêtrière were really exercised and automatized suggestions. Bernheim also showed that Braid's procedure of fixing the eyes upon some bright object does not induce hypnosis because of the object itself or because of the act of fixation, but because of the subject's idea that the procedure must hypnotize him.

5. Today, hypnotism has long since lost the mystic nimbus which once surrounded it. Hypnotism is considered a thoroughly natural occurrence, although this by no means implies that it has been explained beyond all cavil. Still it has been brought into a certain rapport with normal psychology. This is corroborated by the fact that most hypnotists consider at least 90 per cent of all people hypnotizable.

Moreover, the similarity of hypnosis to normal states of the mind has become evident. This is especially true of sleep, from which the very name "hypnotism" is derived. The analogy between sleep and hypnotism has found its protagonists and antagonists. It is more precise to refer the similarity to a dream state rather than to compare hypnosis with sleep, although the variable motility and far greater susceptibility to outer influence in hypnosis also present marked differences.

From another angle, waking suggestion must also be included in this discussion. Some persons are strongly susceptible to suggestion when in a waking state, yet circumstances and states may occur in the life of everyone which greatly limit his logical control over his mental functions and make him the victim of his imagination; this may originate from without, or, in the case of autosuggestion, well up from within. In such cases, even though the superconsciousness is awake, behavior may result that externally closely resembles that of a hypnotized person.

For psychology the most important problem in hypnosis is that of consciousness, and this problem is rendered all the more difficult because the concept "consciousness" has so many connotations. We certainly cannot consider the hypnotized subject as being wholly unconscious, because he performs actions which otherwise can happen only through the intervention of consciousness; he hears and understands the hypnotist's words and carries out performances that imply mental deliberation and a choice of means. If the hypnotized subject has been said to be unconscious, the reason has been partly because many inhibitions and controls of waking existence are eliminated, and partly because the subject on awaking no longer recalls what has happened during his state of hypnosis.

Hypnosis, consequently, may best be characterized as a phenomenon entailing a splitting of consciousness in which the simultaneous and the successive nexus of mental life is partially deranged. That this also involves subconscious data is proved by the fact that hypnosis is not merely characterized by amnesia but also occasionally by forms of hypermnesia, in so far as the subjects recall facts which have disappeared from their waking consciousness. Certain peculiar posthypnotic phenomena are the best evidence of the existence of subconscious activities. When the hypnotized subject still carries out commands days and even weeks after they have been given him during a state of hypnosis, and his waking consciousness knows nothing of these commands, we are compelled to deduce some subconscious mental activity.

6. Reducing hypnosis to suggestion only shifts the problem to another category. We are confronted with the further question: What is suggestion? Its definitions vary widely, primarily because the subject is approached either from the angle of consciousness or from the question of its origin, or from that of its effects. Almost every one of the psychologists and psychiatrists who have occupied themselves with the problem has his own favorite solution. These solutions have been gathered together in A. Herzberg's *Analysis of the Phenomena of Suggestion* (1930). Herzberg's own view of the matter is that suggestion is an external influence conditioned not by content but by the form of transference. The essential point to bear in mind is that the suggested train of thought does not occur by virtue of the logical deliberation of the "I" itself, but by virtue of external influences (usually affecting the emotions) that often prevail against the usually dominant "I." Thus, the forms of suggestion are authoritative, sympathetic, habitual, divertive,

and so forth. The state of preparedness to accept such external influences is called suggestibility, which may be either momentary or permanent.

In this consideration it is important to note that suggestion, to a certain degree, nullifies our assumption of a thoroughly united consciousness, because suggestion represents the invasion of external attitudes. Such an intrusion, however, is only possible because it meets with subconscious susceptibilities and because it is abetted by unconscious impulses and dispositions. Suggestion, therefore, proves that consciousness, or more precisely, the logico-critical consciousness, by no means comprises the whole of our mental life. Suggestion, moreover, compels us to admit that our consciousness rests upon subconscious facts which pervade consciousness.

7. The psychology of suggestion became a matter of public interest as a result of certain therapeutic movements among which Couéism was the most prominent in Europe. "Christian Science" and the "New Thought" movements had already employed suggestion in America. Coué came from Nancy, the hotbed of the psychology of suggestion, and his followers consequently called themselves the "second Nancy school." From 1885 to 1886 he had witnessed Liébeault's experiments. Coué was not an educated scholar but studied the curative effects of suggestion autodidactically. He set down his experiences in a thin monograph entitled *Self-mastery through Conscious Autosuggestion*. From 1910 on, the Coué school began to develop. Its most significant representative, Charles Baudouin, placed Coué's therapeutic method upon a scientific basis in his chief opus entitled *Suggestion and Autosuggestion*.

Baudouin defines suggestion as the unconscious realization of an idea. Suggestion consists in the mobilization, either by ourselves or by the influence of others, of the ideo-cognitive forces of imagination present in everyone. Suggestion can be considered a "force" in the scientific sense. The fact that suggestion is directed counter to the will is of great theoretical importance, for the will often works directly counter to suggestion. This is affirmed by Baudouin's *"Loi de l'effort converti,"* that is, the law of paradoxical effort. When an idea impinges upon the mind so strongly that it induces suggestion, then all conscious efforts opposed to it operate toward the suggestion. This leads to the law of subconscious purposiveness: "Once a purpose or goal is defined, the subconscious also finds ways and means to its realization."

It is not within our province to pass judgment upon the practical utility of Couéism, a system that has been so variously judged. From the theoretical viewpoint, it is interesting to note that here, too, external suggestion is traced back to autosuggestion, and the unconscious is endowed with purposiveness. Thus, the psychology of suggestion empties into the same main stream into which all the other tributaries of modern psychology have flowed.

SIGMUND FREUD AND PSYCHOANALYSIS

1. The studies in hysteria and hypnotic phenomena were the historical forerunners of one of the most influential tendencies in modern psychology, that of psychoanalysis. The name "psychoanalysis," which by no means entirely conveys the essential significance of this tendency, was selected in order to distinguish its endeavors from those of ordinary psychology. To Sigmund Freud, the founder of psychoanalysis, the mind is not identical with the consciousness. He saw his chief mission in the illumination of the unconscious. Psychoanalysis, in spite of its being only a few decades old, already has a variegated history which can be divided, with a fair degree of accuracy, into four phases.

In its first phase psychoanalysis, not yet known under its present name, was a procedure employed for the examination of states difficult of access, that were regarded as "constricted" and designated as psychic "traumata." The chief participant at this stage, besides Freud himself, was the Viennese physician, Josef Breuer, whose merits Freud has always recognized.

In the second phase, beginning about 1900, Breuer retired from the scene and Freud then independently developed the procedure of the first phase into a complicated therapeutic system for the treatment of neurotic disturbances. He evolved new methods, such as the interpretation of dreams, functional errors, and symbolic actions. Strong emphasis was laid upon the investigation of sexuality and its complexes. It was at this time that the entire method received the name of psychoanalysis.

During the third phase, Freud and his constantly expanding school applied the results of psychoanalysis to every possible sphere of life and of science; to pedagogy, law, religion, mythology, and the like. Psychoanalysis became a general cultural science.

Not until its fourth phase, which set in after 1920, was psychoanalysis systematically founded and developed beyond an essentially practical therapy into a totalitarian theory of mental life.

In the meantime, the dissenting schools, headed by Adler and Jung, had left the fold of orthodox psychoanalysis. We shall discuss them separately.

2. The historical relations between psychoanalysis and the studies in hypnotism and hysteria are not solely of a purely theoretical nature. Freud had at one time studied with Bernheim in Nancy, and with Charcot in Paris. In 1886, he returned to Vienna with the experiences he had gained from his foreign teachers. In Vienna he learned from his colleague, Breuer, of a pathological case which the latter had already treated from 1880 to 1881. But it was Freud who first recognized the cardinal significance of this case. Freud also stimulated Breuer to resume his research along the lines of the experiences he himself had acquired abroad. The first fruits of their collaboration was a report called "On the

Psychic Mechanisms of Hysterical Phenomena" (1893), and a book entitled *Studies in Hysteria* (1895).

Since Breuer's pathological case served as a guiding principle, a brief description of it follows. A highly gifted girl, twenty-one years of age, became subject to a number of physical and mental disturbances, although her bodily organs were sound. The symptoms were paralysis of the extremities, impairment of eyesight, and difficulty in keeping the head erect. In addition, the patient was unable to drink in spite of intense thirst. Her powers of speech lapsed. She experienced states of confusion, and there was an alteration of her entire personality. In brief, she presented a picture generally designated as hysteria.

Breuer, however, was not content with determining the symptoms but tried to get at their causes. The disorder had first appeared while the girl had been nursing her dearly beloved father, who was suffering from an ailment that eventually led to his death; and as a result of falling ill herself, she had been obliged to give up nursing him. It occurred to Breuer that the patient, during her deranged and confused states, murmured words which led him to infer some hidden meaning. And so he subjected her to a kind of hypnosis. While in this state, the patient abandoned herself to sad and often poetical fancies whose usual theme was that of a girl at her father's sick bed. What was remarkable was that, after having indulged in such fancies, the patient felt relieved and resumed her normal existence. But the cure at first was only temporary. Other factors entered the situation. While hypnotized, the patient told how she had once seen her governess reach out a glass of water for a dog to drink from, and the sight had aroused her profound disgust. After she had related this incident with considerable emotion, while still in the hypnotic trance, she asked for a drink and then awoke with the glass still at her lips. After this her inability to drink, from which she had suffered so painfully for a long time, disappeared permanently.

Breuer then determined that almost all the symptoms of

this girl's illness were traceable to similar emotionally toned experiences. And in other cases, too, he succeeded in curing such "psychic traumata," as he called them. From all this, Breuer and Freud derived two general theories which were also corroborated in other cases: they noted first, that hysterical types of behavior have meaning and significance, inasmuch as they are substitutes for normal psychic acts; second, they recognized that the disclosure of this unknown meaning coincided with the suspension of the patient's symptoms. This was confirmed in the treatment of other patients.

Breuer and Freud assumed that a mental impulse charged with intense emotion was in some manner prevented from being discharged into the normal channels leading to consciousness and to the appropriate motor abreactions. As a consequence, the "constricted" emotion was shunted into the wrong channels and sought for some outlet in the bodily nervous system. This process they called "conversion." In "conversion" the patient suffers from repressed memories which have become unconscious. The cure follows after the paths to consciousness and to normal discharge have been opened. This was termed "catharsis," an expression used by Aristotle, who saw the effect of a tragedy as a catharsis, that is, a purging of the passions.

3. So far, Breuer and Freud had followed a common path. Their opinions began to differ when Breuer became firmly convinced that pathogenic ideas originate only in "hypnoid states," whereas Freud believed that ideas become pathogenic when their contents counteract the ruling tendencies of the mind and thus arouse its resistance. In practice, therefore, Freud dispensed with hypnosis, since the recovery it produced was not permanent, and substituted free association in its place. He availed himself of Bernheim's proof that what is experienced in somnambulism is only apparently forgotten and can be recalled by assuring the patient that he still remembers it. Freud persuaded his patients to recall

things which they had apparently forgotten, but soon discovered that there was no necessity for any persuasion at all. On the contrary, the patients of their own accord added a wealth of material which enabled the physician to understand the hidden significance of apparently unimportant, meaningless, and irrelevant expressions.

In the course of practice psychoanalysis was developed into a methodical interpretative method. The next important step was to elaborate upon the earlier discovery that neurotic symptoms are substitutions for other uncompleted mental acts. In the interpretation of such symptoms, the so-called functional errors assumed exceptional importance. The forgetting of names or tasks, mistakes in speaking, reading, writing, the misplacing of objects, and similar matters no longer appeared to be accidental, but were discovered to be psychically determined, as expressions of suppressed intentions. Thus functional errors became beacons of light for those groping in the dark realm of the unconscious. Freud's comprehensive treatise on the subject was published in 1901 under the title of *The Psychopathology of Everyday Life*.

Another portal to the unconscious was revealed by the analysis of dreams. Age-old, popular conceptions of the meaning and interpretability of dreams were thus revived. Freud considered the essence of dream interpretation to be the finding of ideas which appeared latent behind the manifest content of dreams. The result of such interpretation was that most dreams resolved themselves into latent wish fulfilments. But since there is a concomitant tendency to preserve the state of sleep, the manifest content of dreams undergoes a change. Dreams are subject to a censorship similar to the one imposed upon waking thoughts. Dreams often revive "day residues" left over from our waking existence. These "day residues" become "idealized"; they suffer mutilation through a process of "distortion" and are transformed into visual images. Such transformations often present themselves as "archaisms." It is the task of psychoanalysis to fathom the latent meaning behind the frequently abstruse symbolism of dreams. Freud's treatment of the problem is to be found in his books entitled *Concerning Dreams* (1901) and *The Interpretation of Dreams* (1900). His pupils Stekel, Silberer, and others subsequently carried on his work in the same field.

In the course of their expeditions into the unconscious depths of the soul, the psychoanalysts encountered a ubiquitous factor which society likes to gloss over even though all life is based upon it: the factor of sex. Freud and his pupils decisively broke away from social prudery and spoke of these matters so frankly that at first they aroused horror and resentment in their audiences. They declared that sex did not emerge in human beings like a flash of lightning with the onset of puberty, but that it was also imperative to speak of an infantile libido. By "libido" Freud meant the dynamic expression of the sexual instinct in the mind. A particularly sensational factor was introduced into the sexual theory of psychoanalysis by applying to the sex life of the child concepts which formerly bore the moral stigma of "perversions." Freud employed the terms of sadism and incestuous desires in reference to children, but without any connotation of moral opprobrium.

Without entering into the particularly moot analysis of the infantile libido, we merely present Freud's conclusion that after a period of autoeroticism, in which the object of sex is sought in the child's own body, a period characterized by the Œdipus complex follows. This lasts from the age of two to five years. During this period, in boys, the mother becomes the object of the libido and the attitude toward the father is one of rivalry and hostility. The designation is not quite correct, referring as it does to Œdipus, who married his mother and killed his father, but who had never even known his parents in his youth, so that he could never have suffered from the complex named after him. According to Freud, however, the Œdipus complex is of the greatest significance in the shaping of the love life. The normal person, of course, conquers this complex; only the neurotic remains enthralled by it. After a long dormant period, the Œdipus complex reawakens during puberty after having previously been suppressed by ethical compulsions. Not until puberty do the sex instincts develop to full intensity. Their direction, however, has already been determined during childhood.

At this point, Freud's theory of sex merges with his other theories. For it is sex that proves itself the most important of the unconscious forces disclosed by the psychoanalytic method. Freud uses the term "repression" to designate the complexes rejected by the conscious mind and forced into the unconscious. The term has become very popular and certainly applies to an important psychological phenomenon. But that which is repressed is not completely put out of commission; it surreptitiously continues to slip back into the conscious sphere. The neuroses arise as a result of the conflict between the conscious "I" and the repressed sex complexes. Should one seek to render conscious by means of psychoanalysis that which has been suppressed, the repulsive forces set up a so-called "resistance." In spite of this, the "repression" often gives way and the libido creates outlets for itself by "regressing" to earlier phases of development. The libido breaks through into consciousness and is discharged at the weak points in infantile object fixations. The result is a symptom that is something in the nature of a compromise between the suppressed sexual desires and the repressive desires of the "I." There is then an incomplete wish fulfilment for both sides in the conflict. This is particularly applicable to the symptoms of hysteria, whereas in the obsessional neuroses the participation of the suppressive determinants frequently expresses itself more strongly by the creation of safeguards against sexual gratification.

Such, in substance, are the facts which Freud himself designated as the fundamentals of psychoanalytic theory at the end of its second phase of development. All those who profess to be psychoanalysts must subscribe to the following:

a. assumption of unconscious psychic phenomena.

b. theory of suppression and resistance.

c. theory of infantile sexuality and of the Œdipus complex.

In this form, psychoanalysis no longer remained the private conviction of its founder, but became an international sensation. Besides Vienna, Freud's home, Zürich became a center of the movement. The Swiss psychiatrists, E. Bleuler and C. G. Jung, allied themselves to the movement in 1906. The year 1907 witnessed the first psychoanalytic congress in Salzburg. At the same time, however, the opposition also became active and contributed in no small extent to the growing notoriety of psychoanalysis. In many countries local groups were formed. Their leaders were: Abraham in Germany, Flournoy in Geneva, Ferenczi in Budapest, J. Putnam in Boston, Ernest Jones in Toronto and then in London. Psychoanalysis fell on fertile soil, especially in the United States. No less a personage than Stanley Hall adopted a favorable attitude toward it. Freud himself crossed the ocean and proclaimed his doctrine in a series of lectures at the celebration of Clark University's twentieth anniversary in 1909.

4. In the meanwhile, a further phase of development in psychoanalysis had already set in, a phase in which it expanded far beyond the field of medicine. Freud himself had from the beginning subjected poetry and works of art to psychoanalytic interpretation. His work, *Totem and Taboo*, applied the same method to racial psychology. Numerous disciples advanced along the same lines. Pfister, and later Bernfeld, applied the psychoanalytic doctrine to pedagogy. Rank, Pfister, Reik, and many others included religion and mythology. Similarly, the psychoanalyzing of creative writers and other artists came into vogue: Flaubert, Gottfried Keller, and Goethe were psychoanalyzed, and at the present day there are probably very few significant person-

alities in world history who have not in some way been analyzed in regard to their Œdipus complexes and their dreams. It is not always easy to sift reason from nonsense in this plethora of analyses. The procedure is often exceedingly distortive. All too often a dogmatism reminiscent of religious sects characterizes the Freudians, which has made the entire movement sensational and brought it into disrepute.

5. The fourth period of psychoanalysis, introduced with youthful energy by the sexagenarian Freud, is more important in the history of psychology than the many digressions of psychoanalysis into related fields. This period is noteworthy for the synthesis of psychoanalytical discoveries into a new "depth psychology" intended to create a total picture of mental life from the standpoint of the new doctrine. Such a system had already been roughly outlined during the second period of psychoanalysis, but at that time it was confined to certain ingenious intuitions and isolated discoveries of Freud's in the realm of the unconscious.

The main work of the last phase was a small volume entitled *The Ego and the Id*, which appeared in 1923. Another important contribution was *Beyond the Pleasure Principle*, published in 1920.

In order to provide a theoretical foundation for psychoanalysis, it was primarily necessary to clarify the relationship between consciousness and the unconscious. Freud began with an unequivocal denunciation of all psychologists who identify all the psychic phenomena with consciousness. To Freud, consciousness is only a quality of the mind which can join itself to, or refrain from joining, other qualities. But the unconscious which does not possess the quality of consciousness is not therefore entirely unitary. The unconscious can become directly capable of consciousness and can emerge within consciousness. In this event, Freud calls the unconscious the "pre-conscious." The unconscious, however, can also be repressed, that is to say, constricted in its capability for becoming conscious. The unconscious is then actually unconscious. It is this unconscious, which is not merely unconscious but actually suppressed, which opposes the conscious ego in psychoanalysis.

It is obvious that Freud's terminology differs essentially from that of other structural psychologists. Whereas the latter consider the structure of the "I" in itself as predominantly unconscious, Freud places the conscious and the "I" upon a fairly equal plane, even though he designates the "I" as the "surface" of the psychic apparatus. Consciousness is primarily the representative of external reality in the psyche.

Below the conscious ego, according to Freud, there is a further stratum which he designates with a term borrowed from Groddeck as the "id." This is not sharply separated from the "I" but often intermingles with it. The ego sheathes the id in much the same manner that an ovum is sheathed by a germinal disc. The "I" represents what can be called reason and prudence in contrast to the id, which contains the passions. In relation to the id, the "I" resembles a rider who is able to control the superior power of his horse, the only difference being that the rider does his controlling with his own power, whereas the "I" exercises control with borrowed power. The functional importance of the "I" consists normally in its control over motor functions. Frequently, however, the "I" succumbs to the id and must transpose the will of the id into action as though it were its own will.

All this, however, does not exhaust the compass of the mental phenomena. Freud makes yet another differentiation within the "I," which he calls the ideal "I" or superego. This superego opposes the remaining content of the "I" and attempts to superimpose itself upon it. The superego dominates the "I" as conscience, for example, and perhaps as an unconscious feeling of guilt, or as a categorical imperative.

Such a notion might align Freud with popular psychology which also recognizes the significance of conscience or of an ideal "I." But the theory of how this superego comes into being is peculiar to Freud. Here, Freud applies his theory of sex and of the Œdipus complex. The child in its helplessness and dependence alternately identifies itself either with its father or with its mother in an ambivalent manner, that is, either in the affirmation or denial of parentage. As a result of the original bisexual nature of the child varying forms of experience occur. But the formation of an ideal "I" is always some kind of union between the father and mother identification. The superego is, therefore, always the representation of our relationship to our parents. As children, we regard our parents as higher beings; we love them and fear them and later incorporate them into ourselves. Thus their influence is not only important in the education of the individual but also in the education of the species.

Since the "I," as we have previously seen, is the representative of the external world or of reality, the superego as the advocate of the inner world or of the id stands opposed to the "I." Conflicts occur between reality and the ideal which reflect the contrast between the external and the internal worlds. As a result of its evolutionary history, the ideal has a strong connection with the racial heritage of the individual. That which is deepest in us becomes the highest, in respect to values. Religion, morality, and the social instinct are rooted in the rôle of the father and in the continuation of this rôle through teachers and authorities.

In order to render the dynamics of mental life understandable, Freud probed even deeper into the murky depths of the id. Here he found, adjacent to the sexual instinct, yet another instinct, the instinct of death. Whereas the sexual drive endeavors to preserve life through the union of life's scattered parts, the death instinct tries to reduce organic life to a state of inorganic lifelessness. Life itself is a compromise between these two tendencies. Frequently the death instinct is transposed into a destructive instinct; it even changes into hate which is counterposed to love. But hate and love also intermingle because of their ambivalence, for both are ultimately derived from an undifferentiated, variable energy. The sublimation of impulses, of which Freud had already spoken, is equivalent to the desexualization of the libido.

We cannot go into the multitudinous conflicts between impulses which Freud holds to be the cause of the neuroses. We should note, however, that mental life appears to be a struggle between the ego on the one hand, and the non-individual powers of both the id and the superego on the other. The "I" develops from the perception of drives to the mastery of drives. This development proceeds with the aid of the superego which is, in part, a reactional formation against the impulse phenomena of the id. Psychoanalysis is an instrument which enables the "I" progressively to conquer the id.

From among the involved and detailed studies in psychoanalysis we select the theory of the unconscious which Freud finally evolved after numerous changes. This theory is quite complicated. If we disregard the previously mentioned divisions of consciousness, we have the following threefold division:

  a. subindividual id.
  b. individual "I."
  c. superindividual superego.

Freud does not present all this in a strictly systematic fashion but with almost aphoristic terseness. His writings are more stimulating than integrated. Notwithstanding this, they constitute a fascinating enrichment of psychology, all the more so since they are indirectly related to the other new theories which we shall meet in our further discussion.

6. We need not at this point criticize the significance of psychoanalysis as a therapeutic method. This has been done to such a broad extent in every country that it would be supererogatory to add another to the arguments for and against. Our concern is only with the evaluation of psychoanalysis in respect to the whole field of psychology.

In its beginnings, psychoanalysis was strongly mechanistic. Freud applied the principle of association and spoke constantly of the mechanisms of mental life. In a subsequent phase Freud seems to have approached closer to vitalism, because his "libido" in its undifferentiated form bears considerable resemblance to a "vital force." Of course, notions of physical energy mingle with his vitalistic conception. Many of his studies give one the impression that the libido undergoes a "metamorphosis" in much the same way physical energy is transformed into other forms of energy. There is no way of knowing exactly whether Freud uses the expression metaphorically or not. We shall see later how this notion of energy emerges even more prominently in the Zürich school of psychoanalysis. However, although Freud fundamentally adheres to mechanism, teleological points of view infiltrate into his studies. Thus it becomes obvious that Freud, the brilliant and original thinker, has very little contact with the philosophical problems of his time. His very latest writings, in particular, betray a rather primitive rationalism that often displays traces of frank materialism, and this naturally greatly limits his psychology.

For all the expansiveness of his interests, Freud has the one-sidedness of a genius who cannot understand the opinions of others and has not even the desire to understand them. Despotically, he subjects all problems to the yoke of his ideas. No matter to what problem he applies himself, it takes on a new aspect for him; he discovers new and hitherto unnoticed features; but, and this is indisputable, he exaggerates these features to such an extent that the final result is a caricature. He views everything from a bizarre and limited perspective that must certainly prove itself inadequate when it becomes the sole method of approach. Presumably, a great many of Freud's discoveries will become the permanent property of psychology, but no theory that appears in such a single-track and exaggerated form as psychoanalysis does today can ever be wholly acceptable to science.

Freud's limitations are also indicated by the fact that he

takes scarcely any notice of the development of other systems of psychology. When he engages in a controversy, his polemics are almost entirely directed against his heretical disciples or against his opponents of the medical fraternity. The surprising thing, however, is that there are nevertheless numerous points of agreement between psychoanalysis and the rest of psychology, so that Freud's doctrines can very well be fitted into its general development. There are marked parallels, for example, to ego-psychology, inasmuch as Freud often speaks of a structure of the soul beyond consciousness.

Freud's theories concerning the functions of consciousness are extraordinarily primitive compared to those of Lipps or Husserl. However, such theories are not at all the pivot of interest in Freud; he is much more interested in the unconscious, which is more important to him than it is to all the other structural psychologists. These psychologists regarded the unconscious, in so far as they treated it at all, as an auxiliary to the conscious, whereas in Freud the exact antithesis holds true. To Freud, consciousness is essentially the mediator between the external and internal worlds. It is not a monopoly of the "I" but it also embraces the dark region of the id. Here, too, Freud's terminology is different from that of most other structural psychologists. He conceives consciousness and the "I" essentially as "content," whereas other psychologists conceive both more as a functional combination which is not consciousness known but only consciousness knowing.

The new factor which psychoanalysis brought into psychology was the discovery of repression and of the unconscious complexes which infiltrate into the conscious. Here Freud was the actual discoverer of new territory. The great significance of sex in repressions cannot be denied, even though it impresses one as exaggerated. Freud is, for all his empirical pretensions, primarily a constructor of logical systems, a man whose approach to irrational problems is that of an extreme rationalist. It will be interesting to learn what the psychology of the future will have to say about him. Freud smashed into the barricades of science as a revolutionist, but his revolution, like all others, will no doubt become incorporated in the deeper and more constant stream of evolution.

ALFRED ADLER AND INDIVIDUAL PSYCHOLOGY

1. In our historical review of psychoanalysis we mentioned another movement that issued from it in 1911 and whose leader is the Viennese physician, Alfred Adler. After his defection from the Freudian school, Adler gave his competitive system the name of "individual psychology," which is an even less apt designation for what it purports to be than was psychoanalysis. Adler's chief difference from Freud is his rejection of the latter's pansexualism—although Freud himself does not accept this designation for his doctrine. Adler replaces the sexual libido with the "striving for prestige," to which he joins the social feeling as a second factor. A further distinction between the two is that Adler makes the teleological factors of the mind the pivotal center of his system to a greater degree than Freud does.

Adler's first considerable work appeared in 1907 in his *Studies in the Inferiorities of Organs*. Here, for the first time, there emerged the concept of overcompensation which later became so important. In 1913, with the publication of a book bearing the title *The Neurotic Character*, Adler's parting of the ways with Freud was accomplished. A work published in 1920 under the title of *The Theory and Practice of Individual Psychology* was a collection of lectures and articles. Not until 1927, in a work entitled *Understanding Human Nature*, did Adler choose to present his theories systematically. A more consistent systematization, however, was achieved by E. Wexberg in his *Individual Psychology*, published in 1928. In the meantime, a *Handbook of Individual Psychology* had already appeared in 1926; an

international society of individual psychology with its own
publications had been founded; and congresses were being
held. In short, like psychoanalysis, individual psychology
flourished into a "movement."

Similar to psychoanalysis, individual psychology is not
primarily a system of theoretical psychology but of medical
practice. Like Freud, Adler belongs to the medical profession and endeavors to cure mental ailments. Nevertheless,
from the very beginning, Adler was governed by certain
theoretical views which gradually coalesced into a kind of
system. We shall not trace the various changing phases
through which individual psychology passed but shall
merely review the system as it exists at the present time.

2. The chief principle of individual psychology is that
human personality is an inherently purposive unity and
totality. To understand a human being is to apprehend the
purposive tendency, or as Adler says, the "guiding principle," of that being's life. Each new observation must be
rationally integrated with this central purposiveness.

The inherent purposiveness of personality is in turn
composed of three subgroups of purposive tendencies:
    a. biological.
    b. social.
    c. rational.
Biological purposiveness comprises the innate reflexes
and emotions which serve for the preservation of life. Social
purposiveness comprises the vital expressions resulting
from human communal life, collectively referred to by
Adler as the concept of social feeling. Rational purposiveness
finally comprises the conscious, planned activity of human
beings. These three subgroups of purposiveness are everywhere subordinate to personal purposiveness even where
an activity appears to be "automatized." Even functional
errors (as Freud had already shown) must be interpreted
purposively. In the same way, Adler uses dreams as the
material for purposive interpretation. To be sure, conflicts

occur in which, for example, an "illegitimate" purposive tendency struggles against the feeling of moral responsibility; but the outcome of the struggle reveals the totality of the character or personality as a determinant of all actions.

Adler also proceeds similarly to Freud by going back to the period of earliest childhood in order to understand the development of the individual. But he does not lay his chief stress upon the factor of sex. The Œdipus complex is left unmentioned. Adler investigated the relationship between the determination of the ego and its experience with other egos, and arrived at the fundamental principle of his doctrine—the feeling of inferiority. The consciousness of helplessness, the fact of being weaker than someone else, and the dependence upon someone else coöperate in producing the child's feeling of inferiority. Counter to this runs the tendency to overcome inferiority. This tendency Adler calls the striving for prestige. It gradually leads to the objective conquest of helplessness. There is also a subjective way of conquering the feeling of inferiority. The child finds it more convenient to satisfy his tendency toward self-assertion (prestige) by fictive means. A great deal in child behavior is to be understood in this subjective manner of doing away with inferiority through self-deception.

Conjointly with the striving for prestige, a second fundamental impulse involved in the development of every individual is the social feeling. If the assertive tendency is centripetal, the community feeling is centrifugal. It is by no means evidenced only in relationships with other people, but also in relationships with objects, with nature, and with art. It reveals itself in the form of objectivity, in the form of a readiness to perform and accomplish real tasks, in devotion and self-surrender, and in personal responsibility. The social feeling can come into conflict with the assertive tendency, but both tendencies can and must be synthesized.

Adler's theory of the "inferiority complex" has achieved undoubted popularity. But his theory of overcompensation is no less important. In his previous studies limited to the medical field, Adler had already determined that the organism not only persists in compensating for the inferiority of certain organs but overcompensates for it. And this overcompensation not only relates to the organ itself (as in the formation of a thick scar in place of a wound) but primarily to the whole "psychic superstructure." The defective organ becomes the pivotal center of all attention. The whole life plan is completed with this inferiority in mind, and frequently the sum total of psychic energy subordinates itself to a compensatory adaptation of the defect.

Adler illustrates this by the example of musicians who, like Beethoven, Franz, Smetana, and many others, suffered from defective hearing. One might therefore paradoxically say that these great men became great musicians, not because they had a particularly good, but an inferior, organ of hearing. The overcompensation of existent defects is important not only in regard to gifts or talents but also in regard to character. Physical ugliness often leads to its compensation by means of mental superiority. A great many subtleties of human nature are hidden in such observations, which we cannot exhaustively present here. Compensatory phenomena cover social life in all its forms. They lead to an understanding of the importance of the family in psychic development, but not in Freud's limited perspective, which encompasses only the Œdipus complex. In addition to the relationship between child and parents, the relations between siblings and their ordinal position in the family are also considered with respect to their significance in mental development.

3. Among the multilateral applications of individual psychology, we mention its contributions to the psychology of the sexes. Here, too, the essential factor is not the organic difference between man and woman but its psychic superstructure. An abundance of types and life forms are interpretively derived from the changing interrelationships of

the sexes. The concept of "masculine protest" has become a kind of slogan.

Like Freud, Adler applies his psychology to the neuroses. He draws no fundamental distinction between character in general and the "neurotic character"; he believes rather that to a certain degree all modern people are neurotic. However that may be, Adler lets us know what he considers neurotic symptoms. Adler refers to such symptoms when physical or mental behavior, subservient to the attainment of a personal goal and ostensibly involuntary and pathological, causes failure in the fulfilment of vital functions. Most neurotics are discouraged slaves of ambition. Their goals have been raised too high and are, therefore, unattainable. Consequently, they flee to an artificial world in which they are the fictive focal centers. They create a gulf between themselves and others, and their sole endeavor is to shield their hypersensitive personal feelings from injury. An abundance of more special pathological symptoms, such as anxiety neurosis, agoraphobia, and the like, are to be understood as an escape from a real task which the patient seeks because of his inability to banish some feeling of inferiority that originated in his childhood. Instead of attaining objective achievements, the patient merely dons subjective masks of escape.

If the patient's insight into his ailment disappears and contact with the external world is lost, the neurosis changes into a psychosis. The obsessive idea becomes a delusional idea. The neurotic is still capable of guarding himself against his obsession because he knows that his behavior is pathological. The insane individual considers his obsessions correct and constructs for himself a private logic which he counterposes to the general logic or the common sense of normal minds. It is certain that inherited dispositions or organic disturbances are frequently involved, but as a whole, according to Adler, every psychosis can be understood in terms of his theory of the purposive structure of the personality even when it has fallen into devious ways.

Individual psychology has been expanded into a philosophy of life and an interpretation of culture not only by Adler himself but also by his numerous pupils, among whom F. Künkel deserves especial mention. Despite its name, individual psychology is anything but the glorification and isolation of the individual; it strives, rather, for the banishment of "rugged individualism." Hence its connection with socialism in the political sphere. Man is not viewed as a disparate being, but within his social nexus.

4. If we were to characterize Adler's psychology as a whole, we would be compelled to admit that it appears extraordinarily simple and transparent when compared to the highly complicated systems of structural psychology, characterology, psychoanalysis, and other modern tendencies. It resembles behaviorism in tending to simplify rather than to complicate problems. Not the least portion of its success is based upon this tendency toward simplification and also upon its general temper of optimism, which it also shares with behaviorism. Whereas Freud achieved his results through the daring and superacuity of his doctrines, Adler achieved his by constantly addressing himself to sound common sense. Compared to the psychoanalysts, whose motto seems to be "Why be simple when you can be complicated?" Adler's manner sometimes borders upon banality.

This, however, should not blind us to the fact that he has actually devised essential and new facts which have become part of the permanent store of psychological knowledge. Adler's concept of the inferiority complex and his theory of overcompensation through fictive subjectivisms are genuine accomplishments in psychology which have also proven themselves extremely fruitful both from the pedagogical and therapeutic points of view.

Historically viewed, Adler belongs wholly to the psychology of the twentieth century which deviates from the pure analysis of consciousness. In his works, there are hardly any of the abstruse distinctions and analyses that were so characteristic of the Wundt or Brentano schools. Like his masters, Nietzsche and Freud, Adler knows that consciousness is often deceptive and that it is a subtle masquerade which the ego performs for itself. Although the unconscious does not play as important a rôle for him as it does for Freud, Adler, too, probes behind consciousness for hidden motives. Primarily through his emphasis on final purposiveness, Adler aligns himself with the phalanx of modern psychologists. His kinship with William Stern, Spranger, and other professional psychologists has often been dwelt upon. From the practical point of view, Adler has had an exceedingly stimulating influence upon medicine and pedagogy.

CARL G. JUNG AND THE ZÜRICH SCHOOL OF PSYCHOANALYSIS

1. Another dissenting offshoot from orthodox Freudianism, tending in a different direction from individual psychology, is the so-called Zürich school of psychoanalysis. Its leader and independent champion is the physician, C. G. Jung. From the very beginning, Jung, like Freud, evinced a predominant interest in mythology and in mythological thought. He developed these interests in his writings with an astonishing display of erudition.

Jung's first extensive essay to attract attention appeared in Freud's *Annual of Psychoanalytic and Psychopathological Research* in 1913, under the title "Metamorphoses and Symbols of the Libido," to which was appended the subtitle "Contributions to the Evolutionary History of Thought." The title in itself is a characterization of the Jung school. Jung distinguishes two types of thinking: first, "directed thinking"; and second, "dreaming and fantasy." Directed thinking aims at verbal communication; it is indefatigable and exhaustive, institutes new forms of adaptation, imitates reality, and tries to influence reality. Dreaming and fantasy, on the contrary, constantly work hand in hand, so to speak, with reminiscences; they turn away from reality, liberate subjective wishes, and are wholly unproductive as regards adaptation to the external world.

Like Freud, Jung believes that dreaming is a fragment of the childhood mind carrying over from the surmounted past. But Jung emphasizes even more strongly that dreaming is a residue of early phylogenetic stages of thinking; it is what he calls "the archaic myth fantasy." All myths and dreams, however, are obviously latent wish tendencies within the mind. Using as an illustration several imaginative poems published by an American poetess, Miss Frances Miller, Jung analyzed the procedure employed in "archaic-symbolic" thinking. Although he discovered symbols of the "libido" everywhere, Jung broadened the concept considerably beyond its Freudian sexual connotations. In doing so, he aired his main differences with the Freudian school, just as Adler had done. It was these differences which led to the schism between Vienna and Zürich.

2. In his second main work entitled *Psychological Types* (1921), Jung went into more profound detail with respect to his problem of objective and subjective thinking, or, as he now calls it, the problem of extraversion and introversion. Rather than viewing these as conjointly functioning within the same person, he distributes them between two polar types, the extravertive and the introvertive. In both types, moreover, there is a sharp distinction between the set of consciousness and the set of the unconscious which he views as "compensatory."

In the extraverted type, the object plays the determining rôle. The interest of such individuals pursues objective events. The extravert acts in order to influence persons and to move and change things. He runs the danger of losing himself in the objective. The neurosis of the extravert is hysteria in which occurs an exaggerated rapport with the individuals who people the patient's surroundings. In the extravert, the set of the unconscious is egocentric, that is to

386   The Evolution of Modern Psychology

say, it compensates for the extraversion of consciousness. The more complete the conscious extravertive set is, the more infantile and archaic is the unconscious set; indeed, it often verges upon the brutal and the ruthless.

The subdivisions in extraversion are two rational types; the extraverted thinking type and the extraverted emotional type, both of which subordinate existence to reason and try to eliminate the accidental and the chaotic as much as possible. But the experiences of these types are irrational because they come from their unconscious, which is exceedingly primitive. In addition, however, there are also two irrational extraverted types: the sensation type and the intuitive type. These types are empirical with respect to consciousness; they are shaped by experience to such an extent that their judgment often outstrips experience. When these types deliver judgments out of their unconscious, such judgments have the appearance of dispassionate profundity, but are mostly naïve and distortive.

The introvertive type represents the polar extreme of the extravert. The introvert is more poorly orientated to objective than he is to subjective factors. Into his perception and action a subjective view obtrudes itself, which prevents the action from assuming a form corresponding to what is objectively true. The subjective factor, according to Jung, comprises those psychic actions or reactions which fuse into a new psychic form under the influence of the object. This subjective factor is the hereditarily provided psychic structure, which is a quantity inherent within the individual. This structure, however, is not merely individual; it is much more comprehensive than the ego. It is a collective unconscious, and embraces the instincts and the form of psychic apprehension of objects which Jung terms the "archetype." By means of the superior position of the subjective factor in consciousness, the inferior tone is given to the objective, a condition that also can become dangerous. The typical form of neurosis in introverts is psychasthenia, characterized by extreme sensitivity and a tendency toward exhaustion.

Objective relationship in introverts, in contrast to extraverts, is infantile and archaic. Objects possess qualities
which arouse fear in the introvert, yet the introvert does
not become aware of such fear through his consciousness
but through an unconscious foreboding.

Corresponding to the psychology of extraverts, introverts are also divisible into subtypes. There are the same
two rational types: the thinking type and the emotional
type. Both are based upon rational, deliberative functions
directed not merely toward the objective but toward the
subjective. Hence they often come into violent conflict with
environment. In addition, introverts are also divisible into
two irrational types: the sensation type and the intuitive
type. These types are outwardly reserved, secretive, and
indifferent; they are enthralled by a wealth of subjective
experiences. Their influence upon the external world is
often inadequate and, in consequence, such types are often
held in low esteem.

Of course, this antithesis applies to extreme types scarcely
to be found in real life. We cannot avoid noting a certain
relationship between Jung's types and those of Kretschmer.
The latter's cyclothymics correspond to the extraverts, the
schizothymics to the introverts, although there are certain
differences of detail. Jung himself has indicated the resemblances of his types to other psychological polar types.
Thus Friedrich Schiller's antithesis between naïve and
sentimental poets, Nietzsche's contradistinction between
the Apollonian and the Dionysian, James's religious types,
and others are related to Jung's typology.

Jung's most significant discovery, although not yet entirely elucidated, is undoubtedly that of the "collective
unconscious." Since this deals with archaic and mythological
matters, a rather frequent mythical vagueness inevitably
creeps into his written presentation. Jung often exceeds the
bounds of rational science in his discussion of irrational
matters. From a purely scientific standpoint, it is difficult to
say just where the threshold leading to solely intuitive

comprehension begins. It is therefore no accident that poets feel themselves especially attracted to Jung's psychology.

3. In his more recent publications, Jung endeavors to present his psychology in a more systematic form by working out a theory of "psychic energy." We have already encountered in Freud a number of metaphors borrowed from modern physics. These metaphors alluded to the transformation of psychic energy much as the physicists speak of the transformation of physical energy. Jung elaborates upon this idea more consistently than Freud.

Jung, nevertheless, contrasts his notion of psychic energy to mechanics. Mechanism is purely causal and conceives phenomena as the effect of some cause. Energy, on the contrary, is final and conceives the relation of cause and effect in such a manner that a unit of energy underlies the changes in phenomena. Energy maintains itself constantly and in the end entropically brings about a state of general equilibrium. The stream of energy has a definite direction—a goal—and irreversibly flows on toward the lowering of the potential. Energy is not a substance but a concept derived from the correlates of motion.

Jung's application of this concept to psychology hinges upon the question whether a quantitative estimation of psychic energy is possible. He answers this question in the affirmative, not in the sense of Fechner's psychophysics, but by invoking the system of psychological values. Values, according to Jung, are quantitative estimations of energy. With reference to psychic energy, Jung also uses the term "libido," of course not in the Freudian, sexual sense, since sex is a qualitative factor and Jung is only concerned with quantitative factors. However, he does not deny the dynamic importance of sex but merely sets it into its proper place. To Jung, the libido is an unknown quantity, a symbol, a pure hypothesis.

Jung's theory of the libido becomes comprehensible only when it is applied. Two accessory concepts are introduced with it: those of progression and regression. Progression is the process of adaptation to the external world. Regression, on the contrary, is the adaptation to the soul, to the inner world of the psyche. Both must be understood as transitory points through which the stream of energy flows. These two new concepts do not entirely coincide with extraversion and introversion. Progression can be extravertive when primarily affected by objective factors; it can also be introvertive when obliged to accommodate itself to subjective conditions. Similarly, regression can be introvertive through withdrawal from the external world, or extravertive through flight into a superabundance of external experience. Thus the libido not only moves forward and backward but also outward and inward.

The energy of certain psychic phenomena can be transformed into other dynamisms only through suitable means. A transformation of impulse energy occurs by means of transference to an analogous impulse object. The psychological "machine" which transforms energy is the symbol. Symbols make it possible for human beings to assume a counterposition to primitive and instinctive nature, in other words, to assume a civilized attitude as against mere instinctive behavior. The function of religion is primarily the creation of such attitudes.

The contrast between Jung's theory of energy and Freud's mechanism is thus brought into bold relief. Freud's theory consists of a causal interpretation of the psychology of instincts. According to Jung, the mind is governed by instincts, to be sure, yet it is not a derivative of some other instinct but a principle *sui generis*. Mind is the inevitable form which the power of instinct assumes. The control of instincts by means of mental processes proceeds in the individual with as much force as it does in the species. Instinct control is a normative process whose power originates from inherited channels of the ancestral line. Thus, the concept of God develops in the course of millennia as the formulation of a mental principle that stands opposed to mere instinctive behavior. Whereas for Freud religion is only an illusion, for Jung it is an historical force that profoundly transforms human nature by revising and spiritualizing innate energy through the agency of symbols. The theories summarized here are most clearly formulated in Jung's treatise "Concerning Psychic Energy," which first appeared in English in his *Collected Papers on Analytical Psychology* (2d ed., London, 1920).

4. Jung has devoted several studies to the collective unconscious. This concept conveys not merely individual connotations but also superpersonal ones in the form of inherited categories or archetypes. Similarly to Freud in his later writings, Jung ascribes relatively vital and collective contents to the subconscious. In conjunction with this, however, he also recognizes an individual subconscious that contains the repressed but potentially conscious parts of the unconscious. The conscious personality is a more or less voluntary section of the collective psyche: it is a "persona," which means, literally, "mask." The individual's differentiation from the collective is not actual individuation but rather a relinquishment of self in favor of some external rôle or imagined ideal. Individuation, however, makes one become one's own self. This self is a quantity superimposed upon the conscious ego; it embraces not only the conscious but also the unconscious psyche. Individuation is not merely the differentiation of one's own "phenomenon" but also of this phenomenon's invisible system of connection with the unconscious, the "anima." The anima is a feminine figure of speech compensating for masculine consciousness. In women, the figure compensating for masculinity is the "animus." The anima as an autonomic complex must be superseded and transformed into a function connecting the conscious to the unconscious. In this way, it loses its "demonic" power.

In order to distinguish between the ego and the figures of the unconscious, a technique is necessary lest abnormalities, conditions of being possessed which range from ordinary moods to psychoses, be produced. When the conscious ego comes to terms with the anima and takes over the latter's "mana," that is, its functional power, the result is the "mana personality." From the historical perspective, the "mana personality" develops into an heroic and divine figure. This type of personality possesses, on the one hand, a superior mentality, and, on the other hand, a superior will. The dissolution of the "mana personality" by means of the conscious realization of its constituents leads us back again to our own "self," an existent and living something which might also be called the "God in us," and which is related to the ego as closely as the sun is to the earth. This is the goal of life, of individuation. It is obvious that Jung's conclusion is one of profound mysticism, although he denies the fact.

5. Jung's is the most profound of all psychoanalytical systems, and also the most difficult one. He departs from the single-track sexualism of Freud, although not to as great an extent as Adler. Jung firmly retains the concept of the libido and expands it far beyond its sexual connotation. Like Adler, he rejects Freud's mechanistic interpretations and stresses the teleology of psychic phenomena. In all other respects, however, Adler and Jung are extreme opposites, not only because the former is a cool rationalist and the latter a brooding irrationalist, but because their whole *Weltanschauung* is completely different. Adler views man as the product of social conditions, of conjacent factors, and tries to minimize as much as possible, although not to deny, the importance of heredity. Jung, on the contrary, sees life as a process imbued with elements of the remote past, and his psychology is the portrayal of a conflict (which every individual must resolve) against this archaic past which he unconsciously bears within him. At any rate, Jung has expanded the sphere of the unconscious tremendously. It no longer means the possession of unconscious, individual memories, but includes the cumulative after-effects

of the whole history of mankind. Nor is the unconscious merely an individual datum; it is superindividual. This introduces the psychology of the unconscious to a group of problems toward which other new schools of psychology have also tended: the problems of the superindividual psyche.

PART SIX

THE PSYCHOLOGY OF SUPER-
INDIVIDUAL PSYCHIC LIFE

THE PROBLEM OF SUPERINDIVIDUAL SUPERCONSCIOUSNESS

1. In our survey of the history of psychology we discovered the astonishing fact that in the beginnings of the science of psychology in all civilizations, whether primitive or Indian, whether Greek or medieval European, the problem of an individual consciousness or even of an individual soul did not constitute a fundamental issue. The basic hypothesis in ancient times was that of a superindividual, cosmic psyche which was considered as an organic whole extending far beyond the consciousness of single individuals. While we were compelled to criticize the unscientific methods of ancient psychology, permeated as they were with theology and metaphysics, we were also compelled to admit that the general approach of the ancients, as such, need not be considered unscientific. On the contrary, superindividual relations between individuals and the question of a superconsciousness represent thoroughly significant scientific problems. As a matter of fact, it would be unscientific to ignore them and even those psychologists who deny the existence of a superindividual superconsciousness must at least prove that they can explain in terms of individual consciousness the phenomena that other psychologists ascribe to the superconscious.

We shall, therefore, begin by enumerating several facts which compel even the most critical of investigators to face such problems as are hereinafter designated as the superindividual psyche, the superconsciousness, or the "mind," the concept of "mind" being contrasted with that of "soul."

An exact investigation must divulge the fact that individual mental life is never solely individual but that in every consciousness and in every soul superindividual factors are co-involved. No individual thinks his thoughts or performs his actions solely as an individual but always as an integer of the social communities and classes to which he belongs.

Robinson Crusoe upon his island was able to exist because he brought with him the whole content of European culture as applied to thinking and behavior. Even in his isolation, he thought in verbal concepts which he had brought along as the heritage of an ancient culture; and when he named his companion "Friday," he was enabled to do so because of his knowledge of the calendar which dominated his habits of thought as an ancient heritage of civilization. Indeed, the most cursory examination into the communal life of a number of people confronts us with data in the way of language, art, custom, law, religion, and government, which, while they constantly pervade the consciousness of the individual, by no means exist solely within, nor are explicable only in terms of individual consciousness.

Today, such superindividual phenomena are designated as "social data" but, as we shall see, this term in itself is not a factual explanation. The nature of the individual's relationship to society can be viewed in a variety of different ways. One thing is certain: it cannot be understood in terms of the pure psychology of consciousness because in the majority of cases the superindividual operates completely unconsciously. Very few people are aware of the fact that they follow the superindividual norms of their social group in their moral conduct, their logical thinking, and in their esthetic evaluations. Their entire existence is dominated by the typical superindividual style of life belonging to their temporal and spatial groups but as individuals they are absolutely oblivious of this fact. It would not do to designate such social data as "unconscious," because they are not unconscious either within the meaning of that word as used by psychoanalysis, or any other psychological discipline that uses this mercurial concept. Moral conscience, logical norms, and esthetic taste pervade consciousness, indeed, they dominate it. Consequently we shall call these psychic factors "superconscious," in order to distinguish them from the individual unconscious and at the same time to denote their dominance over individual consciousness.

There is a further factor to be considered. The above facts are also supersubjective in so far as they objectify themselves. Language, art, custom, science, and religion, in short, all human culture belongs to subjective life, to the psyche. But these categories also exceed the limits of the psyche; they objectify themselves in deeds, works, and institutions occurring as objective facts. Hegel had already distinguished an objective mind adjacent to the subjective mind. The concept as employed here is somewhat similar when we say that language, custom, art, science, government, and religion are not merely superindividual and superconscious but are also supersubjective, even though they inevitably tend to resubjectify themselves in the consciousness of different individuals. As a result of these distinctions, many modern scholars have designated all superconscious data as the "objective mind" or simply the "mind," and have diametrically opposed this "mind" to the "soul."

In speaking here of a superindividual and supersubjective superconsciousness, we do not propose to advance a theory but merely to outline a point of view. We shall see that a whole series of sciences—social and racial psychology, sociology, biology, and cultural philosophy—have occupied themselves with these problems and have endeavored to solve them in various ways. At any rate, it is a thoroughly legitimate procedure to view such problems as existent. They must be included within a history of modern psychology even if their solution can never be purely psychological, least of all from the standpoint of pure consciousness.

2. A review of the past discloses that the problem of a superindividual whole in psychic life has always been dimly suspected but was at first considered only in religious or metaphysical speculation. In primitive man, the "soul" is by no means strictly individualized and connected with a physical being. It can leave the body and exist apart from the body; it can transmigrate to other bodies, or it can be

the product of a nonindividual or superindividual psychic force, of a "mana" or divinity. In Vedantic philosophy, the only true reality is the superindividual, the cosmic Atman, whereas individuation is regarded as an illusion (maya). In a similar fashion, the Eleatic school of philosophy conceived the Divine as the sole reality, while everything individual was considered nonexistent.

Plato's approach to these problems was more scientific, despite the fact that it was veiled in metaphysics. Subsequent psychological research was enriched by Plato's philosophical belief in ethical and logical norms as superindividual, and his concession of a supersubjective reality to these norms considered as "ideas." Plato disputed the contention that our truths and moral ideals issue from individual experience; he viewed them rather as originating from some preëxisting cosmic world.

The Middle Ages designated the superindividual or supersubjective as an *a priori* datum. However, this was not intended to mean that ethical and logical norms are chronologically operative before individuals, but that these norms universally dominate all individual psychic life. Thus far, the approach still remained entirely metaphysical, but facts were touched upon that modern social psychology is forced to treat from its own point of view. We shall see that the problem of an *a priori* recurs in modern science even if it is biologically and sociologically disguised.

With Aristotle, Plato's apriorism assumed a form approaching empiricism. Aristotle located the superindividual within the individual himself. Man as a *"zoon politikón"* contains within himself the state, or at least the capacity for setting up a state. The superindividual is not a primary but a "secondary" substance according to Aristotle. As with Plato, it is also substantialized.

Among the great metaphysicians of the seventeenth century, the problem of superindividual mental life played a significant rôle. To Descartes individual souls were not substance; substantiality, to him, inhered only in the cosmic *cogitatio*, a cosmic consciousness that was individualized only in connection with bodies. But even in their individualized form, superindividual data are decisively involved in the form of "innate ideas." The principles of logic, for example, do not originate in individuals, according to Descartes, but are superindividual and supersubjective.

In a similar fashion, Leibniz, who conceded substantiality to the individual as such, assumed that in every individual soul the *"vérités de raison"* were superindividual and *a priori*. His doctrine of a preëstablished harmony also presupposed a superindividual and supersubjective causality that uniformly governs all individuals.

These theories have their echoes in Kant and in his successors. The various Kantian schools engaged in a violent controversy as to whether their master, in speaking of the ego, had meant an individual ego or a cosmic ego. The latter inference is particularly championed by the Marburg school, led by Cohen. At all events, it is certain that Kant believed that logical, ethical, and esthetic norms, as aprioristic, superindividual and supersubjective causalities, dominated the psychic life of individuals. Kant, of course, was wholly remote from the modern sociological approach, but in a speculative and metaphysical way he treated the same problems that modern science has treated with different methods.

Much more boldly than Kant, Fichte substantialized a superindividual superconsciousness in his cosmic ego; indeed, to such an extent (especially in his first period), that the individual remained wholly in the background. And similarly, in Schelling and Hegel, the cosmic mind appeared as a superindividual, superconscious datum which individualized and objectified itself in many ways. We shall observe later how Hegel brings us to the direct anticipation of modern research. For Hegel attempted to render the evolution of historical epochs and cultural cycles comprehensible in terms of a cosmic mind.

Our historical review shows us that many of the most

celebrated philosophers of the past by no means considered the individual mind a primary phenomenon. They were rather more inclined to regard the mind as a superindividual, superconscious, and supersubjective datum which is *a priori* in contradistinction to individuals. Most philosophers, of course, endowed this superindividual mind with a certain nonmaterial substantiality. It is in this very respect that contemporary research has changed its course into new channels.

3. Opposed to the philosophers who assume a superindividual psychic life there have always been others who have explained superindividual data in terms of the individual psyche. Among these were the Sankhya philosophers, the Sophists, the Atomists, the Epicureans, and the Stoics. Whereas most of these philosophers were pure individualists with respect to all problems of civic and social life, the Stoics attempted to advance a theory of human society derived from the "common sense" operative in all men. In this way they arrived at a system of cosmopolitanism. None of these philosophers, however, contributed a more profound solution to the problem of a superindividual mind, since such a problem was secondary to their individualistic principles.

The Middle Ages laid hold of superindividual problems more vigorously. In contradistinction to the universalism of the Schoolmen, who placed the species before individuals and saw *a priori* essences in universal phenomena, the nominalists emphasized the belief that universal phenomena come after individual particular phenomena; indeed, they viewed universal phenomena as totally devoid of reality. If, however, all universals (the species) in the objective world are only *"flatus vocis"* (purely verbal abstractions), then the universal or common aspect of particulars (individuals) must also be unreal.

The nominalistic tradition was continued even more radically in Hobbes. Hobbes championed nominalism not only in regard to the psychology of the individual but also in politics. Here, however, a certain dualism appeared in his works. On the one hand, he instituted the state as a superindividual entity ("Leviathan"), and on the other hand, he derived the state from the legal subjection of individuals to the power of an absolute ruler. Thus, he founded social life upon the reason of individuals, which recognizes that the naturally bellicose instincts of man must be held in check.

The later English philosophers were also individualists in social and political theory. Locke, in contrast to Hobbes, started from the premise of an original state of freedom and equality, but he also viewed the state as an arrangement, made imperative by reason, to further the welfare of individuals. Hume sought the basis of social life not solely in reason but in innate sympathy, the root of moral impulses. Sympathy derives from the fact that individuals resemble each other in their feelings and actions. In the recognition of sympathy as a socially constituting factor, Hume was succeeded by Adam Smith, who also added to this factor the instinct of gain. Social life, particularly in its economic aspects, is due to the free competition of individuals, according to Smith. Rousseau also introduced a *"volonté générale"* in his *Contrat Social*, not as a substance but as a collective will in which the volitional strivings of individuals are united.

As natural as the individualistic standpoint may appear to the modern person reared in a liberal spirit, historically it arrived later than the universalistic standpoint, and, for the most part, as a distinct reaction to it. We shall see that here too, as in so many other instances, the development has reversed itself at the present time. Philosophers, to be sure, still make the individual their main premise, but see themselves impelled, with increasing frequency, to accept collectivistic and totalistic conclusions.

THE PIONEERS OF MODERN SOCIAL PSYCHOLOGY AT THE BEGINNING OF THE NINETEENTH CENTURY

1. The same contrasts characteristic of the past also stood opposed to each other at the beginning of the nineteenth century. In the interim, matters had become more complicated and new phases of opposition had come into existence. Since these still have their violent repercussions in contemporary research, we shall enter into a more precise discussion of them.

At first, the chief contrast, as in the past, was a national one, and consequently possessed social implications. Whereas the leading English thinkers were of an individualistic-nominalistic persuasion and would not countenance an actual superindividual psychic entity, German thinkers entertained aprioristic-universalistic views and were inclined toward the acceptance of a real superindividual mind. This distinction lasted far into the nineteenth century, and indeed, exists to this very day; although at times the situations were reversed. There were some extreme individualists among the Germans, while Hegelianism flourished richly in English philosophy. Various compromises were also effected. For example, we shall see how Spencer, although an individualist at bottom, nevertheless viewed society as a totalitarian organism; whereas the German racial psychologists assume the existence of a uniform racial mind, but try to understand this mind in terms of individual psychology.

In addition, new and powerful influences issued from France, where Comte had founded the science of sociology in which social phenomena were raised to the level of a new and independent field of research. These influences showed their effect in England in the thought of Spencer, who had already independently developed the biological method begun by Comte. The question now raised was by no means confined to the earlier antithesis: universal vs. individual.

The nineteenth century asked: Are the facts of superindividual mental life to be interpreted in terms of individual psychology, of biology, of sociology, or in terms of pure "ideas"?

2. The individualistic-nominalistic theory of society was continued in its place of origin, England. Bentham's formula of the greatest possible good for the greatest possible number was purely individualistic as a moral and legislative principle. The desire for pleasure was considered a primary psychological motive next to which sympathy was of but slight importance. Notwithstanding this, self-interest, when rightly conceived, was supposed to be conducive to the general welfare. The ethics of J. S. Mill were directed along the same lines, except that he maintained that social feelings were just as effective as egotistical ones. Moreover, he also drew qualitative distinctions among the forms of pleasure and property. But he consistently adhered to an individualistic interpretation of society.

Darwin's doctrine of the descent of man, although at first a purely biological theory, also developed into a social philosophy, essentially in the nominalistic sense. The theory of evolution destroyed the belief in a constant reality of species (universals) by showing that exceptionally well-adapted individuals (particulars) could create a new and higher species. Darwin also exercised a direct influence upon social philosophy. According to him, the moral sense originates from an original social instinct by way of natural selection. Reflective man discovers in himself a tendency toward the commonweal which has its roots in the individual.

In Germany, where individualism was in the nature of an explicit reaction against the predominant universalism, Feuerbach became an advocate of nominalism. Stirner, who rejected everything superindividual as a "mad conceit," was much more radical even than Feuerbach. Nietzsche, too, was essentially an individualist for all his profound insight into the biological determinants of the mind.

In general, it can be said that in the liberal society predominant in most civilized countries during the nineteenth century the individualistic standpoint was considered to be the natural one.

3. In addition to all these views, the universalistic doctrines of the past exerted an after-influence and gave birth to new doctrines. Problems of this nature came into particular vogue in the philosophy of history that flourished during the Romantic Era. The Romanticists did not accept the earlier concepts of a universal mind, but championed the concept of a mind distinguished according to racial groups. A forerunner of this view was Johann Gottfried Herder, who made languages the particular subject of his studies and expressed himself counter to Kant's apriorism. He drew fine distinctions among the most disparate national traits. Herder did not view national character as an entity but as having developed under the influence of climate, geographical situation, and the like.

Wilhelm von Humboldt, who was also primarily a philosopher of linguistics, was greatly influenced by Herder. Humboldt conceived of "ideas" as the forces which mold history and society. At the beginning he followed Herder in emphasizing only the "idea" of humanity, but, later, under the influence of Schelling, he recognized the operation of a plurality of ideas. These ideas are cryptic forces which are revealed also in the individual. The original ideas were considered to be those of truth, beauty, and justice.

The theory of the "idea" emerged in a different form in Hegel. To Hegel the "idea" is the principle which creates the universe. It is the "master of nations and of the world" and resembles God in its unity. But the idea does not remain a unity; it divides by expelling its antithesis and then unites with this antithesis to form a higher synthesis. In this continual process of division and union of ideas we have the history of the world, which is, in its essence, reason. Civilization in all its forms results from the autochthonous movement of ideas, and civilization uses the individual only as a means of attaining its goal. Individuals are not clearly conscious of these universal ideas. The whole metaphysical process reaches its full conscious fruition in Hegelian philosophy.

The metaphysics of ideas propounded by Humboldt and Hegel had its repercussions in Leopold von Ranke, the greatest German historian of the nineteenth century. "Undoubtedly, it is always the force of the living mind [Ranke's synonym for *idea*] which stirs the world to its very depths. Prepared by previous centuries, these forces emerge when their time comes, summoned forth from the unfathomable depths of the human mind by strong and inwardly powerful individuals. It is their very nature to draw the world over to themselves, and to conquer it."

We shall refer to all theories of the Herder-Humboldt-Hegelian order as "ideological." These theories were no longer universalistic in the same sense as they had been in former times; since the superindividual mind that they assume is no longer unqualifiedly universal, but is divided into spatially and temporally different powers that superimpose themselves dictatorially upon individuals. At times, ideological theories are conceived in a more subjective way as the "national soul" or the "national mind," and at times in a more objective way as "ideas"; but in either event, they are superindividual, superconscious, and supersubjective.

4. Although most German theories of this period were still strongly metaphysical, an explicitly antimetaphysical tendency arose in France. This tendency, too, introduced a force in the shape of "society" which was intended to substantiate the problems of the superindividual mind in an empirical way. We refer to the sociology of Auguste Comte. Comte juxtaposed sociology with the empirical natural sciences and called his system "social physics"; but with respect to the motive forces of social life, he was just as anti-individualistic as were the Germans.

To Comte, society is an "organic system." In contrast to the *"organisme individuel"* it is an *"organisme social."* Both are dominated by a *"consensus universel,"* an interaction of all its parts. This pervasive social solidarity is a creative idea (*idée mère*). Social "statics" deals with the "consensus" in a state of quiescence; social "dynamics" deals with progress. The solidarity of social statics depends upon the solidarity of social ideas; a union of sentiments and interests is inadequate. Social dynamics is the result of external conditions such as soil, climate, race, and the like, and also occurs as a result of social competition (*concours*); but it is the human mind which supplies the directive power. Although the mind also needs desires and passions as animating impulses, it still retains its predominance. Every reform must originate as an idea. Ideas transform morals and institutions.

With reference to the manner in which progress takes place, Comte set up his famous law of three stages. These stages of the progress of civilization are stages of the human mind. The human mind first passes through a theological and then a metaphysical period until it finally reaches its last stage in positivism, in which the exact science of sociology, rather than imaginative theories, dominates human conduct.

Comte's sociology, particularly in France, aroused intense interest in social phenomena. Some scholars, such as Littré, De Roberty, De Greef, and Lacombe, developed the intellectualistic aspect of Comte's sociology; others, like Von Lilienfeld, Fouillée, Worms, Izoulet, and Schäffle, concerned themselves with its biological basis. As a result of Spencer's influence the biological phase developed so powerfully that it became a movement of its own.

5. Spencer's sociology was a synthesis of English individualism and Comtean sociology. His point of departure, especially in his ethics, was individualistic; but he strove to exceed the limits of individualism by making the goal of

voluntary human activity not merely the preservation of the individual, but also the preservation of the species. Involved with this was Spencer's idea of evolution, conceived before Darwin's theory. With this idea, Spencer exceeded the bounds of individualism in so far as he assumed the inheritance of acquired characteristics. To this extent, then, he believed in the existence of a superindividual connected whole, so far as the mind was concerned. Intellectual as well as moral dispositions are inherited from the experiences of the species. Logical and ethical norms are therefore *a priori* for the individual. They are at least superindividual biological phenomena operative from generation to generation, if not *a priori* in an absolute sense.

In addition to these views, Spencer gradually arrived at the idea, inspired by Comte, that the forms of human society are to be regarded as organisms. Like Comte, Spencer also employed the rational medium of analogy to a great and detailed extent. The analogy of growth and of structure were the primary analogies by means of which Spencer endeavored to prove that society and the state are organisms.

Let us consider the analogy of growth first. From among the various forms of animal growth, Spencer chose that of multiple growth, particularly as exemplified in polypi. Here we have a development from the cell to the polyp and further to the polyp colony. Analogously, social growth proceeds from the clan to the tribe, from the tribe to the union of several tribes, and thence to the nation.

The second analogy is that of "structure." In rudimentary organisms two cell layers develop: the "ectoderm," the function of which is to regulate contacts with the external world by means of absorption and repulsion; and the "endoderm," which transforms the matter to be assimilated Corresponding to the ectoderm in society is the system of defense which repels the enemy and permits the approach of friends. The system of food supply which provides for the feeding of the population corresponds to the endoderm.

Just as the nervous system evolves from the ectoderm, so civil government is supposed to evolve from the martial order. And just as a "mesoderm" forms between the ectoderm and endoderm, so a system of commerce forms between the defense system and the system of food supply in society.

In conjunction with these analogies, Spencer also pointed out various dissimilarities. He stressed the spatial separation of parts in the social complex as contrasted with the spatial unity in the biological organism. And he also pointed out a cardinal difference in the fact that consciousness occurs only in separate parts of the physical organism, whereas it occurs in all parts of the social organism.

Biological sociology had many important followers in France and Germany. It was totalitarian in its biological and sociological aspects but did not assume the existence of a superindividual mind as a primary substantial totality. This phase of sociology was distinctively characterized by its penchant for formal analogies that left the actual causal relationships completely in the dark.

6. The scientific tendencies we have just discussed did not attempt a psychological solution of social problems. On the contrary, they attempted to interpret psychological data in terms of metaphysical, sociological, or biological data. In the meantime, another movement known as "racial psychology" originated during the middle of the nineteenth century. Psychology, especially Herbartian psychology, utilized this movement for the interpretation of social phenomena. Racial psychology is closely allied with the ideological tendencies referred to above, although their present views conflict.

The Herbartians, M. Lazarus and H. Steinthal, who were the founders of "racial psychology," translated the metaphysics of Humboldt, Hegel, and Ranke into terms of psychology. In racial psychology ideas were transformed from metaphysical "forces" into psychological "ideas."

The very name of this new science was indicative of its

objective. The main issue was no longer metaphysical logic as with Hegel, but the application of psychological principles. In 1860, Lazarus and Steinthal founded the *Journal of Racial Psychology and Linguistic Science*, which was introduced with a programmatic and analytical essay. Its thesis was that the development of the several separate branches of knowledge, such as linguistics, religion, art, customs, and law, has been conducive to their interpretation "out of the innermost depths of the mind, in other words, conducive to the reduction of these branches of knowledge to their psychological bases." This, of course, was contrary to what Hegel had done. To Hegel ideas were the motivating factor; and individual, psychological facts, so far as he even deigned to notice them, were explicable in terms of these ideas. Racial psychology proposed to do the exact opposite: the psychological facts were now accorded the priority and civilization was to be interpreted in terms of these facts.

Of course, the principle of the new movement was not a psychology of individuals but one of races. Compared with modern social psychology, this is a limitation, since only "races" were selected as the subject of research from all the myriad host of social groupings. The selection was justified by the contention that race is the most essential common bond between individuals. The concept of the "racial mind" was viewed as a superindividual entity. Language, mythology, religion, art, customs, and economics were conceived as the "objective forces of the racial mind." Inasmuch as science must trace the different distinctive characteristics of these forms of culture in different races, racial psychology also became a sort of "psychic ethnology." And since it endeavored to learn not only about coexistent forms of culture but also about the evolution of different culture cycles, racial psychology, moreover, became the psychology of "historical life." Its goal was to discover the "elements" and "laws" of the "total mind," and to study the "coöperation" and "inter-operation" of human beings.

Racial psychology conceived the "racial mind" from the

point of view of content, not of function, in much the same way that the older psychology of consciousness looked upon the contents of consciousness. It conceived the unity of races as derivative from common "masses of ideas." Nevertheless, the racial mind was not portrayed as something passive but as an extremely dynamic and active phenomenon. It is not origin nor language which creates the race, but the "racial mind" in its objective facets which creates history and the laws of history. The motivating elements of history are ideas, the products of the objective mind. History is primarily governed by moral and esthetic ideas. Ideas, to be sure, are in a realm high above individual life, but are, in spite of that, not conceived in terms of Hegelian metaphysics.

In the above program, two groups of problems can be distinguished in detail: in the first place there is the creation of a psychology dealing with the history of races and with the general conditions and laws of the racial "mind," without reference to the separate races; and in the second place, the creation of a psychic ethnology, the province of which is to study the separate, actually existent, "racial minds" and their evolutionary forms.

The racial psychology of Steinthal and Lazarus, for all its many ambiguities, led directly toward modern social and cultural psychology. In this development it was aided largely by the intermediation of Wundt, who, at a very early stage in his career, had already clarified his own attitude toward the racial psychologists. Hans Volkelt, who has made a study of the rôle that racial psychology played in Wundt's intellectual development, informs us that as far back as 1860 Wundt had already conceived the plan of "adding a sort of superstructure" to experimental psychology in the shape of a racial psychology. As a matter of fact, Wundt's *Lectures on the Human and Animal Mind*, of 1863, contains studies in racial psychology, particularly in the second volume. Indeed, after concluding his work, Wundt considered the chapters on racial psychology the best he had ever written. Shortly thereafter, nevertheless, he so regretted ever having written them, that he deleted these sections from all subsequent editions.

Wundt's first definition of the scope of racial psychology made clear his position toward Steinthal and Lazarus. He saw the value of racial psychology, not so much in the fact that it utilizes psychology, as in the fact that "it can be utilized for psychology." This view recurred in his essay on the "Aims and Methods of Racial Psychology," which appeared in 1886 in the fourth volume of his *Philosophical Studies*. Critical as Wundt's attitude toward Lazarus and Steinthal may have been, he was none the less tremendously inspired by them, and this inspiration was still evident in the very title of his great work, *Racial Psychology*, which did not appear until the twentieth century.

7. We have presented several of the forerunners of modern social psychology who, while they were not primarily psychologists themselves, nevertheless played an exceedingly important part in the evolution of the newer approach of modern psychology. It is quite possible to demonstrate the after-influence of all these older movements in the contemporary treatment of superindividual problems in psychology, despite the fact that the historical connection is not always realized. Contemporary research can be historically divided into the following movements:

a. Social psychology in the narrower sense or psychosociology, with the emphasis on the first part of the word. Psychosociology is allied to the individualistic social philosophers and their attempts to interpret social phenomena in terms of individual psychology.

b. Biological social psychology or biopsychosociology which, although very unlike Spencer, seeks an interpretation of superindividual psychic life primarily in biological phenomena, and only secondarily in psychology.

c. Psychological sociology, or better yet, sociopsychology (also with the emphasis on the first part of the word). This movement bases its research, in emulation of Comte, on the investigation of autonomous social facts and laws, from the study of which superindividual psychic life is secondarily derived.

d. The psychology of values and culture. This phase of modern psychology allies itself to the ideological philosophy of history, but it is also influenced by the racial psychology of Steinthal and Lazarus. It seeks to understand the subjective superindividual psyche in terms of mental objectivations and cultural values.

These four groups represent the main contemporary fronts along which the formidable problem of the superindividual psyche is being attacked.

PSYCHOSOCIOLOGY

1. The first of the modern tendencies in psychology is "social psychology" in its narrower sense. With Stoltenberg and others, I call this tendency psychosociology. The essential principle of psychosociology is its endeavor to interpret data pertaining to the superindividual psyche in terms of individual psychology. In so far as it follows this line of research it is the continuation of an earlier individualistic-nominalistic social philosophy. This philosophy assumes that the causes of all social and cultural phenomena must be sought within the psychic organization of single individuals. The only difference between this earlier social philosophy and modern psychosociology is that the former sought for the capacities making for social organization primarily within the intellect, while the latter concentrates chiefly upon instincts, feelings, and volitional dispositions. Both tendencies still exist to the present day and are often uncritically confused.

The psychology of consciousness in particular, although it deals with the analysis of individual consciousness, frequently makes cursory mention of social phenomena from an essentially individualistic bias. The psychology of consciousness is warranted, from its point of view, in asking how society, art, law, the state, and the like are mirrored in the individual consciousness, and thereby discovers that ideas, feelings, and volitional impulses are involved with these concepts. Psychologists may emphasize either intellectual or emotional factors according to their fundamental bias. Such is the manner in which the problem is treated in most textbooks on psychology. But does this suffice to explain the origin and meaning of all social phenomena? Such a standpoint implies the preëxistence of social phenomena. But the origin of these phenomena is also an important problem that assuredly cannot be solved solely in terms of individual consciousness, especially since modes of physical behavior, objective data, and institutions also belong to the very essence of such phenomena. For this reason, most of the more advanced social psychologists assume that there are dispositions and tendencies beyond consciousness that, at the very least, are not wholly conscious.

2. Because the psychology of consciousness, especially in its sensationist-intellectualist form, was but poorly adapted to serve as the basis for a genetic social psychology, the latter was obliged to establish itself independently. This was accomplished through the agency of an astounding book which, although it was published as early as 1887, did not achieve fame until the twentieth century. Its title was *Community and Society* and its author, Ferdinand Tönnies. This book provided an amazing solution for the ancient dispute as to whether social life is governed more by intellectual or more by emotional factors.

Tönnies created his own system of psychology by taking Schopenhauer's philosophy of will as his point of departure. It is will that constantly impels man to act; but will appears in two different forms, "essential will" and "selective will," as they are termed in the later editions. Essential will includes all forms of striving, such as instincts, feeling impulses, and the like, that are part of the organic essence of man. This sort of will involves a mode of thinking which is subservient to it. In selective will, on the contrary, thinking has the priority and externally imposes its aims upon the will. Essential will gives rise to all instinctive actions, while selective will is responsible for purposive activity.

All social forms can thus be classified into those that are based upon essential will and are instinctively united, such as the family, tribe, or race; and those that are united by rational purposive interests, such as clubs, stock companies, occupational classes, and the like. Tönnies calls the first group "communities," and the second, "societies."

Communities are united by their organic nature, by their natural kinship and concord, by customs and morals, and also by religious ties. Communities are governed by the biological substance of their members. Societies, on the other hand, are not natural but artificial forms. They originate through set purposes, contracts, and laws. The biological substance of societies is irrelevant. Persons of a very heterogeneous sort may enter into them so long as they are dominated by a common purpose. There need be no sentimental or religious ties. Communities have their roots in the past, in common descent and tradition. Societies or associations, however, are joined in the present for purposes to be realized in the future. In the community, the individual achieves influence through personal probity, personal courage, and personal wisdom. In the society, the decisive factors are impersonal things, such as knowledge, shrewdness, economic superiority, and above all, money. In short, the community is a thoroughly irrational form, whereas the society is a rational form. The community is rooted in the subjective. Society is rooted in objective purposes and goals.

The dualistic social psychology of Tönnies was undoubtedly a significant scientific achievement. It was extraordinarily illuminating as regards the understanding of the factors of consciousness which are co-involved in the creation of social forms. But Tönnies' system was not a pure psychology of consciousness for two reasons: in the first place, it regarded consciousness as rooted within a pre-conscious organization; and secondly, the created social forms were not pure facts of consciousness, but the products of a causality which in itself is not conscious. At most this causality was conscious only to a slight degree, since it did not become conscious until Tönnies made it so. To this extent, then, Tönnies' doctrine was not social psychology but sociology. His principle was an individualistic-nominalistic one (it was no fortuitous circumstance that Tönnies devoted a valuable monograph to Hobbes), but it resolved itself ultimately into a proof of a causality which prevails despite the fact that the individuals involved are unaware of it.

3. We shall see that most social psychologists soon reached similar conclusions. This was primarily the case in a movement, pioneered in America, that ascribed the origin of social life to "interests." The concept was introduced into social psychology by an Austrian named Gustav Ratzenhofer. Ratzenhofer's concept of "interest" is not synonymous with the customary usage of the word in modern psychology. It rather approaches the Herbartian concept of interest, but is nevertheless not very profoundly conceived from a psychological point of view. According to Ratzenhofer, the vital energy of man expresses itself in five different interests:
   a. generic (sexual) interest (that is, race preservation).
   b. physiological interest (in nourishment).
   c. individual interest (in the self and its preservation).
   d. social interest (in the family, tribe, nation, etc.).
   e. transcendental interest (in religion and philosophy).
   These innate "interests" are activated by four "drives"; the material, the selfish, the intellectual, and the moral. The will, which as vital energy of the individual unites the force of the drives, is the *vis a tergo* behind "drives" and interests. Will, in turn, is divided into nine subtypes. "Social evolution is a progressive expansion and elevation of interests from the lowest, most immediate, goals to

higher and more comprehensive goals, which represent an indirect, farsighted gratification of needs. The race preservative interest, developed through didactic experience into social interest, can cause the individual to renounce his innate selfishness and thus behave altruistically, while remaining relatively free."

Ratzenhofer's doctrine is contained in a book entitled *Understanding Society* (1898), and in an incomplete posthumous work bearing the title of *Sociology* (1907), which his son published. Ratzenhofer was an army officer, and he displayed an egregious lack of a finer preparation in the elements of psychology. His definition of concepts and their schematic classification was rather vague. In carrying out his social theory, he also included other factors not purely psychological, such as race, environment, the struggle for existence, and the like, and arrived at a classification of social forms based on common blood, power, ideas, etc. All these theories exerted a stimulating influence, less in Europe than in America, where a group of important scholars allied themselves with Ratzenhofer.

The next social psychologist worthy of note was Albion W. Small. In his *General Sociology* (1905), he praised Ratzenhofer as the founder of a critical study of social science. Like Ratzenhofer, Small regarded interests as the elements of the social process, the "modes of motion" in human behavior. Sociology, therefore, became the science of human interests and their effects upon a changing environment. The chief problem of sociology is the struggle of humans to realize their interests. Interests create the "associational or social process." Society is, therefore, not a substantial concept, but a verbal one.

Small differed from Ratzenhofer in his classification of interests. He considered the "health interest," which expresses itself in nourishing, propagation, and work, as the basis of all interests. Upon this basis he constructed five other interests: well-being, sociability, knowledge, beauty, righteousness. Progress in the social process ranges from narrow selfishness to a constantly broadening altruism. Small conceived the task of social psychology to be the generalizing of typical human purpose reactions into typical situations. In his subsequent publications, the concept of "interests" faded into the background.

Lester F. Ward, whom we align with this group, was a disciple of Spencer, to judge from the fundamental views expressed in his system of sociology. But he freed himself from Spencer's biological bias in not ascribing the formation of society solely to blind, natural forces. Ward stressed the fact that two great advances have been made in the evolutionary progress of society. The first occurred when desire, and with it, feeling, evolved from an insentient world. And the second occurred when intellectual force superimposed itself upon desire. Intellectual force is fundamentally different from desire, although it has not yet reached its full development. Inasmuch as Ward ascribed great significance to desires and to intellectual force, he went beyond social biology to social psychology. It is only in its psychological aspect that we shall discuss Ward's system of sociology.

In his first work, *Dynamic Sociology* (1894), he referred to five social forces which are derived from individual desires or instincts. These five forces are self-preservation, sex, the esthetic instinct, moral and mental force. Due to these forces and to natural selection, growth and evolution in society are produced. In his later work, *Pure Sociology* (1903), desires were regarded as a subordinate class of feelings of the most general vital phenomena to which the mind approaches only as an epiphenomenon. Interest which is the dynamic agent in society grows out of these desires. Besides such psychological interpretations, Ward also employed a great many analogies borrowed from natural science. Ward, however, did not retain his naturalistic viewpoint; in his *Applied Sociology* of 1906, he became the protagonist of a conscious control of society based upon sociological insight.

Edward Ross, too, extensively employed the notion of

interest derived from desires. Such a notion was at any rate more correct than Ratzenhofer's theory, which, conversely, derived desires from interests. According to Ross, social groups originate through a community of interests. These groups form the fundamental subject matter of sociology. Such groups are characterized by a uniform group will which does not always coincide with the separate wills of the group's members. We shall meet with the main discussion of Ross's social psychology elsewhere.

Among the older American sociologists who were essentially social psychologists, F. H. Giddings achieved greatest fame in Europe, largely because of his *Principles of Sociology*, published in 1896. Although influenced by Spencer, Giddings proposed to erect his system not upon biological but upon psychological principles. His manifesto called for a subjective and motivational interpretation of society but also demanded an objective interpretation of society as a dynamic structural form. According to Giddings, the original datum from which all social life develops is "the consciousness of kind," which is simultaneously an idea and a feeling. As an idea, this consciousness creates "like-mindedness" which is imbued with a vast socializing force. From an historical viewpoint, Giddings then went on to describe the growth and structure of society. His description is unimportant for our purposes, but his conception of the physical and psychic phases of the social process is highly significant.

Giddings regarded human beings not as the producers but as the products of society. It is only by means of association that man becomes a social being capable of language, abstract thinking, and other civilized accomplishments. All progress is due to the growth of the psychic factor in society. Only the lower levels of society can be regarded as natural products; higher social organization derives from purposive activity.

In his later writings, Giddings showed the influence of behaviorism, which he critically evaluated in his *Studies in the Theory of Human Society* (1922). He advanced a theory of "pluralistic behavior" based on the fact that human beings, in a given situation, usually react in a uniform manner and but very rarely as independent units. This is what unites men into groups. Giddings' innovation lies in the fact that he did not start with a fixed inventory of innate desires and interests but viewed these as being created by society. In this sense, his studies no longer belong to psychosociology but to sociopsychology which will be discussed later.

In present-day Germany, A. Vierkandt can be regarded as the chief representative of psychosociology, inasmuch as in his *Sociology* of 1922, he derived the nature of society from the social dispositions (*Anlagen*) of man. Not all such dispositions, such as the instincts of fear, fighting, and selfishness, are plastic or capable of attaining social value. Social dispositions often appear in contrasting pairs. Furthermore, there is a difference between fixed instincts and more plastic instincts whose content has not yet been crystallized, so that they bear a rather formalistic character. Such instincts are particularly important for social evolution. In discussing the nature and type of society, Vierkandt laid stress on the psychological phenomenon of the extension of the ego far beyond the personal self. In the concluding portion of his work, a purely sociological approach predominated.

To judge all these scholars who strove to interpret society in terms of interests, instincts, and drives, we are forced to conclude that, psychologically speaking, their ideas were very vague. The fact that none of them was or is a professional psychologist, is extremely significant. All such concepts as interest, instinct, and "drive" are but collective designations for modes of social conduct. They are psychologically indefinite from almost every point of view. In the first place, they do not sharply distinguish consciousness from nonconscious instincts or desires. Secondly, emotional and volitional factors are confused with fixed intellectual purposes. And in the third place, interest is sometimes conceived as an individual impulse and sometimes as a superindividual social force.

To be sure, most of these authors attempted to solve these difficulties by creating many special interests, but this not only failed to better the interpretative value of the basic concept of interest, but actually made matters worse. The above-mentioned concepts nevertheless can be utilized in practice by virtue of their summary vagueness, just as geologists, for example, employ collective concepts which appear inadequate to the chemist. Since we are not concerned here with pure sociology, but with psychology, we must, consequently, recognize the invalidity of these concepts. The interests and social forces referred to by the aforementioned social psychologists are not purely natural phenomena. They are not merely innate dispositions or attitudes of consciousness, but are in themselves created by social life. They are just as much the products as they are the causes of social life and cannot, therefore, be used to explain society. Interests, while they may perhaps possess descriptive value, have no interpretative value. For this reason, it was necessary for psychology to consult other categories.

4. The great success of McDougall's social psychology is based to no small extent on the fact that he approached social problems as a professional psychologist who instituted the more closely defined concept of the instinct instead of the former indeterminate "interests" and "desires." McDougall departed sharply from the pure psychology of consciousness. We have already discussed his psychology of instinct in connection with individual psychology. Historically, his *Introduction to Social Psychology* (1908), which has since undergone many revisions, considerably preceded his *Outline of Psychology* (1923) already discussed above. But he retained the fundamental idea, elaborated in his social psychology, that instincts are the prime motives of all human activity. Moreover, McDougall's work is really

nothing more than its title claims to be—an introduction. It terminates abruptly just at the point where the individual instincts it describes should be applied to society. It is a psychology of instinct with reference to social life, but it is not actually a system of social psychology. With respect to the latter, McDougall, of course, later made valuable contributions, but they deal, as he says himself, with group psychology. This corresponds to what we call sociopsychology and will, therefore, be discussed later.

For all the tremendous acclaim which greeted it, McDougall's instinct psychology did not stand unopposed. Floyd Henry Allport, in particular, contested its claims on behalf of social psychology. Allport's objection to instincts was similar to the one just raised against "interests"; namely, that they are not original phenomena but are the finished products formed by social conditions. In consequence, Allport desired to penetrate beyond instincts and determine those elements which are beyond all shadow of a doubt pure, innate dispositions. In doing so, he arrived at the phenomena of reflexes which he divided into "avoiding and approaching reactions." He assigned infantile "withdrawing, rejecting, and struggling" to the former category, while "responses to the stimulation of hunger and of the sensitive and erogenous zones" belong to the latter. Allport endeavored to explain the more complex instincts employed by McDougall from the elementary data by invoking the aid of learning, habit formation, and conditioned reflexes.

In a similar manner, Luther L. Bernard, in his book entitled *Instinct* (1924), endeavored to reduce instincts to more primitive innate mechanisms. Another sceptical view in regard to the theory of instinct was expressed by C. Murchison in his *Social Psychology* (1929).

The extent to which these theories are correct is of secondary importance to us. It is sufficient to note that the tendency toward the atomization of social life innate in all these individualistic theories is here extended far beyond the individual, inasmuch as the individual himself is further resolved into a complex of instincts, reflexes, and even more rudimentary mechanisms. To this tendency must be added the trend toward schematization which is so characteristic of the individualistic social psychologists.

Just as the individual was first schematized as a whole, so later his instincts and reflexes were catalogued and pigeonholed. These theories present us with a purely numerical multiplicity as a substitute for the empirical qualitative manifoldness of individuals and their impulses.

In opposition to all such schematizing atomization, we must seriously question whether society in all its many faceted empirical nature can be reconstructed from atomic elements derived in this manner. The question can scarcely be answered in the affirmative. There is no doubt that there are omnipresent totalitarian laws which govern individuals, their instincts, and reflexes. Atomistic social psychology is hardly a social psychology. Indeed it is ultimately no psychology at all but biology.

5. Psychoanalysis has also evolved theories which belong to "psychosociology." Freud himself, in his work *Totem and Taboo* (1913), discussed the social institutions of primitive peoples and endeavored to render them comprehensible in terms of psychoanalytic concepts. Freud derived the original import of totemism from infantile residues and from the symptoms of totemistic manifestations in the development of civilized children. Taboos are also negatively cultivated in civilized society and still exist, although directed toward different objects. Freud explained taboos as originating from the ambivalence of emotional stimulations.

In a recent work, *Group Psychology and the Analysis of the Ego* (1922), Freud also occupied himself with social problems. This work begins with the daring premise that libido relations constitute the essence of the mob psyche. "Identification," in which an objective factor replaces the ego ideal, is supposed to explain mob psychology in so far as participant individuals identify themselves with some common objective. Freud exerted a stimulating influence in Europe and in America, but the extremely speculative literature that has come into existence as a result of this influence can scarcely lay claim to being strictly scientific.

We have already mentioned that there are many elements of social psychology in Adler's system of individual psychology.

6. Concurrent with the problem as to which of the psychological forces are responsible for the origin of social processes and social forms, there is another problem that has been discussed less by psychologists than by historians and philosophers. The problem as to the relation between the individual and society can also be viewed from a qualitative angle and not merely from the numerical one as is the custom of most social psychologists. We can also ask whether all individuals are created equally important in regard to the social process; or whether the social process is shaped by certain especially gifted individuals, while the masses behave rather passively.

This question has been answered in two ways. We can designate the solutions in terms of the two extremes of the heroic and the collectivistic. Most social theoreticians attempt a union of the two. According to the heroic theory, all historical and social phenomena are created by great men, heroes, who, gifted above the average, either originate social forms or else place upon them the stamp of their individuality. Collectivism sees in great individuals essentially the exponents of collective phenomena. Strange to say, this approach has been adopted only by historians, sociologists, and philosophers, and but very little by psychologists. There is no special incentive to make us occupy ourselves with these theories.

Most of the heroistic thinkers believe their geniuses have been sent by God or Fate and, in general, avoid all psychological interpretation. Their opponents prefer a psychological explanation. The famous theory of Taine consisted in the belief that every genius could be interpreted in terms of heredity, milieu, and history. Of late, the influence of "generations" has been strongly emphasized, and it has been pointed out by Pinder that prominent men of genius often appear in groups. Many of the collectivistic interpretations of genius do not properly belong to the realm of psychology, but either to biosociology or to sociopsychology. In connection with the latter, we shall encounter the problem again in the works of Tarde.

7. As a whole, the psychosociological theories summarized here, as much as they differ from other theories, seek the causes for superindividual forms of life within the innate psychophysical organization of man. The forces we have discussed, whether they be called will, interest, instinct, or otherwise, are important social factors. Another pervasive attribute which these theories have in common is the tendency to transfer the center of gravity from the intellectual to the emotional sphere. In many authorities this tendency goes so far as to vastly underestimate the importance of the intellect. No state, no language, and no religion has ever arisen without some intelligence being involved, even though emotional factors may enjoy a certain primacy.

Our problem, however, is entirely altered if we ask whether these psychological interpretations are capable of explaining the whole of social reality. To ask this question seriously is tantamount to its negation. Even if we grant that interests, impulses, and instincts play an important rôle in the origin of society, does this explain the essential differences between the civilizations of Greece, China, Germany, or America? Are instincts or impulses solely responsible for the fact that many social groups tolerate polygamy, whereas others insist upon monogamy? Can they explain the existence of patriarchal and matriarchal societies?

The chief fallacy of most social psychologists has been that in taking the individual as their point of departure, they have nevertheless not conceived individuals as qualitatively different beings, but only as numerically separated representatives of an abstract type, the *homo socialis*. The individual in the sense of a unique and particular entity does not exist, astonishingly enough, for these social psychologists. While they view society as an extraordinarily uniform whole, they do not, as a result of this fallacy, explain either the multifariousness of social forms, or the nature of the psychic life developing within them. As soon as one attempts such an explanation, one must necessarily adduce additional data. This was first done by invoking the aid of biology, especially with regard to the explanation of unique racial traits.

BIOPSYCHOSOCIOLOGY

1. No matter which capacities of man we regard as those making for social organization, no matter whether we choose instincts, interests, or intelligence as our focus, the problem necessarily leads finally to the question of how they originate within the individual himself. This, in turn, necessarily leads beyond the bounds of individual life. The superindividual nexus is not merely conjacent in space but is also sequential in time. This nexus can even be said to have a dual existence: one aspect, as tradition, is transmitted by way of consciousness; and the other aspect, as heredity, is transmitted purely biologically without the intervention of personal consciousness.

We shall confine ourselves first to the extensive body of research that approaches the superindividual facts of psychic life from the biological angle. This research has given rise to a science which might be called biosociology but would be more exactly defined by the term biopsychosociology, since it also comprises psychological phenomena.

We have already mentioned the fact that sociological research hoped for the support of biology. Comte, Spencer, and their successors tried to explain the various forms of society as organisms. But they only succeeded in evolving mere analogies of only slight psychological value. Psychology expected the aid of biology from an entirely different quarter. As soon as psychology attempted a genetic interpretation of the mental capacities from which social forms arise, problems of heredity and race were raised. In short, biological data became exceedingly important. Few psychologists pursued their problems to their final biological implications. The problem was left to biologists and to biologically inclined philosophers, who, in turn, exceeded the limits of pure biology by including the psychic effects of race and heredity within their field of study.

We are, therefore, not only justified, but actually compelled to consider such research in a history of modern psychology. The goal of this biopsychosociological research was nothing less than an interpretation of the superindividual psyche, as evolved in society and in civilization in terms of biological data. To the extent to which the categories of race, heredity, and evolution can be correlated to psychic data, they belong within the province of psychology.

2. Spencer's sociology was biological only in a formal sense. His connection with biology consisted in stressing the similarity of structure, that is, societies behave as if they were organisms. Spencer, however, neglected society's biological composition, and failed to understand race in all its vital differentiations.

Since the middle of the nineteenth century, the science of comparative ethnography has developed on a grand scale; the most remote races and cultures have been thoroughly studied and, in the course of this study, the question of the rôle played by the biological composition of social groups, that is, the rôle of "race" in the development of specific forms of social life, was raised again.

The question of racial differences had already received notice in the eighteenth century. Herder rejected the concept of race as being purely biological. But Kant and

Blumenbach used the concept. Comte, too, not only referred to the difference of races but also to their hierarchical order. In Taine, the factor of race was studied with regard to esthetics. Taine showed, for example, that English literature is conditioned by racial factors.

The first systematic attempt to reduce world history to racial differences was made by Count J. A. Gobineau in his *Essai sur l'inégalité des races humaines* (1852). Gobineau assumed the existence of three sharply differentiated and permanent races: the white, the black, and the yellow. As a diplomat in foreign lands, he made many observations which he developed into a "chemistry" of races. His theory was that racial purity represents the highest value, and racial heterogeneity leads to destruction; first to unrest, then to a pathological state of quiescence, and finally, to death. As long as its race remains pure, the thought and culture of a nation follow suit. For culture does not create race, but is dependent upon it. Differences between races presuppose a hierarchical order according to physical and mental criteria. The highest in this order is the white race, which has beauty, intelligence, and strength. The white race values life and honor more highly than any other race, and is least sensual. The yellow race has a very powerful will but is wholly materialistic and intellectually mediocre. The black race is feminine, that is, weak and sensual, although esthetically gifted.

We are not concerned here with a criticism of the minutiæ of Gobineau's theories, which are replete with all sorts of historical and ethnological errors. What we are interested in is his fundamental contention that race, as a fixed hereditary quantity, is the origin of all civilization. Of course, Gobineau maintained his view dogmatically; he did not prove it in all its details nor did he offer any physiopsychological explanations. Yet he exerted an immense influence.

Employing more exact means than Gobineau, a science of "racial anthropology" came into existence. One of the foremost procedures of this science was the computation of the "cranial index," that is, the exact measurement of the shape and proportions of the skull. A Swedish anthropologist by the name of Retzius divided human beings into three cranial types: the long skull (dolichocephalic) type; the short skull (brachycephalic) type; and the medium skull (mesocephalic) type. Vacher de Lapouge, one. of Gobineau's pupils, published two works: *Les Sélections sociales* (1896) and *Race et milieu social* (1909), in which he distinguished three races in Europe according to their cranial index; the long-skulled *homo europæus*, the short-skulled *homo alpinus*, and the heterogeneous *homo mediterraneus*. Like O. Ammon, a German, Lapouge observed the phenomenon of social selection by means of which a hierarchy of races comes into existence. The superior type is the active and independent *homo europæus*. The *homo alpinus*, on the contrary, is passive and dependent. These theories achieved a certain degree of recognition but were quickly exploded by the adverse criticism of such scholars as Niceforo, Nyström, and others.

A great deal of notoriety was aroused by a history of culture based upon the racial theory outlined by Houston Stewart Chamberlain, an expatriate Englishman who lived in Germany. The title of this history was *Foundations of the Nineteenth Century* (1899). In contrast to Gobineau, Chamberlain did not accept the theory of a few constant, indigenous races and their decline through miscegenation, but emphasized the fact that races can also be evolved when a national group lives in a certain isolation for an extended period of time and crystallizes itself by means of inbreeding. Chamberlain believed that any crossing of races with wholly heterogeneous stocks was fatal. According to him, the decline of the Roman Empire, for example, was brought about by indiscriminate miscegenation which resulted in racial chaos. Chamberlain maintained that philosophy is dependent upon race; and that a really organic "culture," as distinguished from an inorganic "civilization," is possible only on a racial basis.

Subsequently, the concept of race was applied to other fields. Whereas some authors like Friedrich Hertz doubted the influence of race upon the mind, or at least regarded it as intangible, other authorities ascribed definite mental traits to the various races.

If we were to weigh this heterogeneous literature, in order to determine its factual value, or its significance for psychosociology, we would arrive at very equivocal conclusions. This literature counts race as a biological datum, as a group of individuals, bound together by a common descent, whose type can be distinguished physiologically. That such groups exist is an indisputable fact. It is an equally indisputable fact that a certain kind of psychological unity also accompanies the biological unity. This psychological unity is evidenced in "racial traits" which represent, at the very least, one of the many important factors in the distinctive forms of specific civilization.

So far our argument rests upon a solid scientific basis. But no further. For as soon as we attempt an exact determination of psychological racial traits, we are confronted with insuperable difficulties because the constant intrusion of physical, human, and environmental influences makes it virtually impossible to isolate the purely racial factor. It is an indisputable fact that certain biological, racial factors are involved in every culture. But the degree and the manner in which they are involved defy analysis because of the tremendous interconfusion of phenomena. This is true at least as regards the individual. A true insight into the etiology of racial traits, moreover, would become possible only when all the problems of heredity, especially those of the inheritance of psychological traits, had been completely solved.

3. As a matter of fact, the next important problem that ethnology essayed to solve dealt with the great historical and ethnographical groups of mankind. Of late, this problem has been studied in smaller social groups because these are more accessible to exact investigation. An important off-

shoot of ethnology which has developed since the end of the nineteenth century is the study of heredity and genealogy. This study is primarily concerned with biological and physiological matters, but inasmuch as it also includes data relating to traits of character and innate capacities, it extends into the field of psychology.

The fact that there is a superindividual, vital connection in heredity has probably never been doubted since man first began to subject these problems to scrutiny. The common sense of practical life far exceeded science in this respect. Although we do not know exactly what the ultimate motives behind totem worship were, and although we have no clear insight into the remarkable codes of honor among primitive peoples, we can safely assume that some regard for heredity and some interest in the determination of posterity were involved in them. The fact that our religions forbid the intermarriage of brothers and sisters may partly be due to man's desire to prevent physical and mental degeneration.

For our present purposes, we are mainly concerned with the question whether the subject of heredity belongs to the science of psychology. From the standpoint of the pure analysis of consciousness this must, of course, be denied, because the contents of consciousness are considered to be noninheritable at the present time. Since Locke no psychologist has believed in the existence of innate ideas in the sense of innate constituents of consciousness. But we have seen that psychology has long ceased to be merely a study of consciousness. Whether we consider the focal problem of psychology is the physical structure of the brain, the modes of physical behavior, or the structure of the soul, or character, we must admit that the lore of heredity must be invoked in order to determine the facts.

The first comprehensive treatise on psychological heredity was the one which Ribot wrote from 1871 to 1872 and later repeatedly revised. Ribot employed the classification of psychic phenomena as offered by the contemporary psychology of consciousness, but provided these phenomena with a substructure of "faculties." He introduced as facts the inheritability of instincts, senses, memory, intelligence, feelings and passions; and also discussed the inheritability of activity, of racial traits, and of pathological phenomena. Ribot derived certain laws of heredity from these data and defended them against the objections of Maupertuis and Buckle.

Ribot's contention was that inheritance is the rule and noninheritance the exception. The laws which he formulated were as follows:

a. The law of direct, immediate heredity. Parents tend to pass on to their children all their general and individual mental traits, both original and acquired.

b. The law of predominance in the transmission of characteristics: one of the parents may have a preponderant influence upon the mental constitution of the child.

c. The law of indirect heredity (atavism). Offspring often inherit physical or mental traits from previous generations, without resembling their own parents.

d. The law of heredity at a corresponding age. Many clearly defined traits, often of a pathological nature, emerge in descendents at the same age when they first appeared in their ancestors.

Theoretically, heredity may be viewed either as a creative or as a preservative phenomenon. Ribot decided upon the second probability. He held the inheritance of acquired characteristics to be possible but left open the question whether man can succeed in improving the race by learning to utilize the laws of heredity.

Whereas Ribot's treatment was rather summary, his English contemporary, Francis Galton, made an intensive and independent study of the problem. Galton invented methods still used today in the study of psychic heredity. Among these were mental tests, the questionnaire, the curve of regression, etc. His first goal was to determine the collective laws of psychological heredity. He studied the inheritance of capacities and other traits more important for the nation as a whole, within the population at large, because his ultimate goal was eugenics. Galton formulated his results in several laws. The law of reversion to type stated that the children of parents who deviate from the average in one trait, also deviate in the same direction as their parents, even though they have a tendency to revert toward the average. The law of ancestral heredity stated that half of a child's traits come from its parents, one quarter from its grandparents, one eighth from its great-grandparents, etc.

Galton's studies were extremely original in their approach and methods, and he found many disciples, especially in England, where Pearson and others followed in his footsteps. In more recent times, the problems pertaining to the theory of heredity became extremely complicated as a result of the discoveries of the Austrian monk, Gregor Mendel. Mendel's discoveries were ignored for a long time despite the fact that they were contemporaneous with Galton's investigations. Modern experimental biology, which does not directly concern psychology, begins with Mendel's achievements. Mendel's chief experiments dealt with the hybridization of plants and animals and demonstrated the very interesting numerical causality governing the inheritance of specific characteristics.

This causality was also studied in human genealogical relationships. The psychological theory of heredity, like the biological theory, distinguishes mixed heredity in which offspring show a mixture of parental characteristics, and alternating heredity, in which offspring resemble only one of the parents. The Mendelian laws of heredity were widely revised as a result of the study of psychological heredity, but they have also been widely corroborated in other respects.

In recent times, the statistical investigation of capacities and personality has been pursued to such a broad extent that we must limit ourselves to the discussion of a few typical studies. Heymans and Wiersma, two Dutch scholars, undertook mass investigations of families in which they compared the results derived from parents with those derived from their children. Their reports were first published in the *Zeitschrift für Psychologie* in 1906–07. They chose complicated qualities rather than simple ones for comparison. The final results indicated that the heredity of mental qualities was no less certain than that of physical ones. Furthermore, the results showed that the inheritance of traits from the same sex was much greater than inheritance from the opposite sex.

We might also mention the extensive data gathered by W. Peters with regard to the grades attained by school children and their relatives. It would take us too far afield to discuss the detailed studies of this nature, many of which are made in America. We must content ourselves here with the mere reference to Peters' book, *The Inheritance of Mental Characteristics and Psychological Constitutions* (1925), in which the vast amount of material he collected is more or less condensed.

Extensive as the study of heredity is in modern psychology, its definitely ascertained results are meager. It has corroborated the fact, already known in prescientific days, that there is not only a general but a specific inheritance of both mental and physical dispositions. A no less important fact is the variability of heredity, so that we frequently find not only resemblances but great dissimilarities between parents and their offspring. The difficulties, far from diminishing, have actually multiplied, especially since Johannsen's discovery of the distinction between genotypical and phenotypical qualities. According to Weismann the only really inheritable qualities are those transmitted through the nuclear germ plasm; i.e., the genotypical characteristics. These, however, cannot be determined directly but only indirectly in the form in which they appear (phenotype).

This line of investigation does not advance us much beyond the point reached in the study of ethnology; in both instances we found that inheritance of a qualitative nature exists, but we find it impossible to fix the definite rôle of heredity within the total form of personality. The apparent exactitude of statistical research, with its endless tables of figures, is largely deceptive. The coincidence of a trait in both father and son need not necessarily imply heredity; it can also be brought about by means of phenotypical adaptation to the same environmental phenomena. In its early days, science placed heredity and environment in diametrical contrast to each other. But we must realize that, as a rule, we also "inherit" environment, to the extent that we are born and raised in, and adapt ourselves to, the same environment that surrounds our parents. If a father and son are both musical, it may of course be due to the fact that the son has inherited his father's musical talent. However, it can also happen that the son was born with a wholly mediocre talent, but that the musical atmosphere in his father's home developed that mediocre talent beyond the average.

4. During the World War a book appeared which shed some new light upon the biosociological problems discussed here. This book exerted a revolutionary influence, particularly in Germany. It bore the sensational title of *The Decline of the West;* its first volume appeared in 1918. The second volume appeared in 1922. The author of this book was a previously unknown philosopher named Oswald Spengler who was far removed from academic circles. Spengler was enthusiastically acclaimed but he has also been harshly criticized. His work, to be sure, displays its flaws in a hundred details. It is often distortive and contains downright misstatements of fact. But as a whole, it bears the mark of genius and must be mentioned in a discussion of the development of contemporary science.

Spengler's work must be included in a history of modern psychology with reservations, since it rejects modern psychology unequivocally. Indeed, Spengler doubts whether there can even be such a thing as an objective and scientific psychology. According to Spengler, psychology can never posit itself upon an Archimedian point outside of the history of mankind, but is itself an evolutionary product of history. Spengler claimed that that which you regard as "soul" is nothing but the image of that which you consider as the "world," and that your concept, therefore, varies according to your individual system of philosophy. That which we today call "psychology" Spengler claims is no more than the application of mechanistic ideas to the soul, which is conceived as a mechanism in much the same fashion that the macrocosm is conceived as a machine.

Despite his rejection of modern psychology, Spengler does employ a system of psychology, even if he calls it by another name. In his *Morphology of World History* and his *Physiognomy of Culture*, he constantly reduces the phenomena of civilization to psychological fundamentals, and thence to their biological roots. It is from this point of view that his work belongs within our context.

The superindividual units with which Spengler is concerned are not races or nations, but "civilizations." He distinguishes eight of these systems of culture: Mayan, Chinese, Indian, Egyptian, Babylonian, Græco-Roman, neo-Occidental (Faustian), and finally, Russian. Each of these civilizations is a fixed vital unit. These units develop like biological organisms and go through the phases of childhood, youth, maturity, and senescence, after which they disappear. This sequence of phases is completed in accordance with an inexorable inner necessity. Each of the eight civilizations developed its own style, manifesting itself in typical forms in each periodic phase. This style is homogeneously expressed in religion, art, society, government, science, and law. Although each civilization stamps all of these cultural activities with the unique seal of its individual nature, certain comparable phenomena occur in the infancy and senescence of every civilization. Thus, for example, the old age of every civilization is characterized by the predominance of science and technology, irreligion and inner chaos, the rise of megalopolitan life, the rule of dictators, and the like.

If we refer to Spengler as a sociobiologist, we do so because he applies biological categories dealing with the maturational phases of organisms to his civilizations. His approach is also psychological because he causally subordinates the thought and feeling of respective civilizations to biological processes of maturation. The factor of race, at least in the form of racial inbreeding, is accorded a minor rôle by Spengler. To him, the concept of "race" is not so much a matter of a pure line of descent as it is vital and dynamic. Consequently, his cultural biology is an essentially formal concept, and the nature of its biological constitution is left wholly in the dark. Of course independent, historico-cultural laws take their place in conjunction with the laws of natural science in his writings. In addition to blood relationship Spengler also includes the mind, and it is in this respect that he betrays his kinship with cultural psychology.

Spengler shed some new light on the problem of evolution. Unlike the sociologists, he does not conceive evolution in mankind as a whole but only within its various civilizations. The evolution of civilizations does not proceed in a straight line toward an unlimited higher evolution, but change can also lead to the devolution which ends in death, just as in the senescence of organisms.

5. The material summarized in this chapter, for all its variability in point of scientific value and purpose, has this in common: it endeavors to offer a biological explanation for the origins of the superindividual psyche. We can undoubtedly agree with the contention that a superindividual whole exists, at least from the physical point of view. The isolation in which the psychology of consciousness viewed individuals is as certainly untenable from the physical aspect as it is from the psychological point of view. Even if the contents of consciousness are not inherited, dispositions are.

We must also agree with biosociology in its contention

that mental traits are inherited not only as quantitative but also as qualitative realities. The moral and intellectual traits characteristic of man are conditioned by the traits characteristic of his ancestors. Viewed in a broader perspective, the traits peculiar to whole peoples and their civilizations, such as the Egyptians, the Chinese, or the British, are essentially conditioned by biological heredity, by "blood," to use the metaphorical expression.

Errors creep into these statements largely because of the bias with which they are propagated. The attempt to use biology as a direct basis for all the psychological traits of social groups is questionable, if only for the reason that it is impossible to define the extent of biological heredity purely and precisely. Moreover, other influences can be definitely traced which, to say the least, are co-involved with biological conditioning.

An inquiry concerning these other influences brings us to constellations of phenomena that have been brought to the fore by other schools of research. These phenomena include, in part, sociological constellations and structures and, in part, the values and cultural developments that influence social evolution. The former constitute the subject matter of sociopsychology; the latter, that of cultural psychology.

SOCIOPSYCHOLOGY

1. The tendency of research that we have called sociopsychology, subscribes to the primary dominance of purely social data over all psychological data. Wherever human beings live together, social constellations exist between them that can be observed independently of the mental and physical traits peculiar to their component individuals. Such phenomena as partnerships, corporations, organizations, factions, hostile or friendly relations, mastery, slavery, and the like must be viewed as such social constellations. Pure sociology treats these factors without considering their real

psychological implications. It adopts an a-psychological approach on methodological grounds. As soon as sociology recognizes the primary importance of external social phenomena upon the mental life of participant individuals, however, it has embarked upon the study of "sociopsychology."

Although the a-psychological sociology referred to above is not directly pertinent to our theme, let us characterize it by discussing some of its typical representatives, because an understanding of the development of sociopsychology is premised on a knowledge of the evolution of pure sociology.

Nonpsychological sociology continued the tradition of Comte and found its most extreme representative in E. Durkheim. Durkheim contended that social phenomena are "things" and not "ideas." To be sure, a "thing" need not necessarily be material: its essential characteristic is that it is known through external observation. On the contrary, the nature of "idea" is that it is known from within. Hence, social data must be sought wholly outside the realm of the consciousness of the participant individuals; social data influence individuals as forms of external constraint. Sociology considers them data only according to their common, external distinguishing traits, that is, independently of their individual manifestations. Sociology, according to Durkheim, is a science dealing with the "objective reality of social processes," and with "institutions, their origin, and their function." These "institutions" impose themselves upon men from without. Hence, psychological considerations must be kept apart from sociology.

Durkheim made the distribution of labor and religious institutions the special subjects of his detailed investigation. But it is highly doubtful whether a system of sociology which eliminates all psychological data can really do justice to the facts, and does not view these data merely as one-sided abstractions.

Georg Simmel also proposed a purely formal science of sociology, rigorously excluding all social psychology. He presented an exhaustive apologia for such methodological delimitation in his main work, *Sociology* (1908), which bore the subtitle of *Studies in the Forms of Social Life*. To Simmel, the only legitimate function of social psychology was to supply an answer to the question: What modification does the psychological process of an individual experience under the specific influences of social environment?

Most modern sociologists are not so radical in their rejection of psychology. We may cite the attitude of L. von Wiese as being typical. Von Wiese employs the two main categories of social "relationship" and social "institution." He firmly adheres to the purely sociological approach but without falling into Durkheim's one-sidedness. To Durkheim, for example, suicide represented only a social and not a psychological phenomenon. Wiese, too, accords the social factor primary importance over the psychological one but by no means eliminates the latter wholly. For a social "relationship" among human beings is scarcely ever purely physical. It must have its psychological aspects. In the same way, a social "institution" can only exist upon the basis of a reciprocal mental and spiritual relationship.

We need not be astonished, therefore, to learn that a new science that not only recognizes the fundamental primacy of social data but also tries to do justice to the psychological processes operating within society was developed to meet the challenge of the facts. Unlike psychosociology, this new science does not interpret society in terms of the individual mind, but conversely, interprets the individual mind in terms of society. For this reason, we shall call it sociopsychology, so that the name itself may convey the primary emphasis placed upon society.

2. Although France was the home of pure sociology, she also produced a group of thinkers whom we can classify as sociopsychologists to the extent that, while they premised given social constellations, they also recognized the influence of such social constellations on their component individuals. Gabriel Tarde, who opposed Durkheim by rejecting

mechanistic sociology, was the most significant scholar of this group. In his chief work, *Les Lois de l'imitation* (1890), Tarde introduced imitation as the chief origin of social processes. Imitation presupposes the purely social constellation of individuals as they exist in social groups in the present, or as they exist in successive generations. To this extent, Tarde accords the social aspect a certain priority. Society, however, becomes a communal existence only through imitation, which can occur either under constraint or spontaneously, either unconsciously or deliberately. In the communal life of the existing present, imitation is expressed by way of mores and fashions; in the communal life of successive generations, it is expressed through tradition.

Next to imitation, Tarde also recognized the extreme importance of "invention" in society. Imitation and invention are the two factors which make for the progress of civilization. Creative personalities are the motive forces in history. They are qualitatively different from the mob, which follows them in a kind of somnambulistic trance.

In a later work, *Les Lois sociales* (1898), in which he summarized all his previous theories, Tarde listed the following as the principles of social life: repetition, contrast, and adaptation. Although he thus related sociology to the natural sciences, Tarde is far removed from Durkheim's mechanism. In so far as he recognized *désir* and *croyance* (desire and belief) as the social constituents upon which imitation is based, Tarde may even be said to approach psychosociology.

One of the most esteemed sociopsychological works in which a given social situation was conceived as the origin of typical, superindividual states of mind, was Le Bon's *La Psychologie des foules* (1895). The "mob," as such, is not a psychological but a sociological datum, yet it causes curious states of mind in its component individuals, states which deviate wholly from the behavior of these individuals in different situations. Whenever many individuals unite into a mob, their individuality seems to be extinguished; their egos recede, they often act directly counter to their own interests, and experience feelings, emotions, ideas, and the stirring of desires which would never come to them were they alone. The crowd, irrespective of the types of individuals that compose it, can act either heroically or criminally.

The most important changes in the life of consciousness within the mob, according to Le Bon, are in the realm of feelings and morals. Consciousness becomes terribly impulsive, variable, and excitable. Every suggestion is carried out. In place of critical deliberation, an easy credulity, intolerance, and a blind feeling of authority make their appearance. Excessive exuberance alternating with simplicity characterizes the mob psyche. Thought is restricted. There are no logical conclusions and the effect of ideas does not depend upon their verity or credibility. Unrestrained imagination becomes the order of the day. The mind reverts to its primitive magical and mythological aspect.

These are indisputable facts. But do they warrant us to speak of a mob consciousness or mob psyche? Indeed not. We can only do so in a metaphorical sense. The mob acts "as if" it possessed a uniform consciousness or psyche, but there is no real unity in its mental constitution. The apparent psychological unity of a mob is brought about by imitation and adaptation through the circuitous channels of physiological expression.

In his other works, Le Bon dwelt at great length upon problems of race and civilization in order to fathom the psychological elements of racial evolution. The very title of his second chief work, *Les Lois psychologiques de l'évolution des peuples* (1894), expressed his sociopsychological point of view.

A typical representative of sociopsychological research was E. A. Ross, whose *Social Psychology* appeared in 1908. We have already mentioned him in connection with social "interests." In this work, however, he followed in the wake of Tarde and Le Bon. Ross envisaged the task of sociology as the investigation of groups and institutions. The task of social psychology, on the other hand, he considered to be the study of social "planes" and "currents"; in other words, those "uniformities in feeling, belief, or volition, and hence in action, which are due to the interaction of human beings, i.e., to social causes." He entered into a detailed study of the mob mind, fashion, conventionality, custom, and similar phenomena which he had observed and gathered during extensive journeys. In a subsequent work by Ross, *Principles of Sociology* (1920), the psychological point of view was given less prominence.

Like Ross, McDougall reached sociopsychology by way of psychosociology. His sociopsychological conclusions were developed in a work entitled *The Group Mind*, published in 1920. In this book, McDougall disavowed any connection with the idealistic theory of a superindividual group mind. He begins with a discussion of the degrading influences which a crowd exerts upon the individual, but goes on to show how the organization of higher groups counteracts this influence and ennobles the individual. He proceeds to the study of national psychological and sociological traits. He analyzes the conditions of the origin and development of a national spirit or mind, and clarifies the rôle of will and idea in this process. McDougall distinguishes what he called a "race-making period." He does not ascribe any eugenic influence to civilization. Civilization does not improve the race, although it does ennoble intellectual and moral traditions. The early stage of national progress differs from the stage of maturity. In the latter, greater tolerance and mutual understanding are developed. It is the group spirit, however, that facilitates this development.

3. There is probably no other field in which the contrast between sociopsychological and psychosociological methods is thrown into such clear relief as in the study of the psychology of primitive man. As a result of the prodigious amount of ethnographical research in the nineteenth century, the external facts covering the life of primitive races became

quite well known. The sociologists, with Herbert Spencer at their head, made it their business to coördinate all these facts into their systems in the hope of proving the theories of evolution. The great works of Tylor, Frazer, and many others might be noted in this connection. From a psycho-sociological point of view, the main task of these scholars was to interpret the primitive mind in terms of the civilized mind. As we have already shown, such an interpretation presupposes that the human mind is universally homogeneous. Thus the great fallacy marring the researches of these psychologists lay in the fact that they did not realize that psychological factors are not original data but are everywhere shaped by social conditions.

A recognition of this oversight was stressed by sociopsychology, whose most significant representative was h. Lévy-Brühl. As a student of Comte and Durkheim, he naturally gave preëminence to social relations. But he did not confine himself merely to the external aspects of social life. He endeavored to penetrate into the inner life of primitive man from a social viewpoint. The mental functions of aborigines depend upon their social environment and are, therefore, fundamentally different from those of civilized man.

Lévy-Brühl laid special emphasis upon "collective ideas." The essence of collective ideas lies in the fact that they are common to the members of a social group, are passed on from generation to generation, and are externally superimposed upon man in the degree to which they arouse reverence, fear, or worship. The characteristic hallmark of the aboriginal mind is its mystical nature. The very perceptions of aborigines differ from ours because they are almost universally pervaded with mystical qualities. They are governed by the law of "participation" according to which ideas of specific things can at the same time denote these things themselves or something entirely different. A man, for example, can also be a wolf. The mental processes of aborigines are not logical in our sense, but are pre-logical.

Lévy-Brühl's book on *Les Fonctions mentales des sociétés inférieures* (1910) shows how the language, the numerical systems, and the conduct of aborigines are wholly dominated by pre-logical thinking. One of his later works, *La Mentalité primitive* (1923), also demonstrated that the causal ideas of primitive man are entirely different from ours.

4. In America, under the influence of behaviorism, a research trend that we may designate as sociopsychology, strongly opposed to similar tendencies that try to interpret social life in terms of innate interests of instincts, was developed at this time. John Dewey may again be mentioned as representative of this tendency because of his rejection of the psychology of pure consciousness.

Dewey does not entirely deny the significance of consciousness. He admits that "conscious" as an adjective may be applied to certain acts; but the promotion of the "conscious" to the status of a noun and to an independent existence is an unwarranted abstraction. Dewey considers the exaggerated value imputed to consciousness to be historically explicable as a result of the individualization of life. The practical effect of individualization, according to Dewey, has been to detach the individual from his social context and from nature. Thus, the forces really animating human nature have been eliminated. The formation of habits and convictions, of desires and values, all of which grow out of the social interrelations of human beings, must be considered the fundamental facts of personal character as well as of social life. Dewey's goal is not merely a system of theoretical psychology. He is far more interested in evolving a social technique subservient to the ethical principle that regards man as inextricably bound up with nature and society. In consequence, Dewey holds that all behavior, even moral behavior, should not be studied in segregated individuals but within the social constellation. The subjective factor is not entirely absent but it means little in comparison with the impersonal forces and the corresponding depersonalized

habits forced upon man by his surroundings. What we call
will, character, or self, only denote the habits which a person has acquired within his environment. But these habits
are not of a subjective nature; they are objective and, in
turn, react upon the environment. Thus it would be a senseless, metaphysical abstraction to speak of the priority of
society in the formation of human character. There are
only systems of interaction, social groups. The problem of
social psychology is not to determine how the individual
or collective mind constructs social groups or mores, but
to determine how different social mores shape and evolve
different minds. The psychology of habit, therefore, is an
objective and social psychology. In itself, every habit is
conservative. It is only when habits collide that instinctive
behavior is activated, with the result that a change in
habits and mores is effected.

This brings Dewey to a discussion of the instincts. It is
his opinion that the reduction of all social life to an instinctual basis is not enough. One must know the social conditions
that have shaped the sensory motor dispositions known as
instincts. Instincts are innate but very indeterminate forces
which assume different forms according to the use to which
they are put. The significance of instincts to society lies in
their ability to keep society from falling into a state of rigid
stasis. Instincts are the cause of social rejuvenation. As
factors of habit, instincts are called motives. But impulses
and instincts cannot be considered in isolation; nor can
social factors, such as economics, be reduced to isolated
instincts. There is no such thing as a separate instinct of
fear. Fear is a condition involving the total individual.

Dewey also recognizes the full value of intelligence in
society, although he also views understanding and thought
as being extremely dependent upon habits. In conclusion,
we may say that Dewey champions the view that unconscious
social phenomena are the determinants of communal life,
yet he does not overlook the importance of conscious acts.
Indeed, he even hopes that a scientific system of psycholo-

gy will effect an essential amelioration of social relations.

This also is the paradox of pure behaviorism; it expects a practical improvement in social relations of science but theoretically tries to eliminate consciousness, and with it science, as a mental datum. However, very few of the scholars who try to base social psychology upon behavior are entirely consistent in their exclusion of consciousness. Whether they speak of "attitudes" like Thomas, of "behavior patterns" like Ellwood and others, or of "interstimulation" like Bogardus, what they are doing resolves itself into a translation of previously employed psychological concepts into physiological terminology. The truth is that they employ this terminology to denote the same phenomena that formerly were called psychological.

5. A more recent development in sociopsychology has developed precise methods with which it hopes to comprehend the psychological traits peculiar to specific social groups. Thus Carl Murchison in his *Social Psychology*, published in 1929, states that the function of social psychology is the determination of the measurable factors relating to individuals and groups, not the study of instincts and the teleological interpretation of social behavior. Only in this way, Murchison believes, can social psychology achieve practical value. Murchison feels that the stereotyped forms of social life occur in infinite variety only upon the basis of individual differences. In general, Murchison's procedure is descriptive. He lists various types of tests and statistically evaluates them.

Of course, a great many studies of this nature never get beyond their material and offer no real causal explanation of psychological data in terms of given social situations. A prodigious number of petty and detailed studies have been devoted to this sort of research with the resultant computation and compilation of endless statistics, tables, and curves. There are very few social groups that have not in some shape or manner been subjected to this method. The favorite categories of these students are school classes, occupational groups, age levels, and families. It is impossible to review, even approximately, the widely ramified literature dealing with sociological statistics. Innumerable periodicals in America, Germany, and other countries, are filled with such studies. As historians, we need merely observe that research of this type is partially governed by the sociopsychological approach. Much of it consists of material gathered with a view to a future revision in terms of sociopsychology.

6. The study of the superindividual psyche goes far beyond human interrelationships. Man not only has relations with those of his kind but also with animals, plants, and with his inanimate surroundings, such as his home landscape, his customary climate, soil, and geographical situation. Herder undertook to explain differing racial traits in terms of geographical determinants. Comte and Buckle also stressed the importance of geography. Ratzel in his *Anthropogeography* (1882–91) attempted a systematic analysis of the dependence of human groups upon geographical conditions.

The first to apply the methods of modern psychology to the solution of this problem was W. Hellpach, in a work on *Geopsychological Phenomena* (1911), in which he studied the influence of weather, climate, and landscape on the psychology of individuals and groups.

Of late, an experimental and statistical science of "environmentology" which aspires to an exact solution of problems in the same field has been born. It is impossible to enumerate all these detailed endeavors. We can merely refer specialists to Busemann's *Pedagogical Environmentology*, in which the vast scope of this material is summarized. The danger of such one-sided sociopsychology lies in the fact that it desires to explain all psychic life in terms of environment, whereas it is often only upon the basis of an individual, psychological attitude, to quote Üxküll, that mere surroundings are transformed into an environment. For "environment" is never a purely physical datum, since it is psychologically modified by the subjective attitudes of the individual who consciously experiences his surroundings.

7. The above summary may have demonstrated that the sociopsychological approach has made valuable contributions toward an understanding of the superindividual mind. Social constellations and institutions are unquestionably a pregnant subject for descriptive sociology. But they cannot be understood with respect to their inner life without psychological insight. On the other hand, sociopsychology is right in its contention, directed against psychosociology, that psychological phenomena do not shape society as given natural factors, but are themselves intensively determined by society, and that at a very early stage in the individual's life. Sociopsychology has proved this fact convincingly in its studies of the psychology of primitive man, the mob, and the institutions of civilized society. Our sole reservations must be aimed at the unrestrained bias of extremists who attempt a purely sociological explanation of the entire superindividual mind. Their bias forces them into an untenable position. The psychosociologists and biosociologists can, with good reason, protest that the existence of innate mental and physical data beside social data cannot be overlooked. We must remember that there is an "objective mind" independent of the individuals and groups that create it, and this "objective mind" must also be included in a true interpretation of society. It is to these problems that we now turn.

THE PSYCHOLOGY OF CULTURE AND THE "OBJECTIVE MIND"

1. Most of the scholars we have already considered were and are primarily social psychologists and only incidentally cultural psychologists. We shall turn now to a group of thinkers whose chief aim is to understand human beings

or groups inferentially in terms of the given cultural works they have created. Whenever earlier thinkers referred to cultural values, such values were conceived as the products of social activity. These thinkers believed that they were able to derive the causal laws of cultural values from general psychological or sociological observations. The scholars now to be discussed adopted a diametrically opposite approach: they considered the rich treasures accumulated in the history of mankind as the end products in which the mind of groups and of individuals has crystallized and objectified itself. Their goal was to fathom the nature of the subjective mind in terms of the objectified products of that mind.

The research sponsored by these thinkers encountered the problem of the superindividual mind even in those instances when their studies focused themselves on certain individuals who appeared as creators of cultural values. These creative individuals bear the typical hallmark or "style" of their times, the distinguishing seal of the nation or group to which they belong. No matter how objective these achievements of civilization may appear at first sight, their true value is based upon the effect they have had upon subjective individuals. A system of culture is not merely created; it is also creative. Systems such as Christianity, Grecian art, and Roman law have not merely been the products of certain groups but they have, in turn, exerted an enormous influence upon other groups and individuals. The intellectual life of mankind cannot be understood without the repercussion of such cultural achievements. Physical heredity is not the only creator of a superindividual nexus which runs through history. Intellectual tradition, also superindividually, creates culture cycles that dominate all biological and sociological unities and construct a world of the mind that can be regarded as a sphere of existence in itself, if only in the abstract.

Only some of the scholars to be discussed here are professional psychologists. They are predominantly historians and philosophers who have, however, employed the conceptual media of psychology, although their terminology is not always identical with that of technical psychology.

2. Our first concern is with that most comprehensive psychology of culture of all time, the ten-volume *Völkerpsychologie* which Wilhelm Wundt compiled from 1900 to 1920, during his last years. To begin with, the title *Racial Psychology*, which Wundt took over from Steinthal and Lazarus, is not a very happy one, because a determination of the psychology of the separate races, which was the goal of the founders of racial psychology, became a matter of minor importance in Wundt's studies. Even when Wundt discussed the social communities that produce cultural values, his classification of "races" was quite irrelevant in most instances. On the other hand, the manner in which he grouped all his material clearly shows that his actual goal was a social psychology of cultural values; for he treated, in sequence, language, art, mythology, religion, customs and law, and finally united them all according to his conception of culture. In spite of this, Wundt clung to the name of racial psychology with a certain degree of stubbornness in the face of critical charges that the name was exceedingly controversial from many points of view.

The reason for Wundt's retention of the name goes back to the early influence of Lazarus and Steinthal, which we have mentioned above. Even in the later stages of his work, Wundt was at pains to clarify his position with reference to these two scholars. He criticized their psychology in particular, and Herbartian psychology in general, for the metaphysical conception of individualism confined simply to "soul," and for the intellectualism implied in their mechanistic conception of ideas. Wundt ridiculed their attempts to justify these conceptions by the introduction of "racial minds." He pointed out that racial minds are merely the counterparts of individual minds, their only difference lying in the fact that they are composed of more complex units.

In doing so, however, Wundt completely dispelled the very character peculiar to social phenomena.

If Wundt did not wholly reject the conception of a "racial soul," the reason was that to him the concept of "soul" signified something entirely different from the metaphysical unity which it denoted in older psychology. Wundt's concept of "soul" was the same as that of the psychology of consciousness of which he was a representative. In 1900, he repeated his contention that "soul" has no other meaning than a designation of the interconnection of the direct facts of consciousness, or of "psychic phenomena." If he spoke of a "racial soul," he intended it to mean no more and no less than it means in individual psychology. The psychological developments resulting from the coexistence of members of a racial group are no less factual components of reality than are the psychological phenomena within individual consciousness.

Wundt defined the relation of the individual soul to the racial soul as follows: "The racial soul is a product of the individual souls of which it is composed; but the individual souls are no less the products of the racial soul which they compose." Although it is impossible for the group to exist without individuals, the group is not a mere addition and intensification of the traits and activities of its individuals. The connections and the reciprocal interrelations of individuals are what the group, as such, contributes; they are the means by which the group stimulates the individual to new achievements which specifically pertain to group existence. "Racial psychology finds its tasks and problems within this medium of reciprocal connections and interrelations."

However, the thing with which we are concerned is far more important than the name we give it. Hence we must note that Wundt championed the principle that cultural values cannot be understood solely in terms of the psychology of individuals. He stressed the fact that language, art, and custom, as objective data, demonstrably precede the historical mention of individuals and even the beginning of historical records. But these forms of culture, in the course of history and because of the initiative of individuals, undergo causal changes that can only be understood as the results of corresponding changes within the culture-bearing groups. In spite of this, Wundt frequently consulted individual psychology in order to explain cultural facts and their evolution, but he also took account of the reciprocal influence of society on the individual.

In spite of his "racial psychological" approach, Wundt laid his chief emphasis on the relation of the fields of culture to individual consciousness. He also adhered to the same radical standpoint with respect to consciousness, which he had defended against all charges in earlier decades. The same psychology of ideas that Wundt had never relinquished in spite of his recognition of many counter-tendencies still dominated his "racial psychology."

According to Wundt, the ideas of man are mirrored in his language. The change in the meaning of words expresses the laws governing the change of ideas occurring under the influence of varying associational and apperceptional conditions. The organic structure of language, the building of word forms, and the syntactical constructions of parts of speech reveal the causal laws governing the association of ideas under the specific natural and cultural conditions of the group in which that language is spoken.

Mythology often endows the ideas thus deposited in language with their specific content. Mythology comprises the still inchoate vital philosophy constructed in the primitive racial consciousness on the basis of primitive perceptions and ideas. It is evident that the imaginative activity operative in myths is constantly and intensely conditioned by primitive emotional tendencies. Fear and hope, wonder and awe, humility and reverence, influence the mythological imagination and its conception of the objective world far more than any accidental perceptions.

Custom, in turn, comprises common volitional tendencies which are transmuted into norms of behavior. But just as ideas, emotions, and will interpenetrate the conduct of the individual being, so do they permeate all culture, so that even those elements which are disparate at first intermingle in many ways and finally merge into a unity.

Wundt gathered a tremendous amount of material under these thematic ideas; whether he mastered it all is another question. While Wundt was hampered by the sheer weight of his material in his magnum opus, he succeeded better in a smaller but separate study, *The Elements of Folk Psychology* (1912). In this work, he classified his subject matter according to a graduated series which corresponded somewhat to the phases of modern culture. This series was as follows: the primitive age, the totemistic age, the age of gods and heroes, and finally the age of humanity. Although the system of psychology that Wundt employed in his works on racial psychology is rather antiquated and only partially includes the multifold innovations of a newer generation of psychologists, his "racial psychology" is a monumental achievement if only by virtue of its sheer comprehensiveness.

3. A Leipzig historian by the name of Karl Lamprecht attempted a psychological interpretation of the history of German culture. While Lamprecht's work appeared prior to Wundt's it was influenced to a certain degree by Wundt's psychological system. Observing a certain "style" which coincides in all the vital expressions of an historical epoch, Lamprecht speaks of the spiritual "diapason" of that epoch, that is to say, a sociopsychological unity which recurs in economic life, as well as in art, politics, and religion.

Beyond this, Lamprecht also finds a series of these sociopsychological diapasons which he claimed were not accidental but determined by a definite causality. This series represents the stages of evolution corresponding to following sequential eras: the symbolistic era, the typico-conventional era, the individualistic and subjectivistic era, to which the contemporary period is appended as the "neurotic" era. Lamprecht's eras, although actually nothing but empirical conclusions resting solely on a frail basis of psychology and sociology, have exerted a powerful and stimulating influence. Of late, however, they have been largely superseded by Spengler's historical periods.

4. Meanwhile, scholars conceived the notion of finding a typically psychological representative of the dominant style of an historical epoch or of a racial group. They evolved the typical man whose psychological structure was to explain the style of a specific time or people. Thus Jakob Burkhardt evolved a typical "man of the Renaissance" as representative of Renaissance culture, and a typical "Hellene" as the representative of Grecian culture. Nietzsche followed suit. In a similar way, scholars began to speak of the "Gothic man" (Worringer) and the "Baroque man." Whether these typical champions have any basis in reality or are merely fictive personifications is a question.

In a similar manner, scholars began to seek for typical representatives of national or racial forms of culture. Alfred Fouillée attempted to determine the typical Frenchman, and, later, the typical representatives of all European nationalities. Müller-Freienfels sought to determine the essential Teutonic man from the totality of German culture. In all these instances, it is difficult to decide whether it is the man who shapes culture or culture which shapes the man. At any rate, the crux of the matter lies in an extremely complex reciprocal interaction of biological, sociological, and cultural influences that extend into individual consciousness only in part.

5. The man who delved most profoundly into the theoretical fundamentals underlying a psychological conception of history was Wilhelm Dilthey, whom we have already met more than once as the creator of an independent system of psychology. In all probability, Dilthey's system of individual psychology was not his ultimate goal but was more in the

nature of a means to an "epistemology of the cultural sciences," which must resolve itself primarily into a psychology of culture. However that may be, we are here concerned only with the psychological aspect of Dilthey's studies.

In order to understand Dilthey historically, we must remember that he was closely related to German idealistic philosophy and had devoted penetrating biographical studies both to Hegel and Schleiermacher. Even though his own systematic ideas did not come to fruition until 1900, they were already adumbrated in his youthful writings, which appeared between 1860 and 1875. As early as 1866, he wrote that his goal was an historical analysis of the totality of the interrelations of all the branches of knowledge evolved by the human spirit.

Dilthey's first important work in which his psychocultural ideas were systematically presented was his *Introduction to the Cultural Sciences*, published in 1883. The very conception of "cultural sciences" (*Geisteswissenschaften*), which Dilthey opposed to the natural sciences, is indicative of a fundamental attitude. Dilthey referred to those sciences that are ordinarily designated as the "historical and social sciences" when he coined the term "cultural sciences." Dilthey's distinction places "mind" in antithesis to "nature." Mind by no means comprises only subjective consciousness but also includes the "objective mind." Whereas natural science has to do with processes which are formed from sensory material by cognitive association, the cultural sciences are primarily concerned with the facts of inner experience. Only by means of this inner experience does there exist that which has value or purpose for us, that which is the experience of our emotions and our will. Out of this inner experiencing grows a realm of experiences that have an independent origin and material, data that must be fundamentally separated from the data of nature. Of course, man as a natural being can also be made the object of scientific investigation, but he then appears only as a dependent manifestation of nature. From the viewpoint of natural sciences, this dependency is only the obverse side of man's mastery over nature.

Now this inner experience is not merely a subjective experience of the individual. It is also the means by which we understand the whole of objective, sociohistorical reality. The individual is not antithetical to this experience but is variously interpenetrated by it. Although the world of objective experience is at first foreign to us, we can understand it by means of inner experience. "Nature is something foreign to us; it is something external, not internal. It is the shadow cast by some hidden reality. Society, on the other hand, is our world. In it we are able to coexperience things with the full strength of our entire being, since we vitally produce out of ourselves the states and forces from which the social system is constructed. We are obliged to master the form of society by constantly adjustable evaluatory judgments, and we must reshape society with an indefatigable force of will, at least in our imagination." This was the essence of Dilthey's teaching.

The cultural sciences, to be sure, do not yield as many clearly defined laws as do the natural sciences. We find very few uniformities in them. Besides, the understanding of the individuals who make up history is infinitely complicated and cannot be understood solely in terms of contemporary human types. This complexity, however, is counterbalanced by the inner vitality of the historic process which is not the play of inorganic operative causes but can be traced back to ideas, feelings, and motives. Indeed, it is not merely the intellect which is here cognitively involved; it is the total human being that is the cognitive subject of the cultural sciences. The decisive factor is the "intensity of inner experience."

The sociohistorical world may be viewed from three aspects: with regard to the separate races, to external organization, and to the systems of culture. Of these three, Dilthey relegated the racial approach to the lowest order, apparently having the racial psychology of Lazarus and

Steinthal in mind. Conceptions such as the "racial mind," the "racial soul," and the "racial organism," he rejected as being too mystical. He also desired to reduce the sciences of external organization, that is, the problems treated by sociology, to psychological factors, referring them in part to the group consciousness and in part to the relationship between the ruler and the ruled. Both these psychological factors stream like blood through the delicate arterial systems of society. They find their limits, however, in the freedom of the individual. Dilthey rejected the notion of an external, objective sociology as projected by Comte and Spencer. A really vital science of history cannot be satisfied with a few general precepts; it must always have an artistic power of presentation.

The best understanding of social reality is obtainable from the analysis of systems of culture, even though such an analysis may at first split up the unity of culture. By his concept of cultural systems, Dilthey meant the great, super-individual "purposive systems" that further the realization of human values. As such "purposive systems" he listed religion, art, justice, science, language, morality, and the like. These systems endure, whereas individuals come and go upon the stage of life. Such systems, to be sure, are embodied in individuals, but each individual is the crossing point of several systems. At the same time, systems of culture express themselves in objective works which crystallize and preserve their superindividual import: art in works of art, science in books, justice in laws. Although the separate "purposive systems" can and must be studied separately, each one of them develops only within the whole socio-historical world, which also includes external organization.

In reviewing Dilthey's system of cultural psychology from the purely psychological point of view, we must measure it against the question of what position it assumes with respect to the problem of the superconscious, super-individual, totalitarian mind. Dilthey personally rejected all metaphysics. He even spoke of the "partivism" (as distinguished from totalism) of his method. As we have seen, he rejected the concepts of "racial soul" and "racial mind." In general, and this was characteristic of him, he was less concerned with psychological factors in their present conjacent state than he was with their sequence in time. After all, he was preëminently an historian and approached psychology from the historical point of view. Therefore, he coördinated the psychic process into a sequential system governed by values. Systems of culture extend primarily in time, and individuals are their rather accidental representatives, no matter how decisively or how often they may break into prominence.

The programmatic nature of Dilthey's thought is also evidenced in his cultural psychology. In this realm, as in pure psychology, he was a source of profound inspiration, and here, too, Spranger continued Dilthey's work. Tröltsch might also be mentioned, although he based his philosophy of history more on sociology than on psychology. In addition to Dilthey's influence, Tröltsch was influenced by Max Weber whose great *Sociology of Religion* represents the converse of Marxism in its endeavor to show how religions influence economic forms. Hans Freyer also essayed a *Theory of the Objective Mind*, which is partly psychological.

6. The most recent extensive system of the philosophy of history to employ psychological conceptions is the three-volume work of K. Breysig entitled *Historical Evolution* (1925). In his graduated reconstruction of world history, presented as far back as 1905, Breysig evolved a sequence of phases in the evolution of culture which largely anticipated Spengler's ideas, although in a less biologistic sense. In Breysig's new work, inspired primarily by Nietzsche, an "heroistic" standpoint is advocated, which is vigorously directed against the current "objectification" of personality. The effect of any creative work is viewed as being based upon the personal force revealed in it. Consequently, the idea of evolution must be conceived in terms of individuals.

The significance of the group is expressed only in the success or failure of its leadership.

Marxism is curtly rejected by Breysig and even Hegel's ideology is recognized only with great reservations. Breysig does not admit the existence of a *Zeitgeist* (spirit of the time) which directs creative effort by its own strength. He prefers to speak of a "soul of the time" (*Zeitseele*) which influences even the greatest creative individuals. The *Zeitseele* is the sum of all forces that become operative within the subjective self below the level of consciousness, that is, social instincts, their tempo and rhythm, the temper of the time; and further, the *Zeitseele* is the tendency to make a single one of the psychological forces of man especially effective, which gives single eras their specific character. Breysig elaborated this idea more fully in a later work, *The History of the Soul* (1930).

Going even further, Breysig assumes a "time body" behind the time spirit, a certain "corporeal attunement" (*Leibgestimmtheit*) which belongs to one and only one era. From these psychological premises, Breysig, in the last volume of his work, endeavors to render the history of mankind comprehensible.

As multilateral and, at times, even profound as modern cultural psychology is, its conclusions are by no means to be taken as gospel. Its indecisiveness is partially due to the weight and complexity of its material, which can never be exhaustively treated from only one point of view. It is possible to take the objective, or better yet, the objectivated mind as a point of departure, but in order to understand it, it must always be subjectified. And not merely within the personal self of the observer! If this were so, then it would fully bear out Goethe's ironic apothegm:

> What you the Spirit of the Ages call
> Is nothing but the spirit of you all,
> Wherein the Ages are reflected.
>
> *Faust* (Bayard Taylor translation.)

In order to understand the historical effect of cultural creations, we must advert to the subjective minds which create cultural values, and also to the subjectivity of all those persons and things which these minds assimilate and revise. This subjectivity, however, is rooted partly in psychological, partly in biological, and partly in sociological factors. In consequence, a psychology of the objective mind would only be possible through the inclusion of all the factors discussed in the preceding chapters. Thus, it is obvious that the various standpoints discussed here, which aim at an understanding of society, are necessarily interwoven.

We have shown in this chapter in how various a manner modern science has attempted to approach the problem of the superindividual psyche. The four main tendencies distinguished here agree in recognizing the fact that there is such a thing as a superindividual psyche; that it is not wholly confined to consciousness but objectifies itself in manifold ways and that, as an objectivation, it in turn reacts upon the subjective individual. With all due respect to the vast amount of labor expended, we are obliged to admit that as yet no exhaustive solution of these problems has been produced. On the contrary, current opinions are diametrically opposed to each other. In general, there is a predominant tendency to divide the superindividual psyche into actually ascertainable processes, but here and there an inclination to substantialize this psyche makes itself evident. Perhaps the differences among the various schools appear to be more irreconcilable than they really are simply because they employ wholly different categories and concepts to denote the same data. This may be warranted for reasons of method but cannot represent the ultimate goal of science. Such a state of affairs, however, is just as true of individual psychology as it is of superindividual psychology.

CONCLUSION

IS THERE A "SOUL"?

CONCLUSION: IS THERE A "SOUL"?

W E have reached the conclusion of our historical review covering the psychological research of the last half century. Our aim has not been to produce a catalogue of the illimitable mass of detailed studies that have been created by the international coöperation of all civilized countries. We have attempted only to trace the broad lines of multifarious development along which research has moved during the past few decades.

A final judgment concerning this prodigious amount of labor would be premature at the present time. In fact, we must admit that the central problem of all psychology, the "soul," today appears more obscure and indeterminate than ever before. Yet this state applies equally to all other sciences. As a result of recent brilliant discoveries in physics, the central problem of matter today presents a far greater complexity than it did to previous generations, who believed they could either define matter or else negate its existence by virtue of a few simple indicative facts. There is nothing to warrant our believing that the ultimate solutions of universal problems are simple. We have no right to reproach either physics or psychology simply because the solutions of their nuclear problems involve other sciences.

The history of psychology cannot, therefore, print a colophon at the end of its tale; nor can it offer its reader a conclusion which, like the keystone of an arch, neatly and definitively completes the entire structure. Least of all can this be done with regard to the central problem of whether there is a "soul." Very few modern scholars, to be sure, still assume the existence of a soul as conceived by the primitive animism of earlier times. But on the other hand, the *ex cathedra* denial of the psyche which was characteristic of the gross materialism of recent years can today find very few advocates. Scholars have recognized that both in the life of the individual and of all mankind there are forces at work that follow their own laws and that cannot be reduced to a purely material process. We have seen how, on the threshold of modern research, the science of psychology began with a lucid definition of what it intended to denote by the concept of "soul." Psychology believed that it possessed exact methods to gain a complete understanding of its subject matter. The "soul" was understood to be "consciousness," and only the study of consciousness was to be the province of psychology. The paradox which then developed was that just this apparently solid basis of research and these very lines of demarcation which were so sharply drawn proved themselves to be more and more uncertain. The result was that consciousness was not only incomprehensible without the inclusion of physiological, biological, and motor data, but that it also became necessary to study unconscious structures and complexes, and furthermore, to place consciousness into a superindividual social context.

Thus, we are confronted with the astonishing conclusion that that science which had at first been called psychology, was not even able to solve its own psychological problems! Even the procedure of occasionally drawing other accessory sciences into consultation proved to be inadequate. And it was futile to divide psychology into innumerable special sciences whose special conclusions, even when summed up, could never be fused into a totality.

Not only has the conception of "soul" undergone a metamorphosis, but also that of "psychology." Psychology has become more and more expansive and also has lived to see the day when it was compelled to include the very data which the "new" psychology of 1870 deliberately rejected. In thus outgrowing its swaddling clothes, psychology was far from being unjustified. It was merely obeying a genuine historic necessity.

There is already a demand for a "philosophical anthropology" or a "general science of life," that would uniformly incorporate all the aspects in which mental life appears. Perhaps the time is not yet ripe for such a science, although the tendency toward totality envisages even broader and more comprehensive organic unities. Perhaps the question of a soul can be solved only in conjunction with the solution of the problem of the nature of the world as a whole. Whether the soul, in any of its meanings, can solve this latter problem is in itself an unsolved problem.

It is a beautiful enthusiasm that again and again impels man to wrestle with these problems. May the studies summarized in this book be viewed in this light, even if none of them has attained its ultimate goal.

APPENDIX

PARAPSYCHOLOGY AND THE UNCONSCIOUS

PARAPSYCHOLOGY AND THE UNCONSCIOUS

1. It is with some hesitation that I add to my history of the evolution of modern psychology a section on that group of problems which are called "psychical research" in England and America, *Sciences psychiques* in France, and "parapsychology" in Germany. The boundaries between scientific research and extra-scientific speculation are so difficult to delimit in this field of study that a great many students consider it beneath the dignity of science to investigate these phenomena at all. Yet even if this study dealt only with fallacies, it would, nevertheless, be an interesting field of research for psychology, if only for the purpose of explaining the fact that so many apparently sincere students feel compelled to study these parapsychological phenomena. Even if parapsychology deals with abnormal phenomena, which most human beings cannot experience, and even though these phenomena do not have the esoteric metaphysical background that some people are inclined to read into them, they are worthy of psychological clarification and study.

Before we proceed to the conceptual definition of these problems, let us approximately delimit the scope of our investigations. Our first consideration will be those phenomena that have come to be called mind reading and telepathy. In such cases we are dealing with a psychic rapport between several people which is effected without the intermediation of speech or other controllable forms of expression. Clairvoyance and prophecy, phenomena in which knowledge of spatially or temporally distant facts is acquired without the intermediation of a third person, are to be considered among these parapsychological phenomena. A third group of phenomena which have been accorded such high-sounding appellations as telekinesis, levitation, and materialization, in which physical effects are alleged to be produced by psychic influences, will also be considered.

One of the chief characteristics of most parapsychological phenomena is the fact that not everyone can experience them. One has to have special gifts to apperceive these phenomena, and even then one cannot always produce or recognize them. People who are thus specially talented are known as "mediums," and the title is retained even in those instances in which it is no longer believed, as the spiritualists certainly do, that the medium is a true intermediary between ordinary men and the spirits and ghosts of a supernatural realm.

Mediums of this kind have existed and still exist in almost all countries. Among the most famous of them were Mrs. Piper who held sway in America, Eusapia Palladino in Italy, Léonie in France, and recently Willy Schneider in Germany. Many a medium has been caught red-handed in deception and fraud, yet those who believe in these mediums claim that such palpable frauds are not valid arguments against their mediumisite talents, but only evidence that they utilize fraud and deception at such times when the unpredictable mediumistic faculty fails them.

For the most part mediums are only capable of producing psychic phenomena in a remarkable condition which is called a "trance" or a "trance state." From the point of view of scientific psychology such a trance is to be considered as an artificially produced or spontaneous hypnosis in which the faculty of automatic writing or speech is commonly present. In these cases the waking consciousness is either entirely eliminated or largely suppressed, with the result that the unconscious functions so much more freely. At any rate mediumism is a legitimate psychological problem albeit a problem which cannot be completely understood unless we also understand the psychology of those who believe in mediums.

From a purely historical point of view the belief in parapsychological phenomena goes back to the dawn of written history. Such phenomena are to be considered a partial component of the magic and sorcery present in the lives of all primitive peoples and in the early stages of civilization. Some evidence of such beliefs may be found in every civilization. Everyone knows the important rôle prophecy and sorcery played in the lives of the Hindus, the Babylonians, the ancient Israelites, Greeks, and Romans. There the prophets and oracles were institutions supported by the state and the prevailing religions. During the Middle Ages in Europe sorcery was considered a very real thing, and was gruesomely punished as a veritable crime in the widespread witch burnings and witch persecutions.

In modern times most parapsychological phenomena have been revived under the banners of Spiritualism, Occultism, Christian Science, Theosophy, or Anthroposophy.

We shall concern ourselves with these phenomena only in so far as they have been examined with a view toward strictly scientific understanding, and under conditions of rigorous scientific control. The first result of such investigation is the finding that many parapsychological phenomena are pure frauds, illusions, or the products of suggestion, and thereby find themselves outside the sphere of our interest. Nevertheless many scientifically minded psychologists admit that, when all fraud and deception have been ruled out, a considerable residue of serious problems remains to be investigated. Experience has taught that the following problems must be solved: (1) a determination of the actual facts of parapsychological phenomena under conditions of strictest control; (2) the relation of the allegedly supernatural phenomena with the findings of normal psychology, and, wherever possible, the explanation of so-called supernatural phenomena in terms of scientific psychology; (3) the construction of an hypothesis wherever possible for the purpose of explaining and clarifying these problems. The opinions of scientists, today, vacillate between the far-reaching beliefs of certain sincere students and the nihilistic scepticism of the whole realm of parapsychology by others.

2. All civilized countries have been the scenes of lively parapsychological research. The most dignified organization for this purpose is the English Society for Psychical Research which was founded in London in 1882. Henry Sidgwick was its first president, and its official organ, the *Proceedings of the Society for Psychical Research* is an important collection of parapsychological writings, some of which have a certain scientific value. An American Society with a similar goal, publishes its own *Proceedings*, and both societies number among their membership scientists of the highest standing, and from the most various fields of work. W. James, R. Hodgson, S. Crookes, F. W. H. Myers, Oliver Lodge, W. J. Crawford, Andrew Lang, E. Gurney, F. Podmore, among many others, were or are members of these two Societies.

An interest in parapsychological problems was awakened in Germany among the romantic philosophers as early as the beginning of the nineteenth century. Schelling, Schopenhauer, G. H. Schubert, the poet Justinus Kerner, J. Ennemoser, and many others, participated in this interest, while the astronomer

C. F. Zöllner and the psychologist G. T. Fechner attempted to reconcile spiritistic phenomena with the phenomena of the natural sciences. Wundt was sceptical of the whole matter, but E. von Hartmann, acknowledged the existence of clairvoyance and telepathy although he refused to believe in spiritism. The leaders of German occultism, which is a more critical form of spiritualism, were Carl du Prel, the Russian Aksakov, who edited the *Psychical Studies* from 1874 on, and Lazar B. Hellenbach. Among the more modern scientists who believe in parapsychological phenomena Schrenck-Notzing, R. Tischner, T. K. Österreich, and H. Driesch may be named, while M. Dessoir, R. Bärwald, R. Hennig and others can be counted among the sceptics, and A. Moll among those who give no credence whatsoever to these phenomena.

France, too, took a lively interest in psychical research. The astronomer Flammarion, E. Boirac, L. Osty, J. Coutier, G. Geley, and above all the physiologist C. Richet have interested themselves in the subject. T. Flournoy, in Switzerland, a ranking professional psychologist, and C. Lombroso, E. Morselli, E. Bozzano and others in Italy have occupied themselves with these problems, Eusapia Palladino being their most interesting and most productive medium. A. N. Chorin and Naum Kotik in Russia, and Ochorowicz in Poland may be named among those who have given time and thought to parapsychology.

3. What were the results of all this research? Let us consider first the phenomena of mind reading and telepathy. In both instances at least two persons must participate: a sender and a receiver. In mind reading the two participants may see each other, whereas in telepathy the participants are so far separated that all sensory relations between them are excluded. The problem of mind reading, that is, of close rapport, can be considered completely clarified today. There is no such thing as mind reading, and what passes as mind reading is really the unconscious reception of unconsciously expressed motor signals. The only abnormal, or rather supernormal, phenomenon concerned in this process is the highly intensified sensitivity which some individuals have for the usually unnoticed unconscious motor activities which accompany all psychic activity. This hyperesthesia for unconscious motor expressions seems to be especially marked in

trance states. In other words, good mediums purposely suppress their waking consciousness in order to be the more sensitive to the transference of these motor signals.

This can readily be explained psychologically. We are bombarded by a multitude of stimuli simultaneously. Of these stimuli our waking consciousness, our "attention," admits only a few, excluding the rest of them. As soon as our attention is suppressed, we begin to apperceive the totality of the bombarding stimuli in a more diffuse fashion. In other words, we react to stimuli that are ordinarily excluded from our consciousness. The usually unnoticed stimuli, together with the reactions that follow them, are amenable to experimental demonstration, and the whole process is not in the least mystical, astonishing as the performance may appear to the layman.

The unconscious motor rapport plays an unconscious and important rôle in the quite normal relationships between people. When we "sense" that a person dislikes us, or is amicably disposed, without being in the least able to state on what grounds we have such a feeling, we can deduce that we derive our "intuition" from such unconsciously apprehended motor signals.

The problem of telepathy is far more difficult. There are innumerable very specific accounts of cases in which an individual, usually at a far distant place, has experienced or has been conscious of the experience of another individual who is suffering some tremendous pain or is in the throes of dying. An attempt was made to supplant these single experiences, which are practically impossible to control, with artificial experiments designed to prove or disprove the existence of telepathy. Such experiments were carried out either when the receiving individual was in a state of normal consciousness or in a hypnosis. The first attempts were made by H. Sidgwick with his wife and consisted in the transference of words and numbers. Nine per cent of the attempts were successful when the two experimenters were in different rooms while 18 per cent were successful when they were in the same room. These attempts are really not, in the last analysis, examples of telepathy but of "mind reading." Experiments by Lehmann and Hansen, who intensified unconscious speech by means of a concave mirror, seem to confirm these results.

Among the most famous experiments in parapsychology were

those which Pierre Janet and other investigators carried on at Havre in the years 1885 and 1886 with the peasant woman who is known in psychical research literature as Léonie. Because of the fact that the scientific controls in these experiments were not recorded, the results are indeterminate and have little scientific bearing on our problem. The same criticism may be leveled at the experiments of the Russian physician, Naum Kotik, who worked with a fourteen-year-old girl and a young woman named Lydia. Lydia used to write down on a "ouija" board whatever she experienced in her trance state. Kotik's experiments were critically annihilated by Dessoir and others.

Today we can safely say that there is no good experimental and scientifically valid evidence for the existence of telepathy, yet this does not indicate that the countless cases of spontaneous telepathy are all based on mistakes. Such telepathy, conceivably, could occur under abnormal conditions which were experimentally not amenable to reproduction. If an experimenter were to demand of Goethe or Keats that he demonstrate his poetic inspiration at a given experimental command, it is quite likely that evidence of such inspiration would not be forthcoming. Consequently science will have to leave the question of telepathy open for the present.

4. Clairvoyance and prophecy are distinguished from telepathy in that there is no need to assume, in them, that there is any transference of thought from a strange consciousness. In these phenomena it is supposed that the medium becomes aware of temporally or spatially removed facts without the intermediation of a "sender."

The faculty of clairvoyance is so often claimed that psychology cannot pass it by without further examination. "Second sight" seems to occur very frequently in some countries, such as Scotland or Westphalia. Scientific control or check-up on most cases is next to impossible, and some very famous acts of clairvoyance, such as Swedenborg's vision of a distant fire, have crumbled under critical investigation. It is certain that many instances of so-called prophetic foretelling are simple frauds or systematic deception, as in the case of the Pythian prophecies of ancient Delphi, which were no more than subtle machinations of the local priests. The alleged prophecies of the Old Testament prophets were either vague and indeterminate statements that were never literally fulfilled, or they are posthumous forgeries.

Turbulent times stimulate prophets to practice their craft, as was proved during the late War, when self-appointed prophets flourished in all countries. In Germany, for example, most of the prophecies foretold the triumph of German arms before the end of the War, whereas after the Treaty of Versailles countless prophets could be found who claimed that they had foretold the bitter end years before the Armistice.

Science has allowed itself to be involved in the careful examination of those who claim the power of clairvoyance. The most famous case is that of the American, Mrs. Piper, who was investigated by such serious students as James, Hodgson, Newbold, and others. The most astounding performances were credited to her. Some of these performances must be considered as examples of telepathy, since the examiners knew in advance what the subject was supposed to do. A true clairvoyance on the part of Mrs. Piper might have been assumed in those instances where she recognized facts that were not known to the experimenters. She told William James facts about the health of two people living in New York, which were later confirmed by letter, and on one occasion she indicated where a lost book could be found.

Examples of the use of "divining rods" which, through their deflections indicate the presence of springs, subsurface oil, or minerals, must be considered as examples of clairvoyance unless we are willing to ascribe magical powers to the divining rod itself. It is certainly true that springs or oil deposits have been found by the use of divining rods, although sceptics have objected that if you dug deeply enough you could find underground springs everywhere. The unconscious observations and conclusions of the divining rod bearers must play a certain part in these performances even though they insist that the bending of the divining rod occurs entirely without their will or knowledge.

There is, moreover, a widespread belief in dreams that come true, prophetic dreams in which the faculty of clairvoyance occurs in sleep. In the *Proceedings of the Society for Psychical Research* of November, 1902, a case is cited in which a laborer discovered, in a dream, the place where a much-sought corpse was finally brought to light. This is but one of the many cases in which persons have discovered facts in their dreams of which they were completely unconscious during a waking state.

Professional clairvoyants have a penchant for taking a watch or a ring from some member of their audiences and reading from it a great many facts about the lives of the previous or present owner. My own as yet unpublished experiments with the famous German clairvoyant Hanussen proved that the man had a remarkable faculty for constructing stories out of thin air. Hanussen, however, was completely incapable of seeing through obviously false clues. In this connection it is interesting to note the statement made by a former police commissioner of Berlin who claimed that every time a criminal mystery baffled the police countless alleged clairvoyants offered to help the police solve the mystery, but that in his experience not a single mystery was ever cleared up in this fashion. As in the question of telepathy we must say with the lawyers, *non liquet*—the case is not clear.

5. Finally a few words may be said about those phenomena in which the psychic influence of certain media is alleged to affect the material world. These phenomena have been described under the headings of telekinesis, levitations, and materialization. Objects move, musical instruments sound, without the presence of any physical agent. Indeed corporeal objects form themselves from the air!

Science must approach these phenomena with the utmost scepticism. The most hallowed laws of nature are put in question by these phenomena! Scientists who are inclined to believe in the verity of these phenomena point to the case of Willy Schneider who has never been caught in any fraud. The sceptics answer that there is no single trick or phenomenon of the spiritualists and mediums that cannot be duplicated by a clever professional magician without the aid and intervention of any occult powers. In many of these cases the controls of the scientific observers have been inadequate. The sceptics add, moreover, that scientific controls are useless—the only technical controls that would be adequate would be controls by professional magicians who understand the tricks of the trade. And even magicians can be fooled! Psychologists must approach these phenomena with especial care, since the data of physics and chemistry are also involved. All that we can say is that even today there are scientists who believe in the genuineness of such phenomena as telekinesis and materialization without in the least being able to offer any explanations that could be incorporated in the body of scientific knowledge.

6. Science can never be completely satisfied with the mere substantiation of the existence of real or allegedly real facts. A phenomenon becomes a scientific "fact" only when its causal relationships are explained.

Explanations of parapsychological phenomena exist, to be sure. The oldest and most honorable, so far as its relationships to primitive human thought processes are concerned, is the explanation of the spiritualists: parapsychological phenomena are caused by the activity of the ghosts of departed human beings. This explanation assumes the existence of uncorporeal ghosts which flit about the cosmos until they incorporate themselves temporarily in the body of the medium and express themselves through the mediumistic activities. Telepathy and clairvoyance are explained on the same hypothesis. This theory has gained so little credence in scientific circles that even those investigators who openly admit their belief in parapsychological data refuse to recognize it.

It is customary to apply the term occultism as the official label to those studies on the fringe of science with which we are here dealing. Occultism denies the ghosts and spirits, but affirms the belief in occult forces, defining them as powers and laws that are not accredited by orthodox science. The *modus operandi* of occultism lies chiefly in the use of analogies borrowed from the physical sciences, the favorite one being the assumption of unknown rays and radiations. The discovery in recent times of radiations formerly neither known nor imagined lends a certain specious credibility to the hypotheses of the occultists. But no exact evidence for the existence of such radiations has ever been adduced by parapsychological research, and, for the time being, we must consider these mysterious rays as nothing more than surrogates for the now happily departed ghosts. The ghosts have simply been dignified with pseudoscientific titles.

A number of serious students have advanced the hypothesis of a cosmic psychic relationship, the oversoul from which the

478 The Evolution of Modern Psychology

individual soul is only partially distinguished and separated. This belongs in the sphere of metaphysical research rather than in the realm of exact scientific study. Myers, James, Osty, and others have elaborated this hypothesis. The assumption is that a sort of universal wisdom which inheres in the superindividual cosmic soul occasionally manifests itself in an individual soul. The portal of entry for this cosmic wisdom is the unconscious of the individual, and this hypothesis leads us directly to the hypothesis which is most frequently utilized as an explanation of parapsychological phenomena, even when the hypothesis of a cosmic oversoul is denied.

7. By introducing the subconscious or the unconscious mind into the solution of parapsychological problems we approach the sphere of exact investigation which attempts to explain these phenomena without the aid of metaphysical hypotheses. The assumption of the hyperactivity of the subconscious mind means no more than that our waking consciousness is built up on the foundations of psychological relationships that are not always directly conscious, but of necessity belong to the total structure of the individual personality. We perceive no object, we think no thought without being influenced by the memories and other latent psychic activities of our total ego. The unconscious is no chaos. It is elaborately organized as is evidenced by the fact that it works as a general rule in a meaningful and appropriate fashion. Psychoanalysis has demonstrated the fact that this same unconscious may be a disintegrating factor in pathological cases.

Many of the cases that are considered parapsychological can be explained by the fact that the unconscious is especially prominent and active, and accomplishes certain phenomena without the participation of the normal waking consciousness. As a matter of fact it seems that the repression of the total waking consciousness accentuates and intensifies the effectiveness of the unconscious, as is demonstrated in the trance states.

This accentuation of the subconscious may manifest itself as an hyperesthesia, that is to say, as a sensitivity to stimuli which escape ordinary consciousness. Mind reading, in which an unconscious receptivity for motor acts exists to a degree unknown in normal waking states, is thus explained to a large extent.

Cases of alleged telepathy may be reduced to this unconscious hyperesthesia to a certain degree.

The accentuation and intensification of the unconscious psychic activities may also manifest itself in the form of an hypermnesia that is, an intensification of the memory. In every normal soul traces of earlier impressions are buried which cannot be voluntarily reproduced, which, nevertheless, may be evoked as lively memories by certain situations. Under such circumstances these reawakened memories have the curious semblance of supernatural influences. Flournoy and others have described authentic cases of hypermnesia and cryptomnesia.

The intensification of the unconscious psychic activities may also appear as an intensification of the faculty of association and combination. Such phenomena are not uncommon in dreams, in artistic inspirations or in visionary experiences, even in the lives of quite average human beings. We could say we were dealing with an unconscious hyperassociability in such cases because the the bridges from idea to idea and the combinations of ideas are more unconsciously constructed than is usually the case in normal mental activity. The analysis of the states of poetic and artistic inspiration has definitely demonstrated an intensified activity of unconscious hyperassociation; such observation renders supernatural explanatory devices needless.

Even though all the mysterious problems of parapsychology are not exhaustively explained by the assumption of an unconscious hyperesthesia, hypermnesia, and hyperassociability, these explanations do serve to clarify a great many cases, take them from the realm of the supernatural and incorporate them in the body of science where they belong.

BIBLIOGRAPHY

BIBLIOGRAPHY

Introductory Literature

1880–84 H. Siebeck, Geschichte der Psychologie (Altertum und Mittelalter).

1894 M. Dessoir, Geschichte der neueren deutschen Psychologie, Vol. I.

1911 M. Dessoir, Abriss der Geschichte der Psychologie (Outlines of the History of Psychology, tr. by Donald Fisher; Macmillan, 1912).

O. Klemm, Geschichte der Psychologie (History of Psychology, tr. by E. C. Wilm and Rudolf Pintner; Scribner's, 1914).

1927 K. Bühler, Die Krise der Psychologie.

1929 E. Boring, A History of Experimental Psychology.

R. Müller-Freienfels, Die Hauptrichtungen der gegenwärtigen Psychologie.

G. Murphy, An Historical Introduction to Modern Psychology.

PART I

How Psychology Became Conscious of Consciousness

1860 G. T. Fechner, Elemente der Psychophysik, 2 vols.

1862 W. Wundt, Beiträge zur Theorie der Sinneswahrnehmung.

1863 H. Helmholtz, Die Lehre von den Tonempfindungen als physiologische Grundlage für die Theorie der Musik (On the Sensations of Tone as a Physiological Basis for the Theory of Music, tr. by A. J. Ellis; Longmans, 1875, 5th ed., 1930).

W. Wundt, Vorlesungen über die Menschen- und Tierseele (Human and Animal Psychology, tr. by E. B. Titchener and J. E. Creighton; Macmillan, 1894).

1865 J. S. Mill, An Examination of Sir William Hamilton's Philosophy.

1867 H. Helmholtz, Handbuch der physiologischen Optik (Treatise on Physiological Optics, tr. from 3d German ed. by J. P. C. Southall, 1924–25).

1870 T. Ribot, La psychologie anglaise contemporaine (English Psychology of Today; Appleton, 1874).

H. Spencer, Principles of Psychology, 2 vols.

H. Taine, De l'intelligence (On Intelligence, tr. by T. D. Haye; Holt, 1871).

1873   J. R. L. DELBOEUF, Étude psychophysique.

C. STUMPF, Über den psychologischen Ursprung der Raumvorstellung.

W. WUNDT, Grundzüge der physiologischen Psychologie (1873-74) (*See* p. 74).

1874   F. BRENTANO, Psychologie vom empirischen Standpunkte, Vol. I.

1875   E. MACH, Grundlinien der Lehre von den Bewegungsempfindungen.

1876   J. R. L. DELBOEUF, Théorie générale de la sensibilité.

G. T. FECHNER, Vorschule der Aesthetik, 2 vols.

1877   G. T. FECHNER, In Sachen der Psychophysik.

1878   H. HELMHOLTZ, Die Thatsachen in der Wahrnehmung.

G. E. MÜLLER, Zur Grundlegung der Psychophysik.

1879   T. RIBOT, La psychologie allemande contemporaine (German Psychology of Today, tr. from 2d ed. by J. M. Baldwin; Scribner's, 1886).

1882   G. T. FECHNER, Revision der Hauptpunkte der Psychophysik.

H. HÖFFDING, Psykologi (Outlines of Psychology, tr. from German ed. by M. E. Lowndes; Macmillan, 1891, 1919).

1883   F. GALTON, Inquiries into Human Faculty and Its Development.

T. LIPPS, Grundtatsachen des Seelenlebens.

C. STUMPF, Tonpsychologie, Vol. I (Vol. II, 1890).

1884   A. MOSSO, La paura (Fear, tr. by E. Lough and F. Kiesow from 5th ed.; Longmans, 1896).

J. SULLY, Outlines of Psychology.

1885   H. EBBINGHAUS, Über das Gedächtnis (Memory, tr. by H. A. Ruger and C. E. Bussenius, 1913).

1886   A. BINET, La psychologie du raisonnement.

J. McK. CATTELL, Psychometrische Untersuchungen, Philosophische Studien, III.

E. MACH, Beiträge zur Analyse der Empfindungen (Analysis of Sensations and the Relation of the Physical to the Psychical, tr. by C. M. Williams; Open Court, 1914).

J. WARD, "Psychology," Encyclopædia Britannica, 9th ed., 1886, and also 11th, 1911.

1887   G. T. LADD, Elements of Physiological Psychology.

1888   G. J. ROMANES, Mental Evolution in Man.

1889   J. M. BALDWIN, Handbook of Psychology.

H. BERGSON, Essai sur les données immédiates de la conscience (Time and Free Will; an Essay on the Immediate Data of Consciousness, tr. by R. L. Pogson; Macmillan, 1913).

1889   A. PILZECKER, Die Lehre von der sinnlichen Aufmerksamkeit.

1890   C. v. EHRENFELS, Über Gestaltqualitäten, Vierteljarschrift für wissenschaftliche Philosophie, XIV, 249–292.

W. JAMES, Principles of Psychology, 2 vols.

1891   T. ZIEHEN, Leitfaden der physiologischen Psychologie.

1892   G. S. FULLERTON and J. McK. CATTELL, On the Perception of Small Differences.

A. LEHMANN, Die Hauptgesetze des menschlichen Gefühlslebens.

1893   O. KÜLPE, Grundriss der Psychologie (Outlines of Psychology, tr. by E. B. Titchener; Macmillan, 1895).

1894   A. BINET, Introduction à la psychologie expérimentale.

W. DILTHEY, Ideen über eine beschreibende und zergliedernde Psychologie.

G. T. LADD, Psychology, Descriptive and Explanatory.

J. REHMKE, Lehrbuch der allgemeinen Psychologie.

1895   H. EBBINGHAUS, "Über erklärende und beschreibende Psychologie," Zeitschrift für Psychologie, IX, 161–205.

T. RIBOT, La psychologie des sentiments (The Psychology of the Emotions; Scribner's, 1897, 1912).

1896   F. JODL, Lehrbuch der Psychologie.

G. F. STOUT, Analytic Psychology, 2 vols.

E. B. TITCHENER, An Outline of Psychology.

W. WUNDT, Grundriss der Psychologie (Outlines of Psychology, tr. by C. H. Judd from 7th ed.; Stechert, 1907).

1897   H. CORNELIUS, Psychologie als Erfahrungswissenschaft.

H. EBBINGHAUS, Grundzüge der Psychologie, Vol. I (Vol. II, 1908).

A. HÖFLER, Psychologie.

H. MAIER, Psychologie des emotionalen Denkens.

E. W. SCRIPTURE, The New Psychology.

1899   G. F. STOUT, Manual of Psychology.

1901   M. W. CALKINS, An Introduction to Psychology.

K. MARBE, Experimentell-psychologische Untersuchungen über das Urteil.

1902   W. WUNDT, Grundzüge der physiologischen Psychologie, 3 vols., 5th ed. (Principles of Physiological Psychology, tr. by E. B. Titchener; Macmillan, 1904).

1903   A. BINET, L'étude expérimentale de l'intelligence.

E. CLAPARÈDE, L'association des idées.

J. ORTH, Gefühl und Bewusstseinslage.

1904   J. R. ANGELL, Psychology.

1905   N. ACH, Über die Willenstätigkeit und das Denken.

E. v. HARTMANN, Die moderne Psychologie.

1905   R. Lagerborg, Das Gefühlsproblem.

E. Mach, Erkenntnis und Irrtum.

1906   A. Messer, "Experimentell-psychologische Untersuchungen über das Denken," Archiv. f. d. ges. Psychol., VIII, 1–224.

C. Stumpf, "Über Gefühlsempfindungen," Zeitschrift für Psychologie, XLIV, 1–49.

1907   K. Bühler, "Tatsachen und Probleme zu einer Psychologie der Denkvorgänge," Archiv. f. d. ges. Psychol.

C. Stumpf, Erscheinungen und psychische Funktionen.

V. Urbantschitch, Über subjektive optische Anschauungsbilder.

R. S. Woodworth, "Non-sensory Elements of Space-Perception," Journal of Philos., Psychol., etc., IV.

1908   E. Meumann, Intelligenz und Wille.

E. B. Titchener, Lectures on the Elementary Psychology of Feeling and Attention.

1909   C. S. Myers, A Text-book of Experimental Psychology.

E. B. Titchener, Lectures on the Experimental Psychology of the Thought Processes.

1910   N. Ach, Über den Willensakt und das Temperament.

A. Michotte and E. Prüm, Étude expérimentale sur le choix volontaire et ses antécédents immédiats.

1911   F. Brentano, Von der Klassifikation der psychischen Phänomene.

E. R. Jaensch, Über die Wahrnehmung des Raumes.

D. Katz, Die Erscheinungsweisen der Farben.

G. E. Müller, Zur Analyse der Gedächtnistätigkeit und des Vorstellungsverlaufes, Vols. I–III (1911–17).

1912   K. Koffka, Zur Analyse der Vorstellungen und ihrer Gesetze.

M. Wertheimer, "Experimentelle Studien über das Sehen von Bewegungen," Zeitschrift für Psychologie, LXI, 161–265.

1913   V. Benussi, Psychologie der Zeitauffassung.

K. Bühler, Die Gestaltwahrnehmungen, I.

P. Révész, Zur Grundlegung der Tonpsychologie.

O. Selz, Die Gesetze des geordneten Denkverlaufs.

1914   A. Meinong, Gesammelte Abhandlungen zur Psychologie.

A. Messer, Psychologie.

1915   T. Ziehen, Die Grundlagen der Psychologie, 2 vols.

1916   R. Bärwald, Zur Psychologie der Vorstellungstypen.

H. Henning, Der Geruch.

J. Lindworsky, Das schlussfolgernde Denken.

G. Störring, Psychologie des menschlichen Gefühlslebens.

1917   J. Fröbes, Lehrbuch der experimentellen Psychologie.

1917　W. Köhler, Intelligenzprüfungen an Menschenaffen (The Mentality of Apes, tr. by Ella Winter from 2d rev. ed.; Harcourt, Brace, 1926).

H. J. Watt, The Psychology of Sound.

1918　C. Stumpf, Empfindung und Vorstellung.

1919　E. R. Jaensch and collaborators, "Aufsätze über Eidetik," Zeitschrift für Psychologie, 84ff.

K. Koffka, Beiträge zur Psychologie der Gestalt.

J. Lindworsky, Der Wille. Seine Erscheinung und seine Beherrschung nach den Ergebnissen der experimentellen Forschung.

1920　B. Erdmann, Grundzüge der Reproduktionspsychologie.

D. Katz, Die Erscheinungsweisen der Tasteindrücke.

W. Köhler, Die psychischen Gestalten in Ruhe und im stationären Zustand.

O. Külpe, Vorlesungen über Psychologie (ed. Bühler).

1921　K. Koffka, Die Grundlagen der psychischen Entwicklung (The Growth of the Mind, an Introduction to Child Psychology, tr. by R. M. Ogden; Harcourt, Brace, 1925).

M. Wertheimer, Untersuchungen über die Lehre von der Gestalt.

1922　O. Kroh, Subjektive Anschauungsbilder bei Jugendlichen.

1923　G. Dumas, Traité de psychologie, Vol. I (Vol. II, 1924).

A. Gemelli, Nuovi orizzonti della psicologia sperimentale.

E. R. Jaensch, Über den Aufbau der Wahrnehmungswelt und ihre Struktur im Jugendalter.

D. Katz, Der Vibrationssinn.

G. E. Müller, Komplextheorie und Gestalttheorie.

1924　G. E. Müller, Abriss der Psychologie.

1925　E. R. Jaensch, Die Eidetik und die typologische Forschungs-methode (Eidetic Imagery and Typological Methods of Investigation, tr. by Oscar Oeser from 2d German ed.; Harcourt, Brace, 1930).

M. Wertheimer, Drei Abhandlungen zur Gestalttheorie.

1926　L. Klages, Die Psychologie Nietzsches.

1927　E. R. Jaensch and J. Schweicher, Die Streitfrage zwischen Assoziations- und Funktionspsychologie, geprüft nach eidetischer Methode.

1928　F. Brentano, Vom sinnlichen und noetischen Bewusstsein

1929　R. Matthaei, Das Gestaltproblem.

1933　W. Köhler, Psychologische Probleme.

PART II

Physiopsychology and Psychophysiology

1860   G. T. FECHNER, Elemente der Psychophysik.

1861   E. HERING, Beiträge zur Physiologie (1861–64).

1863   H. HELMHOLTZ, Die Lehre von den Tonempfindungen als physiologische Grundlage für die Theorie der Musik (Eng. tr. by A. J. Ellis, 1930).

1863–64 A. W. VOLKMANN, Physiologische Untersuchungen im Gebiete der Optik.

1865   H. AUBERT, Physiologie der Netzhaut.

        C. BERNARD, Introduction à l'étude de la médecine expérimentale (Tr. by H. C. Greene; Macmillan, 1927).

1866   F. C. DONDERS, Die Anomalien der Refraktion und Accomodation des Auges (An Essay on the Nature and Consequences of Anomalies of Refraction, revised and ed. by C. A. Oliver; Kimpton, 1899).

1867   H. MAUDSLEY, The Physiology and Pathology of Mind.

1868   E. HERING, Die Lehre vom binokularen Sehen.

        H. MUNK, Untersuchungen über das Wesen der Nerven-Erregung.

1870   FRITSCH and HITZIG, Über die electrische Erregbarkeit der Grosshirnrinde.

1872   E. HERING, Zur Lehre vom Lichtsinne (1872–78; rev. ed., Grundzüge der Lehre vom Lichtsinne, 1920).

1876   H. AUBERT, Grundzüge der physiologischen Optik.

        H. MAUDSLEY, Physiology of Mind.

1879   L. HERMANN, Handbuch der Physiologie.

        W. PREYER, Akustische Untersuchungen.

1880   F. GOLTZ, Über die Verrichtungen des Grosshirns.

        H. MUNK, Über die Funktionen der Grosshirnrinde.

1882   J. v. KRIES, Die Gesichtsempfindungen und ihre Analyse.

1883   T. RIBOT, Les maladies de la volonté (Diseases of the Will, tr. by M. M. Snell from 8th ed., Open Court, 1894).

1884   H. BEAUNIS, Recherches expérimentales sur les conditions de l'activité cérébrale et sur la physiologie des nerfs.

1887   WILBRAND, Die Seelenblindheit.

1890   J. LOEB, Der Heliotropismus der Thiere und seine Überstimmung mit dem Heliotropismus der Pflanzen.

1891   A. MOSSO, La Fatica (Fatigue, tr. by M. & W. B. Drummond; Putnam's, 1904).

1893   C. HAUPTMANN, Die Metaphysik in der modernen Physiologie.

1894   S. EXNER, Entwurf zu einer physiologischen Erklärung der psychischen Erscheinungen.

1895   H. Zwaardemaker, Die Physiologie des Geruchs.
1896   P. Flechsig, Gehirn und Seele.
        M. v. Frey, Druckempfindung und Schmerz.
1898   A. Goldscheider, Gesammelte Abhandlungen: Physiologie
        des Muskelsinnes. Physiologie der Hautsinnesnerven.
1899   J. Loeb, Einleitung in die vergleichende Gehirnphysiologie
        und die vergleichende Psychologie (Comparative Physiol-
        ogy of the Brain and Comparative Psychology; Putnam's,
        1900).
1900   H. Liepmann, Die psychischen Apraxien.
1901   H. Driesch, Die organischen Regulationen.
1904   J. v. Kries, Die Gesichtsempfindungen (Nagel's Handbuch
        der Physiologie des Menschen, III).
        R. Semon, Die Mneme als erhaltendes Prinzip im Wechsel
        des organischen Lebens (Mneme, tr. by Louis Simon;
        Macmillan, 1921).
1905   H. Liepmann, Über Störungen des Handelns bei Gehirn-
        kranken.
        C. v. Monakow, Gehirnpathologie.
        W. Nagel, Lage-, Bewegungs- und Widerstandsempfin-
        dungen (Nagel's Handbuch, III).
        T. Thunberg, Physiologie der Druck-, Temperatur- und
        Schmerzempfindungen (Nagel's Handbuch).
1906   C. Sherrington, The Integrative Action of the Nervous
        System.
1908   H. Driesch, Philosophie des Organischen, 2 vols. (The
        Science and Philosophy of the Organism, Macmillan,
        1907–08).
1909   K. Brodmann, Vergleichende Lokalisationslehre der Gross-
        hirnrinde.
        R. Semon, Die mnemischen Empfindungen in ihren Be-
        ziehungen zu den Originalempfindungen.
1911   E. Becher, Gehirn und Seele.
1912   J. Loeb, The Mechanistic Conception of Life.
1914   C. v. Monakow, Die Lokalisation im Grosshirn.
1915   W. B. Cannon, Bodily Changes in Pain, Hunger, Fear and
        Rage.
1916   A. Biedl, Innere Sekretion.
        H. Driesch, Leib und Seele, (Mind and Body, tr. by T.
        Besterman; Dial Press, 1927).
        R. Reiniger, Das psychophysische Problem.
1919   F. Kraus, Die allgemeine und spezielle Pathologie der Per-
        son, Vol. I (Vol. II, 1926).
1920   E. Steinach, Verjüngung durch experimentelle Neubelebung
        der alternden Pubertätsdrüse.

1921   E. KRETSCHMER, Körperbau und Charakter (Physique and Character, tr. by J. W. H. Sprott from 2d rev. ed.; Harcourt, Brace, 1925).

1922   E. KRETSCHMER, Medizinische Psychologie.

1923   J. v. KRIES, Allgemeine Sinnesphysiologie.

        L. MORGAN, Emergent Evolution.

        H. PIÉRON, Le cerveau et la pensée (Thought and the Brain, tr. by C. K. Ogden; Harcourt, Brace, 1927).

1924   G. EWALD, Temperament und Charakter.

1925   E. ABDERHALDEN, Lehrbuch der Physiologie, 4 vols., 1925–29.

1926   W. JAENSCH, Grundzüge einer Physiologie und Klinik der psychophysischen Persönlichkeit.

1929   E. KRETSCHMER, Geniale Menschen (The Psychology of Men of Genius, tr. by R. B. Cattell; Harcourt, Brace, 1931).

PART III

The Psychology of Action and Conduct

1872   C. DARWIN, The Expression of the Emotions in Man and Animals.

1884   W. JAMES, "What is an Emotion?" Mind, IX.

1885   C. G. LANGE, Om Sindsbevoegelser (German tr., Über Gemütsbewegungen, 1887; Eng. tr., James and Lange, The Emotions, 1922).

1887   C. FÉRÉ, Sensation et mouvement (2d ed. rev., 1900).

1888   T. RIBOT, La psychologie de l'attention (Eng. tr., Open Court, 1911).

1890   W. JAMES, Principles of Psychology, Vol. I (Vol. II, 1892).

1892   C. FÉRÉ, La pathologie des émotions.

1895   W. PREYER, Psychologie des Schreibens.

1896   H. BERGSON, Matière et mémoire (Matter and Memory, tr. by N. M. Paul and W. S. Palmer; Macmillan, 1912).

        J. DEWEY, "The Reflex Arc Concept in Psychology," Psychological Review, III, 357–370.

        K. GROOS, Die Spiele der Thiere (The Play of Animals, tr. by E. L. Baldwin, 1898).

        L. MORGAN, Habit and Instinct.

        T. RIBOT, La psychologie des sentiments (Eng. tr., 1897, 1912).

1899   K. GROOS, Die Spiele der Menschen (The Play of Man, tr. by E. L. Baldwin, 1901).

        A. LEHMANN, Die körperlichen Äusserungen psychischer Zustände.

1900   L. MORGAN, Animal Behavior.

1900 H. Münsterberg, Grundzüge der Psychologie, I.

1901 G. Meyer, Die wissenschaftlichen Grundlagen der Graphologie.

1902 K. Groos, Der ästhethische Genuss (Esthetic Enjoyment, 1902).

1904 S. de Sanctis, La mimica del pensiero.

H. S. Jennings, Contributions to the Study of the Behavior of Lower Organisms (1904–06).

1907 J. R. Angell, "The Province of Functional Psychology," Psychol. Rev., XIV, 61–91.

H. Bergson, L'évolution créatrice (Eng. tr. by Arthur Mitchell; Holt, 1911).

W. James, Pragmatism.

1908 G. Dwelshauvers, La synthèse mentale.

W. McDougall, Introduction to Social Psychology.

1909 T. Ribot, Problèmes de la psychologie affective.

J. v. Üxküll, Umwelt und Innenwelt der Tiere.

1910 H. Piéron, L'évolution de la mémoire.

O. Rutz, Neue Ausdrucksmittel des Seelischen.

1911 W. McDougall, Body and Mind.

D. Roustan, Leçons de psychologie.

1912 W. McDougall, Psychology, the Study of Behavior.

R. Müller-Freienfels, Psychologie der Kunst, 2 vols.

1913 V. M. Bechterev, Objektive Psychologie.

G. Finnbogason, L'intelligence sympathique.

L. Klages, Ausdrucksbewegung und Gestaltungskraft.

E. L. Thorndike, The Original Nature of Man.

1914 T. Ribot, La vie inconsciente et les mouvements.

A. F. S. Shand, The Foundation of Character.

J. B. Watson, Behavior, an Introduction to Comparative Psychology.

1917 L. Klages, Handschrift und Charakter.

1918 R. S. Woodworth, Dynamic Psychology.

1919 K. Dunlap, "Are There Any Instincts?" Journal of Abnormal Psychology, XIV, 395–403.

J. B. Watson, Psychology from the Standpoint of a Behaviorist.

1920 J. v. Üxküll, Theoretische Biologie.

1921 J. Kuo, "Giving up Instincts in Psychology," Journal of Philosophy, XVIII, 645–663.

1922 E. Kretschmer, Medizinische Psychologie.

1923 W. McDougall, Outline of Psychology.

R. Müller-Freienfels, Grundzüge einer Lebenspsychologie, Vol. I (Vol. II, 1925).

1923   A. A. ROBACK, Behaviorism and Psychology.

1924   J. B. WATSON, Behaviorism.

1925   K. BÜHLER, "Die Instinkte des Menschen," Bericht über den 9 Kongress, für experimentelle Psychologie in München.
        P. LUCHTENBERG, Das Lebensrätsel des Instinktiven.

1926   K. LEWIN, "Untersuchungen zur Handlungs- und Affektpsychologie," Psychol. Forsch., VII, IX.

1927   I. P. PAVLOV, Conditioned Reflexes: An Investigation of the Physiological Activity of the Cerebral Cortex, tr. by F. C. Anrep, Oxford Press.

1928   E. TEGEN, Moderne Willenstheorien.

PART IV

The Psychology with "Soul"

1882   W. PREYER, Die Seele des Kindes.

1890   J. McK. CATTELL, Mental Tests and Measurements.

1894   F. PAULHAN, Les caractères.

1895   M. BALDWIN, Mental Development in Child and in Race.

1900   E. HUSSERL, Logische Untersuchungen, 2 vols.

1903   A. BINET, L'étude expérimentale de l'intelligence.
        T. LIPPS, Leitfaden der Psychologie (revised, 1906).

1907   W. DILTHEY, Das Wesen der Philosophie.
        T. LIPPS, Psychologische Untersuchungen.
        C. STUMPF, Erscheinungen und psychische Funktionen.

1910   L. KLAGES, Principien der Charakterologie (The Science of Character, tr. by W. H. Johnston from the 5th and 6th German eds.; Sci-Art, 1932).

1911   K. JASPERS, Allgemeine Psychopathologie.
        T. K. ÖSTERREICH, Phänemenologie des Ich, Vol. I.
        W. STERN, Die Differentielle Psychologie.

1913   M. SCHELER, Zur Phänomenologie und Theorie der Sympathiegefühle und von Liebe und Hass.
        —— Der Formalismus in der Ethik und die materialle-Wertethik.

1914   E. SPRANGER, Lebensformen. Geisteswissenschaftliche Psychologie und Ethik der Persönlichkeit (2d ed., rev., 1924).

1915   F. KRÜGER, Über Entwicklungspsychologie.

1918   F. KRÜGER, Die Tiefendimension und die Gegensätzlichkeit des Gefühlslebens.
        W. STERN, Die menschliche Persönlichkcit.

1919   K. JASPERS, Psychologie der Weltanschauungen.

1921   R. MÜLLER-FREIENFELS, Philosophie der Individualität.

1923   F. KRÜGER, Der Strukturbegriff in der Psychologie.

1924   E. Spranger, Psychologie des Jugendalters.
1925   E. Utitz, Charakterologie.
1926   F. Krüger, Komplexqualitäten, Gestalten und Gefühle.
1927   L. Klages, Persönlichkeit.
1928   F. Krüger, Das Wesen der Gefühle.
        G. Störring, Die Frage der geisteswissenschaftlichen und
        verstehenden Psychologie.
1930   W. Stern, Studien zur Personwissenschaft. Pt. I, Personal-
        istik als Wissenschaft.
1931   H. Prinzhorn, Charakterkunde der Gegenwart.

Part V
The Psychology of the Unconscious

1866   A. A. Liébeault, Du sommeil et des états analogues.
1873   J. M. Charcot, Leçons sur les maladies du système nerveux
        (Lectures on the Diseases of the Nervous System, 3 vols.,
        tr. by G. Sigerson; The New Sydenham Society, 1877–89).
1875   C. Richet, "Du somnambulisme provoqué," Journal de
        l'anatomie et de physiologie, II, 348–378.
1879   H. Maudsley, Pathology of Mind.
1884   H. Bernheim, De la suggestion dans l'état hypnotique et dans
        l'état de veille.
1885   T. Ribot, Les maladies de la personnalité (Diseases of Per-
        sonality, Religion of Science Library, Open Court, 1891).
1889   P. Janet, L'automatisme psychologique.
        A. Moll, Der Hypnotismus.
1890   M. Dessoir, Das Doppel Ich.
        A. Lehmann, Die Hypnose und die damit verwandten nor-
        malen Zustände.
1892   P. Janet, L'état mental des hystériques.
1893   J. Breuer and S. Freud, Über den psychischen Mechanismus
        hysterischer Phänomene.
1895   J. Breuer and S. Freud, Studien über Hysterie (Eng. tr.,
        Hogarth Press).
1900   H. Flournoy, Des Indes à la planète Mars. Étude sur un cas
        de somnambulisme avec glossolalie.
        S. Freud, Die Traumdeutung (The Interpretation of Dreams,
        tr. by A. A. Brill; Macmillan, 1933).
1901   S. Freud, Über den Traum (On Dreams, tr. by M. D. Eder;
        Heinemann, 1924).
        —— Zur Psychopathologie des Alltagslebens (Eng. tr.,
        Hogarth Press).
        E. D. Starbuck, The Psychology of Religion.

1902   W. James, Varieties of Religious Experience.
1903   P. Janet, Les obsessions et la psychasthénie.
        F. W. H. Myers, Human Personality and Its Survival of Bodily Death, 2 vols.
1905   S. Freud, Der Witz und seine Beziehung zum Unbewussten (Wit and Its Relation to the Unconscious, tr. by A. A. Brill; Dodd, Mead, 1917).
1906   J. Jastrow, The Subconscious.
        M. Prince, The Dissociation of a Personality. A Biographical Study in Abnormal Psychology.
1907   A. Adler, Studien über Minderwertigkeit von Organen. (Eng. tr.)
1908   H. Delacroix, Études d'histoire et de psychologie du mysticisme.
        N. Kotik, Die Emanation der psychophysischen Energie.
        E. Morselli, Psicologia e spiritismo.
1909   T. Flournoy, Esprits et médiums.
        S. Freud, Über psychoanalyse ("On Psycho-analysis," American Journal of Psychology, 1910).
1910   S. Freud, Drei Abhandlungen zur Sexualtheorie (Three Contributions to the Theory of Sex, tr. by A. A. Brill; 4th ed., 1930).
1912   C. G. Jung, Wandlungen und Symbole der Libido. (Psychology of the Unconscious; a Study of the Transformations and Symbolisms of the Libido, tr. by Beatrice M. Hinkle; Dodd, Mead, 1927.)
1913   A. Adler, Über den nervösen Charakter (The Neurotic Constitution, tr. by B. Glueck and J. E. Lind; Dodd, Mead, 1917).
        E. Osty, Lucidité et intuition.
1914   M. Prince, The Unconscious. The Fundamentals of Human Personality, Normal and Abnormal.
        V. Schrenck-Notzing, Materialisationsphänomene (Phenomena of Materialization, tr. by E. E. Fournier d'Albe; Dutton, 1920).
1915   T. Flournoy, Une mystique moderne.
1916   G. Dwelshauvers, L'inconscient.
1918   M. Dessoir, Vom Jenseits der Seele.
1919   L. C. Baudouin, Suggestion et autosuggestion (Eng. tr. by Eden and Cedar Paul; Dodd, Mead, 1921).
        G. Geley, De l'inconscient au conscient (From the Unconscious to the Conscious, tr. by S. de Brath; Harper, 1921).
1920   A. Adler, Praxis und Theorie der Individualpsychologie (Eng. tr. by P. Radin; Harcourt, Brace, 1924).

1920 R. Bärwald, Okkultismus, Spiritismus und unterbewusste Seelenzustände.

K. Birnbaum, Psychopathologische Dokumente.

S. Freud, Jenseits der Lustprincips (Eng. tr. by C. J. M. Hubback; Ballou, 1924).

W. H. R. Rivers, Instinct and the Unconscious.

A. G. Tansley, The New Psychology.

R. Tischner, Über Telepathie und Hellsehen (Eng. tr. by W. D. Hutchinson; Harcourt, Brace, 1925).

1921 S. Freud, Massenpsychologie und Ich-Analyse (Eng. tr. by James Strachey; Ballou, 1924).

C. G. Jung, Psychologische Typen (Psychological Types or The Psychology of Individuation, tr. by H. Godwin Baynes; Harcourt, Brace, 1923).

T. K. Österreich, Grundbegriffe der Parapsychologie.

1922 C. Richet, Traité de métapsychique (Thirty Years of Psychical Research; Being a Treatise on Metapsychics, tr. by S. de Brath; Macmillan, 1923).

1923 S. Freud, Das Ich und das Es (The Ego and the Id, tr. by J. Rivière; Hogarth Press, 1927).

—— Gesammelte Schriften, 12 vols. (Tr. of 1st. 4 vols., London: The Institute of Psycho-analysis and the Hogarth Press).

A. Wohlgemuth, A Critical Examination of Psycho-analysis.

1924 C. Blondel, La psychanalyse.

1926 Handbuch der Individualpsychologie, 2 vols.

W. McDougall, Outline of Abnormal Psychology.

1927 A. Adler, Menschenkenntnis (Understanding Human Nature, tr. by W. Béran Wolfe; Greenberg, 1927).

S. Ferenczi, Bausteine zur Psychoanalyse, 2 vols.

1928 C. G. Jung, Die Energetik der Seele.

E. Wexberg, Individualpsychologie (Tr. by W. Béran Wolfe, 1929).

1931 O. Bumke, Die Psychoanalyse.

W. Béran Wolfe, How to be Happy though Human.

1933 H. Künkel, Das Gesetz deines Lebens.

W. Béran Wolfe, Nervous Breakdown.

Part VI

The Psychology of Superindividual Psychic Life

1869 F. Galton, Hereditary Genius.

1873 T. Ribot, L'hérédité. Étude psychologique sur ses phénomènes, ses lois, ses causes, ses conséquences (Eng. tr., Appleton, 1875).

1876   H. Spencer, Principles of Sociology.
1877   A. V. Espinas, Des sociétés animales (Stechert, 1924).
1883   W. Dilthey, Einleitung in die Geisteswissenschaften.
        F. Galton, Inquiries into Human Faculty.
1887   F. Tönnies, Gemeinschaft und Gesellschaft.
1890   G. Tarde, Les lois de l'imitation.
1893   E. Durkheim, De la division du travail social.
1895   E. Durkheim, Les règles de la méthode sociologique.
        G. Le Bon, Psychologie des foules (The Crowd; a Study of
        the Popular Mind, Macmillan, 1925).
1896   F. H. Giddings, Principles of Sociology.
1897   P. Barth, Die Philosophie der Geschichte als Sociologie.
        L. F. Ward, Outlines of Sociology.
1898   A. Fouillée, La psychologie du peuple français.
        F. H. Giddings, Elements of Sociology.
        G. Ratzenhofer, Das soziologische Erkennen.
1900   W. Wundt, Völkerpsychologie, Vol. I (Vol. II, 1905–06).
1903   A. Fouillée, Esquisse psychologique des peuples européens.
        L. F. Ward, Pure Sociology.
1905   A. W. Small, General Sociology.
1906   E. Westermarck, The Origin and the Development of the
        Moral Ideas.
1907   G. Ratzenhofer, Sociologie (posthumous).
        R. Sommer, Familienforschung und Vererbungslehre.
1908   W. McDougall, An Introduction to Social Psychology.
        E. A. Ross, Social Psychology.
        G. Simmel, Soziologie.
1910   L. Lévy-Brühl, Les fonctions mentales dans les sociétés
        inférieures (How Natives Think, tr. by Lilian A. Clare;
        Knopf, 1926).
1911   W. Hellpach, Die geopsychischen Erscheinungen.
1912   W. Wundt, Elemente der Völkerpsychologie (Elements of
        Folk Psychology, tr. by E. L. Schaub; Macmillan, 1916).
1913   S. Freud, Totem und Tabu (Eng. tr. by A. A. Brill; Rout-
        ledge, 1919).
        E. L. Thorndike, The Original Nature of Man.
1917   E. Becher, Die fremddienliche Zweckmässigkeit der Pflan-
        zengallen und die Hypothese eines überindividuellen
        Seelischen.
1918   O. Spengler, Der Untergang des Abendlandes, Vol. I (Vol.
        II, 1922) (The Decline of the West, tr. by C. F. Atkinson;
        one vol. ed.; Knopf, 1932).
1919   T. Litt, Individuum und Gemeinschaft.
1920   W. McDougall, The Group Mind.

1922   J. Dewey, Human Nature and Conduct.
        H. Freyer, Theorie des objektiven Geistes.
        F. H. Giddings, Studies in the Theory of Human Society.
        M. Ginsberg, The Psychology of Society.
1923   L. Lévy-Bruhl, La mentalité primitive (Primitive Mentality, tr. by Lilian A. Clare; Macmillan, 1923).
1924   F. H. Allport, Social Psychology.
        L. L. Bernard, Instinct: a Study in Social Psychology.
        E. S. Bogardus, Fundamentals of Social Psychology.
1925   W. Peters, Die Vererbung geistiger Eigenschaften und die psychische Konstitution.
1926   H. Werner, Einführung in die Entwicklungspsychologie.
1929   C. Murchison, Social Psychology.
1930   R. Müller-Freienfels, Allgemeine Sozial- und Kulturpsychologie.
1933   N. Hartmann, Das Problem des geistigen Seins.

INDEXES

ERRATA

Page 287, line 8 from bottom: ; should be ,

Index

INDEX OF NAMES

INDEX OF SUBJECTS